POSTAL INTELLIGENCE

POSTAL INTELLIGENCE

THE TASSIS FAMILY AND COMMUNICATIONS REVOLUTION IN EARLY MODERN EUROPE

RACHEL MIDURA

CORNELL UNIVERSITY PRESS
Ithaca and London

Publication of this open monograph was the result of Virginia Tech's participation in TOME (Toward an Open Monograph Ecosystem), a collaboration of the Association of American Universities, the Association of University Presses, and the Association of Research Libraries. TOME aims to expand the reach of long-form humanities and social science scholarship including digital scholarship. Additionally, the program looks to ensure the sustainability of university press monograph publishing by supporting the highest quality scholarship and promoting a new ecology of scholarly publishing in which authors' institutions bear the publication costs.

Funding from Virginia Tech made it possible to open this publication to the world.

www.openmonographs.org

Copyright © 2025 by Cornell University

The text of this book is licensed under a Creative Commons Attribution-NonCommercial-NoDerivatives 4.0 International License (CC BY-NC-ND 4.0): https://creativecommons.org/licenses/by-nc-nd/4.0/. To use this book, or parts of this book, in any way not covered by the license, please contact Cornell University Press, Sage House, 512 East State Street, Ithaca, New York 14850. Visit our website at cornellpress.cornell.edu.

Library of Congress Cataloging-in-Publication Data

Names: Midura, Rachel, 1991– author.
Title: Postal intelligence : the Tassis family and communications revolution in early modern Europe / Rachel Midura.
Description: Ithaca : Cornell University Press, [2025] | Includes bibliographical references and index.
Identifiers: LCCN 2024024124 (print) | LCCN 2024024125 (ebook) | ISBN 9781501779916 (hardcover) | ISBN 9781501779923 (paperback) | ISBN 9781501779930 (epub) | ISBN 9781501779947 (pdf)
Subjects: LCSH: Tassis family. | Postal service—Political aspects—Europe—History. | Postal service—Europe—History—16th century. | Postal service—Europe—History—17th century. | Written communication—Europe—History—16th century. | Written communication—Europe—History—17th century.
Classification: LCC HE6925 .M53 2025 (print) | LCC HE6925 (ebook) | DDC 383/.49409031—dc23/eng/20240716
LC record available at https://lccn.loc.gov/2024024124
LC ebook record available at https://lccn.loc.gov/2024024125

Dedicated to Patrick, my favorite person

Contents

List of Figures viii

Acknowledgments ix

Note on Conventions xii

Characters xiii

Introduction: The Posts of the World   1

1. The Tassis Family Firm: Postmaster Generals of Information War   19
2. The Arrest of a Postmaster: Information Sovereignty in the Italian Wars   47
3. Deadly Letters: Brigandage, Plague, and Confessionalization   74
4. The Postmistress and the Spy: Networking the Italian Road   99
5. Breaking Records: Commercialization and Control on the Transalpine Roads   126
6. The Sinews of Society: Coach Travel and the Postal Guide in the Seventeenth Century   154
7. High Towers and Black Chambers: Twin Legends of Postal Service   180

Conclusion: Reinventing Revolutions   205

Glossary 215

Abbreviations 217

Notes 219

Bibliography 283

Index 307

Figures

1. Map of the major routes of the Tassis Spanish and imperial postal systems in the seventeenth century — xviii
2. Giuseppe Maria Mitelli, *Il corriere in lontananza*, post-1692 — 12
3. Selection of the Tassis family tree — 25
4. Bernard Van Orley, *Légende de Notre-Dame du Sablon: La statue de Notre-Dame est conduite à l'église du Sablon*, 1516–1518 — 27
5. *Portrait of Count Simone Tassis*, d. 1563 — 39
6. Page from the Spanish nomenclator, 1556 — 58
7. Page from the Spanish nomenclator, 1556 — 59
8. *Cursor Germanus*, or the German courier, in Enea Vico, *Diversarum gentium nostrae aetatis habitus*, Venice: c. 1558 — 78
9. Map of assaults on postal couriers in northern Italy, 1556–1631 — 80
10. Map of the Italian Road, c. 1582 — 101
11. Map of the transalpine roads, c. 1623 — 130
12. Map of dispatched courier expenses, 1605–1606 — 135
13. Dispatch note, 1637 — 143
14. Rider receipt, 1575 — 144
15. Frontispiece from Ottavio Codogno, *New Itinerary*, 1611 — 160
16. Page from *New Itinerary*, 1611 — 160
17. Page with marginalia from *L'Itinerario per diverse parte del mondo*, 1563 — 164
18. Page with marginalia from *L'Itinerario per diverse parte del mondo*, 1563 — 165
19. Image from Jules Chifflet, *Les marques d'honneur de la maison de Tassis*, 1645 — 188
20. Giacomo Cantelli, *L'Italia con le sue poste*, 1695 — 191

Acknowledgments

Every stage of this book has been made possible by a network of support, for which I am immensely grateful.

First, I must thank the many readers who provided comments on the manuscript, including (but not limited to) Danna Agmon, Brian Brege, Giovanna Ceserani, David Como, Mackenzie Cooley, Filippo de Vivo, Paula Findlen, Wouter Kreuze, Amanda Madden, Margaret Meserve, Laura Stokes, Francesca Trivellato, and participants in the Virginia Tech Historians Writing Group.

This book benefited enormously from opportunities to present work in progress. I treasured discussions at Stanford University's Center for Medieval and Early Modern Studies, the University of Notre Dame's Center for Italian Studies, the University of Rochester Ferrari Humanities Symposia, and the Istituto Storico Italo-Germanico at the Fondazione Bruno Kessler. I further valued the opportunity to share work virtually with the Society for Intelligence History and the Universität München Oberseminar. Finally, I am grateful to the editors, staff, and anonymous reviewers of Cornell University Press, as well as Kate Epstein, Stewart Scales, and Bridgette Werner for their help in making this the best book it could be. Thank you to Bethany Wasik for your guidance and support throughout the process.

Several panels and conferences enriched my understanding of early modern communications, exchange, and statecraft. This included the Early Modern Mobility Workshop, hosted virtually in 2021 with the support of the Stanford-UPS Endowment Fund; as well as several Renaissance Society of America (RSA) and Sixteenth Century Society conferences. Thank you to my co-organizers, Luca Zenobi and Giacomo Giudici, and to the Warburg Institute for sponsoring our "Cultures of Bureaucracy" panel series at RSA 2019. Thank you as well to the Society for Italian Historical Studies for their sponsorship of the "Expertise in Early Modern Italy" panel at the 2022 American Historical Association Conference in Philadelphia.

ACKNOWLEDGMENTS

I am grateful to the Mabelle McLeod Lewis Memorial Fund and the Piggott Scholars Program Fellowship for their support of the initial years of research travel and writing. The Gladys Kriebel Delmas Foundation and Fondazione Giorgio Cini funded research in Venice and the former Venetian empire, as well as providing several enjoyable stays at the Vittore Branca Research Center. I benefited from additional research funding from both Stanford and Virginia Tech Universities, including grants from the Stanford Graduate Research Organization; the Stanford Europe Center; the Virginia Tech Center for European Union, Transatlantic, and Trans-European Studies; and Virginia Tech's Office of the Provost and College of Liberal Arts and Human Sciences. Open Access publication has been made possible by the Toward an Open Monograph Ecosystem (TOME) initiative and the tireless efforts of Peter Potter, Corinne Guimont, and Virginia Tech Publishing.

I must credit my mentor, Paula Findlen, with the idea of investigating the Tassis. Paula continues to be the great storytelling, archive-delving, and community-building scholar that I aspire to become. A global community of historians welcomed me into a fascinating world of letters, couriers, and spies. Thank you to Ruth and Sebastian Ahnert, Júlia Benavent, Bruno Crevato-Selvaggi, Clemente Fedele, Bonaventura Foppolo, Ioanna Iordanou, and Juraj Kittler for generously sharing their time and work. I owe a great deal as well to the professional support of the archivists and librarians in Bergamo, Brescia, London, Florence, Innsbruck, Milan, Turin, Verona, Venice, and Washington, DC. I am especially thankful to the administrators of the Fürst Thurn und Taxis Zentralarchiv and Hofbibliothek (FTTZA), the Tiroler Landesarchiv (TLA), and the Archivo General de Simancas (AGS) for their help in digitizing great stacks of postal records, and the Smithsonian Postal Museum, which helped secure the most esoteric literature one could desire on this side of the Atlantic.

Thank you to Charles McCurdy, Duane Osheim, Erin Rowe, and Adrienne Ward for setting me on this path in life. It has been a delight to walk it alongside José Edwin Argueta, Lara Howerton, Joy Merten, Virginia Olmsted-McGraw, Katherine Roberts, Margaret Wood, and their partners. Thank you to the members of the "Book or Bust" writing group for sharing in all the highs and lows of this process. Maggie Sigle: there is no one with whom I would have rather taken the winding road into postal history.

Finally, thank you to Bryant, Christopher, and Kelly Bembry Midura. I would not have had the courage to take on the archives without the adventuring example set by my foreign service family. Thank you to my in-laws, Kelsey, Marilyn, and Robert Mutchler, who welcomed me into their home, and always knew when to ask, and when not to ask about progress on the book. And finally, for your love, patience, and unflagging support, thank you to my partner in all things, Patrick Mutchler.

Elements of this research have previously appeared in different forms in the following: "Publishing the Baroque Post: The Postal Itinerary and the Mailbag Novel," in *The Renaissance of Letters: Knowledge and Community in Italy, 1300–1650*, ed. Paula Findlen and Suzanne Sutherland (New York: Routledge, 2020); "Itinerating Europe: Early Modern Spatial Networks in Printed Itineraries, 1545–1700," *Journal of Social History* 54, no. 4 (2021); "Italian Messengers and Couriers," in *The Routledge Encyclopedia of the Renaissance World*, ed. Kristen Poole (New York: Routledge, 2023) (Online); and "'They Hide from Me, Like the Devil from the Cross': Transalpine Postal Routes as Intelligence Work, 1555–1645," *History: The Journal of the Historical Association* 108, no. 381 (2023).

Note on Conventions

I have provided birth dates (b.), death dates (d.), dates of marriage (m.), as well as dates of office (o.) where available for postmasters, diplomats, and leaders. I use the most common nomenclature in Anglo-American scholarship for well-known historical figures and the most common self-identification in others, although I have provided additional variations in parentheses. The same logic determines my choice of "Tasso," "Tassis," "Taxis," "von Taxis," or "Thurn und Taxis."

Other general conversions include the following:

1 lira = 20 soldi = 240 denari
1 Spanish/imperial scudo d'oro = 6 Italian lire
1 Venetian ducato = 124 soldi
1 postal ounce = 31 modern grams = 4 sheets of early modern paper
1 imperial (German) mile = 1 Spanish mile = 3 English miles = 5 Italian miles = 7.5 modern kilometers

Characters

A nonexhaustive list of family members who play a significant role in the book and their primary office. Indentations reflect lines of descent.

Tassis Family

- Francesco Tassis (Franz Taxis), d. 1517, imperial postmaster general in Brussels
- Janetto Tassis (Johann Taxis), d. 1517, imperial postmaster in Innsbruck, Austria
- Leonardo Tassis (Leonhard Taxis), d. 1518, imperial postmaster in Rome, Italy
- Ruggero Tassis, d. 1514, notary in Camerata Cornello, Italy

Imperial/Spanish postmaster generalship:

- Giovanni Battista Tassis (Juan Baptista Tassis), d. 1541, imperial postmaster general in Brussels
  - Giovan Antonio Tassis ("Il Zoppo"), d. 1580, imperial and Spanish postmaster in Rome
  - Raimondo Tassis, d. 1579, imperial postmaster in Spain and Spanish postmaster general
    - Juan de Taxis y Acuña, d. 1607, Spanish postmaster general and ambassador to London
      - Juan II de Taxis y Peralta, d. 1622, Spanish postmaster general
  - Baron Leonardo I Tassis (Leonhard I Taxis), d. 1612, imperial postmaster general in Brussels
    - Count Lamoral I Tassis (Lamoral I Taxis), d. 1624, imperial postmaster general in Brussels, m. Ginevra Tassis (Genoveva Taxis), d. 1628

- Count Leonardo II Tassis (Leonhard II Taxis), d. 1628, imperial postmaster general in Brussels, m. Alexandrine de Rye, d. 1666, postmistress general in Brussels
  - Count Lamoral II Tassis (Lamoral II Thurn und Taxis II), d. 1676, postmaster general in Brussels

Imperial/Spanish Post Office of Milan:

- Simone Tassis (Simon Taxis), d. 1562, ducal, imperial and Spanish postmaster in Milan
  - Ruggero Tassis, d. 1588, Spanish postmaster in Milan, m. Lucina Cattanea Tassis, d. 1619, Spanish postmistress of Milan (by lease)
  - Isabella Tassis, d. 1614, m. Seraphin Taxis, postmaster of Augsburg

Imperial Post Office of Venice:

- Davide Tassis, d. 1538, imperial postmaster in Venice and Verona
  - Ruggero Tassis, d. 1583, imperial postmaster in Venice
    - Ferdinando Tassis, d. 1648, imperial postmaster in Venice

Imperial Post Office of Augsburg:

- Bartolomeo Tassis (Bartholomeus Taxis), d. 1549, imperial postmaster of Augsburg and Rheinhausen
  - Serafino Tassis (Seraphin Taxis), d. 1582, imperial postmaster of Augsburg and Rheinhausen, m. Isabella Tassis
    - Ginevra Tassis (Genoveva Taxis), d. 1628, m. Count Lamoral I Tassis
    - Octavio Tassis (Octavius Taxis), d. 1626, imperial postmaster of Augsburg and Rheinhausen, m. Susanna Jakobe von Stauding, d. 1656, imperial postmistress of Augsburg

Spanish Italy

- Francesco Tassignano, postmaster of Lodi and deputy to Postmaster Simone Tassis (o. c. 1536)
- Giovan Antonio Vignale ("Il Sarto"), postmaster of Bologna (o. c. 1536–1556)

- Cardinal Antoine Perrenot de Granvelle (b. 1517-d. 1586), imperial chancellor (o. 1550-1556) and Spanish statesman (o. 1556-1586)
- Ottaviano di Marzi, Venetian diplomatic resident in Milan (o. 1573-1579)
- Bonifacio Antelmi, Venetian diplomatic resident in Milan (o. 1580-1587)
- Antonio Pauluzzi, Venetian diplomatic resident in Milan (o. 1596-1597, 1603-1608)
- Pedro Enríquez de Acevedo, Count of Fuentes (b. 1525- d. 1610), governor of Milan (o. 1600-1610)
- Juan Fernández de Velasco y Tovar, duke of Frías, Condestable de Castilla (b. 1550-d. 1613), governor of Milan (o. 1592-1595, 1595-1600, 1610-1612)
- Ottavio Codogno, d. 1630, postmaster lieutenant of Milan under Postmistress Lucina Cattanea Tassis and sons (o. c. 1600-1630)
- Felipe de Haro, d. 1621, Spanish visitor of Milan (o. 1607-1612)
- Pier Antonio Marioni, Venetian diplomatic resident in Milan (o. 1627-1631)

Rome

- Gian Pietro Carafa, d. 1559, Pope Paul IV (o. 1555-1559)
- Carlo Carafa, d. 1561, cardinal nephew of Pope Paul IV
- Giovanni Carafa, duke of Paliano, d. 1561
- Bernardo Navagero d. 1565, Venetian ambassador in Rome (o. 1555-1558)
- Mattia Gherardi (Mathia, or Matteo da San Casciano), d. 1582, papal postmaster (o. c. 1535-1582)

Venice

- Ludovico Fioravante, d. 1538, redeemed exile, spy, and corriero maggiore (o. c. 1520-1538)
- Ferrante Pallavacino, d. 1644, satirist

Holy Roman Empire

- Jakob Henot, d. 1625, imperial postmaster of Cologne (o. c. 1578-1626)

- Johann von den Birghden, d. 1645, imperial postmaster of Frankfurt (o. 1578–1626) and Swedish postmaster in Frankfurt (o. 1631–1635)

England

- Thomas Witherings, d. 1651, English postmaster of foreign mails (with William Frizzell) (o. c. 1632–1640, 1649–1651)
- Henry Bishop, d. 1691, English postmaster general (o. 1660–1663)

POSTAL INTELLIGENCE

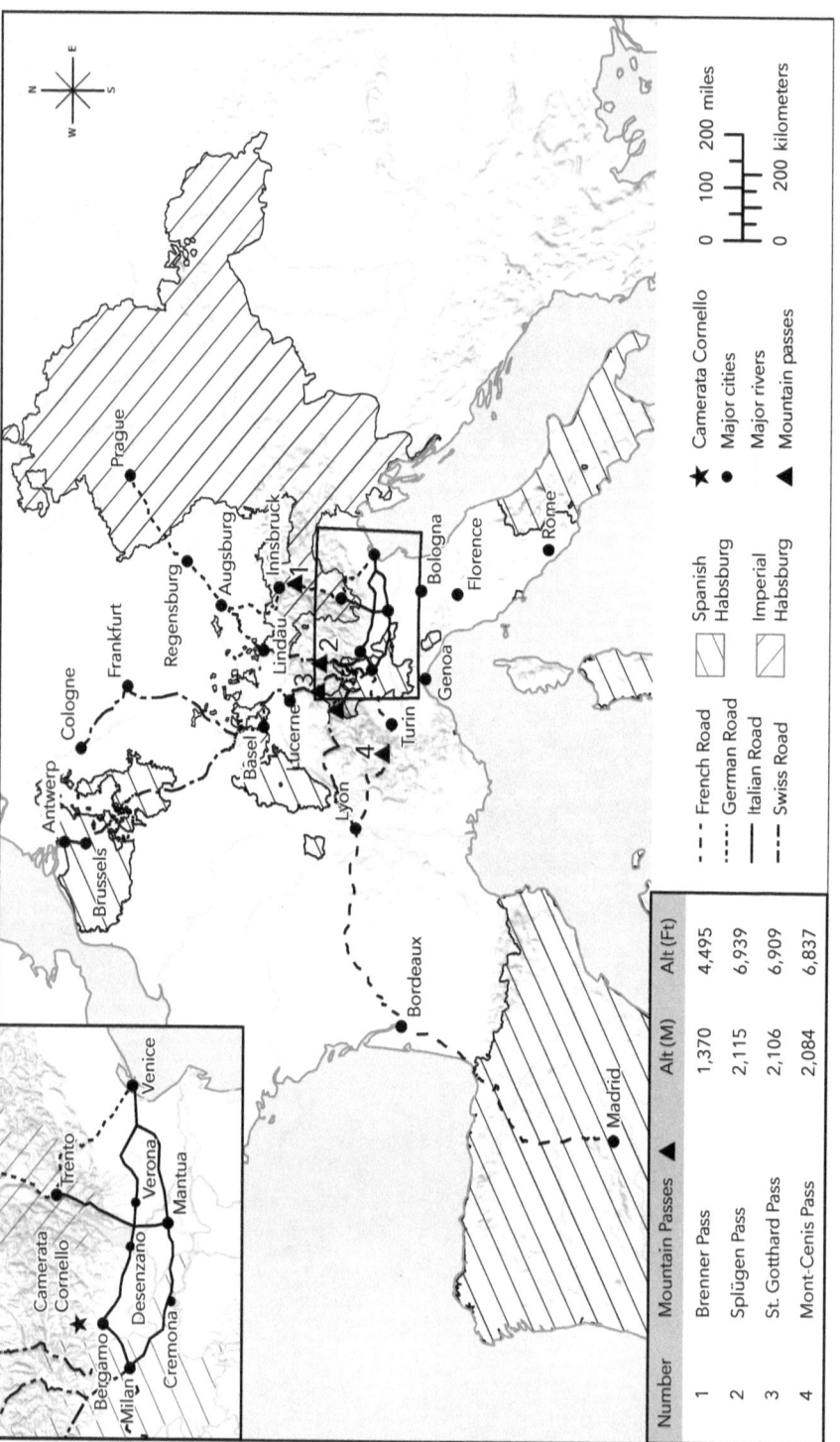

FIGURE 1. The major routes of the Tassis Spanish and imperial postal systems, as published in Ottavio Codogno, *Compendium of the Posts* (1632). Borders here and in other maps in this book represent the territorial extent of polities as of 1600, made available from Euratlas by Jerome Chia-Rung Yang at the Center for Geographic Analysis, Harvard University. Map by the author and Stewart Scales.

Introduction
The Posts of the World

From the city-states of Italy to the Habsburg courts, paper and the written word structured daily life in the sixteenth and seventeenth centuries. Paper was the essential substrate of governance. Miscellaneous slips and ledgers gathered like snow on the desks of Europe's administrators. The management of time, distance, cost, and the all-too-human elements of governance demanded extensive documentation. After all, bureaucracy meant ruling from the desk (*bureau*) as much as from the throne.

The many kilometers of shelves in Milan's state archives monumentalize the ambitions—hubris, even—of this bureaucracy. The correspondence (*carteggio*) of the Spanish period is separated only by year. Jurisdictional disputes, requests for arms licenses, spy reports, and holiday well-wishes jumble together, much as they did in mailbags and on the Spanish governor's desk. A single month of archived correspondence can amount to a substantial stack of paper. Despite the overwhelming quantity, these letters often represent less than half of the conversations that crisscrossed the Italian peninsula and spanned a global empire. My own reading-room table often resembled the desks of earlier centuries, overwhelmed with the particulars. My goal, however, was to reconstruct one desk: that of Ottavio Codogno, Milan's postmaster lieutenant, and the Tassis postmistress he served.

Codogno is best known for his published book, *New Itinerary of the Posts of the World* (1608), and a later version, *Compendium of the Posts* (1623).¹ These are invaluable sources on the post office of Milan and the Spanish system to which it belonged. Codogno combined a guide to the history and professional practice of post office administration with the listed routes run by its couriers. The books advertised the postmaster lieutenant's expertise in regulation, recordkeeping, and geography. They also preserve his uncertainty about pressing issues, such as the invention of a postmaster general: "I have diligently researched in order to identify the inventor, but after having consulted many authors," Codogno wrote, "I still cannot find a name for anyone who served in this role."² We can well imagine the earmarked editions of Livy, Julius Caesar, and Suetonius that Codogno cited for this purpose. These ancient historians told of valiant messengers delivering military intelligence at death-defying speeds. But they offered none of the day-to-day details that comprised Codogno's life in the early modern post house and that fill the archives today.

There was also no clear antecedent to Codogno's role as postmaster lieutenant, nor that of his patrons, the Tassis family of postmaster and postmistress generals. Unlike ancient couriers running between armies, Codogno spent his days catering to the political leaders, businessmen, and diplomats of northern Italy and beyond. Messengers circulated by cart, mule, ferry, and foot on a weekly or biweekly basis. They picked up and distributed mail from a hierarchy of post offices governed by a strict timetable. Mailbags brimmed with familial correspondences, diplomatic dispatches, newsletters, and bills of exchange. Codogno served a widowed postmistress, Lucina Cattanea Tassis, who herself answered to the Spanish postmaster general, a distant relative in Madrid. This was "a world of paper," but it was also a professional enterprise involving thousands of stakeholders, from princes to postmistresses to stable hands.³

Codogno had to venture beyond antiquity for an answer regarding the invention of a postmaster general, or *corriero maggiore*. He used his daily experience to hypothesize instead: "lacking businessmen, lawyers, and merchants, they would not have needed to maintain ordinary couriers (*ordinari*), carriers (*precacci*), or other messengers (*tabellari*), which were invented later, but only the fastest couriers (*corrieri*)."⁴ Codogno spent his days receiving, sorting, redistributing, and recording many different types of letters for many different destinations: the Spanish governor, the stall in the marketplace, or the mailbags intended for Venice, Genoa, Rome, and beyond. These were the responsibilities of a modern postal official to his ruler, his city, and the wider European public. As there had been little literacy, or even paper production, Codogno reasoned, there had not been as much demand for post offices or their many specialized services.[5]

This book follows in Codogno's footsteps. It explores the changing world he inhabited and delineates the powers the lieutenant exercised from his desk. Postal systems take their name from a straightforward technology: the expensive infrastructure of way stations ("posts") with horses and riders kept ready to ride in relay, thereby achieving the fastest speeds possible prior to the invention of modern communications technologies. Yet the early modern institution was both more expansive and more mundane than its Roman precedent, the *cursus publicus*.[6] The new post office operated at a different scale and frequency and with a different diversity of tasks. Codogno, his employers, and his employees innovated and exported new models of public and private services across Europe. They formed a diaspora of postal agents from northern Italy across the Habsburg domains and neighboring lands. This included Codogno's Milan, as well as Naples and Sicily, the Holy Roman Empire, and the Spanish Low Countries.

A distinct brand of postal service evolved during the period at the heart of this book, 1500–1700. Its evolution was primarily associated with one family: the Tassis, later the princes (*Grafen*) of Thurn und Taxis. From humble roots, the Tassis became a ruling dynasty of imperial and Spanish postmaster (and postmistress) generals responsible for overseeing a vast infrastructure of post offices and way stations. With the help of their compatriots and lieutenants, the Tassis family held their positions for several centuries. Individual stories of professionals' self-fashioning—including Codogno's—are woven across bureaucratic documentation, familial correspondence, and legal case files held in the Thurn und Taxis archives of Regensburg and state archives in northern Italy and Spain. In the story that emerges, the Tassis, their collaborators, and their competitors exercised the administration of postal service as far-reaching social and political power.

The shifting distinction between what constitutes public and private communications determines the boundaries between a state and a commercial civil society. The separation between public and private has been called "an essential component of the modern state," and yet historians either struggle to disentangle the two categories or declare the task anachronistic.[7] Early modern postal services offer a concrete measure, as the abstract question of distinguishing state from society came down to the material reality and practices of the post office desk. Sorting letters involved determining whether they were public (state) or private (nonstate) letters. Criteria included: What was the object? Who sent it? To whom? How did it travel, and where? What protections did it carry, and who would enforce them? Finally, and most contentiously, who would foot the bill? In writing his *New Itinerary*, Codogno offered one set of answers. I offer new evidence regarding his work with the Spanish governor, the Tassis postmistress, and even Venetian spies that enriches, and at times betrays, the ideals that he described in his book.

In fact, this book moves beyond Codogno's question of who invented the postal service to consider instead who *reinvented* it, time and time again, and why? From the sixteenth through eighteenth centuries, the technologies of communication remained largely stable: ink, put on a piece of paper by hand or press and carried from one location to another, sometimes (but not always) by a state-sponsored postal system. The role of communications technology in society shifted instead. Acting as information managers and intelligence services, postal officials shaped both international relations and domestic state-building according to their own goals, alliances, and antipathies. If knowledge is power, postal officials were its princes.

To date, postal services have most often been approached as a latent channel of greater cultural, political, and fiscal development. The modern state—a "machine for decision making"—could not exist without internal and external communications networks.[8] Improved communications facilitated making knowledge, money, and empires, but postal officials rarely appear as policymakers in early modern histories. In fact, postal officials carved out space for the state within cosmopolitan society and even interpersonal relationships long before the eighteenth century's age of global trade corporations. Individually, they drove early modern state-building for many of the same reasons as other agents of empire: because the state was an architecture that structured opportunities for honor and lucre. The aggregate effect was that extraterritorial protections and privileges for the courier, the mailbag, and even the individual letter gained widespread acceptance as norms.

Postal history has traditionally occupied a distinct sphere shaped by independent scholars, dedicated museums, or national postal systems. It flourished from the nineteenth century forward in tandem with philately (postage stamp collecting) and regional studies. Histories were sometimes produced with the sponsorship of the national posts themselves—see, for example, *Annales de las ordenanzas de correos de España* (1879), produced by the Spanish director general of couriers and telegraphs.[9]

Like Codogno's, these histories often originate the heroic lineage of postal systems in antiquity, primarily emphasizing the impact of technological revolution on delivery speeds. Herodotus's praise for Persian couriers who were slowed by "neither snow nor rain nor heat nor gloom of night" looms large in postal mythos. The phrase decorates the iconic James A. Farley Building (built between 1932 and 1935) in New York City and serves as an unofficial motto for the United States Postal Service. Stylized postal horns appear as logos for the modern Spanish Correos and German Bundespost systems. Crisply uniformed postal officials on postcards and posters carry everything from love letters to letters from the battlefront. These images evoke a timeless and depersonalized association between the state, exchange networks, and the res publica—the "public thing."

Recent scholarship recognizes that early modern postal systems supported a communication revolution, meaning a fundamental break from antiquity. In the late Middle Ages, news was sparse and sporadic. Mail traveled via restricted channels, and very rarely in formal relay. Elites and institutions generally relied upon their own couriers, while much of the population depended upon miscellaneous messengers including family, pilgrims, or other passersby.[10] With rare exceptions, rulers were more likely to coopt the mail infrastructure of the Catholic Church than establish their own systems.[11]

This was a revolution in the scale and quality, as well as the velocity, of news. By the seventeenth century, Europeans from many walks of life could purchase a printed newsletter with letters from as far away as China or the New World. The fastest couriers could reach Milan from Venice in one day, Rome in a day and a half, and Naples in four.[12] The traffic and sale of news constituted a full-fledged "information economy," spurring the growth of new professions such as journalists, diplomats, and spies.[13] Increasing literacy fed the demand for letters, that demand fed postal innovation, and innovation became a march of progress, whether in the forms of social liberation brought by Marshall McLuhan's Gutenberg galaxy or Jürgen Habermas's public sphere.[14]

Approaching this revolution from the perspective of the state reveals that—for all its liberation—the "letterocracy" of the seventeenth century also demanded a new obeisance to paper. Leaders bemoaned the seemingly endless stream of paperwork: even emperors bowed under the weight of written missives facilitating governance, scholarship, commerce, and interpersonal relationships in the early modern world.[15] Secretaries, diplomats, counselors, senators, and magistrates also took part in the information economy in both official and unofficial capacities. Documentation and its management created new professions and settings, from the diplomat's desk to the merchant's letterboard. Chancelleries and archives armed princes with paper bullets for their dynastic campaigns.[16] Public opinion could be a demanding master for princes while supporting profitable careers for their document-wrangling administrators.

Postal officials and post offices therefore straddled the line between the governing and commercial spheres, and between the public (state-serving) and particular, or private, interest.[17] Early modern scholarship has provided many examples of technocrats who expanded and exercised the sovereign powers now associated with a state in ways more complex than patrimonial profiteering. Revisionist histories of the Gondi financiers of Florence and France or the Höchstetter bankers of Augsburg show that social networks and trade in social capital scaffolded the fiscal state.[18] Military historians have demonstrated that the contractor-state model expanded, rather than hampered, the state's potential for war-making.[19] New histories of trade and empire show that political leaders and investors in joint-stock companies were often the same people.[20] States have always had stakeholders.

Throughout its reinventions, I contend that postal service was the impetus as well as the impact of three major developments of the early modern state. The first was an expanding bureaucracy of empire. While states demanded speed, security, and frequency, they depended on postal agents to provide a faultless communications system with only limited resources. The second was the commercial revolution. Wealthy private patrons were more than willing to pay for a variety of postal services, from carrying packets to renting horses for travel. The third was social discipline, and at times confessionalization.[21] Monitoring dissent, policing travel, and shaping belief drove the search for new controls over civil society.

The Renaissance of the Postal Service in Northern Italy

Jacob Burckhardt called the Italian Renaissance state (c. 1350–1500) a "work of art," and early postal systems were a key component of the masterpiece, complementing new and revived forms of diplomacy, commerce, and legislation.[22] From the duchy of Savoy in the west to the prince-bishopric of Trento in the east, cisalpine Italy was a natural communications zone. The Tassis family and a network of agents from the valleys of Bergamo in Lombardy formulated international treaties that provided the sovereignty of the posts, the extraterritoriality of postal agents, and guarantees of (relatively) reliable service across national and confessional boundaries. This history of postal reinvention shows that northern Italy remained a cradle of statecraft despite its reputation of decline in "the forgotten centuries."[23] The Padan plain had shaped the language of post offices, postal routes, and posting into omnipresent terms by the eighteenth century. The early modern European post and its trappings transcended infrastructure to constitute a cosmopolitan culture of travel and exchange.

In the late Middle Ages, messengership was more of an ad hoc practice than a professional identity. The term *nuncius* predominated, describing any kind of message-bearing envoy. Simple letter carriers included miscellaneous *cursores, tabellari, fanti, varletti*, or even *cokini*—moonlighting kitchen laborers.[24] In some regions, butchers gained a reputation as mail carriers, and in others, innkeepers did. In a 1585 encyclopedia of professions, all messengers were grouped together to describe any job that "entails going on foot, or running the posts by horse, or by boat, or by carriage, & carrying letters, packages, money, goods, chests, bills or similar sorts of things, serving princes, lords, gentlemen, merchants, and whoever else commands him."[25] Mail was just another good, circulated by a varied economy of middlemen.

The explosive growth of universities in the twelfth and thirteenth centuries attracted students and professors from far abroad. They desired mail connections to their places of origin. A regular messenger connected the university city of Padua to Venice and Bergamo on foot as early as 1158.[26] By 1250, imperial universities founded by the Holy Roman Emperor Frederick II (d. 1250) promised to staff messengers for each nation represented among students and faculty. These university messengers enjoyed royal protection, which made them more secure and reliable, but access to their services remained restricted to students and faculty.[27]

The fourteenth century brought affordable paper and growing demand for the conveyance of mail. Europeans imported papermaking technology and supplies from Islamic Spain and North Africa, and many of the first rag-paper mills cropped up in northern Italy.[28] Traveling merchants relied on paper correspondence to administer affairs from abroad. Occasionally, they established mail-carrying services for themselves and their clients.[29] Merchant courier cooperatives known as *scarselle* ran routes between Florence and Avignon (c. 1357), Barcelona and Pisa (c. 1394), and Bergamo and Venice (c. 1440).[30] The international trader Francesco Datini (d. 1410) and his wife, Margherita, maintained an extensive correspondence network from Prato in Tuscany in the late fourteenth century. Surviving letters show that the Datini and their associates nonetheless relied on many informal messengers, from family and friends to domestic servants.[31]

By the Renaissance, Italian governance had a rich late medieval tradition of *communes*, urbanizing *civitates*, and, increasingly, aristocratic *signorie*. The term *stato* came to encompass all this variety, designating a collective gathered, disciplined, and legitimated for the protection of internal peace.[32] The Renaissance in Italy promoted the sovereign state-maker, or *princeps*, as a guarantor of state security.[33] The nexus of the *stato* was the prince's court, which was often on the move. Duke Galeazzo Sforza of Milan (1440–1476) balanced his military campaigns with territorial governance by way of an unparalleled postal system of over fifty couriers between Milan, Rome, and Naples. The steep cost of an on-demand postal system meant that it served only Italy's political and economic elite. Sforza's system cost at least 1,000 lire per month—more than five times what a laborer could hope to earn in a year.[34] Rulers granted their postal services special privileges, such as exclusive access to royal livery, horses, roads, and staging posts to further ensure that their couriers traveled quickly, securely, and reliably.

These were the heirs to the "fastest couriers" of antiquity, and Italy's prince-despots became accustomed to the speedy news enjoyed by their ancient predecessors. Letters bore ample postal markings, such as a hangman's noose to threaten consequences for delay or theft, or the annotated commands "haste haste haste" (*cito cito cito*) or "flying" (*volante*).[35] The ruling families of early modern Italy competed with one another for the best news networks. In 1464, the duke of Milan was furious to learn that his Florentine rival, Lorenzo de' Medici (1449–1492), was the first to hear the results of the papal conclave. He cautioned his ambassador in Rome against a similar lapse: the duke demanded that he be the first to know any news, even if it cost "25, 30, 40, 50 ducats, or more." Papal election in coming decades correlated strongly with miraculous courier speeds.[36] Florentine couriers boasted speeds from 13 to 18 modern kilometers per hour, depending on weather and topography. This could connect Rome to Florence in as little as two days and Rome to London in less than two weeks.[37]

If the Italian *stato* gave rise to postal services, it was Charles V of Habsburg's *imperium* that gave rise to the Tassis postmaster generals. The Tassis were one of several northern Italian families who experienced new prosperity, prestige, and peril in the age of the renewed Italian Wars (1494–1559). Their royal patrons, the Habsburgs, held an unparalleled geographic territory. From their origins in Switzerland and as the archdukes of Austria, the Habsburgs had ascended to elected office as Holy Roman emperors. Strategic alliances and coincidental deaths gave them control of both Burgundy and Castille. Philip the Handsome's young son, Charles, not only inherited the Spanish and Dutch holdings but succeeded his grandfather, Maximilian I, as the Holy Roman emperor.[38] An alliance with the Habsburg and Spanish monarchs provided the Tassis with key competitive advantages for establishing their own administrative dynasty.

The Tassis are central characters of this book, but they are never alone. I adopt the perspective of the best-known princes of the post and their many rivals, such as the Venetian Company of Couriers, foreign diplomats and spies, and even disgruntled employees. Moving beyond a family study of the Tassis (which has been expertly done by Wolfgang Behringer, among others) reveals their astronomical successes and scandalous failures within the context of a wider social network.[39] We also see the disproportionate representation of a single region: the Bergamasco, containing Bergamo and its surrounding valleys. Even as postal service transitioned away from the Renaissance family firm, kinship ties among the Tassis and other mail services continued to shape alliances and antipathies. This story begins with the rise of the Bergamaschi couriers and ends with their gradual replacement as the communications technocrats par excellence by a new class of administrators from the Netherlands. By the eighteenth century, the sun was setting on the Tassis international posts, although in other ways, it was dawning on their reincarnation as princes of Thurn und Taxis.

The Bergamaschi diaspora structures the geographic and chronological scope of the book. We begin with their rise in the Renaissance and end with their gradual eclipse in the later Baroque. We journey from their Lombard homeland to the far shores of England and beyond. Several chapters touch on a rival class of Tuscan administrator-entrepreneurs active in Tuscany, the Papal States, and Savoy as they challenged Bergamaschi dominance.[40] The postal systems of France and England largely did not employ Italians and followed a different pattern and timeline of establishment. I highlight where paths converge, especially in the final chapters of this book, which feature a broader thematic study of travel and public representation of postal services.[41] In addition, the premodern posts were a largely land-based endeavor as supported by the study of itinerary books in chapter 6. Postal officials used rivers and ports when available but distrusted the unpredictability that they introduced to increasingly rigid timetables. Separate administrative bodies handled mail sent to the New World and the Ottoman Empire, such as the postmaster of the Indies in Spain and various rectors and captains throughout the Venetian Stato da Màr.[42]

The Early Modern Information Economy

As central as it was to the expanding bureaucracy of the state, the early modern post office was equally indebted to a globalizing commercial revolution. Post office documents were hybrids of commercial and bureaucratic practice. Surviving documents underscore the chimeric nature of the mail-carrying business. Common forms like double-entry accounting were further adapted to serve a postmaster's, postmistress's, or courier's purposes. The post house patois helped to translate information across the court, the marketplace, and the wider world.

As a result, the process of reassembling the many miscellaneous paper slips, accounting ledgers, and letters from Codogno's desk was often much messier than the polished narrative offered in his books. The diversity and dispersion of post office records also make it difficult to achieve the style of comparative, connective postal history that I undertake here. On its surface, a letter costing its sender a quarter scudo per post seems straightforward enough. Yet defining a sender (a person? an office? a state?), a scudo (of which city? paid to whom?), a letter (a half page? a postal ounce?), and a post (measured by whose distance?) is highly contextual. Even at the time of sending, disagreements on these matters occasionally led to litigation and even blows.

Traditionally, historians have limited the confusion by considering systems in isolation, parsing the Venetian Company of Couriers, the Tassis-dominated imperial and Spanish posts, and the English foreign posts from one another. Nineteenth-century archivists often cataloged material related to "domestic" post offices separate from "foreign" posts that had been established abroad to serve an embassy and expatriate communities. The records of pre-eighteenth-century postal services operated abroad were rarely preserved and often survive only as trace evidence in diplomatic letters or the Thurn und Taxis family correspondence. But separating domestic from foreign mail—and even private from public mail—risks reifying categories that Codogno, among others, were actively defining for much of the early modern era. It is only in reading across the archives kept in Milan, Venice, Regensburg, and Simancas (among other places) that we see how postal systems originated as both fundamentally international and private-public services.

Similarly, the worlds of mercantile and political letters or letter-carriers often preoccupy different subfields of historical study. The letters themselves are most often in separate collections or even archives based on their content and senders, and political and economic historians work in their own subfields. Understanding postal systems requires crossing these boundaries. By the Renaissance, municipal messengers (*cavallari*, or *tabellari*, from the Latin *tabellarius*) had already blurred the line between mail services intended for governance and those intended for commerce.[43] Many cities of the Venetian land empire, including Padua, Verona, and Brescia, appointed a courier corps to ferry correspondence and money to and from Venice.[44] These messengers formed trade organizations to guard the privileges they were offered in exchange for their state service, and were increasingly overseen by their own master (*maestro dei corrieri*).

Like modern mail systems, messengers catered to both private (individual) and public (state) customers. In Florence, the entrepreneurial Antonio di Bartolomeo del Vantaggio (d. 1480) managed an extensive network that spanned all of Italy and reached as far as London. Vantaggio offered subscription services to prominent merchant families, among other notables.[45] The post office was always both a business and an administration, and the postal official was a private-public figure who balanced governance and commerce. Writing in 1608, Codogno recognized that the demands of "businessmen, lawyers, and merchants" were the bread and butter of his office in Milan. Princes could prioritize speed at higher costs, but bureaucrats and other common users desired regularity and reliability at an affordable price. Ordinary couriers who routinely journeyed from Nuremberg to Vienna and back in seven weeks were more important in this respect than the fastest couriers, who rode from Rome to London in two.

State postal systems were further commercialized by their deep ties to news culture. Postal service, like print, worked in concert with oral and manuscript newsgathering. Regular mail routes in turn allowed the regular production of the manuscript newsletter, and eventually, the printed newspaper. Contemporaries lampooned the resulting ceaseless demand for news as nosiness verging on madness or delusional paranoia. Cartoons like Giuseppe Maria Mitelli's *Courier in the Distance* (figure 2) poked fun at war "enthusiasts" who loudly proclaimed their predictions. At the same time, the post brought intelligence with potentially grave political and economic ramifications for its subjects. The term

FIGURE 2. Giuseppe Maria Mitelli, *Il corriere in lontananza* (post-1692). The full title translates to "The courier in the distance awaited by the war enthusiasts." Each character speculates as to the nationality of the courier and places a bet on what news he carries. Image © The Trustees of the British Museum.

for possessing intelligence (*tener intelligenza*) gained traction in Italy in the early modern period. Being intelligent, having intelligence, or sharing intelligence can be defined as gathering or trading politically sensitive information with the aim of strategic advantage.[46] Chatting with the postmaster and courier, or peeking at a stranger's letters, might provide news on the state of the Catholic missions in Japan, settlements in the New World, or the death and succession of monarchs as far away as England. Bribing the courier could mean learning the contents of a personal letter or the current exchange rates in Antwerp before a business rival. Fortunes were made and lost on knowing the arrival of a ship or its loss at sea.[47] This put postal officials in an especially powerful position to intervene and interfere in information, as well as to convey it.

Depictions of early modern mail carriers reflected their power and were far from the Norman Rockwell–style portrait of a dependable, unpartisan, and patriotic public servant. An eighteenth-century French courtier stated, "I would as soon dine with the hangman as with the postmaster-general."[48] Privacy was defined primarily through violation.

The political consequences of correspondence going astray could be severe, from firing to imprisonment or even death. But what of the economic consequences? In the foreground of *Courier in the Distance*, money changes hands. The loser will pay the winner of a bet regarding what news the couriers would bring. In an age of international speculation, knowledge of current events carried economic value.

A burgeoning class of international traders (*negotianti*) demanded the same speed, security, and reliability available to rulers. The growing market share of private (nonstate) correspondence frequently pitted postmasters against preexisting merchant and municipal carriers. As the postmaster Ruggero Tassis of Milan once put it, "Two postmasters for a city are as incompatible as two princes."[49] The success of commercial postal service relied upon restricting other carriers, and postal officials launched a series of aggressive market takeovers, including establishing ordinary couriers to run on regular timetables and postal stagecoaches to ferry travelers as well as letters. The result was ongoing conflict in the courts and on the roads, in which postal officials aggressively lobbied executive powers to expand their privileges while further restricting those of their rivals.

Surveillance and Discipline

The twin forces of bureaucratization and commercialization—and the anxieties they provoked—accelerated a third key function of post offices: surveillance and social discipline. The post office was a crucible for the personnel, practices, and ethics of communication in society. The distinction between privacy—that which should not preoccupy the state—and publicity—that which must do so—dictated postal practice long before it was fully theorized or canonized in law. Anxieties about the contents of a letter, the sanctity of a seal, and the partisanship of the postmaster reveal shifting cultural expectations. Ottavio Codogno emphasized the need for postal officials' prudence, discretion, and equanimity. He advertised these characteristics as a professional culture akin to an ideal bureaucracy, as did other enterprising postal officials in the genre of printed postal itineraries. Books like *New Itinerary* commercialized bureaucratic knowledge, adopting a radical transparency and even ecumenicism toward communications and public service more broadly. A generation of postal lieutenants like Codogno reinvented postal service as discrete brokerage for the masses.

The success of state postal enterprise depended on the trust and, even more importantly, on the distrust of alternative modes of conveying communications. In early modern Italy, much as today, "information war" was waged by securing one's own communications while denying a rival that same security.[50] The nemesis might be a heretical merchant, a foreign ruler, or even a pesky family member. Postmaster generals offered unique expertise in propaganda, counterespionage, and management of public relations, but they could promise their rulers a communications monopoly only if they enjoyed it in turn. If alternative channels such as merchant couriers or rival postmasters remained, the unsupervised traffic of letters and print could continue to pose a threat to state power.

By the second half of the seventeenth century, the post office would ferry new waves of cosmopolitan travelers and tourists by post. The postilion and its private counterparts came to replace the postmaster general as the familiar face of postal services. Yet life in post-Reformation Europe meant balancing an outward public identity with a hidden, private identity for many. State service often meant performing secrecy, adopting a stoic mask. Art, theater, and satirical literature vividly dramatized as much by juxtaposing Harpocrates, the god of silence, and Momus, the god of rumor.[51] The danger of discovery made committing one's secret self—or discovering another's—on the written page even more thrilling. Familiar letters, travel journals, secret histories, and novels composed of stolen mailbags trafficked in the frisson of revelation that came from opening letters and even shooting the messenger.

In fact, moments of letter interception and post office audits gird this history of postal service. Thomas Safley describes how bankruptcy reveals "the *praxis* of counting-houses and marketplaces, where persons made decisions and faced consequences."[52] So, too, do these moments of postal breakdown. The seventeenth century was also the age of visitation, or inquisition, as bureaucracies both enacted and were subjected to surveillance and social discipline. Several chapters of this book draw extensively from a 1612 Spanish audit of Ottavio Codogno's post office. Inspectors demanded that the postmistress and her lieutenant prove that carrying private correspondence facilitated, rather than corrupted, state postal services. The case files of the Venetian State Inquisitors also offer unique insight into postal espionage—real, imagined, or thwarted. It is in moments of frantic document-gathering by contemporaries, in response to an audit or to identify a mole, that the invisible is briefly made visible.

Postmasters had always been public facing, but by the seventeenth century they were also increasingly answerable to public opinion in print.

Notables from the Swedish king Gustavus Adolphus to the Venetian satirist Ferrante Pallavicino questioned whether a Habsburg-dominated postal service could be trusted in an age of free commerce. Dissenters attacked the legitimacy of a communications monopoly. They claimed individual privacy as well as the public's "right to know," both sanctifying and ripping open the courier's mailbag. From diplomatic espionage to brigandage, control over the mail was an ongoing cultural war within, as well as among, early modern states.

Commerce or governance, war or peace, news culture or censorship: these tensions have shaped the history of postal systems since the Renaissance. When Ottavio Codogno wrote his *New Itinerary*, he began by looking backward: Who had invented the postal service? Codogno's next chapters spoke instead to contemporary concerns: Who was the postmaster, and whom did he serve? What kinds of things were sent by post, and what professional ethos guided their management? Victims compared the violation of letter interception to everything from eavesdropping on confession to sexual violence. The same postman who offered to deliver fast, secure, and reliable correspondence could be a spy for a rival or a surveilling state official. Yet the demand for postal service never ceased.

The international "ordinaries"—a term referring to ordinary couriers traveling on regular routes and timetables—wove Europe together for centuries. They depended on guarantees of extraterritoriality, which were in turn derived from hard-won consensus on the collective benefit of communications overlaying geographic, political, and confessional boundaries. Reaching universal consensus on that point was a long and complex process that provides another through line for this book. Postal networks and postal workers would come to represent the civil servants of a primarily domestic enterprise, but this was a far cry from their origins as a multipolar family firm managing international couriers for many rulers. New public relations campaigns obscured their many other functions, such as gathering intelligence, countering espionage, and negotiating foreign and domestic policy.

Maps and genealogies commissioned by postal officials continue to trumpet the role of postal service in nation-building today. The ennobling of the Tassis dynasty and the domestication of postal service—now accountable to a wider public—are two sides of the same coin. Both processes distanced state postal service from an earlier history of espionage and counterespionage work. They also took for granted the state's involvement in offering postal service as a public utility and fiscal mainstay.

Postal services were reinvented as showpieces of modern political economy, much like new road infrastructures. Taxing travelers and correspondents could offer the modernizing state fiscal means of social discipline.

The success of an international state-sponsored system of ordinary couriers, overseen by a postmaster (or postmistress) general, and its involvement in spheres from journalism to border control reflected the alliances, experiences, and goals of a set of postal administrators from northern Italy. Postal officials expanded services to a broader, and increasingly commercial, clientele, but they also provided rulers with new executive prerogatives. Postal agents and the spaces they oversaw, from post offices to the mailbag, shaped how contemporaries thought of the ethics of publicity and their place in international cooperation or conflict. New ideals such as extraterritoriality, information sovereignty, free commerce, public service, and secrecy of correspondence were put into practice long before their Enlightenment theorizations. Postal services were neither a glorious revival of antiquity nor a teleological precursor to our own Information Age. Communications systems, alongside political cultures, are constantly reinvented.

The following chapters proceed largely chronologically, with each considering one major reinvention of postal systems. The Bergamaschi diaspora (and the Tassis family firm in particular) arose from the Italian Wars, when conflict between the Habsburg and Valois dynasties in the Italian peninsula drove the demand for talented brokers on the edges of empires. As hot wars waxed and waned, postmaster generals and, increasingly, foreign postmasters-in-residence continued to wage "information wars," managing public opinion for many patrons. By the turn of the seventeenth century, postal systems had become postal *services*: they conveyed private as well as public (state) letters, in addition to packages and people. This reinvention was an aggressive market takeover to establish monopolistic privileges over letter conveyance.

Two rhetorics cloaked this driving purpose. The first was a counter-Reformation concern for surveillance and control. The second, which took precedence in the post-Westphalian age, was that of universal utility. Postmasters competed to offer unpartisan service in the pursuit of "free commerce." By the end of the seventeenth century, the international postal services had been domesticated. Postal systems were now fully aligned with sovereign power and the consolidation of the fiscal state, as commemorated in print, maps, and new genealogies of Thurn und Taxis. The signals intelligence operation known as the "black chamber" still came to represent the open secret of the post: that the state could and would continue to intervene in civil communications.

It is only in reading across administrative archives, diplomatic letters, and popular print that we rediscover the potential reinventions dreamed up by postal officials and sold to their employers. We also learn that political leaders deliberately obscured the presence of postal agents in politicking, as it fueled distrust of state-appointed officials in a communications system. Then, as now, improved technology amplified early modern culture wars, from political to confessional conflict. The following chapters will explore in depth how and why state postal services succeeded in deliberate campaigns to integrate and then distance postmasters from statecraft and international relations.

This book begins from the origins of the Bergamaschi diaspora and the development of the Tassis "brand" of information management at the end of the Renaissance (chapter 1). The Italian Wars may have ended in 1559, but subtler postal wars continued as states contested the role of a foreign postmaster-in-residence and post offices as institutions paralleling resident embassies (chapter 2). By the end of the sixteenth century, postal services were essential personnel in an age of banditry, plague, and confessional conflict. Postmasters and postal couriers successfully lobbied for expanded protections and privileges that gave them the upper hand against various rivals (chapter 3).

Chapters 4 and 5 each examine different arteries of this international postal network. Shifting perspectives among leaders, postmasters, and couriers illuminates the knotty web of personal antipathies and alliances that shaped long-term infrastructure. The Italian Road connecting Milan and Venice represented one of the earliest international postal treaties with bilateral service (chapter 4). The transalpine roads saw Tassis family members compete and collaborate with one another, as well as with a new generation of lieutenants at the outbreak of the Thirty Years' War (chapter 5). In each case, the question of whether state postal services could successfully balance private and public patrons drove new auditing, resistance, and the attempted reform of post offices.

Two visions of postal service had crystallized by the middle of the seventeenth century. Postal lieutenants and postmasters advertised in print a public-facing, commercialized service that provided a hospitality and travel infrastructure while also ferrying state letters, to the mutual benefit of prince and public (chapter 6). Yet state postal services continued to serve the intelligence-gathering and social discipline goals of expanding state bureaucracies. Public awareness and reaction to the "black chambers" of the ancien régime kept post offices front and center in debates about privacy, the public's right to know, and official secrecy (chapter 7).

These tensions prove key to understanding the blend of private and public interests that define utilities today: namely, as public services attained through private contracting and state-backed monopolistic privileges. Before the Enlightenment development of utility theory, postal officials routinely argued for the common utility of international postal networks, adapting their approach as the contemporary political climate demanded. Utilities exist at the intersection of profit and public service, governance and commerce, national security, and commodity. They defy common market principles of ownership and competition. Expensive and expansive, postal systems depleted state treasuries by their very nature. This was state-funded communication as a common good—if controlled. To understand these warring impulses, we must do as a seventeenth-century Italian proverb cautioned: "Watch those to whom you trust your letters."[53]

Chapter 1

The Tassis Family Firm
Postmaster Generals of Information War

The clowns, or *zanni*, of the Italian commedia dell'arte traditionally shared a common homeland. The wily servant, Harlequin, and the innkeeper, Brighella, hailed from "the valleys of Bergamo." In Carlo Goldoni's eighteenth-century *Servant of Two Masters*, the Harlequin archetype, here called "Truffaldino," attempts to carry mail for two patrons at once to double his income. But if he mixes up the senders and recipients, he will give away the ruse. His masters' requests mount and contradict one another, driving the servant toward a breakdown. Marveling at the servant's folly, another character still infers that as a Bergamasco, Truffaldino is likely a cunning knave rather than the simple fool that he first appeared to be.[1] Bergamaschi knew that it paid to serve many masters—if you could pull it off.

Truffaldino's Bergamaschi compatriots were better positioned to do so than most. Bergamo and its surrounding valleys were located northeast of Milan, above the Lombard plain (see figure 1). The Swiss Grisons and Bavarian hubs of Augsburg and Nuremberg lay to the north. To the south, the Padan valley channeled exchange. Bergamo passed back and forth between the rulers of Milan and Venice in the fifteenth century, reflecting its strategic position. By the sixteenth century, it was a heavily fortified upper city. This liminal homeland produced brokers who were adept at navigating tricky situations.[2]

Like Truffaldino or Brighella, the Tassis aspired to greater things. They rose from merchant bankers to postmasters serving imperial, Spanish, and Venetian patrons. Tassis (also Tasso or Taxis) progenitors are often upstaged in scholarship by more famous descendants, such as a distant cousin, the poet Torquato Tasso (d. 1595), or the later German nobility of Thurn und Taxis. It was nonetheless the "knaves" from the Valle Brembana who translated a northern Italian technology of running mail in relay into a powerful international network. The Tassis built on early transalpine successes to become lauded technocrats across Europe.

Many have praised the Tassis as exceptional entrepreneurs, but opportunism depends upon having opportunities to start with. This chapter begins by considering three structural advantages that enabled the Tassis to serve many masters. First, the Tassis employed their Bergamasco heritage to act as brokers. They cultivated loyalties to many princes and popes. They collaborated with compatriots such as the Venetian Company of Couriers. As "Italian imperials," they routinely bridged political divides, even in times of open war. Second, the Tassis dynasty could be in multiple places at once. Past scholarship amply documents how the Renaissance family firm model transformed into protocapitalist enterprise.[3] The Tassis worked together to acquire monopolistic privileges, cultivate reputation and patronage, and apprentice family members across Europe. Family ties were not always harmonious, but when they worked well, they circulated expertise, built alliances, and fostered trust around shared investment in family fortunes. The postal network's success remained dependent upon a family network. As this chapter will show, eminent leaders mediated Tassis family squabbles to keep communications functioning smoothly. Beneath its new bureaucratic trappings, running the posts remained a family business.

Third, postmasters balanced physical presence in many courts with figurative presence through *intelligencing*, meaning trading in politically sensitive information. Italy had long been torn between pro-imperial and pro-papal factions. In the sixteenth century, a second generation of Tassis postmasters navigated the new and dangerous world of renewed Italian wars. Many Italian dynasties allied with the Habsburg rulers of Spain and the Holy Roman Empire, thereby claiming new territories and titles as the dukes of Milan, Mantua, and Tuscany. State-building popes countered Habsburg hegemony by allying with France's Valois dynasty.[4] The Tassis continued to intelligence for many masters, despite what struck many as mutually exclusive loyalties to Venetian, papal, and imperial patrons.

The Bergamaschi were able to do so because they offered valuable services at a time of great demand. I contend that both licit and illicit intelligencing came to define a Tassis brand of information management in a time of *information war*. "Information war" describes a battle over truth and authority focused on control and disruption of communications technology. While waged between opposing international forces, information war continues in periods of peacetime as a battle for control of the public narrative. In some cases, it features open attacks on communications infrastructure. In other cases, foreign-allied agents exploit existing fault lines of domestic discontent by way of covert operations, blurring the line between combatant and noncombatant. The term information war has gained traction with relation to modern cybersecurity and strategic disinformation, but it well represents the role of interception, propaganda, and disinformation as early modern factions struggled to control Italy.[5]

The Tassis were on the front lines of information war in early modern Italy. Postmasters ensured the security and reliability of a ruler's communications. They also propagated favorable intelligence and occasionally slowed or contradicted unfavorable communications. They administered national, familial, and political networks from London to Madrid. Sources from the English and Venetian archives demonstrate that even these states reluctantly depended upon Tassis intelligence.

Like other diplomatic representatives, postmasters were professional "masters of ambiguity" in the early modern period.[6] This chapter explores the strategic complexity of navigating many alliances through the case of the postmaster Simone Tassis (d. 1563). Simone came of age during the Italian Wars. He cultivated intelligence networks established by his uncles and built out the postal network to reach new extents. Simone also collaborated and competed with his family across Europe, including Bergamaschi compatriots in the Venetian Company of Couriers. In later life, Simone waged a new campaign to establish the autocratic management style of the family firm in the post office of Milan.[7] Structuring the office of corriero maggiore (*correo mayor* in Spanish) required a clearer delineation of privileges and duties. While "hot" wars in Italy may have come to an end by 1559, information wars continued to shape how post offices institutionalized an administrative hierarchy in the second half of the century.

The Rise of a Postal Dynasty

Camerata Cornello may seem like an unlikely setting for the clash of empires. The hamlet sits high on the hilltops of Valle Brembana in the Bergamasco, about a half hour's drive from Bergamo and about an hour from Milan (figure 1). The modern highway follows a gorge carved by the Brembo River farther north into the Swiss Grisons. Rough-hewn stairs lead into a complex of medieval stone buildings, just up the hill from the bus stop and a large inn. It takes a careful eye to spot the worn heraldry carved above an arch or the faint traces of paint by a window: a leg of a badger (*tasso* in Italian) and a hint of a curved postal horn.

The Tassis home at Camerata Cornello (also called Cornello dei Tasso) is now a museum dedicated to the family and to postal history. It contains a restaurant, exhibits, a bookstore, and the Tassis family chapel, with rich frescoes depicting Saint Catherine, the patron saint of messengers. A plaque indicates the remnants of the Via Mercatorum, a late medieval alpine path traveled by many of the families in this region. The Tassis were one among many such merchants who parlayed their location in the alpine foothills and at the crossroads of empires into a Europe-wide reputation for hospitality and brokerage.[8]

Although quiet today, the hillsides were bustling by the late Middle Ages. Bergamo and its northern valleys were wealthy, populous, and central to networks of trade and travel. Camerata Cornello hosted a market and provided a key waypoint for merchants traveling the busy alpine routes with mail and other goods.[9] The Bergamaschi dominated the early Venetian Company of Couriers to the extent that it was often referred to as the "company of the Bergamaschi" well into the eighteenth century. In 1305, Venice further subordinated the company to the Provveditori di Comun, three regulators overseeing commerce within Venice and its subject cities.[10] The couriers adopted a common Venetian corporate form known as a "school" (*scuola*) around 1400, headed by a company steward (*gastaldo artis*) elected from their membership.[11] These developments notably preceded Bergamo's incorporation into the Venetian land empire, the terraferma, in 1426. The people of Bergamo continued to cross the Padan plain between Milan, Venice, and the Swiss cantons regularly.

In 1490, the Venetian Company of Couriers assembled a charter known as the *Mariegola*. We see from its member rolls that the residents of Bergamo, and particularly of the Valle Brembana, constituted most of the company.[12] Surnames repeated across the decades as fathers passed their offices to sons, and uncles to nephews among the Giupponi, Maffei, Benzoni, and Tassis families. The home of the company was the chapel of San Giovanni Elemosinario, located just past the Rialto Bridge in the commercial heart of Venice. The couriers gathered there to hold meetings, celebrate holy days, and distribute charity among widows and orphans.[13] Illustrations of Saint Catherine appear throughout the chapel and charter, receiving offerings from her couriers and benevolently watching over their journeys. Courier companies regularly involved their members in performances of professional and civic pride.[14]

The Venetian Company operated under the purview of the Provveditori and relied upon both state and commercial traffic. Early chapters of the *Mariegola* established that a courier would stand ready in the courtyard of the Palazzo Ducale at the disposition of its councils.[15] The elected bench (*banco*) of the company distributed this responsibility and other journeys on a rotating basis. This meant that a courier would often have several weeks of intensive work over a monthslong period. Competition for jobs grew fierce when war or foreign politics restricted traveling. Conflict led to new sets of legislation aimed at policing the turn system, which restricted the number of offices and provided debt relief for couriers' families. Similar practices existed among the municipal messengers (cavallari) of the Venetian terraferma and a growing body of papal state couriers. By the fourteenth century, papal couriers had also incorporated as a collegium of between twenty and sixty-five members headed by a *magister cursorum*.[16]

Like many trades in Renaissance guild cities, the Venetian Company benefited from monopolistic privileges. These were invariably discussed as ancient "rights" rather than monopoly in a modern sense. They included exclusive privileges to distinguish couriers visually, such as the right to bear the lion of Saint Mark, the symbol of the Venetian state.[17] Trading nations had long negotiated for their own mail-carrying privileges in Venice.[18] By the fifteenth century, the company instead fought for official exclusivity in northern Italy and on the route to Rome, which was their primary source of income.[19] Foot messengers and letter carriers (known as *pedoni*, *procacci*, or *portalettere*) nonetheless offered rates and services that the official couriers would not. Florentine mercantile cooperatives (*scarselle*) also had remarkable longevity, running mail long into the seventeenth century.[20]

Whereas the Venetian Company had strong roots in both merchant and municipal mail systems, the postal system of Milan grew primarily from princely couriers. Historians name the Duke of Milan, Gian Galeazzo Visconti (1351–1402), as the founder of Renaissance state postal systems. References to the Visconti *posta* and *poste* appear in the 1380s. Ducal couriers accessed a system of way stations for rest and exchange of horses throughout the Duchy of Milan.[21] In 1395, the Visconti family purchased the title of imperial duke and expanded their territory from Genoa in the west to Vicenza in the east, and as far south as the gates of Florence. By 1402, the duchy consisted of over thirty cities, including the university at Pavia. Its countryside (*contado*) was among the largest in Italy, at over 4,000 square kilometers.[22] Couriers served a key role tying the outlying cities to the ducal court, as well as keeping the dukes and their captains informed about the duchy's many contested fronts.

The Tassis emerged at the intersection of the Venetian Company of Couriers and Milanese ducal posts, much as Bergamo lay between Venice and Milan. The Tassis family name appears as far back as one "Odonuj de Taxo" in 1146 (see figure 3). An "Omodeo Tasso del Cornello" was one of many Bergamaschi acting as Venetian couriers by the fourteenth century.[23] The "Sandri" branch (named after its progenitor, Alessandro, or "Sandro," Tasso) had parlayed their success into postal privileges in the Papal States by the mid-fifteenth century. This income, combined with a salt-tax collection contract in Bergamo, enabled the family's further investment in land and property, as well as in a Rome-based bank.[24]

Early Habsburg patronage of the Tassis is only roughly sketched by surviving sources. Like the dukes of Milan, the archdukes of Austria ruled over expansive territory, and their diplomatic and financial networks stretched even farther. Frederick and his son, Emperor Maximilian I (1459–1519), employed the first generation of Tassis family traders-turned-postmasters to ferry correspondence and funds as far as from Brussels to Rome. Seventeenth-century genealogists asserted that Holy Roman Emperor Frederick III (1415–1493) had employed a "Ruggero de Tassis."[25] By 1490, Maximilian gave the first surviving postal contract to Janetto (or Zanetto) Tassis (d. 1517). Impressed by the papal and Venetian postal routes, Maximilian appears to have poached Janetto Tassis from Rome on behalf of his own imperial court.[26] He charged Janetto with establishing postal way stations from the Low Countries to Italy through the Swiss Grisons. The route passed through the Tassis homeland, contributing to their suitability for the contract.[27]

Renaissance courts relied on a "master of the couriers" (*magister cursorum*, or maestro dei corrieri), who oversaw the dispatch and reception of a team of (usually royal) messengers riding in relay. A postmaster (*maestro delle poste*), meanwhile, managed the supporting infrastructure of way stations and readied horses.[28] Early edicts referred to the Tassis as "postmasters" and "masters of couriers" interchangeably, as the family subsumed both sets of responsibilities.[29] Like the original master of the couriers, a Tassis brother always needed to be accessible to the

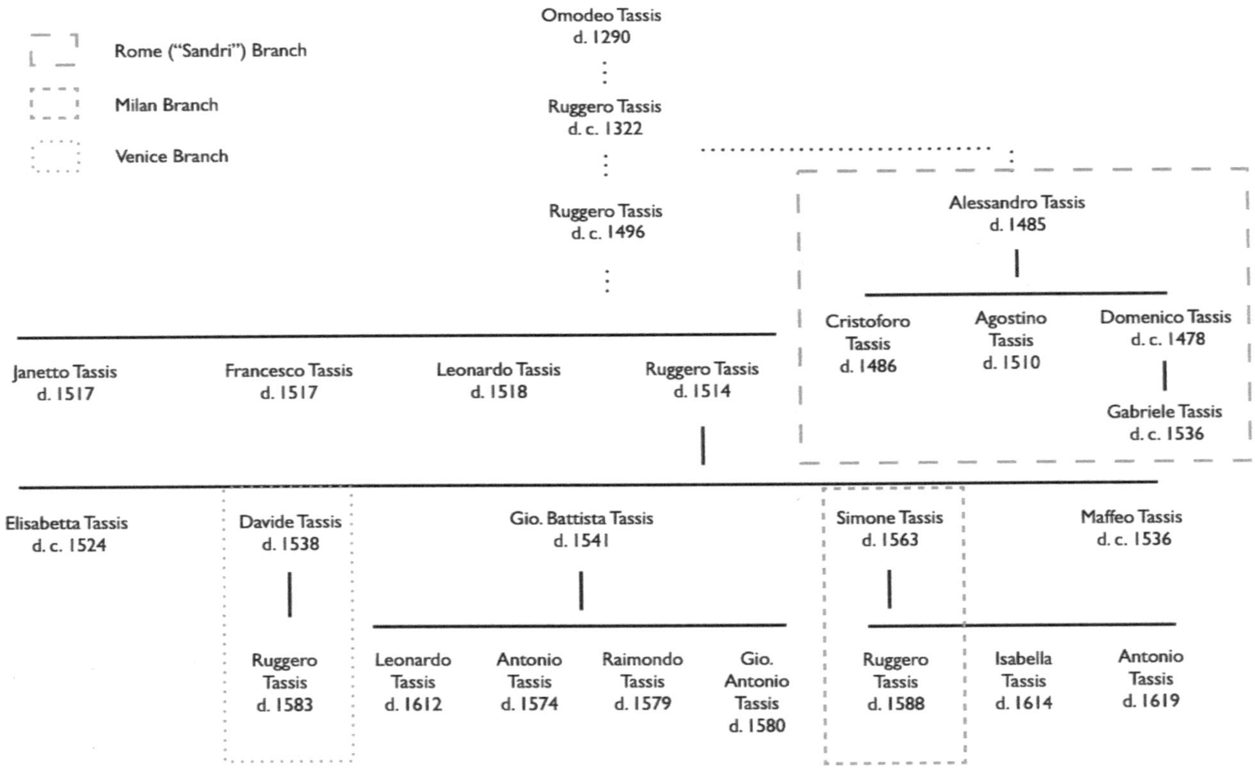

FIGURE 3. Selection of the Tassis family tree. Dotted lines of descent indicate abbreviated lineage. Three distinct branches were active in overseeing postal service in Rome, Venice, and Milan by the mid-sixteenth century. Created by the author.

emperor and ready to dispatch and receive his correspondence at top speed. The master of the posts instead oversaw communications occurring at a distance from the court, inspecting and supervising the postal way stations in person. Rotating roles among family members was a key strength of the Tassis family firm, which effectively permitted them to be in many places at once. The brothers Janetto and Francesco Tassis (d. 1517) held the official titles, but a collection of Tassis family sons and nephews built, managed, and ran the early imperial postal routes on the ground.[30]

Early agreements between Habsburg rulers and Tassis postmasters specified the establishment and maintenance of single routes, such as an edict for the establishment of a postal station in Speyer in the Rhineland-Palatinate region. A similar contract established staging posts every five German miles (roughly 37.5 kilometers) that would support couriers riding in relay. Mail between Memmingen and Rome—a distance of roughly 1,000 kilometers—would take less than five days.[31] By 1501, Maximilian's son, Philip I (1478–1506), had named Janetto's brother, Francesco, as "chief and master of the posts" (*chief et maistre des postes*).[32] Francesco established a semipermanent headquarters for the imperial post near to the Burgundian court, and in 1505, he negotiated a lucrative contract for 12,000 lire annually.[33] This marked a new permanence for both a state postal system and the Tassis as its postmasters.

The Habsburgs contracted the Tassis to move information and funds among their many courts and armies, within and outside the Italian peninsula. Like banking or military provisioning, postmastership involved financial speculation as well as state service.[34] Keeping horses, particularly during the high-demand years of the Italian Wars, was extremely expensive, to say nothing of the salaries and traveling stipends of skilled couriers. Postal staff grew swiftly during these decades, and by 1506, the Tassis postmasters employed around forty couriers at their headquarters in Brussels.[35] The Tassis had limited success pressing their royal patrons for cash but did enjoy a steady rise in their social and political status. Emperor Maximilian granted Janetto Tassis the Istrian fiefdoms of Rachele and Barbana in return for his services.[36] In this way, investment in the early modern state often yielded social as well as financial returns.

Distinguished by new titles, the Tassis moved among a cosmopolitan diplomatic and secretarial milieu by the first decades of the sixteenth century. In the 1510s, Francesco Tassis commissioned a set of tapestries for Notre-Dame du Sablon in Brussels (figure 4). It depicted the kneeling Francesco handing Emperor Maximilian his letters. The tapestries

FIGURE 4. Bernard Van Orley, *Légende de Notre-Dame du Sablon: La statue de Notre-Dame est conduite à l'église du Sablon* (1516–1518). The rightmost panel from the Brussels tapestry shows Francesco Tassis kneeling before Emperor Maximilian and receiving his privileges. Tassis family members based in the Low Countries were notable patrons of the arts, sponsoring this tapestry, as well as an elaborate altarpiece for a chapel in Notre-Dame du Sablon.

announced that the Tassis had "made it," as did the elaborate altarpiece for the family chapel commissioned by Giovanni Battista Tassis (d. 1541) in 1534.[37] Family branches remaining in Italy also did well for themselves. Domenico Tassis (d. 1538), postmaster to Pope Julius II, received a knighthood and the title of count in 1512. He used his fortune to build several finely decorated villas in Bergamo and its surroundings.[38] Within a few short decades, the Tassis family and postmastership were nearly synonymous. Lavish patronage trumpeted the Tassis dynasty, and by extension the postmaster as an honored state office.

The rise of the Tassis mapped onto that of their Habsburg patrons. In 1358 or 1359, Duke Rudolf IV of Austria (known as "the Founder," 1339–1365) had commissioned the *Privilegium Maius*, which designated his family line as "archdukes" of Austria. Over the following century, the Austrian archdukes claimed the title of Holy Roman emperor and the ancient legacies that it represented. By the sixteenth century, many saw the Habsburg dynasty of rulers as the best claimants to a pseudo-prophecy that imperial invasion would unite Italy and expel corruption from the Catholic Church.[39]

These universalist claims did not go unchallenged. In 1494, Charles VIII of France (1470–1498) led an invading army into Italy to press Angevin claims to the Kingdom of Naples. French armies marched to the gates of Pope Alexander VI's Rome, enlisting or toppling longstanding Renaissance dynasties en route. The Habsburg and Valois dynasties entangled much of Europe in their conflicting territorial claims, and Italy would remain a key battleground for the next century.

The Tassis reputation could easily have been one of many casualties of this turbulent period. In 1518, the family was best known in Venice for the scandalous default of their bank in Rome. The widely reported news had all the tantalizing elements of a modern tabloid drama: family betrayal, embezzlement, and even murder.[40] In 1526, the postmaster Simone Tassis and his staff were forced to flee the city of Milan as popular uprisings targeted imperial officials as unwelcome occupiers. Simone and his family sought sanctuary in the Sforza castle.[41] Postal routes might have been overtaken by other contractors or the military, or simply abandoned when active armies withdrew following the death of Maximilian (1519) or the Treaty of Madrid (1526) between the Habsburg and Valois.

Instead, the sons of the third brother, Ruggero (d. 1514), a notary in Bergamo, took on a mountainous task. They not only inherited but expanded and improved the postal service. Family rifts complicated this process. The early modern period brought increasing concern with preserving unified patrimony through primogeniture.[42] The first generation of Tassis postmasters had shared privileges among themselves, such as a 1512 edict that made the Tassis brothers counts and members of the Order of the Golden Spur.[43] By the 1530s, the postmaster general, Giovanni Battista Tassis, was approaching his sixties. He sought to arrange an unchallenged inheritance for his son, Raimondo (d. 1579), as the family patriarch and postmaster general to the king. The resulting family conflict was so venomous and protracted that the Habsburg emperor Charles V (1500–1558) himself intervened in 1534. Later documents allege that

Giovanni Battista and Raimondo conspired to trick the ruler into believing that Simone—the only other surviving postmaster of Giovanni Battista's generation—was no longer alive.[44] The stratagem was only possible because of the widely distributed nature of the Tassis family enterprise. Decentralization was an advantage for the family firm, but physical distance from a court could greatly disadvantage an individual family member. Inheritance of rights and privileges and competition between family branches would be a recurring source of conflict.[45]

Familial strategies such as intermarriage mended the rifts caused by asymmetrical inheritance. Scholars have long emphasized the role of marriage in tying together early modern family enterprises, as well as women's active work toward maintaining family solidarity.[46] Marriage served three important goals: first, it established local credibility and status; second, it fostered alliances with other family firms, and even rival postal dynasties; and third, it consolidated family interests. While this was no less true among the Venetian Company of Couriers and other Italian family firms, women remain largely absent from both scholarship and the family tree at the Museum of the Tasso Family and Postal History at Camerata Cornello.[47]

Marriage established local reputation and forged alliances early in the family's rise. Marrying the wealthy Christine Wachtendoch in the Spanish Netherlands in 1514 integrated the postmaster Giovanni Battista. Marrying Maddalena Renausea (also known as Magdalena von Neuhaus or Maddalena di Castronovo of Gorizia) in Friuli offered a similar advantage for Simone Tassis in 1527. Both women came from local patrician families. Intermarriages with other postal dynasty families—such as with the Bordogna, Zapata, and de Morin families—also grew the Tassis's postal empires.[48] The marriage of Simone's son, Antonio, to Christina Zapata was one of several such alliances between the two lines. Christina was the daughter of Giovanni Battista Zapata, postmaster in Sicily, and Allegra Tassis, daughter of Giovanni Battista Tassis.[49] Like their Habsburg patrons or modern corporations, the Tassis used marriage effectively to facilitate business mergers.

As Tassis family fortunes grew, and inheritance battles loomed large, intermarriages between different branches of the Tassis family became more important. The marriage of Regina Tassis, daughter of Giovanni Baptista, to her cousin, Cristoforo Tassis, in 1549 reaffirmed family ties along a key transalpine route.[50] Similarly, Isabella Tassis (d. 1614), daughter of Simone, married Seraphin Taxis (d. 1582) in 1557 and took over the office in Augsburg on his death.[51]

The scale of the Tassis's success was exceptional, but their methods were not: the Venetian Company of Couriers remained composed of many of their compatriots and distant relatives. Katia Occhi finds the same to be true of terraferma family firms across various logistical industries—namely, that "the need for up-to-date information required an extended network of contacts along all the commercial routes, a network of know-how, agents on site, and members of the family company located in the strategic centers between Venice and Innsbruck, in a transnational context that formed the core of their business and interests."[52] The Tassis further benefited from hitching their proverbial horse to the Habsburgs—another dynasty on the rise—but never discounted service to other masters. In this way, postmasters furthered a long tradition of Bergamaschi cultural brokerage.

(Post)masters of Ambiguity

Proximity to the Habsburg rulers was advantageous, but it could also invite unwelcome scrutiny. Emperor Maximilian and his daughter, Archduchess Margaret of Austria (d. 1530), often referenced Giovanni Battista Tassis in their correspondence. He personally ferried messages and, at times, large sums of money between their courts, as did his brother, Davide.[53] Correspondence between the rulers from 1509 depicts the Tassis's allegiances as politically sensitive. In May 1509, Maximilian wrote to Margaret that, despite Davide's loyalty, "we do not want anybody of this [Venetian] nation in our service." Regardless of his long residence in Brussels, the Bergamasco Davide remained, in the emperor's estimation, "a native of Venice." As a result, Maximilian suggested that "he [might] arouse great suspicion in his duty" and cause "inconvenience and damage to our interest." Maximilian asked that Margaret employ Davide for the time being, avoiding "any duty or service of our posts, for the time of these conflicts," referring to the ongoing Italian Wars. The emperor appeared torn between a personal trust of the Tassis, built during years of personal interaction, and the imperative of managing public opinion.[54]

In a striking parallel, the Venetian Company of Couriers had accused the Tassis members of fraud, treachery, and extortion four years earlier. Members of the Sandro branch, Cristoforo (d. 1486) and Agostino (d. 1510), as well as their nephew Gabriele Tassis (d. c. 1536), had acted as both papal postmasters and masters of the Venetian post office in Rome. The Venetian Company now accused them of "by various means and extortions oppressing" couriers and "inviting and instilling subversion" among the order.[55] Of the seventeen company members present for the accusation, fifteen voted to ban the Tassis. The company went even further, prohibiting any future involvement of the Tassis and entering the ban into the company charter alongside other foundational tenets. Rulebreakers would be "deprived of the privileges of the office," the severest punishment the company could enforce.[56]

Farther east, Janetto Tassis also found a cold welcome when he retired to his imperially granted Istrian fiefdoms in 1516. Both Venetian and imperial forces harassed the elderly patriarch, accusing him of disloyalty. Despite the best efforts of family members, Janetto died in penurious exile, his properties seized by the Venetian state.[57] His brother and heir, Francesco, died the next year, leaving the Tassis family firm in a precarious position. These incidents and many others reflect that the Venetians, popes, and Sforza dukes of Milan were quick to suspect information managers of disloyalty during the Italian Wars.

Simply put, the Tassis were too imperial for the Venetians and too Venetian for the imperials. A fluid national identity and a cosmopolitan collection of titles and offices among family branches had been crucial to early Tassis success. But it also posed a liability, raising suspicions that the Tassis might serve the wrong masters during the Italian Wars. Postmastership demanded constant code-switching from the court to the marketplace, and from Brussels to Rome.[58] The Tassis's challenges in this respect mirrored those of the cosmopolitan Habsburg rulers themselves. The rulers of Europe's composite monarchies struggled to balance rival national factions and their interests.[59] Maximilian's grandson and heir, Charles V, routinely stood accused of favoring one national faction of his sprawling empire over another. His Castilian ministers, for example, demanded that he appoint only native officeholders. Charles obeyed the letter (if not the spirit) of the law by naturalizing several Tassis family members as Spaniards in 1518.[60] Critiquing a ruler's ministers was often a convenient means of obliquely criticizing the ruler himself. Given the strong ties between the Habsburg and Tassis dynasties, we could easily read court suspicions of the Tassis as suspicions of the Habsburgs themselves: namely, doubt regarding whose national interests they would champion when push came to shove.

Distrust of the Tassis also reflected a wider concern about how bad actors might exploit new communications technologies. After all, like Harlequin in the commedia dell'arte, the Bergamaschi had a reputation for duplicitousness and the pursuit of self-interest. Postal agents conveyed specie as well as communications, especially during active military campaigns. Money attracted hucksters, bandits, and spies. The Venetian diaries of Marin Sanudo (1466–1536) chronicled this worrying trend. In September 1520, for example, a "Bernardo Timone" staged an elaborate scenario to defraud a Spanish marquis. Dressed as a courier, Timone showed the nobleman false edicts. The papal treasury allegedly sought a lost gemstone and offered a reward of four times the cost spent to recoup it. Down the road, Timone convinced the marquis to hand over 340 ducats to what turned out to be Timone's confederates in exchange for the "stolen" gem.[61] The elaborate con relied on both the courier's livery and the counterfeit edicts as symbols of authority, not unlike a "phishing" scam in the digital age.

In another incident recorded by Sanudo, an enterprising "Zuan" (Giovanni) Gamba evidently staged his own assault as he entered Rome carrying 2,000 ducats for the wealthy Fugger family of bankers. The Roman governor sent an agent to reveal to the courier that he had been found out. The false friend promised Gamba that if he revealed the location of the "stolen" funds, the governor would simply take a cut, and the Fuggers would be none the wiser. Gamba self-incriminated by divulging that he had hidden the funds in a wine barrel.[62]

Masquerading as a messenger was effective because official messengers moving across enemy lines enjoyed a baseline of respect, even in times of open war. Treaties increasingly specified some measure of protection for couriers, as was the case in the agreements between the English cardinal Thomas Wolsey (1473–1530) and French representatives in September 1521. The Venetians and the Holy Roman emperor reached a similar agreement for mutual protections of couriers in the same month.[63] In 1524, when imperial troops harassed a Venetian messenger, the Milanese lord Teodoro Triulzi returned the letters and apologized in the strongest terms: "Even if I am not at present serving the *Illustrissima Signoria*, I remain a true servant, and it hurts my heart that he was held." The following day, the Venetians sent a *trombetta* to Lodi as a further symbol of accord.[64] Italians were familiar with the mercenary politics of warfare: today's enemy might be tomorrow's employer; the morning's harassed courier might be why no news arrived that evening.

Baseline protections created unique opportunities for letter carriers and postal officials. Able to pass where others could not, they were popular sources for up-to-date information regarding on-the-ground conditions—reporting that bore remarkable similarity to spying.[65] Venetian authorities especially relied on the municipal messengers of the terraferma, known as cavallari. These were Lombard locals of Crema,

Brescia, and of course, Bergamo, who may have attracted less visibility than other couriers and who also knew the local terrain. Sanudo's diaries tell us that when the cavallaro "Rossetto" passed a few soldiers on the road, they asked him, "Where are you going spying?" Rossetto replied that he was delivering a message for a merchant of Saluzzo, but the soldiers warned him away, telling him he would be killed if he tried. The cavallaro reported back to the Venetians, inferring that Spanish forces were on the move.[66] In 1525, Sanudo noted that the Venetian senate dispatched the cavallaro "Bernardello" to Milan to determine why artillery was being withdrawn. Encountering some merchants "who were his friends" en route, Bernardello learned that the Spanish at the castle were celebrating. Confident in their companion, the merchants spoke freely, asserting that if the Venetians and the pope wanted to help the Sforza duke, they should "cut to pieces the imperials in Milan."[67] Cavallari provided states with eyes and ears on the ground, as well as ferrying communications.

As servants to many masters, couriers and cavallari enjoyed unique access and protections. That in turn led to anxiety among leaders about their potential disloyalty—sometimes with good reason. Concerns about the ambiguity of Bergamaschi identity came up repeatedly and explicitly in both the appointment and scrutiny of postmasters and couriers. For the state posts to succeed as monopolistic utilities, they needed to overcome such distrust and even redirect suspicion at their competitors. The life of one second-generation Tassis postmaster, Simone of Milan, well illustrates this evolution of a "master of ambiguity" to a prince of the post.

Simone Tassis: The Postmaster General of Information War

The Italian Wars drew much of Europe into an information war. Imperial allies were primed for Habsburg power in Italy, forming "an imperial Italy tenaciously and absolutely opposed to a papal Italy."[68] Elite "imperials" resisted church censorship through their patronage and protection of critical thinkers, artists, and authors. They exchanged representatives, intermarried, and kept in constant contact, utilizing fanciful literary codes and ciphers in their correspondence.[69] The Tassis played a key role in ferrying correspondence among this Spanish-imperial faction of Habsburg supporters in Italy, including between official diplomatic representatives and governors in Naples and Milan; allied families such as the Gonzaga, Colonna, and Medici; and sympathetic intellectuals among both laypeople and the clergy.

Disadvantageous positions on the frontiers of empires could be nodes of strategic access. Like diplomats and ambassadors, postmasters were public figures representing their patrons abroad. Sources from Venice, the Spanish Low Countries, and England demonstrate that postal officials traded in politically sensitive information. The Tassis routinely measured, reported upon, and influenced public opinion. In this respect, postmastership was closer to a political role than a commercial contract. Postmasters used intelligence to influence foreign policy, often to their benefit.

From the 1520s forward, the necessities of Charles's unprecedented empire and hyperperipatetic court drove a significant increase in the speed, scale, and frequency of postal service. As postmastership outgrew the family firm, it posed new problems and required new solutions. A novel term appeared across Europe by the mid-sixteenth century: corriero maggiore or *correo mayor*. As early as 1518, royal contracts referred to the second generation of Tassis brothers—Davide, Giovanni Battista, Simone, and Maffeo, active in Spain—as corrieri maggiori in addition to *maestri delle poste*. Most historians have simply translated corriero maggiore as "postmaster" or "postmaster general."[70] In fact, the term evoked several traits increasingly identified with a Tassis model of postmastership. It combined the autocratic management style of a family firm with the blended roles of postmaster and master of couriers. The corriero maggiore brought commercial knowledge and experience gained on the road to information management, as well as administrative oversight of personnel and infrastructure. It was a state-appointed office that managed public relations for rulers in addition to the logistics of mail.

The advanced development of the imperial system in northern Italy, pushed forward by the military campaigns of the Italian Wars, enmeshed postmastership within a larger bureaucratic infrastructure of empire. The life of the postmaster Simone Tassis of Milan (d. 1563) exemplifies the complex social and political landscape navigated by an Italian "imperial."[71] Starting as a courier running routes in Spain and the Netherlands, Simone came to oversee a linchpin of the international postal network in Milan. His life spanned several rulers and Spanish governors. Simone's contests with Milanese governance and merchants, other postmasters and administrators, and his own family provide rich sources for understanding a postmaster's shifting place in state and society. The integration of foreign sources, such as Sanudo's diaries and the English State Papers, paint a portrait of a master intelligencer, propagandist, and administrator: in short, an all-purpose information manager.

Like many Tassis men, Simone traveled from Camerata Cornello to the Spanish Netherlands to apprentice to his uncles. He served Charles's father, Philip I, as his master of couriers, accompanying him from the Spanish Netherlands to Castille. On Philip's death, Simone despaired, "abstaining for several days from food, publicly exclaiming that he did not wish to survive his Lord."[72] The dramatic proclamation suggests Simone's early attention to managing public opinion. Following Philip's death, Simone traveled widely, as directed first by his uncles and then by his brother, Giovanni Battista. It was a frenetic life: in 1510, Simone wrote that it had been more than a month since he lay in his own bed, but with service came reward. In 1513, Simone was appointed as the ducal postmaster to an imperial ally, the Sforza duke of Milan.[73]

The Tassis network offered incomparable access for sending and receiving letters across continental Europe. The English State Papers show a constellation of connections linking Francesco and Simone Tassis with correspondents farther north, including the Florentine intelligencer Tomaso Spinelli, the imperial secretary and envoy Louis Maroton, the English ambassador Sir Robert Wingfield, and the newly minted English postmaster Brian Tuke (o. 1510-1545).[74] The English crown paid large sums of money to Francesco Tassis for the development and maintenance of postal routes between the Habsburg Burgundian court and Calais.[75] By 1515, Wingfield complained of Francesco limiting the responsibility of delivering mail to "bayly Damons" (Burgundian court lackeys), whom he considered untrustworthy. In the same letter, he asked for a secretary to help cipher his letters for protection, "for I have written so long that I am almost blind, and clerk have I none that is English."[76] Despite a healthy measure of distrust, Wingfield simply had no alternative to relying on the Tassis.

Simone inherited and cultivated his uncles' intelligencing networks. Spinelli routinely mentioned his letters and personal contact with Simone. In a 1512 letter, Spinelli identified "the Latest News from Italy" (*Ultima Nova ex Italia*) as being from Simone, suggesting that Simone had begun to trade in intelligencing newsletter (*avvisi*). Whereas Simone's letters had once reached figures like Cardinal Wolsey through intermediaries, by 1518, he was writing directly to him.[77] Much like the tapestries or church bells that his uncles commissioned for their home chapel in Camerata Cornello, this direct contact symbolized Simone's rising social status.[78] Simone even acted as a diplomatic envoy: in 1518, he traveled to Rome to help arrange a marriage between the pope's nephew, Lorenzo di Piero de' Medici (1492-1519), and a Spanish bride. By the time Simone arrived, Pope Leo X (1475-1521) had already arranged an alternative marriage to Madeleine de la Tour and a corresponding

French alliance.[79] Later in life, Simone would cultivate connections with key figures in Spanish administration, keeping high company with the Spanish general, Gómez III Suárez de Figueroa y Córdoba, the duke of Feria, and the imperial ambassador, Lope de Soria.[80]

At the same time, Simone maintained important Venetian contacts. The new phase of the Italian Wars, known as the Four Years' War (1521–1526), pitted a French-Venetian coalition against the Holy Roman emperor. Simone was born in Venetian territory and remained on good terms with the Venetian administrators throughout this period; he never disavowed his Bergamasco identity. In the Venetian terraferma city of Brescia, the rectors reported receiving an imperial courier from the army in November 1521 with a request from "the postmaster, who wants free passage for his couriers." After some debate, they conceded the establishment of imperial posts at Santa Eufemia and Martinengo, even giving the postmaster the use of "our *trombetta*."[81] The agreement followed on the heels of a Venetian-imperial agreement for the free passage of couriers.[82] Such favors worked both ways: by 1525, the Venetian diplomatic resident in Milan routinely wrote how difficult it could be to send couriers in and out of the city, but that Tassis aid had been invaluable.[83]

Simone's intelligence was also welcomed—although the Venetians took it with a grain of salt. Much as the Tassis represented unparalleled access to English representatives, Tassis letters were occasionally the only Venetian source about imperial-occupied Milan.[84] Venetians still recognized that Simone represented imperial interests. His news always emphasized Italian solidarity against the French, who rebelled against the emperor. Sanudo described at least one of Simone's letters as "very affected," and dismissed another entirely as "things untrue and embellished by the imperial court."[85] However, the letters are more commonly integrated into Sanudo's reports without such caveats.

Even healthy skepticism could fail against more subtle manipulation. For example, Simone could be selective about what he sent to the Venetians about their French allies and how he sent it. In an October 1523 letter, Simone emphasized that his courier felt great danger of potential assault as he passed the French army some six miles from the city. Later, he reported that the French had been harassing Venetian subjects in the countryside.[86] In April 1526, Simone told the Venetian messenger that there were no letters for him, but the cavallaro remained in the post house to chat. During a discussion of current events, Simone's servant expressed the opinion that "the King of France is well returned to France but will not live two months." Simone slapped him, saying,

"Be silent!" There are multiple possible interpretations of this incident. On the surface, it appears that Simone did not wish for his servant to disclose information about the French king's health to the Venetians. However, his reaction was also conspicuous: Why make his displeasure so visible, as if to advertise insider knowledge? Alternatively, it is worth considering that Simone may have orchestrated the incident to spread disinformation. Such news, verified or not, might serve to nudge the Venetians further toward an imperial alliance.[87]

Overall, Simone appeared to succeed at balancing his imperial and Venetian ties. In November 1525, the rectors of Bergamo commented on sending two cavallari into Milan, saying that "they are faithful servants, the Bergamaschi, who can operate there, but must be cautious, as the Spanish are suspicious."[88] Cross-national Bergamaschi loyalties could be used against Simone as well. In 1532, a Venetian messenger lodged with the Tassis imperial postmaster of Regensburg. That spy passed on an entire conversation regarding the Habsburgs, the Swiss, the Turks, and all other manner of current events to the Venetian lieutenant in Udine, who diligently reported it. The houseguest may well have been a family member, or it could have been another Bergamasco in the Venetian Company of Couriers.[89]

Couriers, like postmasters, seized opportunities to influence higher levels of decision-making toward their own preferred outcomes. In June 1526, Venetian guards intercepted an imperial courier whom Sanudo referred to familiarly as "Battista." Battista readily offered detailed intelligence regarding the numbers and movement of imperial troops. He disliked the trigger-happy Spanish troops and happily reported conversations that he had overheard among Spanish officials, including Simone, which perhaps took place during his time in the post house. Battista thought the people of the terraferma anxiously awaited Venetian intervention. For all those calling for the banner of Saint Ambrose, the patron saint of Milan, he proclaimed an equal number called for the banner of Saint Mark, the patron saint of Venice.[90]

Simone had a vested professional interest in having positive relations with the Venetian state. He depended on Venetian cooperation to extend imperial postal routes from Milan to Trento and Augsburg, which crossed Venetian territory. As early as 1526, Simone planned for an imperial post office in Venice to supplement the prior reliance on Mantua and Verona.[91] It was an unprecedented request, but the postmaster was in a strong bargaining position, as the Venetians also had to cross imperial territory to communicate with France and Spain.

Simone also had a more personal interest: the continuing legal battle to regain control over the Tassis Istrian fiefdoms. He had become the family's executor in 1519, following the death of his last living uncle. He and his brothers presented a letter to the Venetian senate from Margaret of Austria (1480–1530, then governor in the Spanish Netherlands) asking that the properties be restored to the Tassis heirs.[92] In 1523, Simone proposed that such restoration become part of an imperial-Venetian peace treaty. In 1524, the Venetian doge Andrea Gritti did restore the Tassis holdings. Simone retreated to the properties during Charles's Italian campaign, citing poor health. He also removed himself from Italian politics and turned to domestic life, marrying his noble Friulian bride around the same time. It may have been strategic timing since the Italian imperials were in a difficult position as imperial troops sacked the Holy City in 1527. However, the Istrian properties had nonetheless fallen into disrepair, and the Tassis sold them back to the Venetian government a few years later when Simone returned to Milan.[93]

Northern Italy was caught between an imperial Habsburg project on the one hand and a French-Venetian alliance on the other. As servants of many masters, the Bergamaschi earned a reputation for pursuing self-interest and working across battle lines. The Tassis intelligenced on behalf of many patrons, and their brand covered all dimensions of information management, ranging from simple conveyance to active propagandizing. For diplomats and other leaders, access to a Tassis network (much like the networks of their contemporaries, the Spinelli or the Fuggers) was often worth ceding some ground in the ongoing information war. Simone was one of several postmasters and couriers who made the most of the opportunities that this position could offer.

Challengers to the Corriero Maggiore

In 1535, with the death of the last Sforza duke, Milan officially passed into the imperial Habsburg orbit. Charles invested his son Philip II of Spain (1578–1621) with the wealthy and populous duchy of Milan over the next decade.[94] Spanish, Italian, and German agents relied upon the Tassis postal service to keep up to date on the latest political developments across the peninsula.[95] The emperor himself was on the road constantly, passing through Italy en route to and from his campaigns in North Africa and the Piedmont and his trips to address religious upset in Germany.[96]

During the mid-sixteenth century Simone Tassis, the master of ambiguity, settled into his new role as the Spanish postmaster of Milan.

FIGURE 5. Anonymous, *Portrait of Count Simone Tassis* (d. 1563), ducal, imperial, and Spanish postmaster in Milan. Image from Bergamo, Biblioteca Civica Angelo Mai e Archivi storici. With thanks to Jason Rosenholtz-Witt.

A posthumous portrait from the seventeenth century memorializes Simone in these middle years (figure 5). He appears in Spanish court garb, bearing a prominent cross of the religious and military Order of Saint James. Reinvented as a Spanish national, Simone Tassis entered the ranks of a growing state bureaucracy in Habsburg territories as the corriero maggiore of Milan. He could thus fit among the ranks of state secretaries, ambassadors, governors, and military commanders while remaining a businessman at heart.

Simone's postmastership nonetheless saw early instances of the administrative conflicts that would plague European postal services in the decades to come. Postmasters derived their de jure authority from executive-granted monopolies, as well as control over appointments and salaries. De facto power, however, came from the ability to muster capital and mediate among family members or between imperial and Italian powers.[97] When a Tassis postmaster had to leave his office, that authority left with him. The appointment of deputies required clearer institutionalization of the powers that the Tassis had accrued.

Expectations for the postal service also exceeded capacities during the Italian Wars. A 1533 set of imperial regulations required that mounted couriers maintain a speed of at least 4 or 5 Italian miles per hour (roughly 6 to 8 kilometers per hour). The mode known as the *staffetta*, referring to an established relay of riders traveling on horseback at a gallop or trot, could achieve 8 Italian miles per hour (roughly 12 kilometers per hour).[98] In February 1537, Simone Tassis received 9,872 imperial lire for expenses incurred during the past eleven months, which was topped the next year in January 1538 with a payment of 10,769 lire.[99] For comparison, a laborer in Milan earned between 1 and 2 lire per day in the same period.[100] In many cases, these charges involved couriers who traveled in relay to and from the imperial army at Pavia (at a cost of close to 20 lire per dispatch) and Asti (around 16 to 26 lire).[101] Such a system remained demanding enough that it depended upon the unmatched spending and disciplinary power of the state. And despite grand promises, Spanish representatives often complained that the postal service was failing to deliver.

Furthermore, despite steady state business, postal staff protested to political leaders that they were overtasked and underpaid.[102] Two clerks known as *contrascrittori* worked with Simone in the 1530s Milanese post office, as did a treasury-designated chancellor. It was frequently all hands on deck, as clerks often took up the mailbag themselves, carrying important correspondence or money. In 1537, for example, the *contrascrittore* Pietro Martire Borro traveled to Lucerne to deliver money to the imperial ambassador there and returned with several horses that he had purchased for the office.[103] The post office remained dependent upon the personal authority (and capital) of the postmaster to pay its bills, and even that was falling short.

Keeping staff was as crucial to the role of a postmaster as was hobnobbing with elite patrons. The corriero maggiore's responsibilities included overseeing other postmasters in an ambiguous nesting hierarchy. Simone's network included Pitigiano da Felizzano in Felizzano (Alessandria), Giovanni Paolo della Croce in Asti, and Giovan Antonio Vignale (known as "Il Sarto") in Bologna. The importance of a location correlated with the perceived social capital of the appointee. For instance, Sarto managed the flow of mail to and from Rome from his position in Bologna. The strategic importance of that office meant that he enjoyed a higher social status than many postmasters.[104] Like Simone, Sarto occasionally appended personal notes to his deliveries to the Milanese governors. In 1536, for example, Sarto expressed his dissatisfaction with the newly deputized ducal postmaster, Francesco Tassignano (the former postmaster of Lodi), to the newly installed Spanish governor Marino Caracciolo (o. 1536–1538): "I have always served the state of Milan by sending letters to Rome with diligence, and kept your Honor informed, and never failed in this, but your Honor knows that Tassignano failed to pay me my salary for six months. Because I believe that Simone Tassis should pay, it seems to me that he does not wish to pay for my service in the time of Tassignano.... I bring this to your attention simply to know whether I should be paid or not."[105] The question was clearly rhetorical, as Sarto continued to argue that he had "served the state of Milan, and not Tassignano" and, ending on a personal note, that he "did not have another friend in the city, only your Honor."[106]

Much like Tassis, Sarto also traded in intelligence to curry favor. In January 1537, he wrote directly to the governor of Milan regarding the assassination of Duke Alessandro de' Medici of Florence just three days earlier. He included the latest rumors "of which I will not say more than to give news from my own hand to your Honor." He proved true to his word, writing again just hours later that Lorenzino (also called Lorenzaccio) de' Medici had fled "by post" and admitted "from his own mouth" that he had killed the duke.[107] Florentine authorities initially kept Alessandro's death a secret, going so far as to hide the corpse to prevent a potential uprising. It was clear that the death would affect the overall balance of powers in Italy. The governor of Milan would not have been aware of the assassination so quickly without Sarto's intelligence.[108] In this way, Sarto used his own value as an intelligencer to circumvent Simone Tassis's preference for autocratic information control. When Simone attempted to institute a clear hierarchy, utilizing the distribution of salaries as a marker of his superior position, Sarto was one of several postmasters who continued to resist and subvert the hierarchy.¹⁰⁹ In most cases, the Milanese treasury paid Simone, who then distributed pay to his postmasters. The treasury paid only a select few subordinate postmasters directly—including Sarto.

By contrast, the ducal postmaster, Francesco Tassignano, often struggled to wield authority. In 1536, Tassignano wrote a long letter to the governor of Milan. It relayed recent news and troop movements, but the postscript pleaded: "I will not have the spirit to sustain the weight of this office, without the help and permission of your honor.... I beg that you do not leave me in this predicament. I no longer have the respect of my officials in this office." To illustrate his point, Tassignano recounted an incident in which, following Tassis orders to place a new post between Milan and Alexandria, he had "ordered that the post of Voghera coming and going should stop at Vigevano," but the postmaster of Voghera was uncooperative, and he threatened not to handle further mail until "Tassis paid him."¹¹⁰ The absence of the corriero maggiore and slow payment undermined the authority of the deputized postmaster of Milan.

As Tassignano struggled to pay his own messengers, he appears to have looked to Venetian cavallari for aid. The postmaster ordered one "Capelleto" to bring letters to the imperial ally, the duke of Savoy, but "[Capelleto] said, in a nutshell, that he did not want to leave, and that I did not have the authority to order him, and I needed to put my hand in my purse and send another [courier]."¹¹¹ Tassignano's struggles to muster authority reveal how interdependent the Spanish and Venetian systems were, and they also highlight the existence of a growing cultural divide. The Venetian Company was a structure more akin to a trade guild, in which the leader was first among equals. The steward of the company was an elected official with a limited term. Only the collective voting bench or external authority, such as the Provveditori di Comun had the power to punish the cavallari.¹¹² Responding to his insolence, Tassignano ordered that Capelleto "be well punished," but he second-guessed it, saying that "between one thing and another, I do not know who it hurt more, him or me." The governor took pity on Tassignano and discharged him from a position where he evidently was making more enemies than friends.¹¹³

Simone and other members of his generation used the title of corriero maggiore to further differentiate a head postmaster from his subordinates. It was an administrative solution that institutionalized both autocratic management and dynastic inheritance. The Venetian government, familiar with the role that the Tassis played for Habsburg patrons, sought to institute a similar, native oversight of their Venetian

Company.[114] The Venetian Provveditori di Comun had overseen the company since 1305, but it did not begin to regularly intervene until the sixteenth century. Traditionally, the company's voting bench handled its day-to-day business. It was composed of the gastaldo, a vicar, and two counselors, all of whom were elected from the general body of couriers and usually held their positions for terms of one to three years.[115] The gastaldo certainly managed many of the tasks associated with corrieri maggiori, from salary distribution to personally delivering letters to the company's most important patrons.[116]

In a common pattern across Venetian administration, the Provveditori preferred a Venetian citizen (*cittadino*) to the Bergamaschi. This was further indication of the information management role of the office since Venetian citizens staffed much of the Venetian civil service.[117] Yet Ludovico Fioravante, who sought to purchase the newly empowered office of corriero maggiore, was a hard sell. Fioravante was infamous for having murdered his father in the Basilica di Santa Maria Gloriosa dei Frari in 1497 and later engineering a daring escape from prison. The Venetian state banished Fioravante for his crime, but he was eventually granted safe conduct "on account of his service in France," a detail that also appears in his petition for the office. Fioravante's quest for the title of corriero maggiore merited mention in Sanudo's diary.[118] The Provveditori and the senate confirmed Fioravante, but at the time of Sanudo's report, the issue awaited an additional decision by the Venetian Council of Ten. The ongoing debate indicates that there were many eyes on the postmaster of Venice, as well as Milan.

Authorities regarded the corriero maggiore as a powerful and even perilous role. Fioravante's spotty personal history certainly contributed to the amount of scrutiny and pushback that his appointment generated. Mysterious references to the services in France that earned him his return to Venice carry all the trademarks of espionage. That service may have earned him back his citizenship, but it did not instill trust. Early modern governments viewed espionage as "situated somewhere in the hinterland between delinquency and necessity."[119] Making a murderer, prison escapee, and spy the head of the postal service was certainly a gamble, but given that the Tassis corrieri maggiori acted as valuable intelligencers in information war, perhaps not an unnatural one.

The Venetian Company, on the other hand, did not see the upside. The couriers regarded Fioravante as an outsider. In the years following Fioravante's approval, they accused him of superciliously contravening company protocols—most importantly the inheritance of courierships and the system of distributing jobs. The Venetian couriers argued that Fioravante had wrongly kept couriers on the books who had been dispatched abroad to serve Venetian residents in France, Rome, Puglia, and Corfu.[120] This may have been a simple issue of the couriers chafing at management, but a deeper division between the Bergamaschi and Fioravante likely played a role. Much like the unfortunate Tassignano, Fioravante may have lacked the skill to oversee diplomatic couriers and terraferma cavallari in a cohesive system.

At the same time, Fioravante had a formidable task. Europe's imperial rulers increasingly demanded seamless handling of their internal (domestic) and external (international) mail, but they did not provide a framework for how to do so. Whereas higher-level leaders desired a cosmopolitan citizen postmaster, the predominant family firms rebuffed intervention. Lacking the family network, community solidarities, and administrative skill, Fioravante never overcame the couriers' opposition. Much as Tassignano depended upon the governor, Fioravante repeatedly sought affirmation of his authority from the Venetian Council of Ten.[121] On Fioravante's death, the company bench seized the opportunity to elect their own corriero maggiore.[122] While that election was "rejected, revoked and annulled," the Provveditori di Comun did make the next election a public matter, soliciting nominations and information regarding the candidates.[123] Fioravante's failures as a corriero maggiore make the Tassis successes even more remarkable. The intelligencing role of postmasters kept them in the public eye in ways that predecessor offices were not. Many different parties had a stake in the identity and allegiances of the corriero maggiore.

The advent of new information technology often brings lexical uncertainty. Even the postmaster lieutenant Ottavio Codogno, writing in 1608, felt it was necessary to clarify a definition: "This title of corriero maggiore, by which is meant the postmaster general (*generale maestro delle poste*), should only be attributed to those who command all of the posts in a state, and not those who have received offices by concession to receive and dispense letters or dispatch couriers, as many do in Rome, Venice, Lyon, Paris and other places." By this, he meant to distinguish the office from the many deputized postmasters like Sarto, as well as the foreign postmasters-in-residence discussed in chapter 2.[124]

Under varying names, postmasters and postmaster generals had become fixtures of Europe's political landscape over the course of the

Italian Wars. From the medieval "master of couriers," the Tassis exercised new public authority in overseeing a comprehensive infrastructure of posts and riders in relay. Simone and his deputies established mutually beneficial relationships with the English and Venetians, crossing battle lines in an ongoing information war. The Tassis drew on a Bergamaschi diaspora to work across cultural, linguistic, and political boundaries. They succeeded by virtue of a powerful network and alliance with the Habsburg dynasty to cultivate a family brand that persisted for centuries.

The postmaster remained an ambiguous figure, caught between the worlds of the court, stables, and marketplace. The post house required a growing staff: secretaries, couriers, and other (nominally) subordinate postmasters. Maintaining the posts required an enormous financial outlay that warring princes could be slow to finance. The corriero maggiore required a courier's experience, a courtier's polish, a merchant's business acumen, a nobleman's risk tolerance, and an administrator's insistence upon documented hierarchy. A postmaster's allegiances needed to be above reproach, and yet he depended on patronage from foreign powers and employed foreign couriers. He needed to be at his royal patron's side and yet also on the road, inspecting and building new routes, disciplining couriers, gathering intelligence, and fighting legal challenges.

In 1542, a convention of the Tassis family branches reaffirmed the united posts throughout imperial territories, naming Simone as the head of the Italian posts.[125] By 1547, Simone was personally responsible for handling royal mail to and from the Council of Trent (1545–1563) and had reached the peak of his personal power. He oversaw six couriers and received a salary of 14,000 lire, which was intended to cover all expenses he personally incurred. Yet from 1550 to 1555, Simone complained to the Spanish governors several times regarding the lack of payment of his salary, even asking for the intercession of governor-appointed mediators to resolve pay disputes.[126] He claimed to be near bankruptcy, especially when imperial conflict with the French had broken out once more.[127] Even a prince of the post faced constant challenges.

The second half of Simone Tassis's career demonstrated the pressing need to establish more permanent and reliable sources of authority for the postmaster and his office. Deputizing postmastership required firmer markers of privilege, such as pay differentials and power over appointments and salaries. We see contemporaneous debate occurring across postal systems regarding the powers, privileges, and allegiances of postmastership, especially centered on the figure of the corriero maggiore. The sweeping powers of the Tassis model sat poorly with powerful families within the Venetian Company. Political leaders alternatively respected and suspected the intelligencing of couriers and other postal officials. With this in mind, we now move to consider how the dénouement of the Italian Wars centered on none other than a Tassis postmaster.

CHAPTER 2

The Arrest of a Postmaster
Information Sovereignty in the Italian Wars

Shortly before midnight on Sunday, July 5, 1556, a guard spotted a man on the road southeast of Rome. The captain recognized the distinctively scarred face of the Spanish courier. The messenger traveled incognito, in plain clothes, and had eschewed his usual horse in favor of traveling on foot. He carried two packets of letters but refused to provide any further information about where he came from or what he was carrying. The packets had been endorsed by Giovan Antonio Tassis (d. 1580), the Spanish-imperial postmaster in Rome. On the covers, the postmaster had scribbled a warning to his counterparts farther south that "things are becoming more dangerous in Rome," and "it is impossible to ask anyone to remain here."[1] The guard confiscated the letters and sent them to his superiors in Rome.

Disturbing rumors spread through Rome's diplomatic circles like wildfire in the following days. Papal guards had arrested the postmaster and Spanish envoy, together with their servants. The Venetian ambassador tried to investigate at the Castel Sant'Angelo but was turned away. A Tuscan representative overheard that the seized letters invited the Spanish commander, the duke of Alba (1507–1582), to invade the city and "to level this Pope's pride."[2] The following week, rumors reached the Council of Trent far to the north, where the chronicler recorded that "the Imperial representative has been imprisoned."[3] News traveled fast when a fragile peace hung in the balance.

In the following days, Pope Paul IV (1476–1559, o. 1555–1559) held a press conference of sorts. He convened the cardinals and ambassadors in Rome to present an official narrative of events. The pope assured the audience that the evidence of a planned Spanish invasion would be incontrovertible. He promised that the incriminating letters were forthcoming. Meanwhile, the papal fiscal procurator was hard at work interrogating Tassis, as well as other members of a Spanish-imperial faction in Rome. By Thursday, the interrogators were suspending the postmaster by his wrists, which were tied together behind his back, a brutal torture known as the strappado. By hook or by crook, the pope would have his proof of Spanish treachery.[4]

The bishop of Paris, a papal ally, hosted another gathering of expatriates at his home in the Palazzo della Rovere in Borgo on July 14, at which imperial and English representatives expressed their fury over the arrests to Cardinal Carlo Carafa (1517–1561).[5] They demanded that the prisoners be set free, or at least placed under house arrest, as befit their station. The papal nephew replied that "neither man would tell their Princes to release state prisoners, even if they were more important persons than Garcilaso and Tassis." Even the pope's French allies seemed disturbed. The French host confided in the Venetian ambassador his fear that the Spanish king "will bring such powerful forces to Italy that he may defend and attack anyone."[6] By July 12, Cardinal Carafa had recalled his special envoy from the imperial court—a common sign of impending war. Thirty years after Charles V's sack of Rome, it seemed inevitable that Spanish soldiers would once again march toward the Holy City to correct perceived Carafa insolence by force.

Although papal investigators had arrested Tassis along with the Spanish envoy, Garcilaso de la Vega, they focused their efforts on the postmaster. Tassis was interrogated more often and treated more severely than any other prisoner. The story of the postmaster's arrest has usually been a single sentence or footnote in the wider story of papal-imperial conflict.[7] The arrest and dispossession of the Colonna family loom larger in scholarship. Yet early modern chroniclers focused on the captured courier and arrested postmaster, recognizing the violation of *ius gentium* as a key turning point in international relations. This chapter explores why a postmaster-in-residence was both so readily suspected of treachery and so poorly protected from seizure.

The 1547 succession of the French king Henry II and the 1555 election of Pope Paul IV—born Gian Pietro Carafa—opened a new phase in the Italian Wars. Both men were avidly against Charles V of Habsburg and his son, Philip II (1527-1598). The pope refused to recognize either Charles's 1556 abdication as Holy Roman emperor and Spanish monarch or Philip's succession to the Spanish throne. The Carafa family seized the opportunity to dispossess the rival Colonna family and thus endow members of the pope's extended family with the Colonna territories and titles.[8]

The imperial Habsburgs and French Valois staked rival territorial claims in Italy, leading to brutal warfare across the peninsula at the end of the fifteenth and beginning of the sixteenth centuries. The ruling families of Milan, Mantua, and Naples allied with the Habsburgs. Targeting the Spanish postmaster and envoy was a dangerous gambit by the Carafa family to assert papal authority in the face of perceived encirclement. The Carafa and their French allies sought to disrupt the communications networks that united Habsburg partisans from Naples to Brussels, and from Madrid to Vienna. The arrest was a turning point that aggravated the longstanding information war into open violence.

This chapter brings together diplomatic accounts, Tassis correspondence, popular histories, and records of the interrogations of the postmaster to piece together the fateful events of 1556. The Venetian ambassador Bernardo Navagero's version of events gained early traction in news circles, as his colorful dispatches from Rome circulated widely.[9] Later chronicles disagreed on key points, including whether the seized letters were ever decrypted, whether the postmaster was guilty, and when he was released.

Any expatriate postmaster-in-residence faced unique personal and professional risks, as the arrest of Giovan Antonio Tassis vividly illustrates. Linda and Marsha Frey describe how "expediency became practice, and practice became precedent" in early modern diplomacy. Diplomatic extraterritoriality describes the grant of exemption from local law that was accorded to select foreign residents.[10] Yet the diplomatic protection granted to ambassadors did not typically cover ambassadorial staff and diplomatic papers.[11] Ambassadors and other officials instead employed cryptography ("hidden writing") to protect their communications. The use of codes and ciphers, however, still risked accusations that correspondents had something to hide. Rulers, including the pope, asserted a communications monopoly within their domains, equating secrecy with treachery. Despite professional necessity, dissimulation was often equated with immorality, or worse, crimes against the state (*laesa maiestas*).

The arrest of the postmaster serves as an entry point into what I call the "postal wars" of the 1550s to the 1570s.[12] Expatriate postmasters-in-residence, couriers, and even ambassadors widely publicized incidents of harassment, interference, and assassination to attract sympathy in an international court of public opinion, even when legal violations were unclear. Shining light on the perceived victims of state machinations shamed regimes that were at odds with the diplomatic status quo and customary respect for *arcana imperii*, or secrets of state. In fact, Giovan Antonio Tassis was neither a political martyr nor a principled traitor. He was instead an information manager and intelligencer, as his professional role demanded.

Two conflicting paradigms came to a head in the sixteenth century: information sovereignty and communications monopoly. Much like "information war," the term "information sovereignty" has come into vogue only recently to describe claims to secure transnational data transfer in the modern age.[13] Sixteenth-century states also argued for a sovereign right to maintain secure channels outside their borders. From 1556 onward, several militant, state-building popes attacked the legitimacy of the foreign post offices practicing in Rome. The Venetian, Spanish, and French representatives rebutted aggressive campaigns for postal control in the Holy City. They countered that foreign mail should enjoy mutual guarantees of speed, security, and reliability, free of interference by governing powers. This principle ensured the success of a durable network of international communications.

The popes sought instead to establish a *communications monopoly*: total jurisdiction over information shared within the borders of the Papal States. At their most generous, such borders could be construed to extend across the Catholic world. The Papal Index of Prohibited Books (*Index Librorum Prohibitorum*) and its comprehensive program of print censorship constituted a well-known outcome of the Counter-Reformation era.[14] Dangerous personal correspondence, as well as printed books, perturbed church leaders. The papal postmaster Mattia (or Matteo) Gherardi (d. 1582, o. 1535–1572) targeted foreign posts and postmasters, first by physical harassment and later by aggressive commercial competition. In this way, Gherardi's goals of personal advancement were in line with papal efforts to reject and replace foreign information channels within and outside the city.

To some extent, information sovereignty and communications monopoly are mutually exclusive principles. One state had to concede ground for another to establish a postmaster-in-residence. Yet they are better understood as opposing rhetoric, or even bargaining strategies, as states readily employed each in turn in the service of their political goals. While defending information sovereignty in Rome, for example, the Venetians were all too ready to adopt a monopolistic approach to their own territories. Similarly, juxtaposing 1556 with later decades reveals that even the papacy gradually embraced the principles of information sovereignty, especially when arguing for the establishment of a papal postmaster-in-residence in Venice.

The imprisonment of Giovan Antonio Tassis was nonetheless the last arrest of a postmaster-in-residence. I contend that this was the result, in part, of how quickly it kindled the fires of war.[15] The principle of diplomatic immunity had been inherited from Rome as an unwritten law of nations (*ius gentium*), sanctioned by custom rather than codified in law.[16] Yet contemporary and later chroniclers condemned the Carafa for breaching a still-nascent norm by arresting and torturing a postmaster. Venetian-papal conflicts saw the same papal postmaster, Gherardi, constantly toeing the line of diplomatic disaster, but never again eliciting the same public outcry. Commercial competition, instead of arrest and torture, became the weapon of choice. The novel institutions of the international posts and the postmaster-in-residence prevailed.

Campaigning for a Communications Monopoly in Rome

As the hub of international diplomacy, Rome hosted the first foreign state post offices and postmasters-in-residence, but rapid power shifts in the city took a toll on establishing a more permanent infrastructure.[17] Agreements regarding postal offices lasted only as long as a given papacy, which might be a few years or a few months. Pope Adrian VI (1459–1523) was well acquainted with the Tassis from the royal court in Burgundy, where he had served as tutor to Charles V. On Adrian's succession in 1522, he gave the Brussels-based Tassis family branch control over the Roman post, papal and otherwise, much to the resentment of the Roman Sandri family branch and the Venetian Company of Couriers.[18] Adrian's death just fifteen months later cut short the Tassis triumph. The new pope, Clement VII, seized several Venetian posts on the road to Ravenna a few months later for his own newly appointed papal postmaster, the Tuscan Bartolomeo del Vantaggio (o. 1513–1522).[19] The Venetian Company complained bitterly about needing permission to maintain their own horses and posts.[20] Such seizures were nonetheless par for the course when it came to state-building.[21]

Poor reputation further undermined the legitimacy of the longer-term post offices in Rome. The Venetian Company of Couriers routinely fought dereliction, gambling, and general disorder within its Roman office. Sixteenth-century Rome was chaotic, rapidly expanding, and host to a uniquely foreign, unmarried, and male society. Crime ran rampant, from gaming to murder.[22] Separated from the grounding influences of business and family, couriers also indulged various vices while in the city. By 1519, the company required that a postmaster remain resident in Rome. Articles naming Pellegrino Gamba as the Venetian postmaster to Rome in 1533 specified that he would "eat and sleep" at the office. Gamba and his successors kept an inventory of the household goods, handled food provisioning for couriers, and distributed jobs. The terms of appointment for Angelo Longo in 1556 twice emphasized the importance of guarding the keys to the wine storage room.[23]

Another foreign postmaster, Giovan Antonio Tassis (nicknamed "il Zoppo"), was also a fixture of Rome's communications landscape by the 1540s.[24] He was the eldest natural son of Giovanni Battista, the imperial postmaster general. His brother Antonio Tassis (d. 1574) was the postmaster in Antwerp. While Giovan Antonio served under his uncle Simone of Milan—who oversaw all the Italian posts—the relationship was strained. Simone frequently wrote to their shared patron, the Spanish minister Antoine Perrenot de Granvelle (1517–1586), that Giovan Antonio worked against him. "I am ashamed to trouble you, my lord," he wrote, "but until now [Giovan Antonio] has not paid a single soldo, nor shown how he intends to pay, because he has many debts, and has been thrown in prison for them once per year."[25] Simone portrayed Giovan Antonio as living fast and dangerously, like many young men in Rome, but the postmaster of Milan also resented his nephew. The position of postmaster-in-residence in Rome would have been a valuable prize for one of Simone's sons, but by virtue of the inheritance battles discussed in chapter 1, Giovanni Battista had closer ties to the Habsburg court. By 1555, Simone's requests to Granvelle were no longer subtle: "between me and my two sons there are three men, and I have only two offices. One of us needs to take on the office in Rome."[26] Dynastic imperatives would remain a constant source of tension among the Tassis family branches.

Dire financial straits could easily drive a postmaster to intelligencing on the side. Chronic insolvency likely motivated Giovan Antonio to send handwritten newsletters (*avvisi*) to such eminent persons as the duke of Tuscany and the duke of Cleves.[27] Duke Cosimo de' Medici included letters from "il Tasso," meaning Giovan Antonio, to the Spanish viceroy in Naples as early as 1543. By 1544, the Tuscan secretary recommended that Giovan Antonio receive an annual "gold chain, money, silver, or fabrics" from his Medici patrons. The patrons complied, and Giovan Antonio received 25 scudi and a gold chain or bolts of fine satin worth another 25 scudi every year.[28] Medici gifts to postmasters—which also included "Il Sarto," the postmaster of Bologna, and Lorenzo Bordogna Tassis, the postmaster of Trento (d. 1559, o. 1537–1559)—recognized their powerful access. Such gifts were nominally intended to both reward and encourage prompt service, but much like the occasional beneficence shown to foreign diplomats, they often served as bribes.[29]

As the Spanish postmaster resident in Rome, Giovan Antonio was well placed to become an intelligencer. Sixteenth-century Rome was the crossroads of the known world. The postmaster's newsletters reported on events in Rome, but also on the Venetian-Turkish conflict, the French Wars of Religion, Calvinism in Switzerland, and the English throne. Some items originated from as far away as India and Constantinople. Many letters and newsletters from the prolific Giovan Antonio likely remain uncatalogued in European state archives. Spanish archives preserve examples sent to Spanish administrators across the Italian peninsula in the 1550s, and Giovan Antonio's Latin correspondence with Andreas Masius (1514–1573), a humanist scholar and secretary to the duke of Cleves, has been well catalogued and partially published.[30] Masius (whose sister-in-law was a Tassis) also corresponded with the postmaster Josef Taxis (d. 1566) in Innsbruck, thereby gathering news from a wide swath of Habsburg territories.[31]

There are, however, few newsletters from the months just before Giovan Antonio's July 1556 arrest, and for good reason, according to the dispatches of the Venetian ambassador Bernardo Navagero. Renewed campaigning to impose a communications monopoly on Rome began soon after Gian Pietro Carafa's May 1555 election as Pope Paul IV and targeted the Spanish-imperial faction.[32] Navagero reported many letter interceptions and harassment of couriers in his letters to the Venetian state. In October 1555, the Spanish courier of Genoa suffered an assault and the theft of his letters, "held by those of [the city of] Chiusi," located en route to Medici Florence. A few days after the October incident, Navagero reiterated that the pope "continued to open dispatches to the Imperial delegates" and he "held the courier of Naples but did not find the state letters (*lettere pubbliche*), because [the Neapolitans] had taken steps to send them surreptitiously. The secretary to the Florentine ambassador says [the pope] opened the packages of the Duke of

Florence as well." The Medici duke was a well-known imperial ally, having received his title from Charles V in 1537 during the Italian Wars.[33]

Giovan Antonio found Pauline Rome a hostile environment for his intelligencing. He continued to write monthly missives to Masius, which now largely focused on Italian politics. On October 21, he wrote frankly: "I have written more rarely for some time, on account of bad health, as well as the danger of writing. There is nothing that these people do not suspect. If you decide to come here, you will regret it. The fear of war outweighs the hope for peace. . . . No one will be safe from prosecution for crime. This Pope wills everything beneath his feet, so that no one can believe themselves to be safe."[34] The letter closely followed the courier interceptions reported by Navagero. Giovan Antonio continued to send and receive mail, becoming an all-the-more crucial source of news for the correspondence-starved expatriate community in Rome. In December, Navagero reported that Giovan Antonio alerted him to the movement of Spanish troops into the Piedmont. The imperial postmaster may also have been Navagero's source on a "most secret" imperial dispatch sent to Naples in February.[35]

Events were moving quickly at a higher level. The Carafa pursued a secret treaty with the French, reaching an agreement by December 15, 1555.[36] They intended to keep Spanish and imperial officials in the dark by imposing a communications lockdown. In January, Navagero reported further harassment, this time of the courier of Milan, and a growing atmosphere of distrust. The mailbag was seized at Terracina, a port city around 100 kilometers south of Rome. Cardinal Carafa blamed the governor, returned the mailbag, and called it a misunderstanding. Imperial partisans did not believe him, especially since a courier of Naples carrying "28 thousand ducats to pay the Duke of Florence's men" had recently been harassed in nearby Gaeta. French forces similarly detained an imperial courier, "calling him a spy who pretended to be a courier." Papal border controls and surveillance of expatriates grew draconian. Guards turned back anyone attempting to leave the city, including cardinals and couriers.[37] The French sought a less hostile path than the belligerent pope, signing a three-year truce with Spain in February 1556. Rather than following their example, Paul IV redoubled his efforts, relentlessly policing Habsburg allies inside the city.

By the spring of 1556, Spanish and imperial representatives resorted to subterfuge to transmit communications in and out of Rome. In May, papal authorities seized Giacomo Bandino da Curzola, "a member of the household of the imperial postmaster," for eighteen days to interrogate him about how he had sent and received letters. Navagero warned the Venetian postmaster resident in Rome, promising to keep him apprised of relevant developments. By June, the courier of Milan had entered and left the city, seemingly "without letters," but all the Spanish cardinals and the imperial ambassador requested licenses to leave Rome suspiciously soon afterward. That same month, Navagero came to hear "from those who know" that two letters addressed to the imperial ambassador and postmaster had "contained nothing of importance," with the actual message hidden in the shirt of the messenger.[38]

It was in this political climate that the Carafa seized Giovan Antonio Tassis and his household in July 1556. This was the moment that not only tipped the scales toward the resumption of the Italian Wars, but also shifted the balance between information sovereignty and communications monopoly in Rome. Although papal authorities initially attempted to hide the arrest of the Spanish postmaster, they eventually leaked summaries of his confession. Tassis allegedly admitted that Spanish officials had promised to make him "commissary of Terracina, Velletri and Piperno if the Imperial forces seized control of those lands." Tassis confessed that he had sent messengers to Naples by foot so they might sneak by papal guards, and he knew that this was a violation of the protocol requiring that he obtain licenses from papal authorities for all couriers and *staffette* leaving Rome.[39]

Three mysteries surround the arrest of the postmaster. First, were the charges of conspiracy true? The Carafa claimed to have deciphered the invitation for the Spanish invasion of Rome, but later chroniclers presented very different accounts. Second, when was Giovan Antonio Tassis released from prison? In the summer of 1556, world events pivoted on his fate. Just months later, even the most knowledgeable diplomats in Rome were remarkably confused about whether Tassis remained imprisoned, or if not, when he had been freed. I have found that the testimonies of Giovan Antonio Tassis and the Spanish envoy Garcilaso de la Vega, as well as the letters seized from the disguised messenger traveling to Naples, survive in the Spanish State Archives at Simancas.[40] Placed within the context of the postal wars, these documents provide key answers.

Finally, what precisely was the role of the papal postmaster? He did not appear much in Navagero's account, nor in those of later chroniclers, but in administrative sources, the postmaster played a central role. Using the interrogation records as well as later chronicles, I will shed light on each of these questions in turn. The arrest forced to the surface several underlying tensions regarding the intelligencing role of a postmaster-in-residence, the struggle for communications monopoly in Rome, and nascent principles of extraterritoriality and information sovereignty abroad.

Public Secrets: Interrogation and Cryptanalysis

First, consider the incriminating letters. While they had been dispatched by the Spanish postmaster and carried by an established courier, the letter packets smacked of smuggled goods. Who ordered the messenger to travel by foot? It contravened standard procedure, but did it signal conspiracy? Was the postmaster who sent them guilty of treason? Records of his confession show that Giovan Antonio initially implied that Garcilaso de la Vega had ordered him to send footmen (*fanti*). Footmen would often be used for less important letters, and their use in this instance suggests an attempt to disguise the ambassador's correspondence. Tassis's secretary revealed under interrogation that letters to Naples were always delegated to the distinctively scarred courier known as "Franzese." Later, Simone Tassis used this to further suggest that Giovan Antonio had acted not only as a spy, but as a double agent, and he "let important letters fall in the hands of the Carafa, which he could have easily sent by another hand than that of a French courier. Whether done by ignorance or malice, Lord only knows . . . " Simone would later walk back these claims when made aware of Giovan Antonio's torture, although he still suggested that his nephew be pensioned off from his position as postmaster.[41]

Having seized ciphered correspondence, the interrogators had difficulty proving that either Giovan Antonio or Garcilaso had conspired against Rome. As such, they focused on Giovan Antonio's appended notes. Why was the postmaster so concerned about danger or an impending war? The interrogators suggested that Tassis knew more than he was saying; after all, Tassis had publicly bragged that he would receive a commission upon the arrival of imperial forces. At first, Tassis responded by claiming that he was only an eavesdropper to the conversations regarding the likelihood of war that occurred between Garcilaso and the imperial diplomatic representative, Carlo Paceco, in their shared residence.[42] Tassis proclaimed ignorance as to the content of the letters that the footmen had been carrying, and he denied knowledge of the use of cipher, saying that he had received the letters sealed. He explained that his preparations to leave Rome were based only on the possibility of war in the hypothetical sense, much like any other private resident of the city.

By the third interrogation on July 9, as interrogators focused on Spanish-imperial plotting, Tassis argued back, asking, "What do you want, for me to involve myself? I don't have any particular passion for these things that are the affairs of princes."[43] The postmaster claimed ignorance rather than that his position merited special protection. He distanced himself from any public, political role. By this time, the news of his arrest was widespread in the city and the foreign representatives—who felt that he did merit special protection—were outraged. Nonetheless, the torture went forward because the ciphered letters offered insufficient proof of treachery. Giovan Antonio's interrogators hung him by his wrists and likely dislocated or broke his arms. Between his personal pleas to the officials whom he knew well, having worked with them for years, the postmaster provided answers in short order.

The letters did indeed pertain to Spanish invasion. They communicated that the duchy of Paliano, which the Carafa had seized from the Colonna, was unprotected. Spanish-imperial partisans had known about the impending arrival of the duke of Alba from the south since June and had received instructions to remove themselves from the city in preparation for the outbreak of war. Contrary to his earlier descriptions of having merely overheard conversations, Tassis revealed deep knowledge of military intelligence regarding precisely how many Spanish forces would be landed, where, and when. He always claimed to have learned this information from letters brought to the city in the last weeks of June—always by someone other than himself or his staff, he was keen to emphasize—and shared with him as a personal favor by the diplomats. He repeatedly claimed to know only "public knowledge," in the sense of common rumor. The interrogators did not believe him. They questioned the postmaster's sources of intelligence (a relatively early use of *intelligenza* in the modern sense). Given the close oversight of correspondence in preceding months, as well as the small world of Rome's diplomatic circles, interrogators were very likely aware of Tassis's newsletters. Far from a hapless servant, he was shown in these newsletters to be an active purveyor of intelligence and a savvy political actor in his own right.[44]

The records of Giovan Antonio's interrogations seem to resolve the first of the mysteries—namely, whether Giovan Antonio had conspired with the Spanish ambassador. The postmaster's access to intelligence clearly went beyond what he claimed to have placed—already ciphered and sealed—in the mailbag. The Carafa wanted the deciphered letters to substantiate their claims, employing several stalling tactics to delay the news

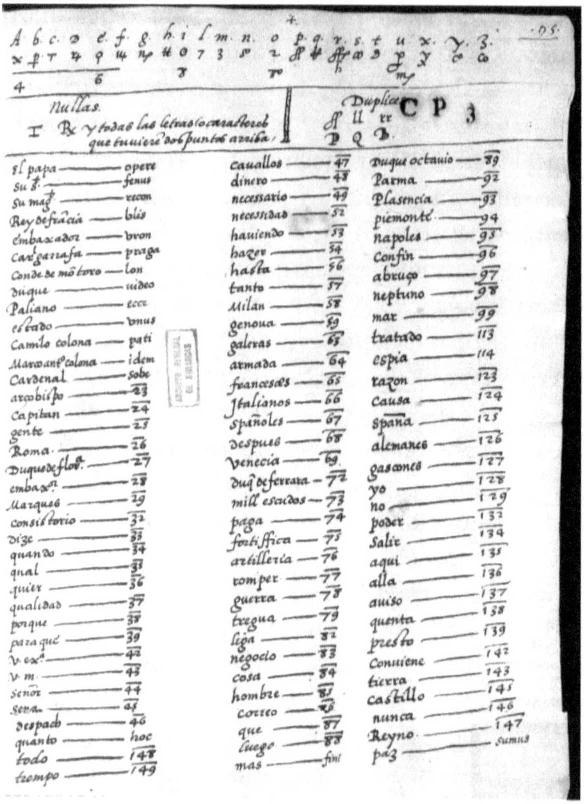

58   CHAPTER 2

FIGURE 6. The 1556 nomenclator used by the Spanish envoy to Rome, Garcilaso de la Vega, to encrypt his letters to the duke of Alba. The top of the page shows a key for the substitution of individual characters. At the bottom are further instructions for nulls and duplicate characters. The remainder of the page provides numerical code for frequently used phrases. Image from Ministerio de Cultura de España, Archivo General de Simancas, https://pares.mcu.es/ParesBusquedas20/catalogo/show/2205381.

of the postmaster's arrest and interrogation as they sought a method to decrypt the letters. This was information war, where control of the public narrative would require more evidence than a coerced confession.

The cipher, however, proved a tougher nut to crack. The surviving key shows that the encrypted letters employed the very latest in nomenclator technology (figures 6 and 7). Sensitive diplomatic correspondence had long employed nomenclators, which were combinations of substitution ciphers and codes for the most common terms. While humanist polymaths publicized newer cryptographic tools, such as the eponymous Albertian wheel and Cardano grille, which were arguably more

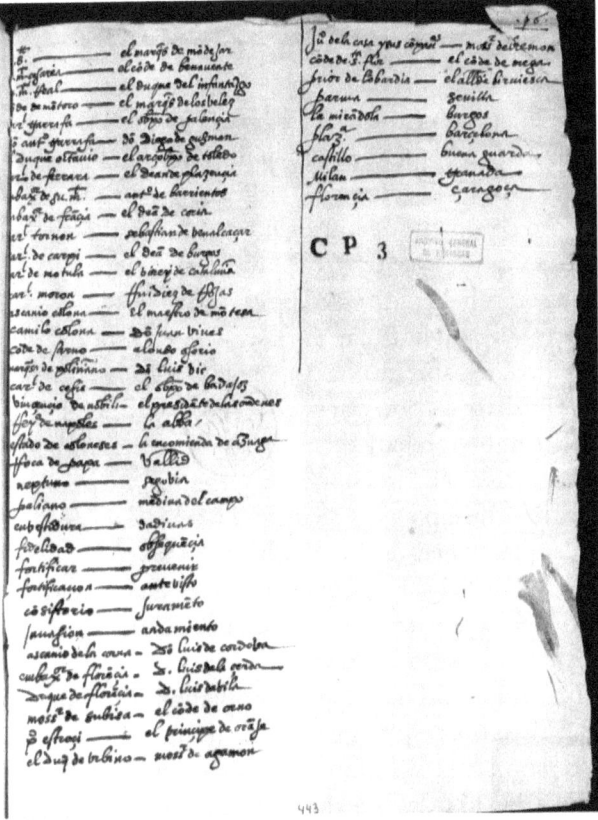

FIGURE 7. The 1556 nomenclator used by the Spanish envoy to Rome, Garcilaso de la Vega, to encrypt his letters to the duke of Alba. The page shown introduces an additional layer of security by substituting important locations and figures, resulting in a ciphered code. Image from Ministerio de Cultura de España, Archivo General de Simancas, https://pares.mcu.es/ParesBusquedas20/catalogo/show/2205381.

secure, security was in constant tension with practicality. Diplomats and leaders alike routinely complained about the time, effort, and skill required to cipher and decipher correspondence. The nomenclator was prized for its accessibility and standardization and remained predominant into the eighteenth century.[45] Philip II had resolved to issue a new general cipher, described by David Kahn as "one of the best nomenclators of the day," in May 1556. He was likely influenced by the spate of courier interceptions that had occurred in Italy. At the king's request, the Spanish Council of State and *Despacho Generale* established a pattern that would be maintained for several centuries: a general cipher (*cifra generale*) would be circulated among all Spanish political leaders, along with individual keys for highly sensitive channels (*cifra particolare*), all of which would be renewed every three or four years.[46] The relative sophistication of the cipher, as well as the still-incipient institutionalization of cryptanalysis, offer some insight as to why the Carafa needed to buy time by keeping the arrest and seizure under wraps.[47]

In 1591, the chronicler Mambrin Roseo suggested that the Carafa had sent the seized letters to Venice for decryption. The French had asked for Venetian help with decryption as recently as 1552, so it is a plausible story, although it may at first seem counterintuitive to send valuable intelligence abroad.[48] Roseo also suggested that the Carafa could not afford to wait for answers, and they therefore seized the postal officials and "forc[ed] them to say by which method they had sent the letters, also seizing Hippolito Capilupi [the bishop of Fano], who had written the cipher." The interrogation records do reveal that Capilupi was questioned on July 11. Like Tassis, he claimed that his only source of knowledge had been conversation, and his reports to his pro-imperial Gonzaga patrons in Mantua consisted solely of common knowledge in the Campo de Fiori, a public piazza and notable news hub.[49] He, like Tassis, argued that his only intelligence had been open source rather than the result of covert communications.

Unlike secret writing techniques that used invisible ink or merchant codes, substitution ciphers like that employed by the Spanish-imperial faction openly advertised the secrecy of their content. A page of numbers or symbols could hardly be anything other than a message in disguise. Jon Snyder characterizes the goal of early modern dissimulation as a "'zero degree' of communication."[50] Or, as the historian Sforza Pallavicino commented on the incident, "nothing indicates a secret as much as dissimulation," meaning that it was as important to disguise a secret's existence as its content.[51] After all, it was the very act of being incognito that had attracted unwanted attention to the courier. Later, the chroniclers Pietro Nores and Sforza Pallavicino (who sympathized primarily with the papacy) called the courier a practiced spy, traveling by foot "without any word of post, or the appearance of a courier," and praised local administrators for seeing through the ruse. Nores also devoted attention to how the performance of secrecy suggested guilt and invited closer attention, describing the cipher as "complex and difficult to penetrate, exciting suspicion and curiosity to discover the contents," as did "the sagacity of the courier who carried them, as he had sought to overcome every impediment that might have detained him."[52]

Pallavicino described the cipher as "most intriguing" and wrote that "curiosity and jealousy grew with every example of obscuring detail." In Pallavicino's view, it was this alarm that drove the pope to detain Tassis, "hoping to shed light on the letters."[53] The timing, the courier's disguise, the cipher: each of these pieces of evidence together formed a clear picture of Spanish treachery. Given Paul IV's predisposition to "jealousy," the detention of the courier and postmaster seemed inevitable.

Yet the same authors were remarkably noncommittal when it came to whether the Carafa had successfully decrypted the letters, and if so, how. Nores claimed the decryption had been completed but did not provide further details. Likewise, an eighteenth-century biographer of Paul IV said that the Carafa "found that the mysterious letters told the duke of Alba that the city was defenseless," but he wrote noncommittally that they found it "through the study of cryptologists, or by forcing [Garcilaso] to provide the key."[54] Chroniclers sympathetic to the Carafa did not address the interrogation and torture directly, suggesting that even they may have seen it as a step too far. Or, perhaps, the removal of relevant documents to Simancas cloaked the events from authors working from Vatican archives.

In fact, the newly digitized documents at Simancas reveal that the letters were eventually decrypted, but evidently by way of the cipher key rather than successful cryptanalysis. By July 23, the papal authorities had Garcilaso's cipher key (figures 6 and 7). A certain "Franciscus Tamaius," originally of Seville, had intimidated Garcilaso's retainer into providing the documents. When the Sevillian had handed them to the papal *castellano*, the man reportedly gloated that "this will be the ruin of Signor Garcilaso." The nomenclator had been issued as recently as late June and featured all the hallmarks of recently tightened Spanish security, such as duplicates, nulls, and a code that switched locations and names to make the decryption seem to pertain to the Iberian Peninsula and the New World (replacing Florence with Zaragoza, for example, and the Cardinal of Motula with the viceroy of California). With key in hand, the cryptological lock was fully open.

As it turned out, the ciphered content of the letters played very little role in the events that followed. The same month as the arrests, the pope excommunicated both the emperor and the king of Spain, placing nearly half the Catholic world of that time under interdict.[55] Diplomats and newsmongers circulated the duke of Alba's public letter of protest (which specifically condemned Tassis's torture), and copies survive in most major newsletter collections from the time.[56] The duke of

Alba went on to lead a successful assault on French forces in the south at the same time that the imperial ally, the duke of Savoy, achieved a decisive victory at Saint Quentin to the north. By September 1, 1556, Alba arrived in the Papal States with 12,000 Spanish troops. The Carafa surrendered, and the Spanish emerged triumphant in Italy, establishing a dominance that they would hold for the next century. Philip II had been formally invested with Naples and Sicily by October 2, 1556. It was during this time, perhaps, that the incriminating interrogations were shipped back to Spain to the hands of the Spanish Council of State, where they would remain, buried in paper.

Throughout the decisive events of later 1556 and 1557, Tassis remained imprisoned. The records of his interrogations continued into August. By autumn, his circumstances saw only the slight improvement of being moved from a tower where he was being held "secretly" to a public prison—"the outcome of which is unclear," a Tuscan diplomatic resident observed in October. The Venetian ambassador wrote in November that Giovan Antonio's friends "fear for his life," although the Carafa assured Navagero that the postmaster would be treated fairly.[57]

In a May 21, 1557, letter to his old friend, Andreas Masius, Giovan Antonio alluded to his repeated interrogations and the damage that they had done to his ability to write. Switching roles, Tassis now begged for news from Masius, asking "how many German soldiers come into Italy; what is reported about me, and where in the world you are." He poignantly signed the letter "From Rome, in Prison."[58] In September 1557, Cardinal Carafa continued to assert that the ambassador and the postmaster were guilty. Carafa pointed out to Navagero that the Spanish had not recognized the treachery of the Spanish envoy and postmaster, and all those "who did not deserve to live, given the poison that they planned to deliver, for which it would be justice to execute them after they have been in prison for some months more, to clarify the process."[59]

By late 1557, copies of the Spanish-papal accord began to circulate across Europe. The third item addressed was the release and reinstatement of Giovan Antonio Tassis. On October 20, Masius mistakenly reported to the duke of Cleves that the postmaster walked free on September 25, 1557, fourteen months after his initial arrest.[60] Yet an October 30 letter from the English representative, Edward Carne, suggested that despite the agreement, Tassis remained imprisoned in Rome.[61] Navagero reported the same, complaining that the pope and his family, far from reinstating Tassis, had instead "revoked what few privileges he had restored" to all the foreign posts in Rome. Given Navagero's close reporting of the case, it seems likely that Tassis was still imprisoned when Navagero left Rome in March 1558. By August of that year, the new Holy Roman emperor, Ferdinand I (1503–1564, r. 1558–1564), officially named Giovan Antonio Tassis as the imperial postmaster in Rome, suggesting that he had been liberated by that point in time, or would be soon afterward.[62] In total, Tassis's imprisonment most likely lasted between eighteen months and two years.

Given that the contents of the letters were clear by late July 1556, why were the Carafa so invested in proving the guilt of the postmaster and envoy? Intercepted letters cast a harsh light on diplomacy. They revealed dissonance—even hypocrisy—between the ambassador's conciliatory acts and his true feelings. Physical proof, in the form of the encrypted letter, raised the stakes by providing evidence for the forfeiture of extraterritorial immunity in a legal court, as well as in the court of public opinion. This was precisely why the postmaster insisted all his intelligence had been gathered from overheard conversations, which would have been indistinguishable from omnipresent rumor. Reading the 1556 imprisonment against a wider papal campaign for communications monopoly—specifically over foreign couriers and postmasters-in-residence—helps to explain why the accords between the Carafa and the duke of Alba did not immediately lead to Tassis's release, even as reports circulated to the contrary.

Initially, public opinion was that the arrest of the Spanish postmaster seemed to fit within a Europe-wide pattern of courier detention for minor infractions. Seized letters were often used to reveal ambassadorial treachery as a casus belli at the beginning of the sixteenth century, as recorded in a contemporary manual on ambassadorship.[63] It was a favorite strategy of the English cardinal Thomas Wolsey (1473–1530), for example, but even Wolsey waited for a court to find an imperial representative guilty of having forfeited his diplomatic immunity. There was a growing awareness that international public opinion did not look favorably on these types of arrests.[64]

For the Carafa, releasing the postmaster would mean acceding to his inclusion among a protected class of public representatives, not private actors. Furthermore, it would confirm that the papacy did not exercise jurisdiction over the foreign posts of Rome. Proving that their actions had been justified was nonetheless an unwinnable battle for the Carafa. Even chroniclers who sided with the papacy avoided addressing the accepted principle of extraterritorial protections head-on: Pallavicino justified the courier's arrest because of his plain clothes, as his insignia "according to custom, would render him inviolable."[65] Pallavicino similarly recognized that Garcilaso would usually be protected by diplomatic privilege, but the chronicler argued that Garcilaso had nullified this protection by acting against the Papal State, as ambassadors swore not to do.[66]

One such chronicle preserves the lengthy oration of Francesco Paceco, secretary to the viceroy of Naples, that well summarized the principles at stake:

> [Giovan] Antonio Tassis, what treachery has he committed? Sending a package to a minister of His Majesty, sending a courier to your Excellency (as is his job as postmaster), for this he has been imprisoned, and removed from his duty? What temerity and villainy the Governor of Terracina has committed in capturing a courier of His Majesty! And for this the Pope will begin a war? . . . What cipher, what letters are these? They must have contained a great secret: to drive Your Excellency to cause such harm to people in so many ways and to declare them enemies.[67]

The florid speech has the marks of a chronicler's rhetorical intervention, but it reveals that the arrest of the postmaster would be primarily remembered as a violation of the extraterritoriality of the diplomatic mailbag and postmaster-in-residence. While still a young institution, the foreign post and postmaster-in-residence enjoyed public support, no doubt aided by the elite patrons who received newsletters and other favors.

Mattia Gherardi, Postmaster Warrior

The 1556 arrest of Giovan Antonio Tassis and the ensuing events took place within a longer papal campaign for communications monopoly. State-building popes of the sixteenth century sought to be rulers of their own postal system rather than hosting a series of foreign posts. In so doing, they hoped to control the means, as well as the content, of print and manuscript communications within their territories.[68] We have addressed two of three mysteries: Giovan Antonio Tassis did seem to have conspired (or at least intelligenced) with a Spanish invading force. His imprisonment continued because his release would have ceded valuable ideological ground. That leaves the third line of inquiry: What role, if any, did the papal postmaster Mattia Gherardi play in these events?

A January 1535 edict established Gherardi's control of the papal posts. He remained a prominent official in Rome for more than forty years. Countless diplomatic letters referred to him by the familiar "Mattia" or "Matteo." He was not a member of the Bergamaschi: Gherardi was Tuscan by birth and sometimes identified as "di San Casciano," a small region south of Florence.[69] His predecessor, Bartolomeo del Vantaggio, was also Tuscan, but Vantaggio had worked with the Tassis to establish the Rome-Florence-Bologna posts. By contrast, Gherardi harnessed existing antiforeigner sentiment to pursue a campaign of aggressive monopolization in Rome.

In contrast to diplomatic letters or later chroniclers, Venetian and Tassis postal administrative records cast Gherardi as the main antagonist throughout the Italian postal wars. Upon his appointment, Gherardi circulated a new set of regulations preventing foreign merchants from carrying mail in the Papal States. In 1539, the papal post rerouted from a primarily Tuscan route north to one run within the Papal States via Bologna to avoid possible foreign interference—a pressing concern considering the recent marriage of the Florentine duke Cosimo de' Medici to Eleanora of Toledo, sister to the Spanish viceroy of Naples. The Sandri branch of the Tassis family—divested of any remaining privileges and perhaps sensing the changing political tides—left Rome to return to Bergamo that same year.[70] In 1540, Pope Paul III (1468-1549, o. 1534-1549) opposed the establishment of a French postmaster in Rome, reportedly because "he does not want anyone but Mattia his postmaster to take letters." A 1542 papal decree prevented the Venetian post office in Rome from directly receiving mail within the Papal States. The following year saw the establishment of a papal Rome-Bologna ordinary courier traveling via Furlo, southeast of Urbino.[71] Gherardi's actions had been consistent with those of Venetian and Habsburg postmasters to restrict foreign mails in their territories in the years preceding 1556.

Gherardi was an outsider to the Bergamaschi cartel and thus lacked the tools that the network provided. He did not have the power base of the Tassis, or even his wealthy Tuscan predecessors in the office of papal postmaster. But he overcame such disadvantages through decisive actions. In 1544, Paul III issued new privileges to the Venetian post office in Rome, but with an important new interpretation: whereas in the past the Venetians had maintained their own horses, they would now need to rent horses from Gherardi.[72] In a letter to the Venetian ambassador, Venetian authorities argued that such a requirement was to the "great inconvenience of couriers and against the intentions of His Sanctity." Gherardi stood firm. The shift had been shortly preceded by the arrest of a Roman courier by Venetian authorities, which likely undermined the company couriers in this matter.[73] The change not only positioned Gherardi as the default rights holder to a key infrastructural asset, but it also ensured a tidy profit for him.

During his first interrogation, Giovan Antonio Tassis had guessed that he had been detained on Gherardi's orders. He was likely correct.[74] In his letter to Granvelle, Simone Tassis even implied that Gherardi had set out to entrap Giovan Antonio. The Spanish postmaster was known to be friends with a man from Viterbo, brother to Giovan Antonio's "woman." This man was none other than a "minister of Mattia, postmaster for the Pope, and spy for the opposing faction." Simone suggested that the man continued to hold such sway over Giovan Antonio in prison that "even if he were my own son, I wouldn't trust him further."[75] While Simone was an admittedly biased source, the Tassis uncle and nephew both immediately suspected their papal rival, who is completely absent from the chroniclers' accounts.

Following Giovan Antonio's arrest, interpostal relations in Rome were grudging at best over the following months. The Venetian ambassador, Bernardo Navagero, reported a standoff with Gherardi in November 1557. The Venetians argued that Gherardi should not have the power to license Venetian couriers, that it posed a disadvantage to both Roman and Venetian merchants, and that in any case, the two offices of postmaster and master of couriers were separate and not intended to pertain to the foreign posts. "I don't believe that the Pope would wish to seize the second office," Navagero speculated, as doing so "would take bread from 500 mouths at least, including the families of the poor Venetian couriers, who live by this *procaccio*, and faithfully serve both the Papacy and the Venetian senate."[76] The debate about postal jurisdictions—which stretched into the following days—seemed like Carafa stalling tactics. Navagero reported to the senate that even papal allies were now frustrated: "I would be remiss not to tell you that the French ambassador had sent a secretary to me to say that this is a matter of the greatest importance, and that his king would never support it, and that I must hold firm. Furthermore, the ambassador has said that he is inclined to send his postmaster outside of Rome to receive the ordinary [courier] from Lyon and take his letters, leaving everything belonging to the merchants."[77] Just as they had in the matter of the

Spanish postmaster's arrest, the Roman diplomatic corps once again stood in solidarity against perceived breaches of custom and principle. Ultimately, Navagero stood down, perhaps sensing that the entire matter had been orchestrated to delay letters as long as possible. He wrote again to the duke of Paliano that he had ordered the Venetian couriers to present themselves to Gherardi, "showing their obedience, receiving their patent and horses until such a time as your Excellency orders otherwise." Gherardi did not make another appearance in Navagero's letters. The Venetian ambassador and the papal postmaster had evidently reached a détente.[78]

It is difficult to say whether the impetus for all-out postal war lay primarily with the Carafa or Gherardi, but Gherardi remained an aggressor under later popes. The election of Pope Pius IV (1499–1565, o. 1559–1565) provided a brief interlude in these violent years. Pius was uninterested in stoking conflict and renewed the Venetian Company's privileges without issue in January 1560. There was still friction at the borders of the two systems, particularly between Ancona and Rimini, where the Venetian postmasters butted heads with their papal equivalents.[79] A 1565 patent specified that the arrangement with the Venetian Company existed because Gherardi found it personally convenient, and further implied that it could be terminated whenever that was no longer the case.[80]

Information Sovereignty and the Papal Post of Venice

Gherardi's most pressing desire in the 1550s was to head the papal communications monopoly in Rome. The 1560s saw him instead press his claims in the language of information sovereignty, meaning the right to establish a secure channel of information in external territory. The pope and papal postmaster sought to establish their own satellite office in Venice, following the model of the foreign posts in Rome. The letters of the papal nuncio in Venice, Giovanni Antonio Facchinetti (d. 1591, o. 1566–1572, later elected Pope Innocent IX), reveal how a seemingly simple request started a new round of conflict.[81] Camerlengo Michele Bonelli (d. 1598) conducted the first overtures on behalf of his great-uncle, Pope Pius V, in 1566. Pius and Bonelli instructed Facchinetti to persuade the Venetians of the utility of a papal post office and an ordinary courier who would leave every Wednesday and provide them with twice the service they currently enjoyed. Facchinetti assured Bonelli that this would be easily accomplished, as "all of the foreign princes" (naming the dukes of Ferrara and Florence) "keep their own couriers who also serve the public good."[82]

To date, the foreign posts in Venice had developed along similar lines to those of Rome. A 1539 edict established monopolistic privileges for the Venetian Company of Couriers but recognized the "reserved liberties of the postmasters of Milan and Florence."[83] The same year, Emperor Charles V named Ruggero Tassis (1513–1583) imperial postmaster in Venice, where he remained active until his death. By 1541, a Spanish/Dutch post office opened with a biweekly ordinary courier, and by the time of Facchinetti's writing, foreign ordinaries ran from Venice to as far away as Poland.[84]

Yet the Venetian response to the papal overtures was lukewarm at best. Administrators replied that establishing a papal post office in Venice "had already been tried."[85] They deferred the matter to their ambassador in Rome, presumably with instructions to bury it. The Venetians evinced disbelief, and then offense and suspicion at Facchinetti's insistence.[86] From Rome, the Venetian ambassador Paolo Tiepolo (d. 1585, o. 1567–1568) reported that the pope remained steadfast, calling the Venetian monopoly "a tax on his subjects." Tiepolo, like the company, saw Gherardi's hand in the whole matter, explaining that the postmaster had grown rich and powerful from his position and recently married his son to a niece of the pope's secretary. In a later letter, Tiepolo even recounted that the pope knew "postmasters in Flanders and Spain who are so rich and powerful that they hold great prestige with princes in the courts of the Catholic King."[87] Whether at Gherardi's prompting or his own mercantilism, the pope sought to import the Tassis brand sans Tassis.

By June 1566, Facchinetti switched to writing about the matter in cipher. Despite the benefits of twice-weekly mail, he now believed that the Venetians did not want to give the papal nuncio a secure channel of communications because it would prevent their own intelligence gathering. "It doesn't matter if one writes in cipher, because [the Venetians] have secretaries who know how to read everything," he wrote at that time. The Venetians were similarly unwilling to send their own mail by papal courier, rendering moot the argument about increased frequency of service. In fact, the Venetians perceived the increased frequency as a *disadvantage*, since the nuncio's frequency of news might outpace their own. Facchinetti grew concerned that pressing the issue was sapping valuable political capital and affecting his ability to convince the Venetians "of matters necessary to proceed against the heretics." Ultimately, he concluded that they held sovereignty in the matter "because in the states of princes you cannot resist their power (*forze*)"—not openly, at least. In truth, the nuncio proceeded to host one of Gherardi's agents in his household, Vergilio Lomboni, "believing tolerance to be a tacit approval."[88] By doing so, Facchinetti effectively dared the Venetians to risk the international condemnation that the Spanish postmaster's arrest had occasioned just a decade earlier. Once again, public letters were a secretive matter.

While Facchinetti waged political battle in Venice, scuffles intensified on the ground at Ancona and Rimini, the designated handoff locations between the papal and Venetian postal systems. Gironimo Simonetti, the Venetian postmaster of Ancona, justified his recent fight with a papal courier as follows: "He said he did not know what moved our Senate . . . he would attribute no vice to Matteo [Gherardi], while you all have shown that these measures do not come from us. Certain badmouthing individuals had given him to understand that Ancona and Rimini (being of the Church) should not allow others to carry the post, and that although we carry the insignia of Saint Mark, we should carry the arms of the Pope, a notion with little foundation." Couriers were keenly aware of the jurisdictional arguments at stake, as well as who was to blame. Real punches and insults accompanied more metaphorical blows delivered in the diplomatic arena.[89]

In 1568, the Venetians caught Facchinetti by surprise: "The couriers of Venice have proclaimed at their benches at the Rialto and San Marco that they will send mail on Wednesdays and Saturdays and are beginning this evening. I don't know what their thinking is, but it is easy to guess that they intend to tire mister Mattia." The "tacit approval" that Facchinetti enjoyed was quickly revoked, as the Venetian couriers attempted to ban Gherardi's postmaster-in-residence.[90] After investigating the matter further, Facchinetti believed that the company was responding to Gherardi's boasts (made *in voce publica*) of a second ordinary to Venice, who would carry mail at the low price of half a *paulo* per ounce (between three and four Venetian soldi). Gherardi intended to ensure that his couriers were sent at the same time or before the Venetian rivals went out. He had even gone as far as to publish his intentions in the Rialto, likely by hanging a printed placard within spitting distance of the Venetian Company headquarters. Gherardi became more provocative, banning the Venetian couriers from the entire Papal States and threatening a steep penalty of a thousand gold ducats and corporal punishment for any courier found in violation. The Venetian Company appealed to the Provveditori di Comun, who, sensing that diplomatic intricacies were involved, deferred the matter to the Venetian Senate.[91]

Whereas the Venetian Company and Tassis postmaster would lobby their governments to crack down on merchant and municipal messengers in the coming decades, a state-supported foreign post posed an entirely different kind of rival. Much like the Carafa assault on the foreign posts of Rome, the affair had explosive diplomatic potential, drawing in ambassadors, senators, the pope, and the Venetian doge. On the ground, postal officials soon turned to the tried-and-true tactic of detaining couriers and intercepting letters. By early 1569, Facchinetti believed that Gherardi had directly ordered the harassment of Venetian couriers at Rimini and Ravenna and was alarmed that the postmaster was acting in such a political capacity: "He must be made aware that opening letters is an extraordinarily dangerous remedy and your Excellency can imagine the consequences."[92] As in the case of Giovan Antonio Tassis's imprisonment and torture, the company sought a wide audience to share in their outrage. Benedetto "Zippone" (Giupponi) testified publicly about how he had suffered at the hands of the despotic governor of Rimini, who had stolen the courier's personal timepiece and two fur pelts, in addition to ransacking his letters.[93] The Camerlengo backed Gherardi to the hilt, tersely instructing Facchinetti, over his repeated protests, to tell the Venetians that the detention of couriers and opening of mail was a natural consequence of their refusal to obey postal edicts. "I love Mattia," Facchinetti wrote in October 1570, after several sentences decrying the man's self-interest, "but I very much ask that your Excellency not show him this part of the letter, because he is a man of his own sense, and I am moved to write at the present for the benefit of the common good, and because I think that it will also benefit his interest."[94] Like the Tassis, Gherardi had profited from strong action. Rome's *magister cursorum* now rivaled the Tassis corriero maggiore.

If the Venetian Company of Couriers originally rejected Gherardi's claims outright, their position modified over time as they were steadily deprived of their primary function and income. By September 1569, they were collecting funds from their own couriers to deliver the 3,000 scudi that Gherardi now demanded in reparations, although the preamble of the entry suggests a continued sense of indignation, beginning, "Aware that we must collect the three thousand to give to M. Matteo Gherardi, the present papal postmaster, in order to reclaim our possessions, and the trip to Rome that he has usurped . . ." The order further lamented the inability to find a patron willing or able to aid them, resorting to instructions that all couriers contribute within a period of eight days to a general fund. Any courier who was unable, or unwilling, would find their position sold out from under them for 100 scudi. Earlier that year, several representatives had been dispatched to Rome to inventory the contents of the post house, likely to hock goods to pay the bill. Four special delegates of the order visited the post house to "see and revisit all the books of our school" and to recall any outstanding debts.[95]

A break in the clouds came in 1572, with the death of Pope Pius V. The Venetian Company threw all their weight behind lobbying Venetian authorities to intervene on their behalf. They petitioned the Venetian College, which the doge forwarded in turn to the Venetian ambassador in Rome with instructions to appeal to the Roman College and a new Camerlengo, "who has the authority given in the vacant seat."[96] The forwarded supplication blamed Gherardi's ambitions for the conflicts of recent years. It stated that he was "extremely audacious and had no respect for the preeminence and dignity of Venice, obtaining with favors kinship and friendship with some of those in the Roman Palace." It even called for the ban of Gherardi and his couriers for traveling in Venetian lands "to punish him for his faults, and for not being respectful," as it alleged the duke of Florence had already done. Finally, it urged rapid movement in the time of the vacant seat, as the papal ordinary "had little respect for the promptness and the secrecy of the news."[97]

The wheels of diplomacy did not turn as quickly as the Venetian couriers might have liked. The company successfully persuaded Pope Gregory XIII (1502-1585, o. 1572-1585) to recognize their ancient privileges in 1572, but he revoked them eleven months later.[98] In 1577, the Venetian Company gave a generous gift (or bribe) to Mattia's successor, Vincenzo Busio Silvestre (o. 1575-1582).[99] The onset of a plague epidemic halted the debate for many months in 1575, resulting in a loss of necessary momentum. It was not until 1585, nearly two decades after the initial bans, that the couriers received the papal protections that they so desired from Pope Sixtus V (1521-1590, o. 1585-1590)—paying 3,500 ducats for the privilege.[100]

The conflicts of the second half of the sixteenth century—from the establishment of the first foreign postmasters-in-residence to the banning of Venetian couriers from the Papal States—constituted an extended period of postal wars. The temperature rose with the establishment of foreign postmasters-in-residence in both Rome and Venice and boiled over with ongoing debates about their respective rights and protections. Incipient principles of information sovereignty, communications monopoly, and diplomatic extraterritoriality in international relations came to a head.

Major battles included the 1556 imprisonment of Giovan Antonio Tassis and the 1568 ban of the Venetian couriers in Rome, but there were countless smaller skirmishes in the form of denied licenses, detained messengers, and intercepted mail. The personal ambitions of the papal postmaster Mattia Gherardi, in addition to those of the Tassis and higher-ranking leaders, further stoked conflict.

Comparing 1556 in Rome and 1568 in Venice reveals one important shift: there would never again be as high profile an arrest as that of the Spanish postmaster in Rome. Postal war still involved officials at the highest levels, from ambassadors and nuncios to the princes themselves, but the public response to the arrest of Giovan Antonio Tassis demonstrated strong support for basic extraterritorial protections for postmasters. Foreign posts were now treated as parallel embassies, and the severance of diplomatic relations was achieved through the symbolic violence of hassling channels of communication rather than the physical violence of torture. The primary weapons of the late 1560s were commercial rather than martial, such as undercutting prices and imposing fines.

Venetian narratives demonized Gherardi and his agents, and his forceful—and perhaps impetuous—personality comes across in the letters of even his allies. The Tassis had succeeded in bridging international boundaries, but Gherardi's claim to fame came instead from surviving the rapid turnovers in mid-sixteenth-century Rome and forcefully expanding the papal posts. Despite his own travails and regular courting of international condemnation, Gherardi's professional expertise and agenda found continuing favor with a succession of popes. Like Simone Tassis, Gherardi was adept at controlling political narrative. Sources disagree on his exact role, but it seems clear that he employed both overt and underhanded tactics to accomplish his goals. Even the papal nuncio carefully masked his criticism, both noting his affection and asking that the letters not reach Gherardi. That hesitancy suggests the shadow of a powerful figure. Gherardi certainly aimed to model himself after the Tassis, marrying himself and his son into the highest echelons of papal bureaucracy and turning his office into a socially and politically profitable one.

The postal wars had a longer impact on the development of international postal routes that stretched beyond their more or less peaceful resolution in the 1570s. After decades of fighting for primacy within the Papal States, neither the Spanish-imperial nor the Venetian systems posed the monopolistic threat that they once had. Restrictions on the Venetian couriers also forced the company to look elsewhere for a constituent purpose, and it became a truly international infrastructure rather than a Venetian-Roman cooperative. This process had already begun with the 1560–1561 establishment of a Venetian ordinary to Lyon. Being deprived of the Roman route shifted the Venetian Company's focus to building postal infrastructure in northern Italy, including the Milan ordinary and transalpine routes discussed in the following chapters of this book. The international ordinaries established in the 1580s relied upon cooperation established during the postal wars, however begrudgingly. Ultimately, the cross-pollination of the postal systems was crucial to their success, as was the exponential growth of long-distance communication and exchange. Clients demanded that postmasters guarantee reliable, secure service, even across borders and in times of hot and cold war.

The postal wars show us the extent to which the Italian Peninsula experienced precocious information wars. The conflict between communications monopoly and information sovereignty forced the practice of new principles such as extraterritoriality before its codification. It affirmed the secrecy of public letters and sanctity of postal messengers, as well as the legitimacy of a postmaster-in-residence. Papal actions against the posts incurred the force of international disapproval, as shown by desperate efforts to avoid a public relations nightmare through secrecy and preemptive jurisdictional justification. Writers and political leaders shaped the historical memory of the incident even as it occurred, transforming Giovan Antonio Tassis from a well-known intelligencer into a martyr. Francesco Zazzera described the postmaster as having earned "infinite praise despite significant danger to his own life, for the sake of his King."[101] Even pro-papal accounts shifted blame from the postmaster to the courier, or described the ciphered letters themselves as exciting a destructive curiosity and thereby unleashing unforeseen political consequences. Yet an undated Roman manuscript addressed to Sixtus V sung the praises of the papal posts, which could "go to new places, such as Prague, and Antwerp, and run more frequently the established routes, such as two trips per week from here to Venice, Milan, Genoa, and Naples, and two times per month to Lyon and Spain."[102] Much like the ideological conflicts of later centuries, all sides of the postal wars declared victory.

CHAPTER 3

Deadly Letters
Brigandage, Plague, and Confessionalization

Peace in the postal wars offered some protection of the diplomatic "pouch"—a term still used to refer to the protected class of mail—but what about the many other mailbags and their miscellaneous contents? Postal couriers carrying state letters remained a small portion of messengers traversing the Italian peninsula. Private letter carriers (*procacci*, *portalettere*, or *pedoni*), as well as municipal messengers (*cavallari*), faced threats that were undeterred by international condemnation.

Lawbreakers, treacherous terrain, and even virulent disease always lurked just around the bend. Historians of northern Italy have demonstrated how the "long tail" of war stretched to the end of the sixteenth century: state efforts to territorialize, confessionalize, and police their respective spheres of influence took place against a backdrop of "global crisis." Many point to a "renaissance of violence" as social breakdown resulting from political, economic, and environmental pressures took a human toll.[1]

Mail systems remained as vulnerable as the humans who carried the letters. Without the demand, protection, and funding offered by rulers waging war, the postal systems of earlier decades could have easily fragmented. Postal systems nonetheless thrived in the sixteenth and seventeenth centuries. Writing in 1608, the postal lieutenant Ottavio

Codogno described "businessmen, lawyers, and merchants" as his clients in Milan. He attributed the transformation of postal systems in scope and scale to the pressing demands of these clients.[2] By the beginning of the seventeenth century, continental Europe depended upon postal systems not just for intelligence, but also to enable the ordinary pulse of commerce and governance. Many private (nonstate) clients chose the state postal systems over miscellaneous competitors. What had started as a state privilege had become a preferred public service.

This chapter explores how we might reconcile the growth of postal systems, and the public investment it represented, with newly prominent challenges ranging from disease to dissent. The history of trust has long preoccupied historians of capitalism and the modern state, who show that family firms made the most of kinship bonds and shared dynastic goals.[3] Credit relations between unrelated individuals demanded new instruments for fostering trust. Early modern states also needed to be creditworthy, quite literally, to exercise sovereign powers. Military contractors, bankers, and civil servants invested in the project of state-building, expecting social and financial rewards in return.

A popular distrust of alternative investments, however, has long been overlooked as a key part of any decision-making process. Adding postal systems to our consideration of state-building shows that a first step toward monopolizing trust is sowing distrust. State affiliates fashioned themselves as trained information management professionals, while emphasizing the dangers of alternative modes. On the one hand, they promised a relatively reliable service to a widening clientele, even in troubled times. On the other hand, postal officials promised princes that they could securely deliver mail while also strategically gathering, intercepting, delaying, and surveilling the mail of enemies, real and imagined. The potential for strengthened control over communications justified the expansion of state posts into handling nonstate letters in ever-increasing quantities. Postal officials sold the expansion of state postal service into private mail-carrying as the best option among many untrustworthy alternatives. This chapter argues that the international system of state postal services therefore succeeded precisely *because* of the religious, political, and even epidemiological dangers of the late sixteenth and early seventeenth centuries.

Early modern states had a strong interest in controlling public opinion by the second half of the sixteenth century. Recent decades had demonstrated that letters and their manuscript or print enclosures could spread the poison of religious and political unrest. *Sola scriptura* (by the scripture alone) was the rallying cry that resounded across Protestant Europe and trumpeted the power of the holy word. Evangelical "flying papers" (*Flugschriften*) and "pamphlet wars" carried powerful words and even reached illiterate audiences by using evocative cartoons, songs, and sermons.[4] High-profile assassinations of clergy and political leaders loomed large in early journalism and diplomatic letters. Protestant rebellions within the Holy Roman Empire, the Swiss Confederacy, the Spanish Netherlands, and France vividly demonstrated the radical threat of religious conviction to political order. Governors feared that secret networks formed "fifth columns" that fed unrest in the contested cities of the Italian peninsula. Milanese inquisitors sought "a type of merchant sent throughout the world with secret intelligence and correspondences, not just related to their business, but to take up arms and rise against their princes."[5] Such "secret intelligences" might arrange for the publication of banned books or guide evangelists, like a map of safe houses for evangelists confiscated from a Milanese merchant in 1575.[6]

Postal officials lobbied to control international mail-carrying, citing the new threats of the late sixteenth and early seventeenth centuries. In this way, state-run postal systems encroached on a communications sphere previously dominated by other mail carriers. Licensed cavallari, or municipal messengers, had operated across Europe since the Middle Ages, while merchant carrier cooperatives (such as the Florentine *scarselle*) offered private subscriptions for longer-distance mail.[7] Milan and Venice granted nations mail-carrying privileges as part of the constituting capitulations for resident trade groups.[8] Many of these merchant organizations offered ordinary services run on a regular route and timetable to their associates.

The Tassis and the Venetian Company of Couriers were the innovative outsiders in the realm of private mail-carrying by comparison to such established bodies. Postal officials had faced distrust themselves in the years of the Italian Wars, but they had marshalled kin networks and intelligencing to forge key alliances with Europe's rulers and diplomats. State postmasters and couriers called on these connections in new monopolizing campaigns by the second half of the sixteenth century. They portrayed their mercantile and municipal rivals as either malicious foreign agents or hapless abettors, in contrast to their own loyalty to "the prince." In this way, foreignness and its threat to information security became a constant refrain in the late sixteenth century. Postmasters exploited the growing distrust between sovereigns and their unruly subjects in the age of confessional conflict in Europe.[9]

This chapter will consider three major threats to communication systems in turn—brigandage, disease, and social unrest—and how they were turned to the competitive advantage of a state-sponsored postal service.

Shooting the Messenger

The courier was as familiar a sight as the foreign soldier in mid-sixteenth-century Italy. The symbols of their office made them immediately recognizable. Tassis couriers claimed white croupiers and the symbol of the family heraldry, the badger (*tasso*); the Venetian couriers bore the lion of Saint Mark; and the papal couriers donned the twin keys of Saint Peter. Whether traveling on foot or horseback, a courier wore thick leather boots and carried a distinctive curved horn (figure 8). Blowing the horn would alert the next way station to ready the relay, but it also could be used to sound an alarm, indicating a courier in distress.

An Italian proverb went: "He who rides by post, plays with death."[10] The crime of attacking a courier was so prevalent by the mid-sixteenth century that it acquired its own Italian term: *svaligiamento*, from the verb *svaligiare*. The word pairs the common "s" prefix structure in Italian, indicating opposition, with the term *valigia*, meaning "baggage." The strong association likely derived from the messenger's characteristic saddlebags of thick leather known as *valigie*. John Florio's 1611 bilingual dictionary defined *svaligiare* as "to rob," but also more precisely as "to uncase one by the high-way."[11] The second translation draws a further connection to the "highway," a raised road along which state protection was offered, if not always effectively delivered. *Svaligiamento* occasionally appeared with reference to other travelers, but that usage appears to be slippage from the association with couriers rather than vice versa.[12]

Historians of violence have long read banditry like *svaligiamenti* as a form of resistance to the centralizing, monopolizing impulses of the state.[13] By the end of the sixteenth century, state postal systems bridged public and private service in one of the first commercial state utilities. They did so at the expense of many existing bodies of local messengers. As states sought to distinguish and protect the post, they strengthened the association between couriers and occupying power. This was true for the Spanish in the duchy of Milan, but also the Venetians in their extensive land empire. Rather than a political act, however, most assaults on couriers in northern Italy seem to have simpler motives

FIGURE 8. *Cursor Germanus*, or the German courier, in Enea Vico, *Diversarum gentium nostrae aetatis habitus* (Venice: c. 1558). Image courtesy of the Rijksmuseum, http://hdl.handle.net/10934/RM0001.COLLECT.443486.

for theft. Banditry is parasitic, and so logically it occurs along the most heavily trafficked trade and exchange routes. Policing reports reveal that letter carriers of all stripes also carried money, jewelry, and other fine goods. Some brigands attacked messengers, merchants, and travelers indiscriminately, but during the sixteenth century, some groups also tracked and targeted the postal courier. Planned ambushes were a new possibility in an age when ordinary couriers followed predictable itineraries.

Prosecution of banditry enjoyed a strong public mandate. In a study of early modern homicide, Colin Rose suggests that the strongest punishments were reserved for crimes with nearly uniform public disapprobation.[14] The strengthened protection of state postal service by state authorities reflected broad consensus concerning the importance of commerce generally and postal communications specifically. Even today, mail theft is treated as a crime against the state in many legal contexts.[15] Elite responses to sixteenth-century brigandage demonstrate a consensus that postal service represented the public interest. Shooting the messenger escalated from classification as an attack on an individual to an attack on society.

State archives preserve many accounts of assaults on messengers (figure 9) that also convey rare details about the postal system. First, such documents reveal that couriers carried large quantities of money for both public and private patrons from an early date. Municipalities had established their messenger corps (*cavallari*) to move money as well as communications between the center and periphery of empires. Tassis postal couriers also frequently carried funds as well as letters for bankers. When the courier Zuan Gamba attempted mail theft, as discussed in chapter 1, he did so from the Fuggers of Augsburg, who were bankers to the Habsburg rulers.[16] Second, while bills of exchange were becoming more popular, couriers often moved funds in the form of hard cash. The records of losses confirm that couriers carried large quantities: in 1551, more than 110 scudi disappeared as a courier transferred 8,000 scudi from the treasury of Milan to that of Fornaro.[17] In 1568, a Venetian courier was robbed of nearly 7,000 scudi outside Goro, on the boundary with Ferrara.[18]

By the 1580s, robbery accounts reference an even greater variety of fine goods. In 1587, brigands assaulted the courier of Mantua in Moradega outside Verona, likely traveling to or from Venice. The inventory of losses included "a golden parrot with many jewels and pearls, a golden girdle, a great quantity of silver spoons and forks, many diamonds and fine rubies in a small box, a silver plate of about 13 pounds, a few gold necklaces, two silver ewers (*bronzineti*) and a good deal of Mantuan coins (*mocenighi*)."[19] In October 1585, the Mantuan ambassador in Milan remarked that "these couriers are constantly assaulted." He called it "a miracle" that the thieves in a recent attack had not located the separate container that carried the mail in the carriage.[20] Travelers also journeyed on postal roads and experienced its dangers. In 1589, a set of Genoese travelers had just left the postal inn of the Three Falcons outside of

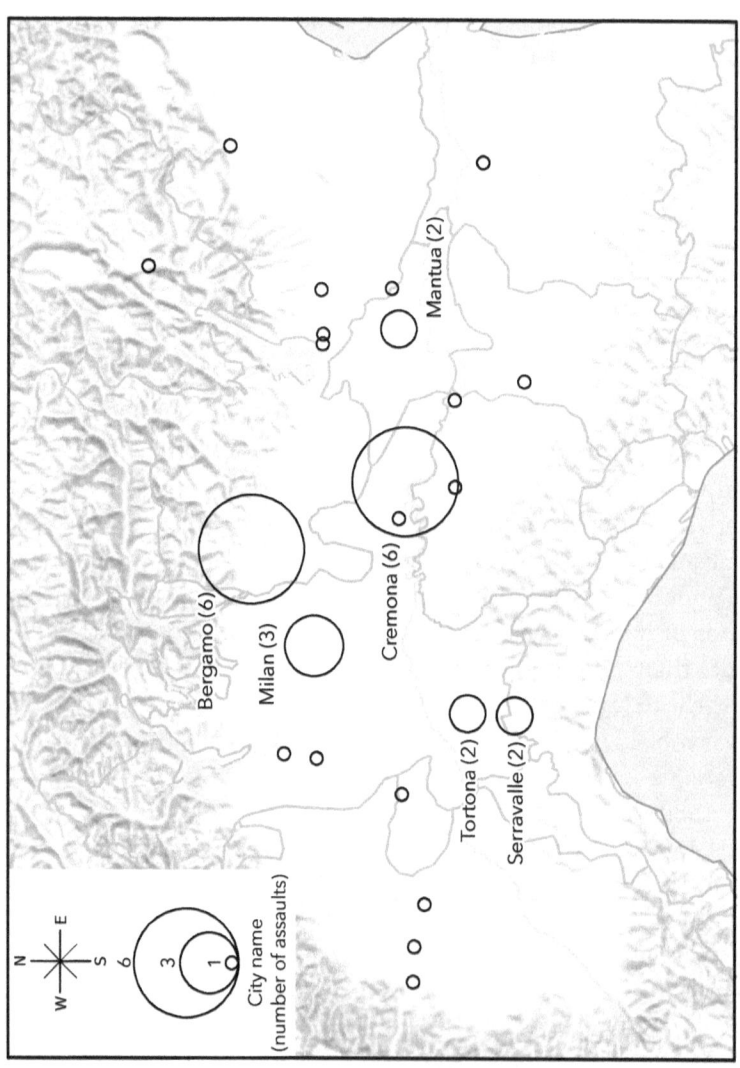

FIGURE 9. Assaults on postal couriers in northern Italy, 1556–1631. Points are sized by the number of incidents. More than half of the identified attacks (twenty-four of forty-eight) occurred in just thirteen years, 1598–1611. The greatest number of assaults (six) took place near Cremona and Bergamo. Many more occurred along political boundaries that facilitated escape across jurisdictions. Map by the author and Stewart Scales.

Cremona when a group of men approached wearing false mustaches and handkerchiefs over their faces. " 'Halt, halt' they cried as they approached with rotary guns, with a dog trained on us. . . . Seeing ourselves surrounded by seven horses and three or four men on foot, we gave them the money."[21] Overall, the travelers reported the loss of more than 2,000 scudi worth of personal belongings. Such accounts are reminiscent of later stagecoach attacks in the American West. They also suggest that many, if not most, *svaligiamenti* were symptomatic of the wider brigandage epidemic rather than episodes of targeted espionage, although such motives were sometimes suspected.

Routine postal service led to equally routine robbery. In 1601, many such assaults concentrated along the Mantuan borders. In July of that year, four men carrying wheellock firearms and wearing false beards and leather masks stopped a carriage carrying a Venetian courier. "With great force," they brought the courier and carriage driver to an inn at Salvaterra, northwest of Ferrara, and stole goods worth around 400 scudi. The carriage driver guessed them to be soldiers from a cavalry company, which would explain why they had turned their clothing inside out to evade identification.[22] The same week, a Roman ordinary and accompanying postilion were assaulted at night on the Mantuan border with Modena, near Concordia sulla Secchia, and left "tied to two trees." The unfortunate courier was the same one who had been assaulted between Bologna and Modena earlier that year.[23]

Policing the posts involved a unique tug-of-war over the mailbag. In January 1604, four armed assailants ambushed a Spanish postal courier along his ordinary route between Rome and Milan. The robbers held up the courier at gunpoint just north of Cremona and then fled by boat on the River Po. Pursued by the Cremonese guards, the bandits threw the mailbags into the river, betting that their pursuers would feel obligated to recover the letters. The bet paid off: the podestà called off the pursuit and recovered the mailbags with the help of local peasants. He had been forewarned that the two bags would contain letters from the duke of Parma and other "assorted things." The peasants "fished [the bags] from the Po in very poor condition." Cremonese authorities then tasked the local postmaster with copying the salvaged letters as well as possible. They asked the governor of Milan for help in sorting out the goods, whose senders, destinations, and recipients had been lost to the river. In the days following the attack on the Spanish courier, the podestà of Cremona dispatched the sheriff (*bargello*) into the countryside. He learned that a nearby surgeon had treated two men with gunshot wounds in the stables of a house at Cornavecchio. The officer held off from further action, now needing permission to extradite the criminals from Lodese territory. As for the slain bandit, the podestà visited the body himself and confirmed it to be one Stefano, known as "Il Longo," a resident of Castelnuovo.[24] The other assailants were the sons of a former innkeeper along the road to Piacenza, as well as one Giulio Mantovano, whose surname indicated that he came from the countryside surrounding Mantua.[25]

Gangs routinely posted up at inns (*osterie*), which is especially noteworthy given that inns were also the staging posts of the postal systems. Local postmasters were often also innkeepers who could stable the horses, as well as feed and give shelter to weary couriers. With the regular flow of gossiping travelers, inns no doubt also served as intelligence hubs to identify and follow heavy-pursed targets. Civic authorities already regarded inns with suspicion, located as they were on the outskirts of town and filled with dangerous foreigners. Milanese legislation routinely forbade city residents from dining at inns, for example.[26] The quartering of soldiers in inns furthered both their disrepute and danger to travelers. That appeared to have been the case in 1612, when a Venetian innkeeper testified to seeing soldiers pass by shortly before they attacked the courier of Milan.[27] Following a July 1601 incident involving an inn at Salvaterra, authorities concluded that since "it does not serve another purpose than the entertainment of young men, for which it is very appropriate . . . it seems appropriate to demolish this place, where otherwise it will require the utmost diligence to prevent murderous robberies."[28]

Other details about how the assaults played out were remarkably similar across cases. First, in most incidents, the bandits were armed but the courier was not killed. Bandits did not commit murder when they could accomplish the robbery without it. Tying the courier to trees prevented him from raising an immediate alarm—otherwise, the courier might return to the nearest town to ring the church bells and raise a posse. However, when couriers escaped relatively unscathed, this fed suspicions that they had colluded or held back information about their assailants. Authorities often imprisoned and interrogated couriers after attacks. In this light, the emphasis that couriers placed on disguises in witness statements may have played an exculpatory role: such details made couriers' insistence that they did not recognize their assailants more plausible.

Second, attacks often took place at river crossings, where bandits could quickly escape across nearby borders. In such cases, authorities could do little more than send sheriffs on information-gathering missions to support extradition requests. Finally, summer months heralded higher rates of criminal violence across the board.[29] One reason for this may have been the prevalence of fairs in the summer, where traders and, increasingly, bankers met to negotiate international exchanges. Two such fairs took place in Mantuan territory during August, which meant increased traffic of wealthy travelers in the preceding weeks.[30]

Prosecuting *svaligiamenti* brought states together in a shared pursuit, even during periods of otherwise-tense relations. Venice and Milan adopted two major extradition agreements, the first in 1572 (modified in 1580) and the second in 1595. Highway robbery and "unlawful wounding by a wheellock arquebus" were featured among the fifteen crimes named in the agreement.[31] In 1604, the Spanish governor assured the Venetian resident that he "did not even need to speak of the agreements" when it came to the bandits because the governor would always be ready to hand them over promptly.[32] This proved important at least twice in the case of one cohesive gang that targeted couriers in the early seventeenth century. In 1601, the Venetian Council of Ten sought to extradite a set of bandits captured by Milanese authorities named Giovanni Battista Martinengo, Bartolo Tealdo, Baldo Furlani (or Furlan), and brothers Ortensio and Bartolomeo Furlan. The Milanese secretary, podestà of Bergamo, podestà of Citadella, and Paduan rectors received instructions to find the bandits "wanted for the number of robberies and murders committed by them" and soon to be tried by a state prosecutor.[33] Their crimes covered a wide swath of Venetian terraferma following the route taken by the postal ordinary. The involvement of Venice's most formidable political and policing bodies underscored the seriousness of the bandits' crimes, but also the delicacy of navigating among the many parties invested in retribution.[34]

By 1604, the same gang was active once again along the Lombard frontier, consisting now of Giovanni Battista Martinengo, Bartolomeo Furlan, and a "Geronimo Fabretto"—an alias used by Giuseppe Bertoldo. The gang harassed both the Spanish and Venetian ordinary couriers. Once the Cremonese succeeded in capturing the highwaymen, the Spanish governor was true to his word, readily signing orders to extradite the bandits to the Venetians for prosecution. In fact, he issued edict after edict that condemned brigandage in the strongest terms.[35] Yet by September 1604, the Spanish ordinary headed to Rome barely made it out of the city gates before being assailed and, as in Mantua three years earlier, tied to two trees. The governor offered a sizable reward: immunity from prosecution and 1,000 scudi for information leading to the criminals' capture.[36] The scale of the damage to both public (i.e., state) and private clients, "none more so than to the businessmen (*negotianti*)," merited this sizable reward. When bandits attacked a courier en route to Lyon the next spring, authorities similarly noted that they were targeting the bankers who had gathered in preparation for the fairs at Piacenza.[37] Official responses indicate that private and public interest came together behind a strong mandate of prosecution against these attacks.

In this way, even when attacks were not about the politics of the post, the official responses were. Furthermore, postmasters and couriers took an active role in petitioning for their own protections. The Spanish postmaster lieutenant of Milan, Ottavio Codogno, worked closely with the governor and even proposed his own edict following an October 1604 attack on the Roman ordinary. Codogno saw both local rivals and resentful local authorities as blameworthy for the lack of enforced protections for the courier. He routinely argued for the adoption of a community penalization approach: if bandits were not captured, the nearest locale should be fined the appropriate amount to make restitution.[38] The postmaster lieutenant saw a clear connection between Cremonese authorities' failure to curb assaults—or perhaps even collusion with their perpetrators—and their disobedience of the office of the corriero maggiore of Milan. The feud between the Spanish post office in Milan and the messengers of Cremona was bitter and longstanding and included accusations of mail theft and several suits and countersuits regarding their respective privileges.[39]

The privileges of the post had been paid for in blood. Postal couriers wore the threat of death or injury in the line of duty as a badge of pride. In 1620, for example, the Venetian Company of Couriers protested competition from rival carriers along the northern Italian route. The couriers cited a recent attack on one Zuanne (Giovanni) Benzoni, who, "without regard for his own life, was happier to die right there on the road rather than voluntarily give the state letters to assassins sent by princes. When asked for the state letters, he pulled out a pistol, shooting one, and was then killed by the others." The company cited the selfless act as proof of the "disposition of the couriers" to be "truly faithful to their princes."[40] Such petitions framed attacks on couriers as an act of war. The Company of Couriers held up the courier's willingness to give his life to defend the mail as a rebuttal to accusations that he might instead conspire with his attackers to defraud the state. Instead of wily knaves, the assaulted couriers were martyrs. Both the Spanish and the Venetians proved to be sympathetic audiences and offered additional protection as a result—protection that further distinguished postal couriers from miscellaneous messengers who were victimized as private, rather than public, individuals.

Yet postmasters and couriers never fully succeeded in one aspect of their petitioning: namely, their desire to carry defensive weapons. In 1568, the postmaster of Vigevano sent his son, Giovanni Giacomo Liscati, to carry letters for the Spanish governor of Milan. The local podestà seized Liscati for carrying "a sword and dagger without light." Traveling in darkness and carrying arms were enough for the podestà to treat the younger Liscati as a potential bandit himself—not unreasonably, given that the sons of innkeepers had been the assailants in aforementioned incidents. The elder Liscati protested that "in 40 years of being postmaster, in carrying out this office, I have never been prohibited from carrying arms."[41] This was the downside of expanded policing for postmasters and couriers. Some officials, such as the postmaster of Serravalle, did succeed in obtaining licenses for themselves and their male relatives based on the travel they did by night.[42] Such a license might not be recognized throughout their journeys, however, and new governors might issue a blanket revocation of licenses granted under their predecessors.[43] Increased state intervention did not always play out in the way that postal agents desired.

Assaults on postal couriers show the persistent dangers that couriers faced, but they also highlight a new international consensus concerning the need to protect postal service. Political and commercial elites across Italy, regardless of nationality, needed to transport letters, money, goods, and even themselves securely and reliably.[44] The state expanded its policing with this mandate, in accordance with lobbying by its postal officials. New measures, from extradition to community penalization, nonetheless favored the state postal services over smaller-scale carriers. Postal officials further asserted their primacy in petitions and even drafted executive orders, thus exercising enviable power over policy.

Policing the Post in a Time of Plague

Plague was much harder to police than bandits, and it was endemic in early modern Europe. Northern Italians had a hard-earned understanding of contagion since the fourteenth century. The Visconti dukes of Milan promulgated some of the earliest plague quarantine laws in Europe in the 1370s. By the sixteenth century, both Venice and Milan had offices of public health issuing bills of health that functioned much like their modern equivalents. Both cities also constructed and maintained large plague hospitals, or *lazaretti*, outside the city walls.[45]

A new, devastating wave of plague first appeared around Trento in the early 1570s and had spread to Milan by July 1576. As of 1574, the population of the city of Milan was around 115,000. By 1577, some estimates place the plague deaths at nearly 25,000—or 18 to 20 percent of the city's population. The numbers were similar in nearby Venice. They were even worse in terraferma cities like Bergamo, which saw about 40 percent of its population die during these plague years. In 1630–1631, a second outbreak had similar results, killing as much as 60 percent of the population of Verona.[46] The fear and real devastation of contagion invariably restricted travel and exchange.

Academic scholarship to date offers surprisingly little information about the broader ramifications of plague at the heart of the budding postal network. Postal routes overlaid the pathways of disease: couriers and contagion naturally intersected along highly trafficked routes among densely populated cities. Some authors suggest that it shut down routes entirely, but plenty of historians of information see this period as especially rich for news flow.[47] Manuscript newsletters flourished, carrying news of Calvinist rebellions, discoveries in the New World, Turkish advances in the Balkans, or, significantly, the spread of disease. Authorities relied on couriers to bring news of plague sightings, even as they feared that the couriers might carry contagion themselves.

The postal wars had seen countless instances of couriers detained for petty, spurious, or retributive reasons. When public health authorities began to detain couriers to stem the spread of plague, leaders and diplomats regarded the tactic with suspicion and annoyance. In October 1575, the Venetian diplomatic resident in Milan, Ottaviano Marzi (o. 1573–1579), complained that Milanese authorities had detained the ordinary courier en route from Bergamo to open and "fumigate" all his letters.[48] Contagion theory of the time linked foul odor to ill effects. In prior plagues, letters had been kept for days in a sealed box with strong-smelling spices. The disinfection of ship cargo similarly employed fragrant woods, juniper, and sulfur. Despite the diplomat's annoyance, the Venetians took a similar approach: just a few days later, a Venetian edict ordered that "all papers from the Lazzaretto Vecchio are subject to fumigation, and all strings and cords should be removed before transfer to the central office of the health magistracy."[49] Popular belief held that such "soft" materials were more likely to act as vectors of disease.

The Venetian ambassador in Rome later reported that Roman officials would allow only letters "closed with wire" from Venice; any "sealed with wax and tied with string" would be burned.[50] In the years that followed, increasingly aggressive disinfection measures would be adopted, such as exposing letters to high heat or dipping them (and sometimes, the courier himself) in vinegar.[51] In addition to requiring that letters be opened or seals removed, thus compromising security, these methods were more likely to make the text illegible.[52]

In 1575, the Venetian resident met with the Spanish governor of Milan to complain about the "little respect" that the overzealous ministers of public health had shown to his government by delaying their mail. The governor asked the resident in turn what the state of plague was in Venice. Marzi responded that "the rumors [of devastation] were not true, not for several months, and everything was improving rapidly; that there was no reasonable cause for alarm nor to prevent trade."[53] The resident's assurances did little to ease the governor's concerns, though. Milanese ministers of public health dispatched their own couriers into Venetian territories to spy on conditions. Only after receiving a positive report would they allow the Venetian couriers into Milan. Whereas foreign couriers posed a potential threat, one's own postal courier remained a valuable source of on-the-ground intelligence abroad.

The courier detentions continued throughout November and December, watched by an anxious public as well as officials. A Roman newsletter reported that Florentine authorities had detained the Spanish courier of Milan.[54] It suggested that the duke of Florence retaliated for the delay of his own courier by the Spanish. The courier then died in Florentine custody just a few days later, and another newsletter reported that his body would be examined for signs of plague.[55] In a similar instance in 1579, tensions rose in Rome to levels not seen since 1556. Papal commissaries held the courier of Milan and opened the letters that he carried in front of Spanish postal officials. They then took the deliveries from afflicted locations to outside the city walls and burned them.[56]

Disease posed a real threat, but so did political opportunism. Plague hospitals and the disinfection process necessitated active counterespionage measures. In 1620, the Tassis imperial postmaster in Venice traveled to meet the mail in person at the lazzaretto, with confidential letters separated from the rest under his watchful eye. Venetian documents reveal this was a wise move, as State Inquisitors had tasked a hospital prior with intercepting the letters. Thwarted by the postmaster, the agent instead expressed his frustration: "Twice I have been able to observe the letters of postmaster Ferdinando Tassis ... I have done everything possible to have the letters. It is not possible, because they come from the lazaretto, secured in the presence of this Tassis." He finished by recommending the appointment of an "expert person" to the lazaretto to succeed where he could not in intercepting the letters.[57] The Venetian ambassador in Turin was not as savvy in countering espionage at the lazaretto. The Savoyard archives preserve a nearly uninterrupted series of confidential Venetian diplomatic letters from 1630. The decrypted letters even include the ambassador's suspicions that his correspondence was being intercepted in this manner.[58] Public health measures could easily compromise secure channels.

In other cases, plague restrictions could also challenge state surveillance. The life of a particularly famous correspondent offers an illustrative example. In 1633, the Roman inquisition called the famed scholar Galileo Galilei (1564–1642) to testify regarding his recent publication, *Dialogue on the Two Chief World Systems*. Church guidelines dictated that Galileo receive preprint permission for his works, but plague had broken out in Rome while Galileo was in Florence. Galileo explained that "commerce was stopped; so, seeing that I could not come to Rome, by correspondence I requested permission for the book to be printed in Florence."[59] Instructed to send the manuscript for review, Galileo encountered further difficulties: "Despite having used every possible care and having contacted even the highest secretaries of the Grand Duke and the directors of the postal service, to try and send the original safely, I received no assurance that this could be done, and it certainly would have been damaged, washed out, or burned, such was the strictness at the borders."[60] He referred to the methods of disinfection, vinegar baths and "toasting" of letters, that were employed on the borders of the Papal States. Evidently, postal couriers carried manuscripts along with letters, coins, and jewels.

Galileo had plenty of other reasons to evade his Inquisition censors. But his account nonetheless hints at why, in a time of plague restrictions, reliance upon postal service increased, even among nonstate users. While Galileo indicated that "commerce was stopped," the postal routes remained active, if subject to inconvenient restrictions. Alternative messengers were neither willing nor allowed to run.[61] Official postal couriers might be the best option, but that did not mean that they were guaranteed. Skilled users could strategize for a better chance of success. For example, in normal times, administrators generally preferred that couriers go by land because speeds were more reliable. Plague changed the calculus: multiple borders meant multiple health regimes that might or might not trust the documentation provided by their neighbors. Officials instead opted to send couriers by sea, especially on routes that linked Genoa, Naples, and Spain.[62] Travel by sea could also minimize potential exposure to disease for the courier in comparison to passing through many way stations on land.[63] Alternatively, letters could be sent to friendlier cities not yet associated with outbreaks, from which they could be forwarded to their final destinations. Correspondents often employed all these strategies and more, sending letters in two or three copies and along different routes at great expense.

Not all the costs were financial. Later acts commemorated the members of the Venetian Company of Couriers who had fallen to plague. A special place was given to those who had died "in the public service," carrying the state letters.[64] Many more would fall in the years to come, often in the terraferma cities that constituted the main routes. At the same time, campaigns to rebuild, reform, and expand postal systems with renewed political will took place during both the 1580s and 1630s. The plague years illustrated that postal couriers were "essential personnel," to borrow a term from a modern pandemic.[65]

The longer-term impacts of recurring waves of plague are not always as obvious as short-term disruptions. They were nonetheless in the background of key infrastructural shifts. By the 1580s, the Venetian Company began to work with Tassis Spanish postmasters of Milan to establish a new postal ordinary connecting their two cities. Couriers left twice weekly: once on Wednesdays via Bergamo, and once on Saturdays via Cremona and Mantua. The new ordinary established a continuous circulation of information in northern Italy. This collaboration was likely spurred by financial necessity and the Tassis posts increasingly relied on Venetian couriers. The financial strain of running postal systems even during times of crisis led postal officials to cultivate new alliances, much as the postal wars had forced the Venetian Company to look beyond Rome.

The demographic impact of plague and violence also contributed to the increasing pattern of widows of postmasters serving as postmistresses. These women exercised newly prominent authority over the post office. Women had always played a role in courier trades, much as they did in any Renaissance family firm or guild. Marriages contributed to communal solidarity among the Bergamaschi diaspora and dynastic alliances for the Tassis. In the post-plague decades, several powerful postmistresses staffed Europe's postal network hubs, including Lucina Cattanea Tassis (d. 1619) in Milan, Alexandrine de Rye von Taxis (d. 1666) in Brussels, and Lucia Ropele Bordogna Taxis (d. 1688) in Trento. After their husbands' premature deaths, these women partnered with male postal lieutenants to oversee the office, sometimes well past the point at which their sons had reached the age of inheritance. After all, even when spared by disease, Tassis sons could be the victims—and instigators—of endemic interpersonal violence.[66] Post offices were often in more capable administrative hands with postmistresses, who had often been raised in an office or married into one in their teenage years.

Policing against plague—much like policing against banditry—disproportionately favored state-sponsored postal systems over alternative modes of mail-carrying. Venice and Milan routinely reminded subject cities to give unimpeded passage to postal couriers even in times of strict lockdown, but private and even municipal carriers did not receive the same government backing.[67] Even if local messengers were not explicitly punished for traveling during plague or attacked by highwaymen, they did not receive the same privileges and protections that their postal competitors did. This had the practical effect of further attracting private users to state postal systems, but it also reinforced a new notion that the systems were themselves a "public service"—after all, couriers risked their lives on behalf of a clientele that extended beyond their rulers.

Channels for Dissent: Cavallari and Merchant Carriers

The spring of 1568 seemed to confirm Milanese authorities' worst fears of spiritual contagion from abroad. Giovanni da Martinengo was one of the four Bergamaschi messengers who ran the route between Milan and Venice. He was a well-known figure who worked from "an inn, at the sign of the peacock above a moat at the porta Romana." At some point, Martinengo left several bales of cloth and other merchandise at an inn outside Verona, apparently by accident. Several years later, the innkeeper opened one of the boxes and found several printed books from that city of heresiarchs, Geneva. Recognizing the danger, the innkeeper turned the stash over to local inquisitors. The famed Counter-Reformation leader Cardinal Charles Borromeo (1538-1584) himself received a report regarding the discovery. Martinengo had evidently been smuggling heretical literature for many years. Kevin Stevens suggests that he had used his professional knowledge of customs procedures to deftly avoid them.[68]

Martinengo was a common surname, derived from a town located between Bergamo and Brescia. Members of a Martinengo feudal nobility routinely challenged Venetian and Spanish authorities in northern Italy during the early modern period.[69] This Martinengo belonged to the merchant carriers of Milan. Merchants had long negotiated for letter-carrying privileges as a part of the capitulations that allowed them to reside and work in foreign cities. The Milan chamber of merchants had formed agreements with Venetian guilds as recently as 1522 and 1525 that established ordinary couriers traveling between the two cities, and even nominated a Milanese merchant *maestro dei corrieri* to reside in Venice.[70]

Merchant carriers were a rival system that predated and coexisted with the Tassis state posts. A rare set of pay records show that the Venetian diplomatic resident of Milan used both systems to carry his letters. From December 1580 to March 1581, he recorded 145 mail-related payments, of which 60 were made to "the Tassis postmaster," totaling around 300 lire.[71] The resident made a nearly equal number of payments (51) to "Bollino," the *maestro dei corrieri* of the merchant carriers.[72] The roughly 250 lire paid to Bollino included sending dispatches to the Venetian senate, as well as letters forwarded from representatives in Spain and Savoy, showing that the Venetian resident did not prefer one to the other when it came to sending his state correspondence.[73]

Yet the book-smuggling incident demonstrated the exploitability of these merchant carrier systems. In the social and religious climate of northern Italy in the Counter-Reformation, governors increasingly associated foreign merchants with disruption, rebellion, and heresy. From the perspective of occupying authorities, subversive foreign couriers spreading uncontrolled communications were a disaster waiting to happen. That the Venetian resident utilized the merchant carriers—thereby potentially avoiding Spanish surveillance—was a perfect example of authorities' worst fears.

The Spanish crown and state council instructed governors to maintain order in northern Italy at any cost.[74] Rich, populous, centrally located, and home to the finest arms production in Europe, Milan had been a keystone of Habsburg policy for the better part of a century. Yet Spanish authorities feared networks of influence from Swiss Protestants, Francophiles, or the partisans in Venetian or Savoyard employ.[75] A 1578 edict expressed concern that "many people riding under many colors of the ordinary couriers of the Dutch, French, Lyonnaise, Venetian and Genoese merchants come and go as they please without notice to their superiors or state officials."[76] Who could say what they were carrying?

Martinengo and the mail-carrying merchants of Milan were not, in fact, very foreign. They were Bergamaschi, just as the Tassis continued to be, for all their Spanish trappings. Unwary messengers nonetheless could, wittingly or unwittingly, invite a foreign threat. They might let their letters be stolen, carry disease, or even purposefully ferry prohibited ideas. Associating carriers with a foreign fifth column was a powerful allegation that state postal officials wielded to great effect. Postal officials and couriers portrayed their services as the best alternative to these untrustworthy messengers. In doing so, they aligned themselves with the confessionalizing, territorializing goals of executive powers in Venice and Milan.

By the 1580s, the son of Simone Tassis, Ruggero Tassis of Milan (d. 1588), aggressively campaigned against merchant rivals. "Two postmasters for a city are as incompatible as two princes," he began a letter to the then governor Don Sancho de Padilla. The postmaster then played to the greatest fears of the Spanish rulers of Milan: "All of the foreign couriers direct themselves in their own house, and secretly and publicly collect letters and dispatches, and distribute them in contempt of your Majesty and the Illustrious Governor, from which derives much gossip and scandal."[77] The governor was not hard to convince. He forwarded Ruggero's petition to the Spanish crown soon after, adding his own thoughts:

> In Your Majesty's states at every time, not just in war, when letters and newsletters are in frequent use, messengers are not free to travel wherever, nor is it often suitable to send them, lest secret actions be discovered; but also in times of peace, when [the enemy] conspires war, not to mention the danger posed to our religion. Your lords and ministers close the roads to these miserable, insidious sects, who seek to oppose us by every means with their false doctrines, which are scattered and sown in souls by way of letters and newsletters. They make the wonderful invention of writing and letters, so necessary to human society, something pernicious and loathsome.[78]

Ongoing spiritual threat broke down prior distinctions between governance in peace and war. Conspiracy was everywhere, seeded by dangerous newsletters (*avvisi*). Padilla cited recent rebellions in "Genoa, Florence, Venice and Rome" and attributed them to merchant conspiracies. He likened Milan's situation to that of the rebellious Low Countries, where the Tassis notably enjoyed monopolistic privileges. The governor claimed that a foreign, sectarian threat necessitated an extension of executive power, akin to times of martial law. The only solution was to control mail by supporting the Spanish post office of Milan in its bid for total control over public and private mail in northern Italy.[79]

The governor was also motivated by his recent experience working with Postmaster Ruggero Tassis of Milan to conduct surveillance, which he recounted in detail:

> I wrote in past days to your Majesty about people sent from England and other places to disseminate heresy in Italy, and to do other things in disservice to God, and your Majesty. It is my charge to use every possible diligence to discover their correspondences, and to have in hand the letters that they write, for which purpose I am sent the names and signatures (*contrassegni*). I communicate with a few ministers because they aid me, but they have nothing satisfactory to report to your majesty, nor myself: the postmaster says that such exchange is disguised as merchants' letters (*sotto coperta de' mercanti*), which he cannot investigate: but if the letters pass through a single hand, as is suitable, it will be easy to tell this and other things, from which I may be warned of important things that he discovers.[80]

Communications monopoly in exchange for unparalleled state surveillance was a mutually beneficial proposition. Padilla's postscript reiterated the strategic importance of information received from the postmaster. Unlike opening letters, which alerted correspondents that a third party was reading their messages, the secret surveillance of correspondents and addresses did not arouse suspicions, facilitating further monitoring. The letter from Padilla nominally sought the king's approval, but the governor had already attached a printed edict affirming the monopoly of the Spanish post office. The gubernatorial edict notably bypassed the Milanese senate, which tended to be more sympathetic to the merchants. Spanish governors routinely distrusted the Milanese elites as potential rebels themselves.[81]

The central argument for monopolization by state postal officials was that all objects and personnel needed to be picked up and deposited at the post house under the watchful eye of the *corriero maggiore*. Much like a customs office or tollhouse, postal officials proposed that channeling all mail through a single location would prevent the smuggling of goods, but also ideas, like Martinengo's books from Geneva. It would also, incidentally, cement the *corriero maggiore*'s primacy over all mail, including that of his commercial rivals.

The Spanish post office of Milan warred for years with both the Milanese merchants and the *cavallari* of Cremona over control of private letters. Merchant messengers accused the Spanish postmaster in Cremona of stealing mail, allegedly under the orders of the postmaster in Milan. Milanese authorities appeared to side with the merchants and chastised the Spanish postmasters for their interference, who in turn found allies in the Spanish governors.[82] Cremona would remain the center of jurisdictional struggles going forward. Much like the Venetian terraferma cities, Cremona had a strong cavallari tradition because it was a key geographic location for mail traveling from east to west as well as north to south, such as to Tuscany and Rome. This was the same region where postal couriers were repeatedly attacked, although it remains difficult to draw firmer conclusions about whether that rivalry motivated attacks, or, as Codogno suspected, at least inhibited prosecution.

Ruggero's campaign against the merchant carriers of Milan had clear Venetian parallels. The Venetian Company of Couriers battled both municipal and private carriers across the terraferma.[83] In theory, cavallari held licenses granted by their respective cities to carry state letters. Anyone else fell into a broad category of carriers of letters, goods, and people by various modes: *procacci*; *portalettere*; *pedoni* (by foot); *carozzeri* and *nolesini* (by coach); or simply "others."[84] Postal officials offered a much simpler vision of communications in which postal agents would be overseen by a corriero maggiore sanctioned by executive power, and every other type of messenger would be approached as restricted competitors.

Fascinatingly, the Venetian Company of Couriers joined with the Tassis in the battle against the merchants of Milan. They wrote a supplication directed to Venetian authorities as well as the Spanish governor, accusing the merchants of "usurpations." Allegedly, the merchants had bypassed the governor to petition the Milanese senators who, "tricked by them," proceeded to grant them undue favor. The supplication declared that the merchants had engaged in a mudslinging campaign (e.g., spreading the false rumor that the Florentine couriers would be banned).[85] The merchants launched a counterclaim in the same vein, pleading to the Milanese senate that the governor, the marquis of Ayamonte (d. 1580), mistreated them by favoring Tassis. The governor of Cremona, they claimed, had turned against them, as had the Venetian senate, "instigated, perhaps, by Tassis."[86]

The Bergamaschi diaspora had succeeded as servants to many masters by making the most of every opportunity, on the road and at the court. They frequently gathered evidence of perceived violations while abroad and presented examples of edicts with their complaints circulated to their political patrons. The petitions framed a binary choice:

either the authorities support their postmasters in a monopoly, which was "a source of great benefit to the public and public reputation of this state's posts," or "foreign princes" would exert control within their territory.[87] "Mantua, Ferrara, Florence, Rome, France and Spain, and all other princes favor their own in the same fashion," the Venetians reported, and all princes held the matter of the posts as "a sacred and inviolable jurisdiction."[88] Much as the papal posts had learned the language of information sovereignty, the Venetian Company was now proclaiming a communications monopoly. The Tassis in Milan used similar strategies against the Cremonese, but also against merchant rivals in Genoa. They enlisted the Spanish governor's aid to overturn an agreement between the Genoese and a consortium of German and Italian merchants.[89]

As states countered threats to their communications systems, they listened to their technocratic specialists, even letting them write the regulations. Official decrees adopted their language, describing how other princes monopolized international mail-carrying within their territories, "with much benefit."[90] A 1582 Venetian act declared that "anyone, of any station, should not presume to carry mail in this city or surrounding territory, nor collecting, accepting, or carrying mail along the routes of Milan, Mantua, Cremona, Genoa, and other foreign states.... The couriers of Venice will carry everything, except for the letters, and other things, which belong to the cavallari."[91] A similar version posted above the stairs of San Marco and the Rialto banned the procacci from collecting mail that awaited the company couriers at those locations.[92] At stake was the profitable business of carrying private letters and goods. Both groups had their own officially recognized exclusive rights over certain types of public letters, but the question was which group would be *limited* to them. While nominally protecting the cavallari, these measures nonetheless boxed them in.

The cavallari viewed the state postal system as offering a raw deal. The cavallari of Verona—a city with commerce and geographic access rivaling Bergamo—provide a particularly rich case study for understanding how state postal systems succeeded at the expense of alternative modes. Cavallari originally carried Verona's official state missives and funds, traveling once a week to and from Venice.[93] Verona took the lead in arguing that enforcement of the Venetian Company monopoly unfairly favored the Bergamaschi over other terraferma subjects. From their perspective, such measures threatened them and their families with poverty and overturned centuries of inherited privileges.[94] This was common rhetoric in Venetian governance of the terraferma, as well as against early modern state centralization and modernization more generally.[95]

Venetian authorities—at the company's urging, and always for the "public benefit"—sought to standardize postal rates and prevent other carriers from undercutting the official posts. They carried out interviews with many procacci and cavallari to determine their familiarity with the measures. Authorities found that many messengers pled their ignorance, or that they had misunderstood the regulations as applying only to mail of foreign origin. This, too, was a form of resistance against the increasing restriction of their market share. Occasionally, the competition broke out into open disputes: in 1583, Piero da Porto, a Veronese cavallaro, confronted Domenico di Longho, identified as a portalettere of Padua, in a local postal inn. Porto called Longho a "spy and a thief . . . a spy because he had tried to see his letters," presumably to determine whether Porto was within his rights to carry them. The encounter devolved into a shouting match of "similar insults."[96]

This was not the first time that Piero had come under scrutiny. In July of that year, printed tariffs with the prices and modes for mail-carrying to and from Verona had appeared around the city and in Venice. Ordered by one Lauro Tasso and Piero da Porto, the printing had not been cleared by Venetian authorities. When asked "to what effect" these tariffs had been printed, Piero answered "the public benefit." He steadfastly denied any knowledge of ongoing fights with the city's portalettere and maintained that he had intended to bring a copy to the rectors for review. Authorities continued to press him, asking, "Does it seem fine to you, to print public tariffs with the sign of Saint Mark without license or orders from the rectors?" and suggesting that the quantities produced looked like more of a campaign than a preliminary draft. Piero snapped back: "I did not order the printer to make a hundred or two hundred, but just that he print it. What [symbol] would you want me to have him add, a Turk?"[97] The rectors thoroughly chastised Porto that he had no business doing such "public things," but it would prove a losing battle. This was competitive professionalization. Appointed officials such as cavallari and postal couriers lay claim to whatever advantages they could, including state insignia and the right to set rates for all mail-carrying. It would be difficult for more miscellaneous carriers to play the game, so long as their rivals wrote the rules.

Around the same time as the struggles among the mail carriers of Verona, the council of Verona took and inventoried a portalettere's mailbag. A sample of the inventory provides a rare glimpse into the variety of goods being carried by Italy's more miscellaneous messengers:

- A package of small breads addressed to Alessandro Ariprete of San Marco
- A package addressed to Simon Ruffo as "S+R"
- A little book addressed from the order of preachers in Venice
- A package addressed to Bartolomeo Benzon with letters[98]
- A purse with a letter signed "S+R," directed to Bartolomeo Zenobio
- Letters addressed to different people with 130 lire: one to Madonna Agnola; one to Vicenzo Curion; and one to Lodavico, which is signed "O. Rosso"[99]

From money to "small breads," the records generated by postal disputes indicate the material variety of things sent by mail. Paintings, books, and scientific instruments traveled across European postal systems. In moments of breakdown, we catch early glimpses of a system that had quickly grown beyond state letters sent by the fastest couriers and toward ordinary service.

In the history of technology and infrastructure, a precipitating crisis often precedes system renewal. The decades between 1575 and 1630 saw several such overlapping crises. Postal agents faced a variety of dangers, from gun-toting brigands to public health roadblocks. Postal systems adapted, offering a greater variety of services to a wider clientele than ever before. The running of ordinary couriers on a cohesive network of routes, as explored in the next two chapters, was born from this crisis. It came at the expense of many longstanding alternatives, replaced by a system that might be better protected, surveilled, and controlled by executive authorities.

State-sponsored postal services turned crisis to their rhetorical advantage, especially in their desire to expand into more forms of mail-carrying. Courier petitions memorialized their fallen companions as proof of their dedication and loyalty to the state. Each incident of smuggling or theft became further evidence of the need for enforced protections, not just against physical threat but also against so-called foreign competition. Officials argued that attacks on postal couriers challenged the authority of the state, but also threatened the material ties that bound together an elite, commercial society.

In this way, the threats of banditry, plague, and rebellion did not cripple the posts; instead, they made the backing of the state a crucial advantage against entrenched competition. The cavallari and merchant messengers posed serious obstacles to the expansion of state posts into ordinary mail-carrying, and the alternative mail-carrying modes of the late Renaissance were never fully quashed.[100] Legal-commercial debates continued wherever state posts might be found, from the Protestant regional competitors to the famed London Penny Post of a later century.

The Spanish post of Milan and the Venetian Company of Couriers succeeded by convincing their respective executive authorities that unlicensed mail-carrying posed a threat to state security. They offered new mechanisms of surveillance, from reporting on senders and recipients to opening, copying, delaying, or forwarding private mail. Sources rarely explicitly note the personal relationships among the postmasters, couriers, and state authorities, but as chapter 4 will argue, they undoubtedly formed a powerful network of ties.

If distrust of foreign threats dominated the 1580s, corruption preoccupied Habsburg rulers in the decades that followed. Fear of treachery from within the ranks of officialdom came to rival that of foreign, spiritual, and pestilential dangers. Corruption was the disease of bureaucracy. Factions within the court and across the empire were rocked by the rise and fall of court favorites. With Spain continually teetering on the edge of bankruptcy and its foreign policy seeming to shift from one minute to the next, intelligence was a valuable currency. It was in this context that the post house of Milan became not just the instigator but also the focus of distrust.

CHAPTER 4

The Postmistress and the Spy
Networking the Italian Road

Early sixteenth-century contracts between princes and the Tassis corrieri maggiori were top-down: rulers commissioned limited-term infrastructure according to the location of their courts, armies, and envoys. The agreements of the late sixteenth century differed: Bergamaschi couriers and postmasters negotiated agreements in the post house as ongoing treaties rather than limited contracts. Routine exchange along the Italian Road would outlive both the Spanish duchy of Milan and the Venetian Republic. Indeed, the continuous circulation of information, people, and goods along these routes persists as modern infrastructure: a modern traveler between Milan and Venice would likely take the train or A4 highway through many of the same locales traversed by late-sixteenth-century couriers.[1]

The postal systems' enduring foundations withstood a range of threats during construction from the postal wars of the 1550s and 1560s (chapter 2), to the plagues, brigandage, and social unrest of the 1580s (chapter 3). By the end of the sixteenth century, postal systems were thriving. Post office records show astounding growth in the volume of mail and the power of postmasters over these turbulent decades. Three key factors drove this expansion: first, there was a growing international consensus concerning protection of the courier and the mailbag. Second, the budding alliance between postal officials and local governors strengthened bureaucratic authority over communications. This chapter will analyze a third reason: the transition of postal service from an extraordinary (*straordinario*) to an ordinary (*ordinario*) service.

The extraordinary/ordinary binary existed across early modern governance. Extraordinary taxes required individual authorization, for example, while ordinary taxes might automatically renew.[2] At the outset of postal services, all couriers were "extraordinaries," or as Ottavio Codogno framed it in his *New Itinerary*, "the fastest couriers." The contents, dispatch, and funding of each mission received individual authorization. However, in the second half of the sixteenth century, postal service was increasingly oriented toward "ordinary" services, meaning prearranged couriers who traveled interlocking routes on a regular timetable. These were generally slower messengers, but in contrast to the expensive extraordinaries, ordinaries were increasingly available and affordable to a wider public, as well as to princes.

This chapter takes the Italian Road as a case study of shifting postal priorities. The Venetian Company of Couriers and the Tassis Spanish postmaster of Milan established a bilateral postal ordinary in 1582. "The Italian Road" (figure 10) consisted of two primary routes: a northern route connected Venice and Milan by way of Vicenza, Verona, Brescia, and Bergamo, while a southern route connected the two cities by way of Cremona, Mantua, and Verona.[3] The agreement consolidated mail-carrying under the steward (*gastaldo*) of the Venetian Company of Couriers to the east, and the Spanish postmaster of Milan to the west. It was one of the earliest international postal treaties proposed, negotiated, and formalized by the Bergamaschi across political boundaries. The Venetian Company even referred to it as "Our Project."[4]

The origins of the Italian Road demonstrated how officials wrote foreign policy from the post house. Traditional political history emphasizes the decision-making leadership of official politicians in matters of foreign and domestic policy. The "Contractor State" modifies this model, describing the state's relationship with outside agents as akin to that of a purchaser to its suppliers. Contracted providers specialized in recruiting, victualing, and equipment provisioning on behalf of the state, especially in times of war.[5] The Contractor State model roughly fits the Tassis postal systems of the Italian Wars until 1559, although the Tassis already did much more to manage information for states than just providing "good information about the market."[6] Postal officials made decisions on the ground with wide-reaching financial, policing, and policy implications. To extend the market metaphor, postal

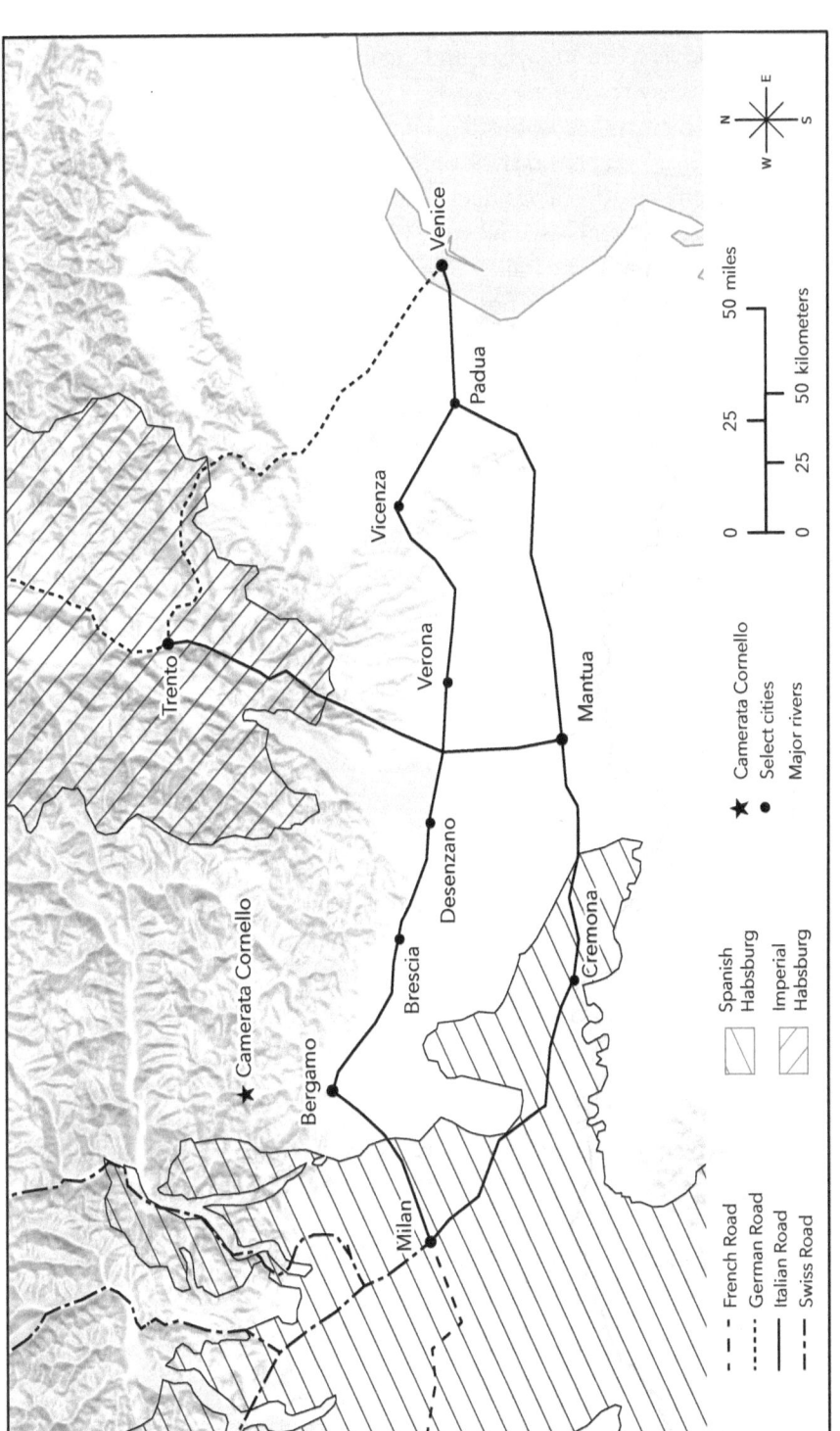

FIGURE 10. The Italian Road. By 1582, the Venetian Company of Couriers and the Tassis Spanish postmaster of Milan oversaw couriers carrying mail between their respective systems. From Milan, mail could continue through Savoy or Switzerland. The imperial Tassis postmaster in Venice oversaw a transalpine route that ran north through Trento, discussed in greater detail in chapter 5. Map by the author and Stewart Scales.

officials were advertisers, lobbyists, and incubators as well as suppliers—in a word, they were technocrats.

Diplomatic history has also often emphasized the role of political leaders and official representatives such as resident ambassadors. The "New Diplomatic History" considers a wider cast of agents but continues to emphasize the embassy and council chambers as the crucibles of international relations.[7] The Italian Road demands instead that we look to both the post house and the post road as key settings that shaped foreign policy from the bottom up. Rather than receiving orders from their rulers, postal officials and couriers presented the Italian Road to their respective governors and ambassadors as a done deal.

Postal agreements deeply interconnected the cities of the Padan plain, although Habsburg Milan and Venice were rarely allies. During the period in question—roughly 1580 to 1612—battle lines hardened between a Habsburg-dominated Italy and the anti-Habsburg coalition that frequently included Venice.[8] Postal ordinaries like that of the Italian Road guided economic, political, and cultural relations in ways that were at odds with official state relations. Telling the history of northern Italy in these fractious years requires looking past political rhetoric to see the deep cultural connections and continuous movement of correspondence, goods, people, and ideas along this central axis of European transit.

Three relationships charted the course of the Italian Road, beginning with a pair of battling cousins who were both named Ruggero Tassis. Their family rivalry began with the 1556 abdication of the Holy Roman emperor and king of Spain, Charles V, which split the Tassis postal system as well as Habsburg crowns. The heirs of different Tassis brothers served as Spanish postmasters on one side of the Padan plain and imperial postmasters on the other, vying with one another for prestige and profit. The younger Ruggero, who was the Spanish postmaster of Milan (d. 1588, o. 1556-1588), benefited from how the Italian Road undercut his rival, the elder Ruggero, who was the imperial postmaster in Venice (d. 1583, o. 1539-1582). Ruggero of Milan's choice to ally with the Venetian Company of Couriers rather than his own cousin, Ruggero of Venice, flew in the face of both official instruction and conventional wisdom. Considering the Italian Road in terms of personal rather than political gains contextualizes why this early postal ordinary took a bilateral form.

Addressing the social and political challenges of the late sixteenth and early seventeenth centuries required new types of administrative relationships. After the premature death of Ruggero Tassis of Milan in 1588, the office then passed through several hands before the Spanish postmaster general leased it to Ruggero's widow, Postmistress Lucina Cattanea Tassis (d. 1619). A royal audit of the post office of Milan offers an unparalleled view of her postmistresship and asymmetrical partnership with Ottavio Codogno, an enigmatic postmaster-lieutenant-turned-author. The legally, economically, and emotionally complex relationships of the post house resembled an expansive Renaissance *famiglia*. Partnerships like that of the postmistress and Codogno nonetheless transitioned the family firm into a depersonalized administration. For the postmistress and other stakeholders, "the office of the postmaster" was a legal fiction: the title could be leased, sold, and, importantly, shared among multiple individuals of different sexes and social statuses. Distancing the individual postmaster from the title ensured continuity but, as the Spanish visitation would discover, thwarted ascribing individual culpability.

Visitations periodically pitted governing bodies against one another in the Spanish provinces. They were intended to diagnose corruption and mismanagement, air grievances, and prevent collusions at the margins of empire that might threaten the center. In the first decade of the seventeenth century, following the governorship of Pedro Enríquez de Acevedo, the Count of Fuentes (1525-1610), the Spanish visitation accused the post office of Milan of having committed negligence and fraud. It assessed damage at a staggering 118,000 lire, more than the annual income of the office. Much as family rivalries shaped the postal routes, so did this political battle fought by proxy among Spanish statesmen. The charges, the defense, depositions, and financial records survive today at the Spanish state archives in Simancas. Telling silences and forgeries—supplemented by the keen observations of a Venetian diplomat—trace a web of espionage and counterespionage that further complicated the shifting alliances of the Italian Road.

The introduction of new, public-serving ordinaries at the end of the sixteenth century tested the strength of existing postal networks. Family ties and other communal solidarities might foster trust, but they also could inspire deep rivalries, especially in the rapidly commercializing communications trades.[9] This chapter blends the spatial history of the Italian Road with the interpersonal ties that structured the same route systems. The antipathy of rival cousins, the partnership of a postmistress and her lieutenant, and the fraught alliance of a post office and the governor all left their mark. Conflict and collaboration, as well as topography, shaped how mail traveled.

Family Rivalries: The Postmasters Ruggero Tassis and the Venetian Company of Couriers

Tassis postal officials thrived across the realm of Charles V. The brothers Janetto and Francesco Tassis employed their nephews, Giovanni Battista, Simone, Davide, and Maffeo, to establish a communications network that spanned Europe, from Antwerp to Naples and Madrid to Innsbruck. State letters remained the driving purpose for this postal service and were often carried in relay (*a staffetta*)—at the fastest speed and highest cost. The six couriers of the post office of Milan received a flat 6 scudi per month, or around 120 lire, intended to cover their expenses on the road as well as their wages.[10] Postal rates from 1545 show that sending a courier in relay between Milan and Venice cost 45 scudi, or approximately 7.5 lire—roughly a week of a laborer's wages. Officially, only members of the governing bureaucracy could use the service to send state letters, or *lettere pubbliche*.

In 1555 and 1556, the unthinkable happened: Charles V of Habsburg announced his intent to abdicate, gradually dividing his domains between his son, King Philip II of Spain (1527–1598), and Charles's brother, Ferdinand, archduke of Austria and soon-to-be the Holy Roman emperor (1503–1564).[11] Emperor Ferdinand first used the term "Imperial post" (*Reichspost*) in 1559, implying a separated system bounded by the Holy Roman Empire. A few individual post offices, such as the Augsburg post office, vacillated between the now-distinct imperial and Spanish systems. In Italy, the Tassis postmaster in Milan became the Spanish postmaster, while the Tassis postmaster in Venice became the imperial postmaster.[12] The allocation made sense given the respective geographies: Milan traditionally oversaw the mail to and from the Spanish Habsburg courts in Valladolid and Madrid, while Venice managed mail traveling across the Brenner Pass to and from the Austrian Habsburgs in Innsbruck, Regensburg, and Vienna. Rulers still expected the Tassis postmasters to work across systems in service to both Habsburg branches.

By the 1560s, eleven Tassis postmasters and mistresses headed offices across Europe, not counting additional relatives employed by the Venetian and papal posts.[13] The third and fourth generations of Tassis postal officials consisted of many cousins on either side of the Spanish-imperial division. Many bore the title of corriero maggiore in their respective domains, but the heirs of Giovanni Battista Tassis remained the patriarchs. Giovanni Battista's eldest legitimate son, Raimondo Tassis (d. 1579), inherited the role of postmaster general of Spain. Raimondo's younger brother, Baron Leonardo Tassis (Leonhard I Taxis, d. 1612), and his heirs acted as postmaster generals in Brussels, Regensburg, Innsbruck, and Prague.

Several postmasters bridged the eras of the united and divided Tassis postal systems, two of whom have featured in previous chapters: Simone Tassis (d. 1563) in Milan and Giovan Antonio Tassis (d. 1580) in Rome. Ruggero Tassis (d. 1583), the elder of the battling cousins, also had a long and illustrious career as the resident imperial postmaster in Venice, where the Spanish/Dutch post office opened in 1541.[14] Ruggero oversaw couriers running missions to Germany, Poland, and the Spanish Low Countries.[15] While his father, Davide, had moved between Verona and Venice, Ruggero took up more permanent residence in the Venetian neighborhood of San Cassiano, a short distance from the Venetian Company of Couriers office on the Rialto by the Riva del Carbon.[16]

Ruggero of Venice corresponded with major political figures of the period, including the Spanish minister Cardinal Antoine Perrenot de Granvelle (1517–1586). Ruggero regularly provided the famous leader with books, Oriental luxuries, artwork by Titian, and even the cardinal's favorite foods, such as Lombard truffles. In 1547, the postmaster attempted to call in a favor. Amid the celebrations of a recent imperial victory at Piacenza, he requested that Granvelle support his bid for postmastership of the captured city.[17] Simone also attempted to claim the office as his own; it was one of several similar disputes between Ruggero and his uncle.[18] Conflicts like these led Ruggero to resent Simone, calling him "impious and obstinate" and "the number one enemy of my family" in a letter to Granvelle.[19]

The conflict between Simone and Ruggero of Venice precipitated the conflict between the cousins, as Ruggero of Milan (d. 1588) was Simone's son and heir. Control over the northern Italian posts was at stake. In 1571, the postmaster in Venice prevented his cousin from establishing a Spanish post office in Venetian Brescia. He later appointed an imperial representative to the same station. In 1573, a Spanish official reported new tensions over the post office of Castelnuovo del Garda (located between Desenzano and Verona), where the cousins now battled over whether couriers should carry imperial or Spanish insignia. Leaders from both the imperial and Spanish systems frequently referenced the family ties and suggested that they were the root cause of the rivalry.[20]

The informal arrangements within the Tassis family worked if the parties saw one another's success as a common benefit. However, the formal break between the Spanish and imperial systems from 1556 forward and the growing enmity between individuals meant that the Ruggeros did not. In their letters, statesmen still held out hope that family bonds would win out. Yet the government never directed the postmasters to establish a postal ordinary between Milan and Venice—Spanish and imperial officials simply assumed that the Tassis cousins would cooperate as needed to guarantee the swift and secure delivery of state letters.[21]

Instead, Ruggero of Milan chose to work with his cousin's rivals, the Venetian Company of Couriers. The Venetians likely approached the Spanish postmaster first. The company had been seeking new revenue sources since the postal wars of the 1560s and 1570s disrupted routes through the Papal States.[22] In March 1581, the company circulated among Venetian authorities a document titled "Institution Proposed by the Couriers in Service to the Venetian Dominion of an Ordinary for Milan by Way of Mantua and Cremona." The proposal described an ordinary postal service run twice weekly across Italy: one leaving Wednesday toward Milan via Bergamo, and one leaving Saturday and traveling to Milan via Mantua and Cremona (figure 10). The steward of the Venetian Company and the Spanish postmaster of Milan would oversee their respective jurisdictions. Receiving and recording all mail in the post house, they would regularly balance their books by reimbursing mail that was carried for one another's patrons. Couriers would exchange letters at Cremona and Desenzano.[23] In April 1581, the most prominent families of the Venetian Company of Couriers and a representative of the Spanish postmaster gathered and notarized the agreements.[24]

Sources are surprisingly sparse on the response from Milan. Governor Don Sancho de Padilla's 1582 letter on behalf of the Spanish postmaster—which defended his monopolistic privileges as a necessity in the ongoing Counter-Reformation—is a rare exception.[25] On the Venetian side, couriers argued that a postal ordinary was the next logical step in serving "the public good." Offering an ordinary courier was still a significant expansion of state postal service into an arena traditionally dominated by more miscellaneous messengers. The Venetian Company of Couriers offered to carry mail for free among the doge and the rectors of the terraferma. The articles of the agreement also advertised that the ordinary would serve merchants and traders as well as political leaders. After all, the company argued, funds paid to foreign carriers could be better spent employing Venetian subjects.[26]

Investigating these claims in 1581, the Venetian senate reviewed the last three month's worth of mail expenses from their representative in

Milan, Bonifacio Antelmi (o. 1580–1587). It was the job of the Venetian diplomatic resident in Milan to manage the western hub of the Venetian communications network. This meant constant dispatches, as Antelmi forwarded correspondence from the Venetians to their embassies and back again, as well as handling correspondence to and from the Venetian rectors in Bergamo and Brescia. From December 1580 to March 1581, Antelmi spent over 700 lire forwarding letters among Venice's diplomatic network and terraferma governance.[27] He reimbursed couriers coming and going from royal courts and Venetian embassies in Madrid, Rome, and Prague. The payment for letters carried between Milan and Venice was almost evenly split between the merchant carriers and the Tassis postal system. Payments to "the Tassis postmaster" represented around 300 lire (43 percent of total mail expenses) while he paid roughly 250 lire to the merchant maestro dei corrieri, "Bollino" (36 percent). Sending mail by the merchant ordinary often cost Antelmi 3–4 lire per journey within the terraferma, while the faster *cavalcata* and *staffetta* (by relay) cost a flat rate of 6 lire. Antelmi often opted for the merchant ordinary. Even at the lower rate, the median recorded payment to the merchant carriers—likely representing multiple dispatches—was nearly twice that paid to the Tassis. One note from January 5, 1581, gives a sense of the quantity: Antelmi noted that the mail given to the merchant carriers included "three hands (*mani*) of letters" from the Venetian senate to Genoa.[28]

In addition to considering cost, Antelmi and other clients likely opted to employ whichever messenger was next to depart. Wednesday, Thursday, and Friday were the busiest mail days for all messengers, with most payments to the merchant carriers taking place on Thursdays, and to the Tassis on Fridays.[29] Antelmi's records nonetheless center on state (public) letters and can only hint at the quantities of private letters. Some entries blurred the lines: see, for example, the frequent letters between the Venetian captain in Verona and the Venetian representative in Turin. Antelmi repeatedly noted that the two were brothers, seemingly prompting the senate to consider whether Antelmi should be picking up the tab for fraternal correspondence.[30]

Antelmi's accounts supported the Venetian Company's claims: Venetian money was going into the pockets of foreign carriers when it could easily go to Venetian subjects or, better yet, never leave state coffers. At the same time, progress was slow on state recognition for the new postal ordinary. Deliberations lasted several months. The doge gave his general approval but noted that "there are many articles to this subject, which require diligent consideration" and delegated the matter to the senate. He may have sensed the difficulty of implementing a sweeping measure that would cross many jurisdictional boundaries during a contentious period in Venetian politics.[31] The Italian Road ordinary significantly expanded the company's role in handling both public and private correspondence across the terraferma, and placed its couriers in direct conflict with other messengers.[32] By March 1583, the senate had reached an agreement that evidenced wrangling from both the company and the cavallari of the terraferma. In June 1584, the Venetian senate accepted the interpretation advanced by the cavallari that the Venetian Company monopoly should be limited to Venetian state mail alone (*al servicio pubblico*), with private letters remaining a nominally open market.[33]

Postal couriers would call upon their respective states to protect the postal ordinary against a variety of threats in the ensuing decades. We can add commercial competition to the dangers of brigandage, plague, and rebellion discussed in chapter 3. Couriers gathered evidence of perceived innovations or violations while abroad and presented them to the authorities with their complaints. They condemned competition from the imperial posts, as well as from the merchant carriers.[34] Either the Venetian authorities supported the company, which was "a source of great benefit to the public and public reputation of this state's posts," or "foreign princes (*principi alieni*)" would once again exert control within Venetian territory while native couriers went hungry.[35] After decades of fighting the papal post's claims to postal monopoly, the company was surprisingly ready to argue that all princes held the right to control the posts within their domain as "a sacred and inviolable jurisdiction."[36] The Spanish postmaster in Milan used similar strategies to enlist the Spanish governor against the Genoese corriero maggiore and a consortium of German and Italian merchants in Milan.[37] By and large, these appeals appear to have persuaded these leaders, and official decrees often echoed the language of their petitions for privileges and protections.[38]

The alliance between the Spanish postmaster of Milan and the Venetian Company of Couriers provided the rhetoric and motivation for state control of mail on the Italian Road. The two groups united against their perceived rivals, which included the imperial postmaster of Venice, as well as miscellaneous messengers across the Padan plain. The Italian Road postal ordinary was a market takeover sold to authorities as a project that would improve the speed, security, and cost of mail.

And, in truth, by the end of the sixteenth century, the cost of sending mail by even "extraordinary" (*straordinario*) postal service along the Italian Road had dropped precipitously. In 1545, sending a courier by *staffetta* between Milan and Venice had cost 7.5 lire. By 1584, sending a letter at the same speed cost just three-quarters of a lira—a little less than a single day's common wages. Private letters could be sent by the new ordinary for 8–10 Venetian soldi or 7–9 Milanese soldi per postal ounce, roughly equivalent to the cost of three or four loaves of bread. Later tariffs even specified costs for single-sheet and half-sheet letters. Sending a letter by post came within reach of even a middling class of northern Italian society, and mail by the "ordinary" (*ordinario*) that once took up to two weeks now predictably arrived in five days. Venetian diplomatic letters arrived from Milan in as little as two days.[39]

Operating at an economy of scale lowered the cost of postal service. The following chapters will provide further evidence of the growing scale of the operation, as shown in the postal ledgers of the seventeenth century and beyond.[40] Neither Ruggero lived long enough to see this transition through, however. The next generation would bring its own complications, including a direct reckoning with the commercialization of not just the mailbag, but the office of the postmaster itself.

Worthy Lieutenants: Postmistress Lucina Cattanea Tassis and Ottavio Codogno

The initial success of the Italian Road ordinary depended upon many factors, including a network of interpersonal relations. That interpersonal matrix that established the Italian Road ordinary in the early 1580s had undergone a generational shift by the end of the decade. Ruggero of Venice (d. 1583) and Ruggero of Milan (d. 1588) had passed away, as had the last of the first and second generations of Tassis brothers. Administrators born in the second half of the sixteenth century now held the most important post offices in Europe. Few had direct experience of the Italian Wars. Far more had come of age in Spanish Italy, tied by constant mobility and exchange to political-confessional conflicts across Europe, including the Dutch Revolt (1568–1648). New officeholders tended to be leaseholders and many were women.

Milan would become one such postmistresship, but only after a decade of rapid turnover. After Ruggero Tassis of Milan died in 1588, the rights to his office passed to Juan de Taxis y Acuña, count of Villamediana, the Spanish postmaster general (d. 1607) based in Valladolid.

That inheritance was complex and contested, in part due to the struggles between Giovanni Battista Tassis and his brothers discussed in earlier chapters. Ruggero Tassis had been wealthy and powerful and was survived by his young sons, but the Spanish branch of the Tassis family had intermarried with powerful nobility and wielded greater influence at court than the postmasters of Milan.[41]

Office leasing—or *arrendamiento* in the Spanish, meaning the resale of state contracts to third parties for limited time periods—proliferated in the seventeenth century.[42] The sale of offices provided cash-strapped states with liquidity, but in the case of the post office, we can identify two additional push factors behind such sales. First, rifts among the Tassis disrupted interpostal service. The rivalry between the Ruggeros was one of several personal grudges and intrafamilial legal disputes that dragged out over generations. Thus, third-party leaseholders offered an alternative to family drama. Second, the state was an increasingly unreliable source of funding.[43] Office leasing shifted the burden of funding postal service from the state to the individual lessors, who were then motivated to run a profitable system to recoup the initial investment.

Postmaster-lessees faced many of the same issues that had afflicted the Tassis postmasters of earlier decades. In addition to their distance from the royal court, they were often foreigners: outsiders to both Milan and the Bergamaschi social networks. A string of deputies leased the office in Milan, including Jacopo Filippo Zonio (o. 1590–1593), Oliver Panizone Sacco (o. 1593–1596), and Ercole Appiano (o. 1596–1599). All were residents or natives of the city of Cremona, on the border between Lombardy and the Papal States. Each would face accusations of theft, espionage, and cronyism linked to their "foreigner" status in Milan.

The Spanish governor, Juan Fernández de Velasco y Tovar, the duke of Frías (o. 1592–1600), had high hopes for the postmaster, Oliver Panizone Sacco, whom he had handpicked for the leased postmastership of Milan. Panizone promised to reduce expenditures and tighten accountability, especially among the unruly staff.[44] This soon proved easier said than done. When Panizone attempted to replace the brothers d'Adda as postmasters of Voghera in 1593, they fought back. Panizone appealed to the governor, explaining that the d'Addas were continually drunk and belligerent, and supporting the accusation with testimonies from couriers, passengers, and a secretary. The brothers had even come to Panizone's house to curse and threaten him. Eventually, a local magistrate permitted their removal from the post, but Panizone had to overcome the judge's knee-jerk rejection of an innovative outsider.[45]

Incidents like this show that locals scrutinized and even attacked the national identity and allegiances of postmaster leaseholders. Panizone's successor fared no better. Ercole Appiano was a merchant with strong French family ties and support from within the governor's household.[46] Bollino, the merchant maestro dei corrieri of Milan, declared that Appiano was a "vile" man whose goal was to enrich himself and return to Lyon. He allegedly "always spoke French," had a French wife and doctor, and favored select (and presumably French) merchants. He opened the mail, interfered in local posts, and harassed the Venetian ordinary couriers to Lyon, Genoa, and Turin. His employees were little better, including a "bastard son" who rented out carriages and a clerk guilty of past bookkeeping discrepancies.[47] Another unsigned letter decried Appiano's favoritism, "opposing by every force the public service, valuing his own interests over those of his Prince," and placing all the Italian posts "under the signs and custody of foreign Princes, as it had been in the past."[48]

Interestingly, this letter opposing the Milanese postmaster was not sent to the Spanish governor or senate of Milan, but rather to the Venetians. This was because of the Italian Road ordinary. The merchant postmaster of Milan hoped that the Venetian Company of Couriers would abandon their prior arrangement with the Spanish post office.[49] Unhampered by family rivalry, Appiano had come to an agreement for a new ordinary route through Cremona and Mantua by working with the imperial postmasters in Venice.[50] It seemed clear that the Venetian Company of Couriers would soon be edged out of the market entirely, much as they had attempted to do to Bollino.

Appiano's tenure ended in October 1599, and after a tumultuous decade, the count of Villamediana seemed ready to rid himself of the post office of Milan. He negotiated for the right to sell the title to the Genovese captain-general Ambrosio Spinola (d. 1630) for the use of his nephew, for a price of 25,000 Spanish reales. Spinola was a powerful financier and, by some accounts, the largest lender of his day. Together with the Grimaldi and Fugger families, the Spinola extended some 40 percent of all loans granted to the Spanish crown.[51]

Milanese and Spanish officials nonetheless feared Spinola's Genovese connections. The idea that Spinola would unduly favor Genoa's interests, and especially its merchants, appeared again and again in claims and counterclaims about the office. Similar allegations arose in later decades as the equally powerful Genovese Serra family began to purchase the office. The nativism of the Milanese authorities is perhaps unsurprising, but Spanish governors were similarly uneasy. Many Spanish leaders were uncomfortable with the growing power of a Genovese lenders' coalition. Ten families—several of whose names come up in relation to the post office of Milan—provided as much as 70 percent of all funds lent to the Spanish state. "Every day we discover new evidence against the Genovese," the president of the Council of Finance of Castile had once commented on Genovese collusion. "I couldn't possibly have enough of their blood."[52]

For decades, the offices of the Milanese ducal postmaster and Spanish postmaster of Milan had been held by a single Tassis postmaster and thus united.[53] For this reason, a Tassis postmistress offered appealing continuity. In 1599, Villamediana leased the office back to Ruggero's widow, Lucina Cattanea Tassis (d. 1619). She would act on behalf of her minor sons for an initial term of eleven years.[54] Histories of the Tassis family have long overlooked the postmistress of Milan, focusing instead on the nobler branches of the family or her postmaster lieutenant, Ottavio Codogno. Even a recent work offhandedly concludes that Codogno performed much of the real work of the office; however, the archive does not support this interpretation of the history.[55]

Lucina Cattanea descended from an aristocratic family from the Bergamasco and minor Milanese nobility.[56] She married Postmaster Ruggero Tassis in 1572 when she was about thirteen years old. Cattanea Tassis appears under different titles in the archives, but often as *conductrix seu administratrix* of the post office of Milan. In April 1598, even before her lease of the office, Cattanea Tassis received a rare privilege from Philip II: the right to represent herself in notarial transactions. Usually, a woman would need to be represented by a male relative in such situations, but Cattanea Tassis could act in her own name.[57] She made the most of this privilege to advocate on behalf of herself and her sons. She also gained a reputation among her critics as a "capricious woman with a temper."[58]

It took a team to run a post office, especially one as busy as Milan's. Cattanea Tassis had a trusted partner in her postal lieutenant, Ottavio Codogno, whom she promoted to the role in 1599.[59] By his own account, Codogno began working for the post office around 1595. He appears in state records by 1598, running missions to Ferrara and other locations. In a study of widows in Milan, Jeanette Fregulia finds frequent partnerships between widows and male appointees, occasionally formalized as a *società*, or a limited-term investment agreement. She proposes that this was at least partly the result of the demographic crisis created by the 1575–1576 plague, which necessitated that some women fill traditionally male roles. The *società* provides the closest model for the initial agreement between Cattanea Tassis and Codogno, although by 1604, Codogno had taken the lead in managing post office relations with the Milanese government and Spanish governor.[60]

In 1610, Codogno, Cattanea Tassis, her sons, and a variety of staff lived and worked out of the Palazzo Tassis, which also served as the post house. The building was near the Porta Tosa, not far from the Piazza dei Mercanti in the southeastern quadrant of the city.[61] Over the decades of his service, Codogno had two wives and several daughters—the youngest named Lucina—as well as one son, also named Ottavio. Cattanea Tassis provided for the education of Lucina Codogno, the youngest daughter, and willed that upon her death, her sons must provide 1,200 lire for her namesake's dowry.[62] Together, Cattanea Tassis and Codogno oversaw around fifteen couriers from the office in Milan and around twenty subordinate postmasters located in the duchy of Milan, the duchy of Mantua, the Venetian terraferma, and the prince-bishopric of Trento.[63] While the postmistress nominally exercised the office in their name—a premise that appeared only sporadically in legal documents—none of her sons replaced the postmistress during her lifetime, even when they were well past the age of majority. After Cattanea Tassis's death in 1619, her two surviving sons, Ottavio and Francesco Tassis, continued to employ Codogno as the procurator of the office.[64]

Postmasters had rarely exercised the singular authority that they claimed, relying instead upon a distributed familial network to run postal services. The postmistress position made visible the many stakeholders of a post office: previously implicit relationships required documented authorization. Legal documents frequently referred to Cattanea Tassis and Codogno as jointly holding "the office of the postmaster." Codogno was certainly the face of the post office in print, including in a series of printed timetables and edicts, as well as in his popular itinerary book, *New Itinerary of the Posts of the World* (1608). Codogno frequently wrote petitions from the "office of the postmaster," which is likely why administrative notes and historians have often mistakenly identified Codogno as the postmaster.[65]

Absent as it may be from modern political history, the postmistress position was nonetheless a sustained and largely unquestioned phenomenon across the sixteenth and seventeenth centuries.[66] Lucina Cattanea Tassis was one of the earliest to hold that post, followed by Susanna Jakob von Stauding und Taxis of Augsburg (d. 1656, o. 1626–?) and

Lucia Ropele Taxis Bordogna (d. 1688, o. 1651–1688), who took over offices in Augsburg and Trento, respectively. Postmistress Marchioness Victoria Zapata Tassis of Sicily (1560–1635, o. 1612–1634) purchased the office from Villamediana around the same time as Cattanea Tassis did in the first decades of the seventeenth century. While the marchioness was a Tassis by birth, she petitioned for the office based on her marriage to Don Diego Giacomo Zapata (d. 1613, o. 1574–1610) of a parallel postal dynasty.[67] The postmistress position, along with print publishing and even espionage, highlight women's activity in early modern communications trades.[68] These were individual business partnerships to which women brought their own portfolio of skills, assets, and networks, as well as familial alliances.

The status of postmistress held several distinct advantages over other leaseholders in the age of general crisis. First, the Tassis remained, to some extent, a family firm. To this end, postmistresses offered dynastic continuity. They kept the office connected to the Bergamaschi networks that had so benefited rulers over past decades. Lucina Cattanea Tassis continued to work with the Venetian Company of Couriers to maintain the Italian Road ordinary, for example, in ways that prior leaseholders had not.[69] Cattanea Tassis also appears to have been a more popular choice with other Milanese and Venetian agents than were foreign alternatives. This was vividly illustrated in 1603, when Villamediana once again attempted to sell the title of postmaster of Milan. The prospective purchaser was a Genovese banker, Giovanni Battista Serra (d. 1643), and later his uncle, Hieronimo Serra (d. 1638). The Serra moved in the same milieu as the Spinola, having handled provisions for the Spanish Netherlands since 1594.[70] The Milanese chamber of merchants protested, and Cattanea Tassis wrote to the governor several times to plead her case. First, she labeled Serra as a "foreigner." As the sale of the office proceeded, she changed tack, arguing instead that she should now continue to lease the office from Serra, as she had from Villamediana.[71] The Spanish governor evidently agreed, expressing to the king that the office would be better occupied by his "subject or vassal, than a foreigner."[72] Serra leased the office back to the postmistress, who held it for a three-year term that began in September 1605.

While postmistresses' initial claims to power derived from their guardianship of their young sons—the heirs apparent to postal dynasties—mothers did not always relinquish control when their sons came of age. This suggests a second benefit of being a postmistress, at least in comparison with the postmastership of designated heirs: competency.

For instance, by 1605, Cattanea Tassis's oldest living son was twenty-seven and her youngest was at least twenty. While her sons had reached the age of majority, Cattanea Tassis had spent the past thirty-three years overseeing key aspects of the post office of Milan. Running a post house was, in effect, household management. It involved overseeing staff, bookkeeping, and negotiating for bread and candles as well as international treaties. Indeed, Ottavio Codogno's *New Itinerary* patterned its guidance for running a post house after popular contemporary treatises on household management, or *economica*. Many scholars have traced the development of modern economics from the allegorical relation of the state to the household, and the prince to the patriarch. Some guides even reversed the parallel between the household and state, declaring the wife to be the natural "castellan or lieutenant" of the household's master.[73] In the absence of the *maestro della casa*, it was only natural that his chosen lieutenant step into the role. Postmistress widows had effectively apprenticed from adolescence to manage the post house as an extended household.

By contrast, economic historians have often commented on the danger posed by the incompetence of a third generation of a family firm. The tendency even has its own diagnosis, derived from a Thomas Mann novel: "Buddenbrooks Syndrome."[74] Traditionally, the founding generation—in the case of the Spanish post office of Milan, Simone Tassis—sets a high standard that the second generation struggles to follow. The second generation—Ruggero and Lucina Cattanea Tassis—raises its heirs in relative wealth and high social standing, shielding them from many of the hardships that they themselves had faced. Whether disinterested in the family business or kept away from the helm for too long, the third generation proves incapable of continuing the success of the family enterprise.

In fact, at the beginning of the seventeenth century, many of the would-be Tassis heirs had caused international scandals. The most infamous by far was Count Juan de Taxis y Peralta (d. 1622), son of the count of Villamediana who first leased the post office of Milan to Lucina Cattanea Tassis and her lieutenants. Whereas the senior Juan Taxis (d. 1607) became a distinguished ambassador, his son was a poet who had been banned from the royal court in 1617 and 1618. Implicated in both a sodomy scandal and an affair with the queen, Juan the Younger came to a gruesome end by assassination in 1622. Among his other black marks, he had been forced to sell many of his Spanish postmasterships to pay his debts.[75] The sons of Ruggero and Lucina Cattanea Tassis of Milan also flirted with violent crime: the eldest, Filippo (1574-1603), murdered a man in a tavern brawl and fled to the family's property in Friuli in 1592. His younger brothers Vittorio (1581-1606) and Ottavio (d. c. 1632) followed his example, also engaging in brawls and fleeing Milan in 1601.[76]

Tassis women did employ male representatives as postal lieutenants, but that may well have provided a third benefit of the postmistress position—opportunities for meritocratic promotion. Family firms risk ossification, even more so when they form part of a rapidly advancing industry like communications. Ottavio Codogno was one of several innovative postal lieutenants whose embrace of print pushed postal service increasingly toward a public-facing role. The postmistress widow Susana Jakob von Stauding of Augsburg would similarly rely on her lieutenant, David Fray, and the postmistress general Alexandrine von Rye und Taxis would rely on Gerard Vrints, among others.[77] This nonetheless could prove a frustrating path for lieutenants, who struggled for the recognition and legitimization of their own administrative accomplishments.

As for Milan, hiring the postmistress may have steadied the boat, but it did not entirely quell the waves of controversy. In 1612, the Spanish visitor Felipe de Haro (d. 1621) presented the postmistress and her lieutenant with a set of formal charges of negligence and fraud—to put it in terms of contemporary economic thought, they were charged with household mismanagement.[78] The documentation gathered by the visitation, which audited the imperial administration on behalf of the crown, offers an unparalleled view of the operations of a major postal hub at the beginning of the seventeenth century. To begin, we will consider why the visitation happened in the first place and what it said about the post office's alliance with the Spanish governor of Milan.

Executive Espionage: Count Fuentes and the Duke of Frías

Couriers and postmasters may have initiated the arrangements for the Italian Road in the post house, but they needed to secure the approval of executive power to implement it, meaning royal authority or the permission of its nearest representative. As discussed in chapter 3, Postmaster Ruggero Tassis of Milan succeeded in his bid. The Spanish governor supported the postmaster's exclusive privileges vis-à-vis merchant rivals. The doge and Council of Ten supported the Venetian Company of Couriers through challenges from the senate and representatives of the terraferma cavallari. Postal officials had convinced executive authorities that state surveillance of private communications was a necessary as well as inexpensive means of countering threats and taking a protectionist stance against foreigners. In exchange, royal, ducal, and gubernatorial decrees significantly extended the postmaster's sphere of influence.

But emphasizing postal privilege as an executive prerogative could still be a double-edged sword. The investigation of the post office of Milan vividly illustrated the downsides of involving the post office in courtly politics and international affairs. Patronage could cut through bureaucratic red tape, overriding challenges from local institutions, but from the perspective of state auditors, it looked remarkably like corruption.[79]

The Spanish visitation (*visitacion*) had existed since the late Middle Ages as an institution that investigated and rectified corruption in governance. At the beginning of the seventeenth century, however, the governor of Milan believed that his enemies were behind the investigation of his administration. Pedro Enríquez de Acevedo, Count of Fuentes (d. 1610), was governor of Milan from 1600 until his death in 1610. Born in 1525, Count Fuentes was a veteran statesman and military leader. He had led Spanish troops in successful campaigns in Portugal and the Low Countries. He had previously served as governor of Milan from 1555 to 1556 and was already in his late seventies when he returned for another term.

The uncompromising Count Fuentes was frequently at odds with both the Venetian diplomatic representatives and other Spanish officials.[80] The count's tenure in Milan was a delicate time in northern Italy, as the Venetians reacted with growing hostility to the prospect of Habsburg encirclement. He also had rivals within the Spanish imperial apparatus. He fought a court battle by proxy with his rival, Juan Fernández de Velasco y Tovar, duke of Frías (d. 1613), the president of the Council of Italy (o. 1601–1612). Frías was the count's predecessor in the office of governor of Milan and ally to the appointed visitor, Felipe de Haro (d. 1621).[81] From the outset, Count Fuentes resented Haro's investigations, declaring himself "unwilling" to accept the visitor's aid and saying that the investigations were detrimental to royal authority.[82] The governor frequently sought to control Haro's access to information: in one instance, he expressly forbade the entire government of Milan from providing the visitor with documents. Count Fuentes also requested that he be the one to receive Haro's orders from Madrid, ostensibly so that Haro and the governor would not be at odds with one another. In fact, he was likely more interested in monitoring and controlling Haro's communications.[83]

Alliance with the post office of Milan fit into Count Fuentes's overall concern with control over information flow. The count knew the Tassis well from his prior posts in the Netherlands and Italy, and maintained a collegial correspondence with the postmaster general Leonardo Tassis (d. 1612), as shown by a box of correspondence that survives in the Thurn und Taxis archives.[84] He also prioritized the security of his correspondence and the secrecy of his political actions, much to the consternation of his colleagues, rivals, and superiors. "Secret," from the Latin *secretus*, was associated with administration, in addition to its more cultural connotations of hidden matters. It is the stem word for "secretary," and in Italian and Spanish the adjective can refer to both "secret" and "secretarial." Count Fuentes relied heavily upon "secret payments" (*gastos segretos*) to cover his operations with minimal oversight.[85] In the context of the post office, secret payments were often for espionage and counterespionage. Secret payments financed couriers that he did not want observed or intercepted; but from the perspective of the visitation, this was one of many unacceptable efforts to avoid oversight by the Spanish Council of State.

Despite Count Fuentes's focus on keeping both his letters and couriers secret, the Venetians were on high alert. The Venetian diplomatic resident in Milan, Antonio Pauluzzi (o. 1603–1608), paid special attention to the count's relationship with the post house, frequently recording the arrival and dispatch of couriers. In September 1606, Pauluzzi briefly referenced two of the governor's confederates, a Spanish doctor and "one Ottavio who governs the post office," calling him "a spy for His Excellency, the Count."[86] In a letter dated April 25, 1607, Pauluzzi provided further information on "Ottavio of the post," who seemed so well informed, "particularly on Venetian matters." He "marveled" that Ottavio had been the first to get ahold of printed versions of anti-Venetian propaganda.[87] Pauluzzi investigated further and found that Ottavio regularly received information from "Vitale," one of the couriers on the Rialto. "[Ottavio] attempts to overhear everything and has done much damage to me already in this matter," Pauluzzi concluded darkly.[88]

The "Ottavio" in question can be identified as Ottavio Codogno, as Ottavio Tassis was serving in the Netherlands from 1606 to 1607. No other figure by the name Ottavio appears in the post office's financial records.[89] Pauluzzi knew Codogno well because of the close relationship between the Venetian and Spanish state posts. The Venetian resident in Milan continued to oversee Venetian correspondence traveling west to France and Spain, as well as north to the Netherlands and England.[90] Previously unknown to scholars, Pauluzzi's reporting offers new biographical detail on the author of the *New Itinerary*. It also offers a tantalizing secret history of the post office of Milan, which was deliberately kept hidden from the Spanish visitors.

The Venetian Inquisitori di Stato, who played a similar role to the Spanish visitors, directed Pauluzzi to learn "the kinds of intelligence that are captured by this Ottavio for the Governor." They demanded to know Ottavio's nationality, the condition of his person, and the nature of his work in Milan, in addition to "what friendships and correspondents he has in Venice, if he receives letters regularly from others as from this Vitale; if these pass by his name or others, and to whom he writes, and addresses his letters in Venice."[91] The Venetians were on guard for these types of intelligence leaks.[92] Budding state intelligence services saw spectacular successes and failures at the beginning of the seventeenth century. The Spanish were particularly hard-hit: rumors of embarrassing security compromises—often caused by carelessness in handling cipher keys—pervaded diplomatic correspondence. In 1605, it was revealed that the secretary to the Spanish governor of Genoa had been selling state secrets for more than two decades.[93] Early modern states had seen the potential damage of intelligence leaks in their communications systems. The political inclinations of the acting postmaster of Milan were therefore a matter of state security to the Venetian inquisitors.

By May 6, Pauluzzi had some answers: "Ottavio is a man of the lowest condition," he replied to the inquisitors, "born in the Netherlands and come as a young man to Italy." Pauluzzi called his position in the post office a great "subterfuge," commenting that "his brother is a cook, and now he governs the entire post, and is a spy for the Count, however, few like him. In Venice he has other correspondents of news, not just Vitale, who receives the letters from the Spanish Ambassador [Íñigo de Cárdenas y Zapata (d. 1617, o. 1603-1607)] and makes copies and sends them to him from there. Meanwhile Ottavio makes copies of the Count's letters and sends them to Vitale, who takes them where they are meant to go."[94] It was as the Venetians suspected: the Spanish post office maintained intelligencing contacts within the Serenissima on behalf of the Spanish governor.

Count Fuentes was not the first governor to benefit from an intelligencing alliance with the post house. Prior chapters have referenced Ruggero Tassis's off-the-books relationship with Governor Padilla, through which he provided Padilla with lists of correspondents from suspect regions. Count Fuentes and the postmaster lieutenant, Ottavio

Codogno, regularly collaborated, including during an extensive effort to reroute Spanish mail away from traveling through Savoy.[95] At times, Codogno even seemed to draft the governor's edicts, such as in responses to courier assaults.[96] Pauluzzi's investigation had turned up something more concerning, however: the count's use of the post office to observe the correspondence of other Spanish officials. In other words, Frías may have used the Spanish visitation to have an inside channel on his rival, Count Fuentes, while the count may have used the post office to read Frías's letters to and from other Spanish officials in Italy.

The Milanese archives do preserve other suggestions of this alliance between postmaster lieutenant and governor, or at least of Codogno's attempts to make the most of their relationship. Codogno encouraged the governor that all decisions regarding the post office's privileges should be "at the judgment of Your Excellency."[97] Codogno also put himself forth for favors.[98] In 1606, Codogno submitted a petition for monetary recognition of his years of service, first to Count Fuentes and then to Spain. The lieutenant recounted his work over the previous ten years, including "providing valuable services" as ordered by Frías and Haro.[99]

In an ill-advised gambit for favor, Codogno also laid claim to unmasking a spy. Codogno's petition described his discovery of Mario Quattrocavi, "who was a confidant of the Count Fuentes who advised both the Venetians and French of what he heard from court and in the Palace."[100] Count Fuentes was unlikely to admit to his employers that he had let a spy infiltrate his household, never mind to his enemy, Frías. The count's secretaries excised the cornerstone of Codogno's petition before forwarding it. Meeting minutes of the governor's council simply note that "it does not seem appropriate to put down in writing the treachery, and the part regarding the Venetian should be removed forthwith from this relation and from every other document." No other mention of Quattrocavi appears in the documents of the period.[101] Espionage and counterespionage were important parts of the post office's mandate, but as the Quattrocavi incident demonstrates, there was pressure and even active intervention to keep this activity undocumented. The governor had nothing to gain by sharing Codogno's spy-catching victories, and everything to lose.

Codogno's relationship with Count Fuentes had frayed by this time, and the indiscrete petition may have played a role. January 1607 marked the beginning of the Spanish visitor's investigation of the post office, which the governor was either unwilling or unable to fully prevent. The Venetian Pauluzzi also recorded a May 1607 incident in which the governor publicly berated Codogno, "scolding [him] mightily, saying that he must not send any further expedition without giving notice, nor write everything to Venice."[102] Count Fuentes distrusted Codogno's professional latitude. Like the Tassis before him, Codogno's Venetian ties made him both useful and untrustworthy as a confidante, especially as the possibility of renewed Spanish-Venetian warfare loomed on the horizon.[103]

Codogno's spying and spy-catching left trace evidence, but if the postmistress played a role, she left no traces at all. Lucina Cattanea Tassis and her sons passed unobserved by the Venetian resident. Only the Milanese notarial archives give a sense of the postmistress's activity, but records of financial arrangements preserve few backroom politics. Women's invisibility could prove a key advantage when it came to covert intelligencing, but their activities remain absent or obscured in the archive for the same reasons.[104] If we take into account that Cattanea Tassis worked hand in hand with her lieutenant in all other aspects of the office—and that intelligencing was itself a core function of the "office of the postmaster"—it seems more likely than not that she did play a role in, or was at least aware of, Codogno's activity. That, however, is a story that remains undocumented.

On July 22, 1610, Milan's political terrain shifted once more. Count Fuentes passed away in office at the age of eighty-five, leading to administrative chaos. Milanese authorities sent an urgent dispatch to Spain seeking instructions. A surviving note in Codogno's handwriting indicates the ironic consequences of the visitation's scolding: "The Secretary has sent this dispatch through Vigevano, and because I have orders from the Council not to send couriers, or add to the King's bill without his consent, I've sent it back."[105] Civil war had exploded in France two months before with the assassination of King Henry IV and succession of his nine-year-old son as King Louis XIII. The disruptions of mail routes necessitated sending three different couriers to Spain, which increased postal expenses exorbitantly. Count Fuentes had previously covered the cost, but in his absence, the council hesitated, bowing to necessity only after long debate.[106] As a result, it took much longer than usual for the crucial news of the governor's death to reach the royal court.

As travel options narrowed and costs increased, Milan bore the burden of supporting Spain's widely distributed communications network. The visitation's investigation over the following months showed that Count Fuentes had owed more than 13,794 lire and 50 soldi to the post office. Extraordinary letters to Spain constituted the minority of charges at 2,232 lire. By February of the next year, the total charges remained unpaid and had grown to 30,495 lire and 78 soldi. There were 608 charges labeled "expenses" (*spese*) in the inexact manner that so frustrated the post office auditors and may have disguised any number of intelligencing functions.¹⁰⁷

Frías succeeded his rival as the governor of Milan in December 1610. That succession made it expedient for Frías to blame present bankruptcies on the extravagancy and secrecy of the deceased Count Fuentes. This provides key context for the accusations of corruption and incompetency that the visitation leveled at the post office of Milan in 1612. Furthermore, if the off-the-books alliance between Count Fuentes and Codogno was (as Antelmi reported) common knowledge, that may have trained the visitation's crosshairs on the post office. Like the Venetian diplomat, Frías may have even learned that Codogno had helped Count Fuentes to monitor Frías's own correspondence with other Spanish representatives in Italy.

The post office responded to the visitation by trying to shift the blame for their vast and vague expenditures to the Spanish governors of Milan. Cattanea Tassis and Codogno claimed that "express orders by both [the Duke of Frías] and Count Fuentes"—not their mismanagement of funds—had delayed the dispatch of ordinary couriers. They further defended themselves by pointing out that even these delays had been minimal, with the ordinaries still leaving the same day that they were scheduled. Codogno and Cattanea Tassis presented corroborating documents signed by the governor's secretaries. The Spanish ordinary was also rerouted through Genoa by gubernatorial command—"the governors wanted their letters more quickly." The exercise of executive privilege and not administrative negligence, Codogno and Cattanea Tassis argued, had caused recent failings in postal service. Even "when the governors patiently waited," delays and rerouting resulted from "rivers, bad horses, the arbitrariness of Princes, assaults, and many other ills, which occurred, at times, because [letters] came by sea."¹⁰⁸

Unfortunately, the archives do not offer a clear resolution of the case against the post office of Milan. The visitation records were recalled to Spain with the visitor, where they seem to have remained. The postmistress and Codogno continued to work together, only interrupted by Codogno's illness in 1618 and Cattanea Tassis's death in 1619. A payment on July 1, 1611, to Ottavio Codogno indicates that Frías continued his predecessor's practice of secret charges.¹⁰⁹ Regardless of the fungibility of administrative ethics, the postmistress and her lieutenant had survived a significant tug-of-war between regimes, indicating that they were granted significant professional latitude—Frías evidently knew how difficult it would be to replace them.

The postmistress's death in 1619 may have provided the impetus to finally close the book on the visitation's charges, much as Count Fuentes's death had proved politically beneficial.[110] Codogno had continued to enjoy a successful career as special procurator for the Tassis sons.[111] He had overseen new publications of his itinerary in 1611 and 1616, and he undertook a 1623 reworking titled *Compendium of the Posts*. It was while he was present at the Spanish royal court in 1620 that Codogno received a letter of commendation for his twenty-six years of service. It was signed by the former visitor Felipe Haro, among others, providing perhaps the strongest sign that the matter had been laid to rest.

The story of the Spanish post office of Milan has often ended there. Following the infamous assassination of the count of Villamediana, the office gradually moved from Tassis control to that of the Serra and other leaseholders and their appointed lieutenants. Yet again, widening our lens to consider both the Spanish and Venetian sides of the Italian Road offers further clues regarding Codogno's intelligencing activities. Ottavio Codogno died at the age of sixty in the devastating plague of 1630, in mid-September of that year.[112] On August 21, 1630, the Venetian diplomatic resident Piero Antonio Marioni (o. 1627–1631) wrote in cipher: "I have been unable to find out more, the corriero maggiore having died this past month, as well as all the principal officials of the post, who served me as the means and secure instrument of learning news which came from the army from time to time."[113] Venetian representatives frequently only encrypted the most sensitive portions of their dispatches; in this case, Marioni only encrypted the sentence describing his arrangement with the postmaster, suggesting that it was not aboveboard. While Codogno was actually still alive on August 21, he may have already been forced from office by illness. Or Marioni may have been misinformed, or alternatively, misdated the letter.[114] Whether Marioni intended Codogno or another official, the letter demonstrates that the post office of Milan remained an intelligence hub.

Is it possible that later in life, Codogno continued to spy for the Venetians as he once had for the Spanish governor? National allegiances rarely overcame the potential profitability of serving multiple patrons. As prior chapters have explored, the Tassis had often succeeded by carefully balancing their identities as both imperials and Venetians. Postal officials used intelligence as valuable social currency, and it would not be surprising if Cattanea Tassis's lieutenant did the same. For all its ups and downs, the relationship between the Spanish post office of Milan and the Venetian Company of Couriers remained central to its functioning. Perhaps, spurned by his former ally, Count Fuentes, and then audited by his distant employer, Codogno determined that his Venetian ties were a more reliable source of income than the Spanish governors. Ultimately, the archive offers few definitive answers.

If the visitation ever discovered concrete proof of Count Fuentes's espionage and counterespionage alliance with the post office, it never made it into the final charges. But the dossiers at Simancas do preserve one strange piece of evidence, slid into the back of a case file: a single letter from March 1607, addressed to Count Fuentes from Cattanea Tassis's son, Ottavio Tassis. The letter seems normal enough at first glance: it recounts the most recent letters received and sent forthwith, with a polite request for reimbursement for "letters sent at my cost." The third paragraph, however, complains about the visitation and its increasing inconvenience: "The visitor investigates this matter and thinks that couriers are always sent following procedure, and this is not true, as you know, and they will not find anything else in my ledgers that they have taken.... It would suit your Honor to tell everything that you have received specially (*a fabor particulare*) because I do not permit misconduct in this office."[115]

On their surface, the complaints were those that would structure the post office's official rebuttal to the visitation—namely, that executive prerogative and everyday exigency required administrative leeway. There was something strange about the tone of the letter, however, which was familiar, even threatening. It clearly bothered Haro, who took it upon himself to investigate further. In fact, the cryptic letter was a forgery. Haro, who had pored over the post office's records, recognized the handwriting as Ottavio Codogno's. The visitor showed the forgery to others to confirm his suspicions, taking his notes on the original letter. Confronted, Ottavio Codogno confessed to having adopted the signature of Ottavio Tassis. He signed a confession to that effect, explaining that "I am practiced in the hand, having seen [Ottavio Tassis] write many times." Cattanea Tassis defended her lieutenant, saying that "he was often ordered to similarly sign letters and other documents in his capacity as special procurator" and "at that time, Ottavio [Tassis] was in the Netherlands in service to his Majesty."[116] There is no evidence that the letter informed the official charges against the postal officials, but it concerned the visitor enough that he kept it on hand along with the signed confessions. While struggling to translate Codogno's malfeasance into a financial penalty, Haro suspected that deeper intrigues tied the post office to the Spanish governor of Milan.

Even if the letter was a simple miscommunication rather than a smoking gun, it speaks volumes regarding the shifts underway along the Italian Road and in the post office of Milan. The personal authority of the Tassis *corriero maggiore* had often been a rhetorical ideal rather than a reality. By the beginning of the seventeenth century, the model seemed especially fractured. The postmaster was an alias: the office was exercised instead by a network of heirs, leaseholders, and lieutenants. Codogno lived and worked within the Tassis enterprise as part of the Tassis *famiglia* in all but name. Perhaps it simply did not seem that different for Codogno to assume the persona of Ottavio Tassis in the same way that he frequently assumed the title of *corriero maggiore*.

One thing is clear: the cultural, political, and administrative ties along the Italian Road determined both how mail traveled and why. Implementing the Italian Road postal ordinary amplified the longstanding collaboration between Venetian and Spanish-Milanese agents, as well as conflict between Tassis family branches. It ensured that the Spanish and Venetian postal systems continued to develop in tandem, with innovations in one system quickly replicated across a wider geography. Reading across the Venetian, Milanese, and Spanish archives proves essential for understanding how the individual offices worked, while diplomatic letters provide even further insight into telling absences in administrative and gubernatorial archives.

From the outset, social networks structured postal practice, but distrust played an equal if not greater role than trust in determining the channels by which intelligence traveled. A select network of postal officials benefited from the distrust that they cultivated against merchants and "foreigners," however defined. Their alliances with executive powers could nonetheless make them objects of suspicion, especially to auditing bodies tasked with identifying corruption, such as the Spanish visitor and Venetian State Inquisitors.

Postal service remained deeply shaped by personal alliances and antipathies. Records diverge in ways that demonstrate the strength of what were often secretive social ties. But if relationships shaped the documentation of the Italian Road, documentation also shaped relationships. Chapter 5 will move to consider the quantitative and qualitative accounting of ordinary postal service. Here, we see how couriers, in addition to postal officials and politicians, intervened in foreign and domestic policy, advocated for their interests, and shaped new notions of a transparent public service.

CHAPTER 5

Breaking Records

Commercialization and Control on the Transalpine Roads

The official opening of international state postal services to private users came slowly in many parts of Europe. Scholars often infer the presence of private letters in postal mailbags from state efforts to forbid or limit carrying such mail.[1] Rulers disliked that private mail might threaten the speed or security of state communications. In 1573, King Philip II of Spain (1527–1598) expressed concerns to his ambassador in Venice that "things intended for private persons (*particolares*, or in the Italian, *particolari*) pass within packages addressed to me." Anxious recipients were rifling through the mailbag prior to its royal delivery.[2] Brigands might similarly rip through the courier's mailbag searching for money or other valuables sent by private users.[3] Both activities threatened the security of state letters.

The easiest way to determine whether private users employed state postal systems would be to open a mailbag directly. In 1889, Frankfurt city workers made a startling discovery in an old administrative building: they uncovered mail from two or more imperial mailbags from 1585. The letters within were delightfully mundane. A Hanseatic student in Rome teased his wealthy father. A merchant in Bologna informed his counterpart in Cologne about the latest trends in fabrics. Friends of many stripes (but especially wealthy Italian businessmen) shared news about the latest papal election, bread riots in Naples, and deaths in the family. These letters show that state postal systems were a practical option for private users, even if the cost remained high. But of course, the Frankfurt mail trove is a rare documentary cache: its very existence depended on failure of delivery, when far more mailbags were successfully dispersed.[4]

Another option would be to digitally reconstruct the original assemblages found within mailbags. The Cultures of Knowledge, Tudor Networks of Power, and Medici Archive cataloging projects facilitate large-scale quantitative analysis through extensive digitization and linked metadata.[5] Letters, and especially early newspapers, featured datelines providing the time and place of dispatch, receipt, or both. When extracted, this data can support models of what traveled where and when across wide temporal and geographic spans. That is certainly true about the handwritten newsletters produced and shared among the associates of the Fugger family network of merchant bankers (known as the *Fuggerzeitungen*). Scholars can match information such as "the letters arrived from Rome this Tuesday" to postal timetables in order to find that the Fuggers indeed often relied on state postal couriers.[6] At the same time, such individual examples do not indicate what proportion of the mailbag consisted of private letters.

Furthermore, these digital collections repeat and amplify the survival biases of their constituent archives. Letter collections are not random samples of early modern communications. Rather, cosmopolitan intelligentsia circulated, assembled, excised, and published their own correspondence. Digital catalogs draw upon these curated collections and edited volumes, which are themselves often "ego networks" constructed around a single person or a handful of well-connected individuals. Based upon the canonical cast of the seventeenth- and eighteenth-century intellectual community known as the "Republic of Letters," we might conclude that this remained a rarified milieu.[7]

Rather than relying on letters or legislation to understand private users of state postal systems, this chapter approaches the commercialization of postal service through post office administrative recordkeeping and publication. The seventeenth century marked a distinct shift in orientation from extraordinary to ordinary postal service. The partnership between the Spanish post office of Milan and the Venetian Company of Couriers expanded into a commercial sphere previously dominated by merchant carriers, municipal cavallari, and a variety of *portalettere, pedoni,* and *procacci.* The Italian Road postal ordinary was at the vanguard of this shift: it provided a model for international postal commerce whereby office leaseholders pursued more reliable sources of income than princely beneficences. State funding alone was increasingly insufficient to meet the demand of a pan-European communications system, never mind the pressure added by commercial competitors and the dawn of the Thirty Years' War (1618–1648).

There were several structural reasons that quantitative recordkeeping improved along with the commercialization of international postal ordinaries. First, records were essential for maintaining oversight. Governments along the transalpine passes had appended recordkeeping requirements to monopolistic privileges by the end of the sixteenth century. Recordkeeping imposed fiscal oversight on powerful postmasters and their executive allies, much as it did in the case of the Spanish visitation of Milan, as discussed earlier in this book. That oversight could benefit postmasters in turn when records provided evidence in jurisdictional disputes with competitors or rebuttals to employee grievances.

Second, records stabilized practice across systems. Rulers often issued executive edicts providing new instructions to postmasters when approving new postal ordinaries. As chapter 4 showed, this was frequently a pro forma recognition of the treaties negotiated in the post house. The printed edicts nonetheless standardized and publicized timetables, routes, and postage, including for private senders. We see here a concern not just about recordkeeping, but about communicating its mechanisms to a wider, invested audience.

Finally, good records enabled mutual reimbursement across systems. Mail handoffs between post offices had to happen without delay. Instead of exchanging cash, postal officials recorded transactions and balanced their books on a quarterly basis. Rider receipts and dispatch notes helped postmasters to continually audit the routes they oversaw, identifying potential danger or proven tardiness. As this chapter will show, postal records also facilitated intelligencing and, increasingly, journalism.

The complexity of interlocking systems and their recordkeeping demanded new types of expertise—not just experience, but the ability to anticipate and shape the present based on a speculative future, especially using the language and tools of financial bookkeeping. An *audit culture* describes the employment of such expertise to study, measure, and iteratively intervene in complex systems.[8] Postal systems were among the first domains of governance to experience the impact of a modernizing audit culture. Postal officials pioneered new forms of documentation of time and space, but that also meant that they were some of the first to experience the persistent dysfunctionality of poorly fit models.

BREAKING RECORDS 129

To read the postal records, we must understand how contemporaries kept as well as read them. This chapter contextualizes recordkeeping within a rapidly shifting culture of expectation. Postal agents and their governor allies had defended working off the books as a matter of state security. By the seventeenth century, two up-and-coming groups were challenging this basic premise. First, the cosmopolitan businessmen to whom governments were increasingly beholden demanded reliable service. Sympathetic governments heard their complaints regarding mail interference and delays, and leaders pressured postal officials to optimize, rather than merely control, the posts. Second, ambitious new postal lieutenants, postmasters, and leaseholders in key commercial hubs such as Milan, Cologne, and Frankfurt challenged the dynastic family firm. Some even accused the Tassis of unsound decisions—including in their management of personnel—resulting from their dangerous "passions."[9] In publishing their claims to expertise, these new postal lieutenants challenged the dynastic claims of the Tassis family brand.

This chapter considers what three types of postal recordkeeping and publication tell us about commercialization along the transalpine postal roads (figure 11). This means looking beyond the individual gripes of misreported missions or price discrepancies in postal ledgers. Instead, ledgers can be read alongside the postal dispatch note, sometimes referred to as the "postal newsletter" (*postavvisi*). Correspondence among postmasters conveyed both quantitative and qualitative information in the closest early modern approximation to "real time." In this sense, dispatches enabled postal officials to continually diagnose and address problems in the system.

Postal systems remained a human infrastructure, however, and assigning blame was frequently more fraught than fixing a machine would be. The postal newspaper became a particular point of tension as postal lieutenants, postmasters, and rulers debated the proper audience for post office records. From recordkeepers to record publishers, postal lieutenants adapted their expertise as communications professionals to print. That choice reflected the desire to communicate with the many private individuals—the *particolari*—whom they now saw as their clientele.

On paper, postal systems translated the abstract act of human communication into something measurable in weights, miles, hours, and funds.[10] In fact, the transition from "the post of the king" to "the post of all" was neither straightforward nor peaceful.[11] It added commercial profit to an already potent mix of religion and politics. Litigiousness over recordkeeping was a direct result of the runaway growth of private

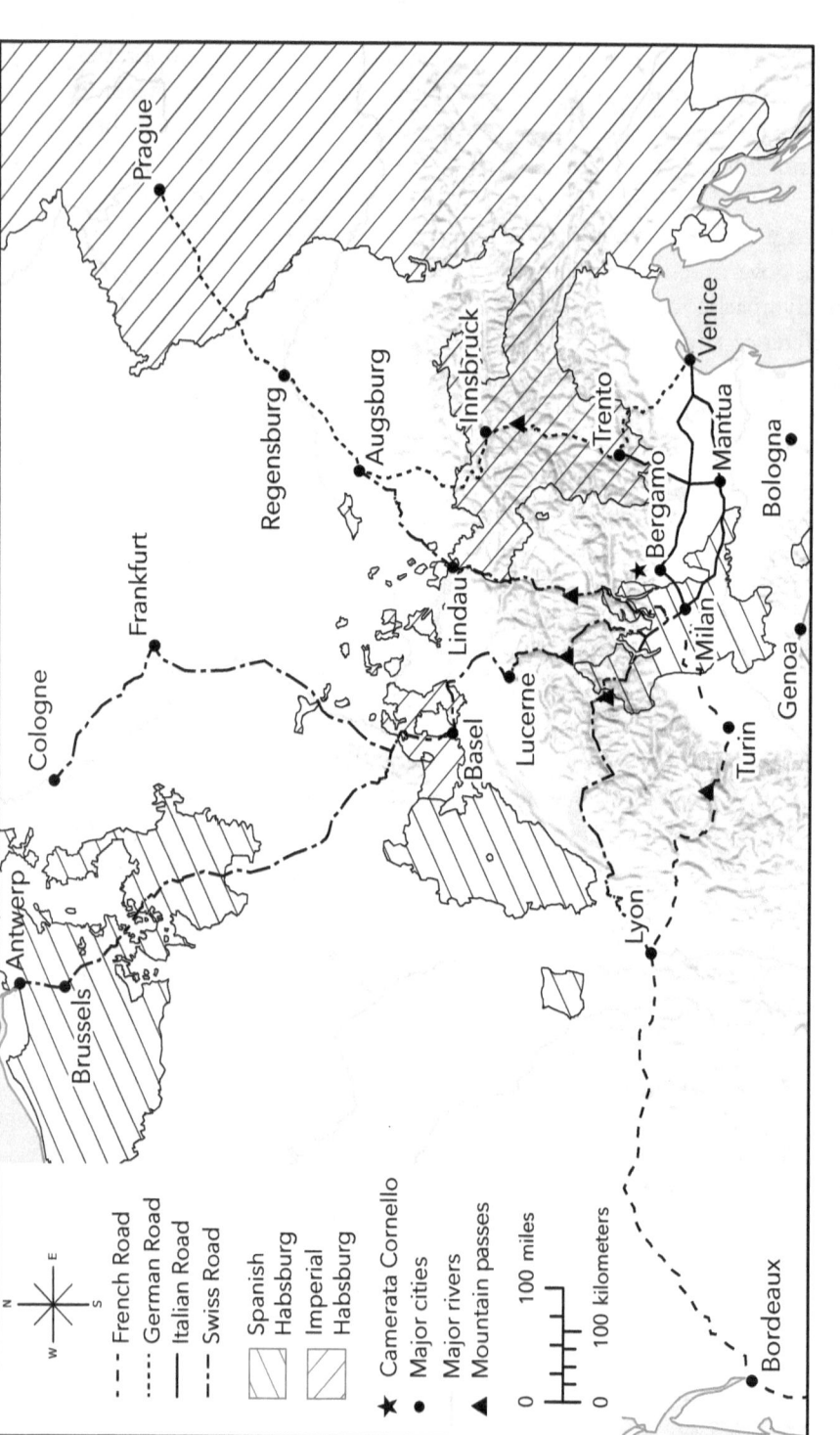

FIGURE 11. The transalpine roads as documented by Ottavio Codogno's *Compendium of the Posts* (1623). Transalpine postal routes can be grouped into three major arteries, here called the German Road, French Road, Italian Road, and Swiss Road, and their variants. The German Road ran along the Brenner Pass, passing from Venice through Bavaria and the Tyrol. The French Road linked Milan to Lyon through the Mont Cenis Pass and the duchy of Savoy. The Swiss Road linked both Lombardy and the Veneto north through the St. Gotthard, St. Bernard, Splügen, Simplon, and St. Gallen Passes. Map by the author and Stewart Scales.

mail-carrying in the seventeenth century. In the words of Carolyn Boyes-Watson, "the concern about the power of record keeping emerges in response to the technological developments which appear to fundamentally alter the social relations among human beings."[12] Post office recordkeeping sat at the heart of the contemporary debate over whom postal systems should serve, and for what purpose.

Challenges to Post Office Bookkeeping

Postal accounting, like most information technologies, relies on redundancies. From the time of Simone Tassis, clerks (*contrascrittore*) worked with the postmaster of Milan as recordkeepers and intermediaries with the state treasury. Ideally, a postmaster submitted a request for a license (*patenta*) to the clerk before dispatching any extraordinary courier. After the mission, the post office paid the courier directly—sometimes requiring notarized proof of the courier's satisfaction—and submitted the signed license to the treasury for reimbursement. The process generated many records: the slip with the initial request and signed permission; the postmaster's record of the dispatch and arrival times; receipts documenting money changing hands among the treasury, postmaster, and courier; and the final record of reimbursement in the treasury's account books (*mandati*).

In 1607, the Spanish visitor Felipe de Haro began to gather all the records kept by the Milan post office. His duty was to reconcile them into a single narrative and investigate any discrepancies as evidence of corruption. Ottavio Codogno handed over his books. Codogno had worked as a postal clerk before his promotion to postmaster lieutenant. He even published his recordkeeping methods in his 1608 book, *New Itinerary of the Posts of the World*. There, he described the postal lieutenant as responsible for "the keeping of the double-entry books, master books, journals, and others." The journals, or "daily books" (*giornali*), recorded "when any courier, ordinary, or *staffetta* leaves." Codogno further instructed readers: "Diligently note it in the journal with the year, day, and hour from whence they depart, to where they go, at what price they are sent, to whom the letter is addressed, what packets they carry, from whom, and to whom they write. If they are the ordinary courier who leaves, note the state packets, especially how many, and to what places they are sent."[13] Postal journals could then be summarized in the "master books" (i.e., secondary and tertiary records).

By the beginning of the seventeenth century, postal service was a profession, with its own specialized knowledge. Literacy and accounting skills had always been preferred, but they were increasingly required of both postmasters and their staff. A 1593 petition described a "modern *postiglione*" as one who "writes down the *staffette* and *cavalcate*."[14] Contemporaries were aware that the postal system was undergoing a meaningful reinvention within their lifetimes. The growing complexity of postal service required a unique combination of book learning and hands-on experience. On the one hand, Italian state chancelleries, including that of Milan, kept similar registers (*registri*) for their own bookkeeping.[15] On the other, the use of double-entry ledgers reflected the post office's position at the intersection of state and commerce. Double-entry bookkeeping features two columns corresponding to debit and credit and was widely utilized by merchants and bankers across Europe by the end of the fifteenth century. Central bodies of state did not adopt the method for financial management until the eighteenth century.[16] Postal officials were early adopters because of their commercial ties. In publishing his recordkeeping practice, Codogno claimed his own expertise as a technocrat or an information infrastructure specialist who was embedded in state bureaucracy as well as the marketplace.

The journals and master books may still be buried in the Spanish archives at Simancas, but drafts of Codogno's accounting survive in Milan, stuffed in the back of the notebooks of the post office's preferred notary.[17] Codogno's records for April 1605 to June 1606 show that couriers' wages ranked alongside those of skilled artisans by 1600. Unskilled labor in Milan was recompensed at around 1 lira per day, while skilled labor earned closer to 2 lire.[18] Worked out across a year, a median wage for Milanese couriers was around 2.6 lire per day of work, although this amount included reimbursement for the courier's expenditures on the road. Whereas couriers under Simone Tassis had received a flat 6 scudi per month (around 120 lire), by the end of the sixteenth century, the post office paid couriers for their journeys by using the number of postal way stations as a measure of distance. By 1599, couriers on state missions were promised 40 soldi for the shortest journeys of a single post, a scudo (120 soldi) for two, 12 lire (240 soldi) for three, and so forth. In practice, the postmistress, Lucina Cattanea Tassis, and her lieutenant, Codogno, often paid at an older, reduced wage (e.g., 9 lire, or 180 soldi for journeys of three posts).[19] These stagnant wages also failed to account for steady inflation in the costs of food and lodging incurred by the couriers at home and on the road.

Codogno's records also show roughly three tiers of professional couriership. The first tier consisted of three couriers who were reimbursed more than 3,000 lire within the roughly yearlong period assessed. The Mariano family (Giovanni Battista and Ambrosio) ran several extraordinary journeys to Valladolid and Brussels. Couriers who took on these long-distance international journeys resembled the diplomatic couriers of past centuries. The position held higher status and required knowledge of various national customs and procedures, such as currency exchange, language, customs, and legal or political conditions that affected mobility. Such couriers interacted directly with their elite patrons and could receive generous tips if they carried good news or achieved record speeds. The records of the Venetian Company of Couriers show similar specialization, as couriers who accompanied ambassadors were often members of prominent company families and ascended to leadership positions in the company.[20]

Most of the Milanese couriers occupied a second tier, receiving between 1,000 and 1,400 lire, in the same period. Nine such couriers appear in the records, including multiple members of the San Martino and Maffei families. These couriers ran a long-distance journey at least once or twice (often to Lucerne, Prague, or Graz), but many of their journeys were south of the Alps. Short, consistent work may have led to a more reliable career. For instance, the courier Gerolamo Landriano ran two missions to Valladolid, but he earned more from many small missions within Italy, sometimes taking as many as four jobs in a month. When couriers were not on the road, there is also evidence that they acted as dogsbodies for the post office. Codogno frequently reimbursed Giovanni San Martino for purchases of bread and other staples.[21] Similarly, Viano Marcandato was paid twice as a courier in April 1605, from which point forward he was only ever reimbursed for household purchases; this suggested a change in employment related to age, illness, or injury.

A final tier of couriers included a wide variety of individuals who received anything from just under 1,000 to less than 100 lire over the year. These likely included family members of couriers, who stepped in to run missions for their relatives or collected pay on their behalf.[22] Some couriers served intensively for brief periods, like Giovanni Angelo di Rossi, who earned close to 140 lire in a four-month period. He ran many short (under 40-kilometer) missions to Novara, Cantù, Vigevano, and Alessandria. In the same period, Francesco Bellone rode longer-distance missions to Lucerne (245 kilometers) and Prague (870 kilometers), earning over 780 lire. Age, seniority, illness, injury, and simple preferences may have played a role in whether couriers took on greater risks.[23]

In contrast with the Venetian Company, few Milanese couriers were associated with single routes, indicating that the post office was not generally subcontracting to local messengers (procacci, portalettere, or pedoni). There were a few exceptions: members of the Secco family (i.e., Giuliano, Francesco, and Antonio) were only ever paid for missions run to Alessandria, and they do not otherwise appear in the post office archives, which suggests that they were more like subcontractors than direct employees.

The post office of Milan was a costly operation (figure 12). Total expenses between April 1605 and June 1606 totaled around 113,000 lire. The office's largest expenditures were the extraordinary couriers, sent on command for state officials.[24] Extraordinary couriers to Rome and Spain each constituted about 20 percent of total costs, followed by couriers dispatched to Venice (7 percent), Brussels (7 percent), Lyon (4.7 percent), and Genoa (4.5 percent). The Milanese treasury remained the most important source of funds for the office, providing over 90 percent of recorded income. The post office received roughly 2,500 lire per month from the treasury to reimburse their expenditures.

Extraordinary couriers sent on behalf of the state continued to represent about half the post office of Milan's total expenses, but ordinary couriers now constituted about a third.[25] Thirty-odd years after the formation of the Italian Road ordinary, the Venetian and Milanese postal systems were deeply interconnected. The Spanish post office of Milan paid nearly as much to the Venetian Company of Couriers as it did to its own ordinaries. Records of payments for letters carried by the Milan-Venice ordinary also recorded the weight of letters, which were often 200–300 postal ounces per trip—the rough equivalent of 1,000 letters traveling from Venice to Milan every week.[26] Codogno even recorded payments to the ordinary couriers of Venice and Lyon by their given names, showing a special collegiality with them. By way of comparison, it is difficult to identify any direct payments made to the papal posts, although the Spanish ordinary did travel from Milan to Rome. The Italian Road remained uniquely interconnected by virtue of personal as well as professional ties.

A scribe writing on behalf of the Spanish visitation confirmed that Codogno "has a book where he keeps the notes of each month of the year, and the time at which the courier arrives and leaves." However, he further noted that "this allows him to note things differently for any given interest (*per alcuno Interesse*)."[27] Recordkeeping, the visitation seemed to recognize, meant the power to obscure as well as to record.

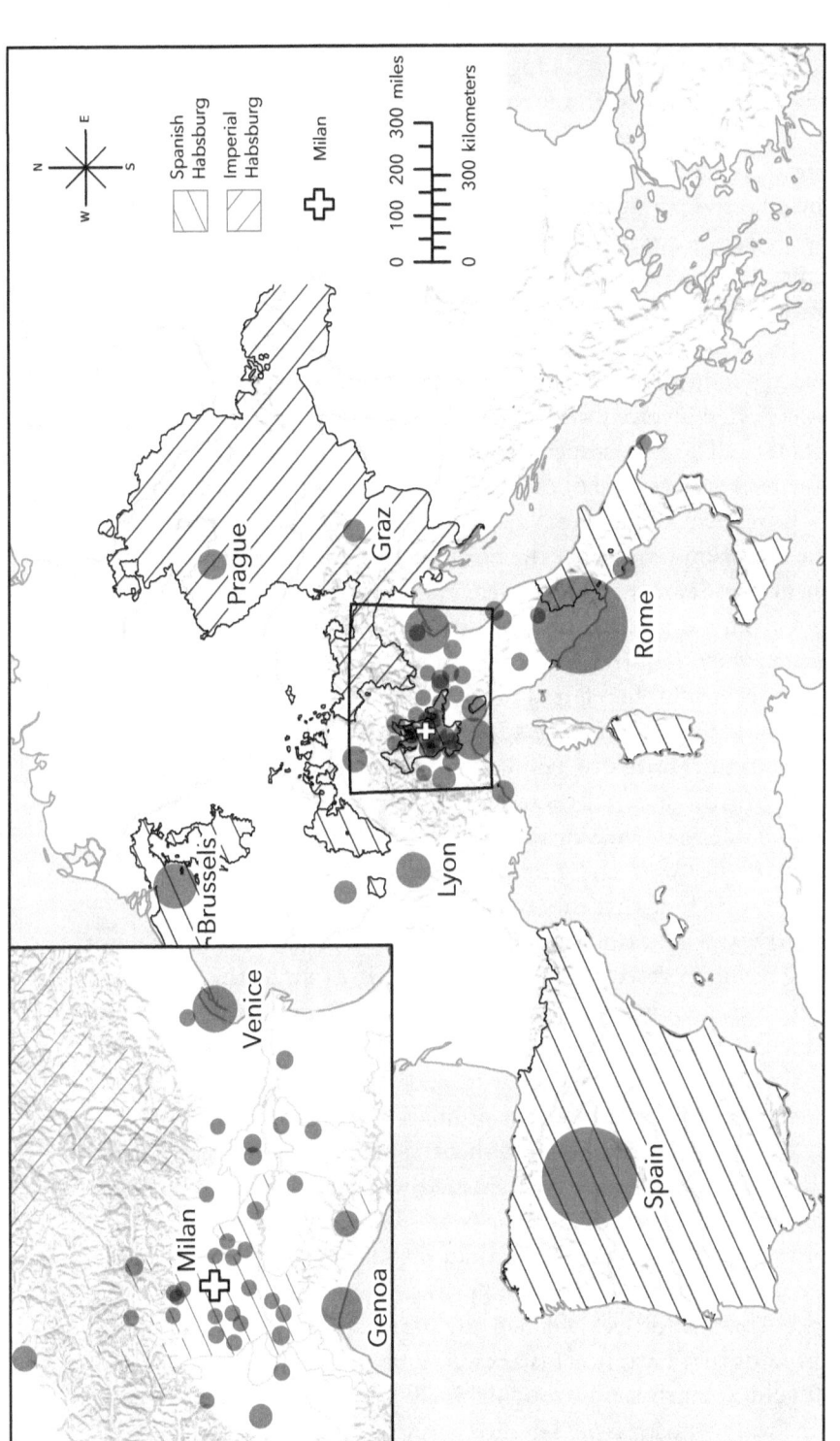

Figure 12. Map of dispatched courier expenses as recorded by the Spanish post office of Milan from April 1605 to June 1606. Location marks are sized by the overall expenditure of missions run to a given location. Dispatches to the Habsburg capitals of Valladolid and Brussels remained relatively infrequent but constituted a high proportion of the office's expenditures. Couriers to Rome were frequent and high cost, while couriers to Lyon and Venice were high frequency and relatively low cost. Map by the author and Stewart Scales.

Investigators pored over Codogno's books to locate discrepancies as well as missions run without correct instructions and permissions in place, especially those that might reflect the influence of dangerous "interests," whether personal or commercial.

The adjective *particolare*, often used to refer to clients as "particular persons" (*particolari*), is often translated to the English "private." The term distinguished nonofficeholding actors who could nonetheless wield significant power and influence in governance. In postal discourse, the term carried similar weight as "interests" in eighteenth-century England: it indicated individuals, most often wealthy businessmen and financiers, who were often involved with state business.[28] Businessmen and traders (*negotianti*) had largely escaped the charges of heresy made against lower-status merchants (*mercanti*) in the 1580s, but the possibility that they might be receiving preferential service was nonetheless worrying.

The visitation found that the businessmen of Genoa, who financed much of the Spanish empire, were regular users of the state posts. Income from the international private letters of Genoa may even have motivated the establishment of the Spanish-Venetian postal ordinary. Venetian records often referred to the Italian Road ordinary as "the trip to Milan and Genoa," and the agreement with the Spanish post office devoted an entire article to handling Genoese mail.[29] If post offices were not charging the state for these private dispatches, there was little reason to include these missions in the records that they presented to the treasury. If they were charging the state—as visitors feared—they had every reason to hide that they were doing so.

In 1612, the Spanish visitation accused the post office of Milan of altering or misrepresenting their records, either to hide the amount of income from such interests, or to artificially inflate the weight of mail for which they billed the state. Postmistress Lucina Cattanea Tassis had allegedly sent unauthorized mail to and from Genoa for these businessmen, sometimes delaying the ordinary courier to Spain in order to do so. The visitation even alleged that the post office had received and distributed mail for these businessmen without notifying the governor and before distributing public (state) letters. The visitor estimated that the post office made more than 60,000 lire of essentially unreported income from carrying such private goods and letters and other favors.[30] The post office defended any profit accrued off the books on the grounds that Cattanea Tassis owed Villamediana an annual rent of 6,000 gold Spanish scudi (roughly 36,000 lire) for the office. Simply put, the widow-postmistress needed a way to earn it.[31]

Another method that Cattanea Tassis and Codogno employed to accrue funds was leasing subordinate postmasterships through individual notarized agreements. Pietro Francesco Villano, the postmaster at Tortona, testified that he had initially paid the postmistress 12 lire per year for his office, then 300 per year for another three years, and most recently, 400 lire. His son, who was horrified by the rising cost, corroborated his statements. Giacomo Monte of Serravalle testified to paying 700 lire for his postmastership—equivalent to approximately a year of a skilled laborer's salary.[32] Leaseholders nonetheless purchased the offices hoping to profit, whether from the mail itself or from the increased traffic that being the postal inn, for example, might bring. The fact that they accepted the raised rates, however begrudgingly, showed their faith that officeholding would eventually pay dividends.

The Spanish visitation found it difficult to reconcile this unabashed pursuit of private clientele with the post office's state affiliation. At the same time, Cattanea Tassis's status as a leaseholder and the push-pull forces that held the post office between the state and the market complicated a simple charge of corruption.[33] The Tassis postmistress in Milan connected the Spanish state to key political and economic centers in Rome and the Spanish Netherlands. On paper, at least, the extraordinary couriers sent for state officials remained the focus of post office expenditures. Ordinaries, especially the Italian Road ordinary from Venice, nonetheless constituted a substantial and increasing source of revenue for officeholders.

Courier depositions provide further insight into the Spanish post office in ways that the financial records—deliberately or innately—do not. Haro and his secretaries conducted interviews with couriers and clients of the post throughout 1607, preserving many otherwise-lost voices of the post office of Milan.[34] These included the seven couriers who had been fired in a general turnover in 1604, among them Giovanni Tirazzo of Genoa, Giovanni Poccapaglia of Genoa, Luigi (Alosius) Maranetto of Piedmont (called Piemontese), Hieronimo Violino, Horatio da Lodi, Giuseppe Rosso, and Cesare Appiano (called Meschino). Whereas Codogno and Tassis argued that these couriers were greenhorns fired for misconduct or other misdeeds (including being foreign immigrants to Milan, as their surnames suggest), the testimonies unanimously agreed that they were relatively experienced couriers who were dissatisfied with their pay.

The visitation was concerned about a pattern of delayed couriers, which threw a wrench into the increasingly complex patterns of interlocking routes. A courier who arrived late to Milan from Genoa might miss the departure of the next courier for Rome, for example. Couriers testified that the root cause was chronically unstable cash flow. Francesco dal Monte maintained that the ordinary couriers to Rome and other places were generally timely but had been delayed occasionally because of a shortage of funds. He confirmed that his fellow couriers resented Codogno and Tassis due to their low wages, which frequently did not cover the journey on horseback: "They have to return home on foot, but they don't dare say so for fear that they will lose their place as couriers."[35] Giuseppino declared: "I remember four hundred times that the trip to Rome was delayed because of lack of money."[36] The courier Dioniseo Gallarato remembered when Postmistress Cattanea Tassis gave the courier Luigi Suardo a silver vase and cistern to sell to raise the funds to complete his journey. Another time, Cattanea Tassis had given the same Luigi a "brocade dress of silver and gold."[37] This was, to borrow a modern phrase, a "gig economy" without the safety nets provided by guild structures or the Venetian Company of Couriers.

Many of the couriers knew that the postmistress's shortage of funds came from the financial burden of leasing the office: "I know well that because of this tax it is in her interest to earn more than two thousand scudi than Ruggero Tasso, Olivero Panizzone, and Ercole Appiano ever did."[38] The couriers nonetheless argued that low wages forced them to carry unregistered private mail. Giuseppino recalled one instance in which the courier Baldessare Binaglio had been sent to Prague, and for fear of running out of money, had carried a clock for one "Don Guglielmo" to Trento.[39] Couriers' critiques were never framed in gendered terms: no courier implied that the failures of the office resulted from there being a postmistress rather than a postmaster. While the couriers resented the times that they had been berated or short-changed, their complaints focused on how the financial records and their associated timetables failed to represent the experiences and pressures of the postal service.

The couriers, guided by the investigators, did note the strong relationships between the post office and businessmen of Genoa. The visitor collected names and followed up with these private clients of the post office. Giuseppe de Caravaggio, who used the office to take care of affairs in "Genoa, Rome, Venice, Naples, the Netherlands, and Lyon," was important enough to merit personalized postal service. Caravaggio testified, "I often go in person to the office, or they bring the mail to me in person, and often I send some servant to pick it up and take down a list of what I will pay when they wish."[40] The courier known as Giuseppino informed the visitors of the close ties between Tassis, Codogno, and a Genovese businessman known as Cesare Pallavicino. While Pallavicino died before he could be interviewed, Giuseppino recalled at least once when Codogno sent a courier to the Netherlands for Pallavicino without notifying the governor, saying, "I know this because Codogno has many similar merchants who give him bribes (*dano le manze*), in particular to see the letters that come from Genoa."[41]

Genoa was the Spanish Wall Street of its day, and businessmen valued even the slight advantage that speed could provide.[42] In fact, Codogno's 1608 guide emphasized the importance of speed and reliability for such clients, saying that "delay causes the greatest harm to businessmen, some who need letters to know how to conduct their business; others who await money or family matters; others who await news of defaults, purchases, deaths, inheritances, victories, offices, and a hundred other things." He equally cautioned the postmaster against being a spreader of news (*novellista*) regarding the businessmen's letters, especially taking care around their rivals.[43] While Haro concentrated on service to merchants, he had also turned up evidence of more dangerous clients: the courier Alosius Marinetto stated that Codogno occasionally gave similar preferential service to foreign ambassadors.[44] Occasionally, the office had sent special extraordinaries on demand, including one for Alessandro Pico I (d. 1637), the prince of Mirandola and the agent of Prince Henry IV of France.[45]

Codogno's records for the post office of Milan are likely some of the best of their time. They nonetheless served the purposes of the postal officials who were caught between a cash-strapped government and an eager, wealthy, private clientele. Political leaders, postal officials, and even couriers reacted to, and at times rejected, the commercialization of postal service, especially for the historically state-dominated, long-distance transalpine postal routes. When these same stakeholders argued over the proper content and form of financial records, they were in fact waging a debate about the core purpose of postal service. They adapted an older language of concern for foreign influence and internal corruption of the post office to the relatively novel problems of the seventeenth century: office-leasing and the influence of private interests in the state.

Dispatch Diagnostics on the German Road

The ledgers of the post office of Milan show that it remained a nexus for connecting Genoa to Spain and the Spanish Netherlands at the beginning of the seventeenth century. The imperial post office of Venice sat at a second crux of transalpine communication by land, connecting Italy by way of alpine passes to central and eastern Europe. The Tassis postal infrastructure coopted preexisting transit and exchange networks where possible. The German Road, the Via Claudia Augusta, or the Roman Road (*Roemerstrasse*) historically linked the Tyrol to Italy by way of Trento and Verona. At an elevation of 1,370 meters, the Brenner Pass was far easier to cross than the Swiss passes, all of which topped 2,000 meters.[46] Running the "German Road" (Via Alemania), as postal officials commonly referred to it, still involved coordination between three Tassis postmasters and several semi-independent subordinates, such as the postmasters licensed by the Gonzaga dukes in Mantua and the prince-bishop in Trento.[47]

Despite the perceived novelty of Genoa's *negotianti*, the German Road had always served private clients, including an earlier generation of merchant bankers financing the Habsburg states. The Tassis carried mail for the powerful patriarch Anton Welser (d. 1557) as early as 1506. In 1509, the Fugger offices in Milan served as the imperial postal headquarters.[48] Augsburg-based patricians financed road improvements and collaborated with the Tassis family to convey large sums of money.[49] The Fuggers even financed rebuilding the Augsburg portions of the German Road, as well as indirectly funding other major portions of the Tassis enterprise.[50] The appointment of Antonio Tassis (d. 1543) as postmaster of Augsburg and Rheinhausen in 1515 and construction of the Augsburg post house in 1549 further cemented the partnership between the Tassis family and Augsburg merchant bankers.[51]

The postmaster verified the contents and timing of a given mailbag and kept an active tally of dues and payments between offices using dispatch notes. A series of such notes from 1608—the same year that the Spanish visitation began reviewing the post office books and Ottavio Codogno published his *New Itinerary*—recorded the weight of mail carried by the German Road ordinary.[52] The notes categorized mail by its destinations, which included Augsburg, Antwerp, and Cologne.[53] Based on these notes, the German Road carried more than 133,000 letters from Venice into the imperial system in 1608. At least 61,000 letters (46 percent) were destined for parts now unknown, but the remaining portion was nearly evenly divided among Antwerp (17 percent), Augsburg (18 percent), and Cologne (18 percent). On a weekly basis, this totaled around 2,500 letters—on top of the estimated 1,000 letters traveling weekly from Venice to Milan, many of which would then cross the Alps via Switzerland or Savoy, or depart by sea from Genoa.[54]

It would be hard to overstate the vast discrepancy between the quantities of surviving letters and the scale of the postal service as recorded in dispatch notes. Recorded weights enable only a very rough estimate of the number of letters, but even these approximations underscore the poor survival rates of correspondence. The largest digital union catalog for correspondence, *Early Modern Letters Online*, features records for 423 letters dated between December 1607 and January 1609 at the time of writing.[55] Based on postal records, that number, encompassing all of Europe, constitutes significantly less than the contents of a single ordinary mailbag traveling a single route. At a weekly pace, the weight of 3,500 letters traveled into the Spanish and imperial posts from just Venice. Even if this weight included goods other than paper, dispatch notes record postal service at a very different scale than that suggested by surviving letters alone.

This is, of course, how a contemporary historian reads these records. For the postmasters who wrote, sent, and received dispatch notes, however, they served a different purpose. Ferdinando's intended audience included his family members and colleagues along the German Road, among them his counterpart, the imperial postmaster Octavio Tassis of Augsburg (1572–1626, o. 1604–1626).[56] Large quantities of Octavio's dispatch notes and other correspondence survive in the Thurn und Taxis family archives. In contrast with the Italian Road, where family rivalries had split along political lines, the Augsburg office represented successful collaboration among offices aided by intermarriage.[57] Furthermore, Octavio's biography captured the intersection of the private and public services of the Augsburg post office: his godfather was none other than Hans Fugger (1531–1598), and he briefly considered marrying into the distinguished Welser family of merchant bankers.[58]

If we think of intermarriage as a strong tie in network analysis terms, the dispatch notes represent the aggregate strength of many weak ones.[59] The Tassis of the German Road used dispatch notes to affirm the familial bonds of their enterprise across Europe. Dispatches passed on local news, greetings from family members, and gifts such as favorite foodstuffs. In a typical missive to Lamoral I Tassis (d. 1624) in 1605, Octavio wrote:

> With the opportunity of adding a dispatch note to the small package from my mother [Isabella Tassis] to Leonardo [either Leonardo I (d. 1612) or Leonardo II Tassis (d. 1628)], I would like to pay my respects to your Excellency and advise you that those in Trento write to say that they will send two mailbags, because otherwise the big mailbag will be ragged. I would regret it if the packages were treated poorly, and there would be the danger of losing something. . . . My sister [Ginevra Tassis] sends me a small package for the Count of Ferstenberg [likely Frederick IV of Fürstenberg-Heiligenberg], that I send with the note to your Excellency, as I have noted, and nothing else occurs to me just now, so I finish and wish you the best from Augsburg.[60]

Notes like these demonstrate the role that Tassis women played not only as administrators, but in maintaining the core structures of a family firm, especially across the Alps. These material and textual connections replicated friendships made in person, often at the family homestead in Camerata Cornello. In other notes, Ferdinando Tassis (d. 1648), the imperial postmaster in Venice, fondly recalled that Octavio's sister and Lamoral's wife, Ginevra Taxis, had cultivated a friendship with Ferdinando's mother, Angelica Albani, during their time "at our villa [in Bergamo]." He regularly conveyed Angelica's best wishes to Ginevra in his own letters to her husband. The letters of all three family branches—Augsburg, Venice, and Brussels—demonstrate constant contact that blended business and family.[61] In this way, dispatch notes more closely resemble merchants' letters, which also oiled the human components of commercial infrastructure.[62]

The letter weights provide valuable quantitative insight to the contemporary historian, but they say much more in combination with the appended text. There, we see that the quantity of goods being sent by the official posts, particularly across the Alps, overwhelmed post offices. Writing one 1609 dispatch note, Ferdinando Tassis passed on the complaints of the messengers of Cologne and Frankfurt that those offices were sending "too many money purses, which are heavy, and cause the postilions to complain of being overloaded. . . . What's worse, if bandits assault a single ordinary, every poor postilion will face the danger of being murdered."[63] Less than a year later, he reported an attack on a courier outside of Bassano, in which the robber "took several heavy packages, for which Signor Carlo [Charles Taxis] blames me. The merchants said that there were 400 gold ungari coins in one, 420 gold zecchini coins in the other, and in another, jewels worth 700 scudi—in total, around two thousand scudi in damages." The assaulted courier was thrown in prison, and as the postmaster wrote rather disgustedly, he was "subject to such torments that he won't serve [the post office] for any salary, even if I assure him that they won't send heavy packages."[64]

Dispatch notes reinforced the social networks that had structured mail exchange for more than a century (figure 13). With time, however, they also became a fundamental information technology for audit culture. That evolution is more visible when compared to a parallel form of documentation: rider receipts (figure 14). These slips of paper, signed by the postmaster, indicated when and where a rider had been dispatched. The Milan archives preserve rider receipts from as early as

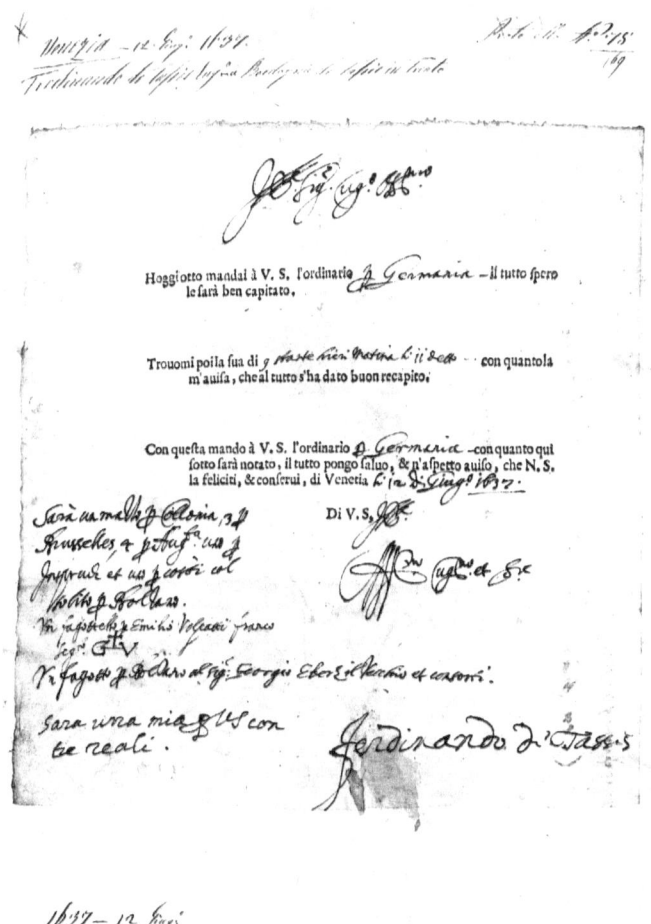

FIGURE 13. An example of a printed postal record from the transalpine roads—a dispatch note describing letters sent to Germany by way of Trento (June 12, 1637), signed by the imperial postmaster of Venice, Ferdinando Tassis (d. 1648). Image from Tiroler Landesarchiv, Taxis-Bordogna, 22, 2.

the Italian Wars.[65] Postmasters signed off as the riders passed through their way stations, proving that the riders had kept to their scheduled routes or, when that was not possible, providing an authoritative explanation. By the end of the sixteenth century, the Tassis post offices of northern Italy were employing preprinted forms for transalpine routes that could be filled in with the day and hour. Rider receipts could then be compared against the promised timings and routes.

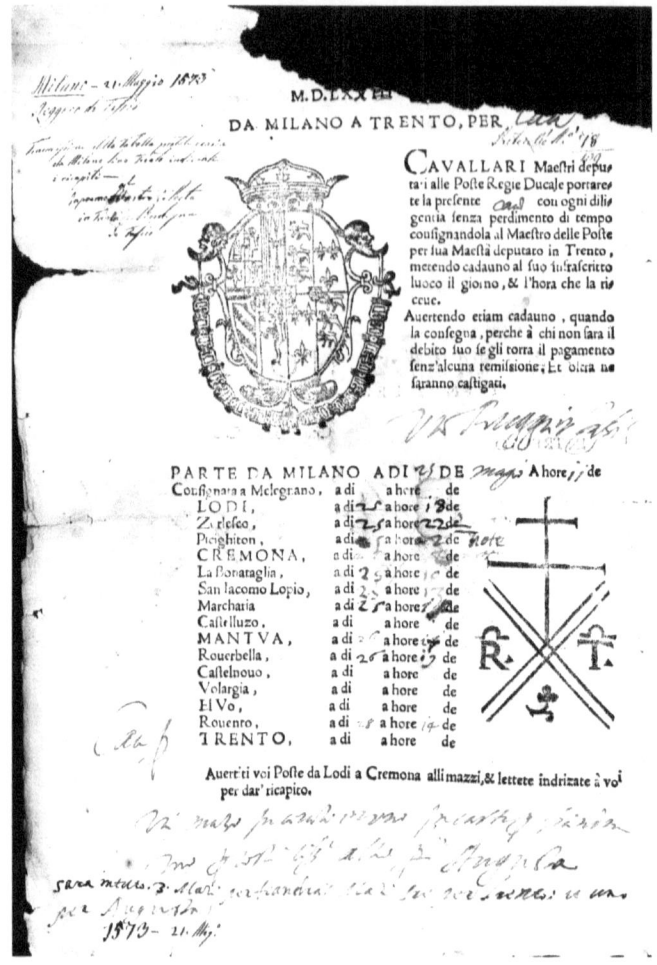

FIGURE 14. An example of a printed postal record from the transalpine roads—a printed rider receipt recording a journey from Milan to Trento (May 21, 1575), signed by the Spanish postmaster of Milan, Ruggero Tassis (d. 1588). Image from Tiroler Landesarchiv, Taxis-Bordogna, 22, 2.

While rider receipts continued to be used for courier accountability, dispatch notes were both a record of breakdown and diagnostic tools. Postmasters along the transalpine roads used them to collaboratively identify and rectify breakdowns in the system. Assigning blame was a key component of this documentation: in the aforementioned 1609 case, Ferdinando noted that while authorities blamed the courier for his own assault, Charles Taxis (d. 1610), in Antwerp, blamed Ferdinando for overburdening the courier in the first place. At the same time, the imperial postmaster in Venice was often between a rock and a hard place. In 1623, Ferdinando complained that Venetian authorities had given him a blistering dressing down, writing that "the letters from Holland are opened every week, including those of the Dutch ambassador. I must write to every Imperial postmaster to remedy these errors, or else they'll seize my office."[66] Venice's substantial ultramontane commercial and diplomatic communities relied upon the imperial postal service, to the point of pressing for Venetian state intervention when the Tassis-run posts failed them.[67]

Overtasked couriers, bursting mailbags, and bloodthirsty bandits were downsides to operating at an economy of scale. The truth was that postal officials were not always able to say no to private clients. State funding was unreliable. Sometimes commercial patrons were also powerful political allies: in another set of dispatch notes, for example, Octavio Tassis referred to a clock carried over the Alps for his Fugger patrons.[68] This type of service raised fundamental philosophical tensions in addition to logistical challenges. From the state's perspective, carrying private mail opened the Tassis up to the very dangers that they had promised to control. Money and fine goods overburdened couriers and attracted bandits, which threatened the speed and security of state mail. These private clients might themselves interfere in state letters or seek to spy upon one another.

In many cases, postmasters did not perceive any conflict between their duties to state and nonstate clients. It was a postmaster's job to ensure the speed, security, and reliability of all mail, as Codogno's 1608 guide stated. Protection of state missives continued to be a top priority, particularly at the dawn of the Thirty Years' War. In a 1623 letter to the postmaster general, Octavio Tassis of Augsburg diagnosed recent delays in these terms: "in the matter of the Mantuan ordinary by which the letters come from Rome, which today arrived all ragged and ruined, with many letters ruined: there is no remedy because the jealousy of the Venetians does not permit it, nor do they wish to accept any blame."[69] Just as bandits looking for easy pickings would negatively affect state letters, political interference meant unwelcome delays of merchants' letters. It was postal officials' job to foresee and prevent letter interference of both varieties.

In the case of the German Road, there was, in fact, one possible remedy: shifting from reliance on the Via Alemania to the Via Svizzera (the Swiss Road). By utilizing the Swiss alpine passes, imperial couriers might avoid Venetian territory entirely. In a sign of the commercializing times,

Octavio Tassis described having met with influential merchants in Milan to discuss the best alternative route. It would involve a significant shift of infrastructure, negotiations with the Swiss Grisons and the carriers of Lindau, and increased capacity of the imperial offices in Ulm and Nuremberg. Octavio graciously offered to take on the last task in exchange for postmasterships there for himself and his sons. It would be expensive, but as he recommended to the postmaster general, "I believe that your honor sees the great difficulty of leaving the Mantuan Road, to which I can only say a single reason: that all Catholic princes are loath to see their letters traveling by the Venetian road."[70]

All the debate, negotiation, and decision-making regarding the shift in transalpine roads took place amid the unfolding political crisis of the Thirty Years' War. In an audit culture, the act of recordkeeping is constantly shaped by a speculative future. Records are interpreted not just by what they show about the present, but by information that they provide about how the human machine might be further optimized in alignment with expert predictions. Dispatch notes were a key information technology that not only recorded and reported information, but also affirmed ties, assigned blame, and proposed solutions. Postal administrators had to guess both where their princes would need news delivered most urgently and reliably and where armies and other causes of upheaval might disrupt routes.

Yet dispatch notes were also understood as an *internal* diagnostic system. Frank and often contentious discussions of politics or personal matters indicate that Tassis postmasters still thought of postal systems as a family firm along the transalpine roads. At the same time, commercial clients had always been stakeholders in this system, and they often benefited in parallel with their princes. By the seventeenth century, *particolari* were holding the postmaster accountable to an ever-higher standard. Further challenges came from within the post house. The new lieutenants would confront the Tassis dynasty and the Bergamaschi cartel not just by keeping the books, but also by publishing them.

The Age of Confessional Warfare and the First Postal Newspaper

In a forward-looking article, the postal historian and Thurn und Taxis archivist Joseph Rübsam dubbed the dispatch notes *"postavvisi."* By this, he meant that they resembled the manuscript newssheets shared among Italian expatriates beginning in the Renaissance, which have often been characterized as an early form of journalism.[71] Journalism depended upon the post: as early as 1527, a German broadsheet cited a Tassis postmaster regarding the imperial sack of Rome. Letters from Constantinople, Vienna, and the New World frequently appeared in print as stand-alone newsletters.[72] Even the term "journalism" indicates the importance of regular dispatches, originating from the Latin *diurnalis* (daily). In addition to their diagnostic role, dispatch notes served an important intelligencing role, as postmasters passed news bulletins to one another and their favored patrons.

The first decades of the seventeenth century brought the newspaper, which introduced the dateline format of its manuscript predecessors to the sensationalism and scale of print distribution. The Frankfurt post office gave rise to the first printed postal newspaper beginning in 1619, after the outset of the Thirty Years' War. The periodical was later dubbed the *Frankfurter Postzeitung*.[73] This early example of a postal newspaper inspired imitators in Leipzig (1632), Stettin (1632), Stockholm (1643), and Danzig (1657). By the end of the seventeenth century, more than 200 printed newspapers had appeared across central Europe, reporting on everything from miracles to military maneuvers.[74] The strong and early ties between postal networks and newspaper production are echoed in modern mastheads, such as the *Daily Mail* or the *Washington Post*. The case of the Frankfurt post office, home to the first printed postal newspaper, shows us that by the mid-seventeenth century, states were no longer as preoccupied with forbidding private use as they were with regulating it.[75]

The Frankfurt post office was relatively new when the Tassis leased it to the Aachen-born Johann von den Birghden in 1615. Birghden was one of several postal lieutenants who earned their stripes under the Tassis, running missions, apprenticing at a major office, and finally attaining a postmastership. He had earned additional honors for his service in the Spanish military. As early as 1615, the elector prince-bishop of Mainz paid Birghden 100 gulden a year for carrying his mail and another 40 for the regular provision of a "weekly newsletter," which Birghden produced. This was likely a type of manuscript *avvisi* in the style of news sent by Simone Tassis to his northern patrons a hundred years before.[76]

Birghden had received an imperial commendation and coat of arms as recently as 1625. Yet just two years later, the Holy Roman Emperor Ferdinand II of Habsburg (d. 1637) called for his resignation. The emperor cited Birghden's inclusion of "suspicious and dangerous correspondence with the supporters of the Count Palatine, Frederick V (1596–1632), in Strasbourg, Basel, Durlach, and Holland in his weekly prints. These newspapers, some of which were spotted in France, have interfered with many matters."[77] Birghden allegedly had a network of distributors and received payment from the Protestant Union. The edict accused him of receiving a medal from the Count Palatine himself, the Winter King of Bohemia and an open rebel against the empire.[78]

Birghden's biographers have interpreted the charges of espionage as a mere pretext for action against the postmaster. They see religious intolerance instead as motivating the Tassis in their machinations against the Lutheran Birghden. From the outset, Birghden's appointment had been a point of tension between the postmaster general, Count Lamoral I Tassis (d. 1624), and his son, Leonardo II (d. 1628).[79] Leonardo routinely attempted to oust Birghden, seeking to replace him in the office with Gerard Vrints, a longtime (and Catholic) lieutenant of the postmaster general.

Operating at an economy of scale meant bringing non-Tassis family members into positions of power and eventual competition. Many of these new administrators originated from the Spanish Netherlands, where they had come of age in the aftermath of the Dutch Revolt. In 1566, the largely Protestant United Provinces of the Netherlands (or Dutch Republic) declared independence from the domains of the Spanish king, Philip II. The resulting conflict led to an exodus of well-educated administrators from the north.[80] Bloody campaigns such as the "Spanish Fury" (1572–1579) were within living memory for the generation of emigrants employed by the Tassis posts. Even Octavio Tassis in Augsburg, who would routinely butt heads with foreign rivals, asked his cousin to send a "youth" to help him with office work, but noted, "I would prefer that he be Flemish to German, because the Germans are given to wine, and therefore not as suitable as the Flemish."[81] Northern émigrés found steady employment in the rapidly expanding postal systems of central Europe and Italy, much as the Bergamaschi diaspora had a century earlier.

Another up-and-coming Dutch refugee prefigured Birghden's rise and fall. Jakob Henot began working at the post office of Cologne three months after its opening in 1577.[82] He eventually gained the postmastership of Cologne from Emperor Rudolph, bypassing Seraphin Taxis of Augsburg, the father of Octavio. Henot went on to oversee much of the "Postal Reformation" of 1595–1596, financially restructuring the imperial posts and negotiating new agreements among the post offices of Milan, Venice, Mantua, Augsburg, and Frankfurt. That work put him in good company, working with the Fuggers and Welsers, among other notables.[83] Henot's son, Hartger, was later appointed imperial counselor and served in several prestigious positions across the Holy Roman Empire.[84]

The postmaster general, Baron Leonardo I Tassis (d. 1612), worked well with Henot, relying on his administrative and diplomatic acumen. Henot still had significant detractors, though, including the Tassis branch in Augsburg. Leonardo's son, Lamoral I (d. 1624), was naturally allied with the Tassis of Augsburg through his marriage to Octavio's sister Ginevra. Lamoral virulently opposed the Cologne postmaster, as did Octavio.[85] The two frequently referred to *"Henotisti"* and "clowns" in their correspondence.[86] Most revealingly, Octavio described that he "prayed to God that [the postmaster general] would trust his family over foreigners," and "it is the ruin of this house when foreigners come to know how to manage these offices."[87] Such statements made clear that the Tassis family concerns remained dynastic in nature. The rise of ambitious postal lieutenants to postmasterships fundamentally challenged the family nature of the Tassis firm. Octavio Tassis expressed that sentiment in 1604, a mere four years before Ottavio Codogno published his *New Itinerary*, which promised to reveal to all the method behind a post house, even providing mock examples of the type of bookkeeping for which a postal official was responsible.

Unlike Birghden, Jakob Henot never launched an explicit attack on the Tassis family or their Habsburg patrons. All the same, the Henots' ascendancy was itself a threat to the Tassis "brand." The Henots gained powerful defenders among the private clientele of the post, including Tassis allies—in 1604, Octavio warned that the Welsers regarded the Tassis treatment of Henot as "ingratitude."[88] The Tassis perception of a zero-sum game set the postmasters against their lieutenants. In 1604, Lamoral made his move, now attempting to replace Henot in the post office of Cologne with Johann von Coesfeld (the husband of an Anna Taxis). While Hartger and his sister Katharine triumphed in reinstating their father to the postmastership of Cologne in 1623, the victory was short-lived. Both faced accusations of witchcraft in coming years. Katherine Henot would be burned at the stake, along with another Henot sister.[89] It is impossible to draw any direct connection between the two sets of events, but whatever political capital the Henots had accrued appears to have been exhausted in earlier battles.

Octavio Tassis's conflicts with Birghden certainly echoed his earlier conflicts with Henot. He accused Birghden of capriciousness, "doing one thing one day and undoing it the next," but he bitterly commented that his opinion never seemed to matter since Birghden was among "the favorites." With the death of the postmaster general Lamoral in 1624, however, Octavio made his true feelings known: "I have never shared it," Octavio wrote to the more sympathetic Leonardo II, "but I know it well from rebel correspondence in the Palatinate, and I have it from Rheinhausen that [the rebels] have complained about not being able to control [the Swiss Road] due to the number of routes on which people arrive. But then I saw Birghden's reply that having considered the current circumstances, it would be difficult to alter the route not knowing where the storm is about to go."[90] While rarely explicitly suggesting that Birghden sabotaged the postal service, Octavio implied again and again that Birghden was a liability, and perhaps even an abettor to Protestant forces. At the same time, he admitted that he was jealous of Birghden's station. The success of the Frankfurt office had come at Augsburg's expense. Frankfurt steadily overshadowed the city as the crux of not just a north–south route but also a newly important east–west axis that would connect Prague to Cologne.[91]

In 1629, the Swedish Lutheran king, Gustavus Adolphus (r. 1611–1632), invaded central Europe, much to the benefit of the Protestant Union. Birghden had not given up the fight after the Tassis succeeded in ousting him. In the following years, he had continued to handle mail for the city of Frankfurt and the elector of Mainz, despite complaining that the imperial Vrints withheld his mail and insulted him.[92] Upon the Swedish arrival, Vrints fled his office, allegedly leaving it in a state of complete disrepair. Swedish forces occupied Hamburg, Frankfurt, Augsburg, and Nuremberg. By 1632, Adolphus had designated Frankfurt the center of the Swedish posts and reinstated Birghden, establishing a Swedish system across central Europe that generally emulated the Tassis model.[93]

In a 1632 letter, the postal lieutenant David Fray (o. 1615–1656) in Augsburg described Europe as being divided into faithful agents and "Birghden's faction." Fray continued Octavio Tassis's campaign to shift portions of the German Road westward, this time adding new posts between Cologne and Nantes. By securing and speeding the posts, he hoped to move business away from Nuremberg and Frankfurt, thereby "playing a lovely trick (*una bella burla*) on the heretic messengers who traffic through Nuremberg."[94] "It really is a shame," he noted about Birghden, "that there be a person so perfidious and inimical ... because if this was not the case, we could send everything that way, especially the merchant's letters."[95] By 1628, the imperial post office sought to avoid Frankfurt as well as active battlefronts. Rather than crossing the Brenner Pass, the new course would run north from Milan through Lindau and Memmingen.[96]

Accusations of espionage and foreign treachery were not new in the battle to control post offices. For decades, Tassis officials had advocated for monopolistic privileges based on the danger of an open communications ecosystem and information economy. The desire to control "pernicious newsletters" had motivated Governor Don Sancho de Padilla of Milan to consolidate the Spanish postmaster's monopoly. Birghden could be tarred by Lutheranism in the same way that Milan's merchants, and even the Henots, were associated with dangerous heterodoxy. Birghden's newspaper simply came to represent the newest threat, part of a longer trajectory of subversive intelligencing in the post office. And while the royal edict gave Birghden's "espionage" top billing, the ongoing legal contestation of his firing—which continued all the way through the Peace Conferences of Westphalia—boiled down to bookkeeping. As with the case of Ottavio Codogno and Lucina Cattanea Tassis in Milan, disputes about inaccurate ledgers stemmed from deeper discomfort about who was using the posts and for what purpose.[97]

We might also compare Birghden's newspaper to Ottavio Codogno's *New Itinerary*. Whereas later authors praised Codogno for making clear all the operations of the post office, doing so was akin to publishing the corporate secrets of the Tassis family firm. Octavio Tassis had warned that it would be the "ruin of this house" if foreigners learned how to run post offices. Birghden's Swedish ascendancy certainly seemed to fulfill this prophecy. Similarly, if we consider intelligence as one of the "goods" trafficked by the Tassis, Birghden's newspaper was like selling on the side, or even on the black market. Furthermore, Codogno and Birghden both expressed sincere belief in both the public service element of their profession and an ecumenical approach to their clientele, perhaps shaped by their shared experience in the Netherlands.[98] It is undeniable that their side ventures also provided them with additional income, status, and patrons, which in turn rendered them a greater competitive threat to their Tassis employers.

Shifting postal service toward an economy of scale had brought decades of logistical and philosophical crises, which are well represented in the debates over post office records and officeholding. Returning to the question of the significance of Birghden's newspaper, we should add a final development: Gerard Vrints, Birghden's successor as postmaster, continued to produce Birghden's postal newspaper after taking office in 1627. Vrints did turn its focus toward imperial propaganda and no longer included France in the distribution, but it was nonetheless an important signal of a sea change on the part of the Tassis and their agents toward public-facing service.[99] As the Thirty Years' War began to resolve, so did the question of whether a postal service might be both private and public. A new ideology of free commerce incorporated the ideas floated by postal lieutenants like Codogno, Henot, and Birghden. The postal itinerary and the postal newspaper were the early markers of an orientation shift toward postal service as civil service.

Surviving records—and the recordkeeping habits that they evidence—show how postal service worked on a day-to-day basis as a bureaucracy, business, and social network. On a strictly quantitative basis, we see the impressive scale of a system that not only reached far and wide but also did so on a roughly predictable basis. Predictability was essential for running the machine of state, but regularity of information flow was becoming equally essential to the global markets that sustained empires. The post was undeniably beholden to both public governance and the commercial sphere. That was true for the letters that the post office handled, but also the information technologies that it employed, and perhaps most importantly, the money that paid for both office leases and nights on the road.

Beyond letter weights and courier schedules, postal records were a key technology of a dynamic postal administration. Audit culture meant that recordkeeping skills and the ability to diagnose, predict, and optimize performance became the new measures of postal professionalism. Arguments over recordkeeping, therefore, went beyond accounting quibbles. Officials competed and collaborated through their records. Contesting the accuracy of a post office's recordkeeping meant attacking the core of the office's information management function. Validation of recordkeeping legitimized one's approach to postal service as both profitable and honorable. Challenges to recordkeeping, whether because of its accuracy or its legitimacy as a pursuit, threw into question the expertise of the officeholder. Debates like these later came to characterize the modern technocratic state, but they made an early appearance in the post office.

Criticizing the post office's books was thus shorthand for critiquing the shifting purpose and ethos of state postal service. Ordinary postal service as public service, in the sense of a utility, marked a major transition from the extraordinary couriers of the Renaissance. The very process of establishing ordinary couriers marked formal recognition of private mail-carrying by state postal services. As Ottavio Codogno recognized in his *New Itinerary*, states of antiquity needed only the "fastest couriers." It was the "businessmen, lawyers, and merchants" that demanded a slower, regular, and affordable service.[100]

Chapter 4 explored how Spanish state auditors objected to the influence of executive prerogatives on the system; they were equally concerned by the role of private interests (namely, powerful businessmen). By the end of the Thirty Years' War, however, private use of state posts was widespread, and states even began to embrace such service as a potential source of revenue.

Debates among postal officials focused on recordkeeping discrepancies, but always with an eye to an increasingly invested audience. Post office print publication shows early communication to a wider audience of stakeholders. As early as 1612, the post office of Milan had rebutted the charges of the Spanish visitation in print. The disgruntled postmaster of Frankfurt did the same in the 1640s. Even Birghden's postal newspaper essentially opened up post office records, advertising his expertise in ways similar to Codogno's work. This widened audience was not only a sought-after clientele for state postal services; it was also an increasingly vocal one. Dispatch notes show how officials felt the daily pressure of demand for reliable, secure, and affordable postal service in peace and war. A new generation of postal lieutenants cannily wielded this pressure for their own professional advancement, with greater and lesser degrees of direct conflict with the Tassis family.

Chapter 6

The Sinews of Society
Coach Travel and the Postal Guide in the Seventeenth Century

Knowledge of and access to good mobility infrastructure were basic obstacles to travel in the early modern world. Travelers expected to be pursued by bandits, harassed by guards, defrauded by innkeepers, and delayed by warfare or their own dwindling funds. One author compared his experience in a leaking French stagecoach unfavorably to riding a snail. Another put a rare positive spin on the trip between Rome and Naples: "It's true, a man is ill lodged, and badly treated in that journey, but it doth a gentle man good to be acquainted with hardship."[1] The history of travel has long been written from similar complaints.[2]

At the same time, during the late seventeenth century, two relatively new phenomena reached a new scale: public transportation and tourism. The commercialization of postal travel (known as "posting") took place in parallel with the commercialization of mail service discussed in chapter 5. If the coach was the major innovation in public transportation, the postal guide was a turning point in the history of tourism. Early modern Europeans associated the sign of the post house with their own travel, as well as that of their letters and goods. How and why did two seemingly distinct functions—carrying state correspondence and ferrying private passengers—merge so widely?

Both seventeenth-century developments further integrated a comprehensive mobility infrastructure involving hospitality, transit, and exchange under the sign of the post house. Mobility infrastructure often falls into one of two categories: the "hard" infrastructure of physical assets such as roads, bridges, and way stations, and "soft" infrastructure, such as training, personnel, and centralized organization and administration. Postal infrastructure defies easy categorization. Take the earlier titles of the master of the posts (maestro delle poste) and the master of couriers (maestro dei corrieri): state officials often perceived this as a division between administering the hard infrastructure of way stations and the soft infrastructure of personnel. The Tassis corrieri maggiori brand succeeded in large part because it blended these predecessor offices. Access to and the security of hard infrastructure depended upon constant brokering among people. Innkeepers, coach drivers, and couriers shared family ties and managed shared assets, such as horses and roads. Information technologies such as the ledgers, rider receipts, and dispatch notes discussed in chapter 5 reinforced both the social networks of postal systems and the material networks of mailbags and routes.

This chapter contends that postal officials and their representatives were held to a high standard precisely because they had become prominent guides to the world of European culture, commerce, and geography. Or, put another way, the post office contributed a pre-Westphalian soft infrastructure that would be essential for the development of the post-Westphalian state's hard infrastructure. By the 1620s, postal systems were well positioned to dominate travel in the same way that they had monopolized mail-carrying. This time, they made their case to the public as well as the prince. Published postal documentation administered and publicized the sprawling clockwork of the international courier routes. Officials created innovative postal forms, timetables, itineraries, and conversion tools. They published this documentation in many forms, including popular itinerary books for travelers to carry on the road (known as the "post-book"). From the timed stagecoach to standardized postage rates, postal officials promoted their systems as more accessible and reliable options for transit and exchange, especially in contrast with private providers.

It was, by and large, a marketing success if not a fully realized reality. Clients were dismayed by the difference between the precision that they saw on paper and their experiences of poor service, inadequate infrastructure, and faulty communication.[3] Messengers were also frequently "unruly" and postage "extortionate," but the greatest ire was reserved for the postilion.[4] The postilion and his private counterpart, the hackneyman (*vetturino*), showed visitors the sights, helped them navigate local customs and geography, and liaised with local authorities and businesses. This was a transition from public relations to full customer service. From the middle of the seventeenth century forward, the postilion thus replaced the postmaster as the public face of the post house.[5]

It is easy to underestimate the value of accessibility and predictability in daily life. When it works well, an ideal infrastructure is an almost invisible scaffold for routine. It is only when we break patterns that we become keenly aware of flaws, such as when we travel abroad. The "culture shock" experiences of early modern tourists illustrate as much about the expectations of postal service as they do about the experience of it—this is why northern travelers, or *tramontani*, are featured heavily here and in chapter 7. The "Grand Tour" describes a pattern of travel by northern Europeans to southern Europe, especially Italy, as a means of acquiring education, experiences, and collections of art and artifacts.[6] By the mid-seventeenth century, British postmasters worked with the Tassis to link the British and imperial systems, extending service coverage for letters throughout Germany, Scandinavia, eastern Europe, Italy, and beyond.[7] Travelers were encouraged to produce journals and letters, many of which appeared in print. Their accounts offer valuable outsider insight, while indicating how pan-European postal culture spread through expatriates' experiences.

A wide clientele took postal officials at their word that the monopolistic services were to their benefit and did not shy away from voicing their opinions as stakeholders. Travel by post furthered the notion of postal service as a *public* service, or a utility. Far from their martial origins, postal systems now featured in political economic debates about roads, waterways, and free commerce, in everything from traveler's letters to debates at the Westphalian Peace Conferences.[8] States turned to technocratic administrators to provide infrastructure for surveilling, controlling, and taxing mobility. By the end of the seventeenth century, states embraced distinct classes of postal service, using associated fees as a means of privileging certain uses over others. This proved to be a promising source of revenue, but also a way of subsidizing activities perceived as politically and economically advantageous to the state.

Before the Thirty Years' War, states feared that private and especially foreign users might take advantage of state infrastructure. By the eighteenth century, they actively guided such users to their postal systems as both a source of revenue and a showpiece of technological advancement. This reinvention, like so many before it, had its origins in grassroots lobbying by postal officials. Yet by the mid-seventeenth century, the Tassis and their Bergamaschi compatriots were no longer leading the field. Northern Italy and the transalpine roads continued to innovate, but the Tassis will be largely absent from this chapter: instead, their efforts would go toward shoring up their existing titles, as discussed in chapter 7. The promotion of the postilion filled in for the aristocratic withdrawal of the postmaster and postmaster general. This was a longer trend that began with office-leasing at the end of the sixteenth century and culminated in the ennobling of the postmaster general by the beginning of the eighteenth century.

The Post-Book in Your Pocket

Language evolves in parallel with the technologies that it describes. Postal systems naturally evoke movement, but the name "postal" derived from its hard infrastructure: the post (*posta*), or the way station. The modern use derived from the Italian *posto/a*, commonly designating a place, or in the phrase "at the ready" (*a posto*). The traveler John Evelyn recorded the wordplay found on a sign outside the Italian city of Acquapendente in the 1640s:

L'insegna della Posta, é posta a posta
In questa posta, fin che habbia à sua Posta.
Ogn' un cavallo a Vetturi in posta.

The sign of the Post, is posted at post
In this post, until you arrive at your Post.
Every horse rentable by post.[9]

Locating postal way stations at inns was mutually beneficial. Postmasters were often either innkeepers themselves or their family members were, and foreign inns had often served as mail hubs before the formal establishment of post houses and postmasters-in-residence.[10] Innkeepers had stables to keep horses at the ready for couriers riding in relay, but as advertised on the sign at Acquapendente, they also regularly rented horses to other travelers. There was evidently ample demand: couriers often complained about arriving to find that no horses were available. This practice flouted regulations that required innkeepers to maintain postal horses at the ready.[11]

Renting a horse from the postmaster or innkeeper was the earliest and most common meaning of "going by post" or "posting." The postmaster himself or a trusted lieutenant would accompany elite travelers. There was safety in numbers, especially in regions known for banditry.[12] The postal guide could also return both mounts to the post house. Diplomatic letters show that posting was a common practice for rulers and other important officials by the end of the sixteenth century. Passports provided authorization for travel using postal horses, roads, or inns.[13] This assured a monitored itinerary for foreign dignitaries, as well as a baseline standard for service. The French scholar Michel de Montaigne (1533–1592) found postal inns especially commodious when he traveled in the 1580s. He praised one at Piacenza as "the best inn that I came across between this and Rome."[14]

A well-developed postal travel infrastructure composed of networks of inns, post houses, and transportation professionals could be found across continental Europe by the end of the sixteenth century. This was especially true on either side of the Alps and along well-traveled mercantile and pilgrimage routes. Despite hearing tales of bandits and "savage" inns, Montaigne judged the Alpine roads so safe and well provisioned that he would have trusted his eight-year-old daughter to travel along them.[15] In Milan, the Inn of the Three Kings served as an additional post house for mail to and from Germany. Located between the cathedral and the Roman gate, it was the most internationally famous of the city's fifty-eight inns. The mid-seventeenth-century traveler Richard Lassels described it as "the best and handsomest Inn in Europe."[16] At the same time, locating postal way stations at inns naturally embedded the post in commerce. Channeling travelers, and most importantly, their funds, was a profitable endeavor. Keeping a postal inn could merit additional privileges, such as the right to produce and sell food or wine.[17] We see, for example, why the Spanish visitation of Milan found that postal leaseholders were willing and able to pay higher and higher leases for their offices.[18]

Yet while making the most of postal inns, sixteenth-century travelers rarely traveled by post. The availability of travel "posthaste"—changing horses in relay—remained limited to state officials by law in much of Europe. Even the price for renting a horse from the post office of Milan was a half ducatone—a substantial cost for even a wealthy traveler.[19] The English writer Thomas Coryate claimed to have walked for much of his pan-European journey, likely to avoid such costs. The Scotsman traveler Fynes Moryson bargained with whoever had a vehicle headed in the right direction, often organizing impromptu groups to share costs rather than finding a ready means of public transportation or hiring an individual means of travel.[20]

Accessing hard infrastructure went beyond legal or financial feasibility. It required knowledge and often a personal connection. Montaigne lamented two aspects of his transalpine travel in the 1580s. First, he had not found or brought a proper companion, "for to live at the mercy of a blockhead of a guide I found to be an amazing inconvenience." Second, he had not brought or read more books pointing out "the rare and noticeable features in each place."[21] Traveling abroad always involved information asymmetry that was inconvenient at best and dangerous at worst.

Postal officials, however, saw information asymmetry as a commercial opportunity. They had always traded in information and provided logistical expertise. When a new generation of postal officials sought to open their infrastructure to the traveling as well as corresponding public, they turned to the printing press. Printed itinerary books popularized postal systems as an infrastructure for public transportation and tourism. We have already introduced one such book: Ottavio Codogno's *New Itinerary of the Posts of the World* (1608) (figures 15 and 16), and its reworking, *Compendium of the Posts* (1623). In addition to his prose chapters on the history of postal service and instructions to would-be postmasters or couriers, Codogno included tables of routes across Europe. He punctuated these with his own opinions about the quality of the roads, inns, and even local sights. He advertised his book on the front page as "most useful not just to secretaries, but to clerics and merchants."

Codogno's itinerary is perhaps the most famous of the genre, but overall, the postal itinerary has received little attention in histories of travel in comparison with traveler accounts. Nonetheless, itineraries are rich sources for understanding the fungibility of hard and soft infrastructure in the early modern context. Several titles were published continuously for close to two centuries, including the *New Itinerary*. Often produced by couriers and postmasters, these books catered to diverse audiences of private and professional correspondents, merchants, and travelers. They popularized the verb "to post," but also the use of "post" as a noun to describe the distance unit between each way station as regulated by a given state. Intended as reference literature, they propagandized state postal routes and agents as the most professional, and therefore most reliable, means of travel and exchange.

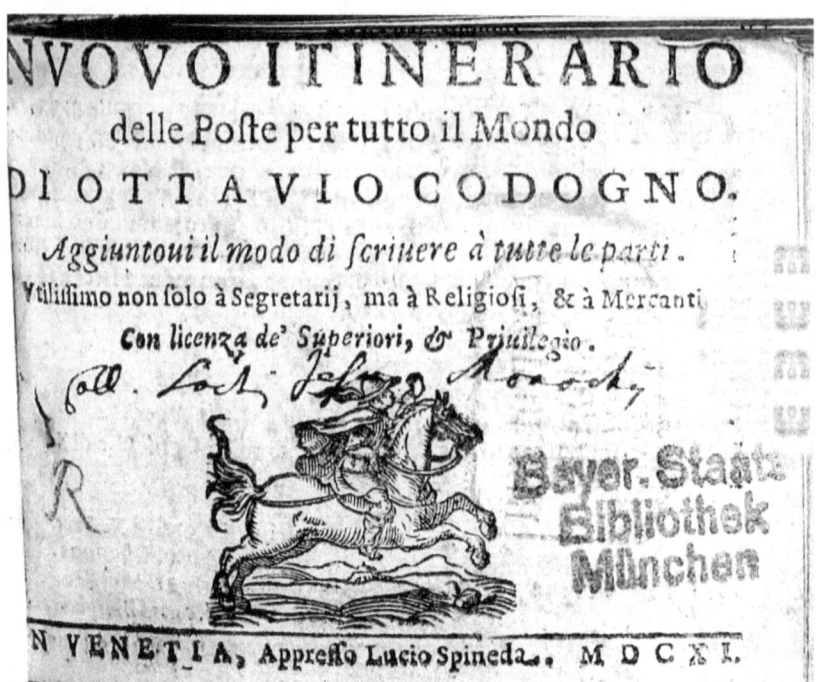

Figure 15. A page from a Venetian edition of Ottavio Codogno's *New Itinerary* published in 1611. The front page advertised the book as "useful not just to secretaries, but to clerics and merchants." Image from Bayerische Staatsbibliothek, München, Res/Geo.u. 87.

156 *Poste per diuerse*

Poste da Milano à Madrid per altra via, da Cunio, & Auignone, ma i Francesi non la lasciano fare.

Milano Città.
Alla Rosa. p. 1
Passarete il Nauilio sopra il Ponte, dipoi il Tecino *Fiume.*
A Vigeuano Città. p. 1
A Mortara Terra grossa, & antica. p. 1
A Cozzo. p. 1
Dapoi passarete il Pò *Fiu-*

me.
A Casal di Monferrato, Città di questo Stato la Metropoli. p. 1
A Aste Città di Piemonte. p. 2
A Alba Città del Monferrato. p. 2
Alla Vittoria. p. 1
Alla Trinità del Piemonte. p. 2
Passarete il Grez *Fiume.*
A Cunio Città del Serenissimo Signor Duca di Sauoia. p. 1
A Borgo Borgo. p. 1
Pas-

Figure 16. A page from a Venetian edition of *New Itinerary*. Route tables frequently featured observations on borders, scenery, and historical or religious sites of interest. Image from Bayerische Staatsbibliothek, München, Res/Geo.u. 87.

Antecedents to the postal itinerary include pilgrimage guidebooks, like the *Marvels of Rome*, and the *Pilgrim's Guide to the Path of Saint James*, which mixed routes with prose descriptions of notable sites.[22] The word "itinerary," from *itinerarium*, originally described a list of cities with their relative distances. Three postal itineraries survive from the mid-sixteenth century in Italy. They appeared in quick succession along the Italian Road. Damiano Turlano and Giovanni Battista Bozola first published *The Necessary Posts* (1562) in Brescia. Within a year, Cherubino Stella, the former postmaster of Perugia, published *Itinerary of the Posts throughout Different Parts of the World* under the patronage of the Genoese postmaster of Rome, Giovanni da l'Herba (to whom it is often attributed). An anonymous author produced *Different Posts of Italy, Germany, Spain, and France* in Milan, likely in the first decades of the seventeenth century.[23] Unlike earlier guidebooks, postal itineraries were firmly based in the travel infrastructure provided by the Spanish, imperial, papal, and Venetian postal systems, featuring routes that were run by postal ordinaries.[24] Pilgrimage guidebooks tended to be narrative prose, but itineraries were often simple lists punctuated by annotated observations. Their authors prioritized speed and comfort as measured by the relative density and maintenance of postal way stations.

Postal itineraries were intended to be carried on the road and accordingly printed in pocket-sized octavo or sextodecimo formats. The books were likely more affordable and more legible to the common traveler than unwieldy cosmographies or maps. Giovanni Torriano's *Introduction to the Italian Tongue* (1657) offers a rare example of a postal itinerary in use. The book provided English travelers learning Italian with several practice dialogues in both Italian and English. In one of these, a traveler asks his companion if he fears he will lose his way. His companion responds: "I have the giurnal (*l'Itinerario*) in my pocket / What, *Scottus*? / No, the post-book."[25] "Scottus" referred to Franciscus Schottus's *Itinerary*, which more closely resembled older pilgrimage guides with its narrative prose, urban perambulations, and small illustrations.[26] The post-book was similar but functionally distinct, and it was the post-book in his pocket that gave the traveler the confidence to navigate Italy's roads and major cities.

Spanish and German itineraries began to incorporate postal routes soon after the publication of the first Italian postal itineraries. Their places of publication were also hubs of the Tassis postal network. Jörg Gail's *Travel Booklet (Raißbuechlin)* (Augsburg, 1563) was more like the postal itineraries than a traditional German *Reisebuch*, or travel journal.

The *Booklet* was a palm-sized book organized in an easy-to-reference format. Gail, its creator, was a schoolmaster and notary in Augsburg who sought imperial permission for his book from Ferdinand I of Habsburg.[27] Gail quickly faced publishing competition from Georg Mayr's *Route Booklet* (Augsburg, 1576) and Daniel Witzenberger's *New Travel Booklet* (Dresden, 1578). Witzenberger identified himself as a postal official on the front page and included several postal routes centered around his home in Dresden.[28]

From its roots in pilgrimage, mercantile, and humanist reference literature, the postal itinerary came into its own as a subgenre in the second half of the sixteenth century. Creators translated, replicated, and supplemented one another's books, building a canon of geographic knowledge based on postal systems. Publishers experimented with targeting different audiences through illustrations or religious and historical supplements. Italian books also incorporated texts and maps from the Netherlands, Holy Roman Empire, and Spain. They were translated and imitated in those locations in turn. The postal itinerary even made it to the British Isles before the public-serving state postal system did; see, for example, *The Post of the World* (London, 1576) and *The European Mercury* (London, 1641). In fact, the English renegade Richard Verstegan's *The Post of the World* (1576) was a close translation of Mayr's *Route Booklet* (1576).[29] Histories of travel have often concentrated on select nationalities of travelers and destinations, but the published itineraries, and the postal travel infrastructure that they advertised, were transnational phenomena.

Despite their pocketability, itineraries were increasingly dense with information. Publishers frequently appended popular ephemeral works to new publications. When Stella and Herba included a calendar of trade fairs in 1563, it was republished in dozens of titles for the next hundred years. Sometimes these supplements were reprinted exactly, but more often they were translated culturally as well as linguistically, much in the way that modern books or movies are both internationalized and localized. *The Post of the World*, for example, featured a list of Welsh and English fairs, and the Germans Gail and Witzenberger included the electors of the Holy Roman Empire. Many seventeenth-century itineraries included prose guides to pilgrimage, conversion tools for currency and mileage, and even quick-reference vocabularies in multiple languages, including Polish and Turkish. Utility remained the guiding principle: publishers kept formats pocket-sized, despite adding tools such as glossaries, tables, clear headings, and multiple indexes.[30]

Marginalia in postal itineraries allow us to peek through the window of the postal inn, much as other postal records conjure the missing mailbag.[31] Many readers were foreign travelers and often were associated with state business. A blank leaf of a 1615 example of Schottus's *Itinerary* reads "I, Guliellmo Jeffera [William Jeffrey] bought this book in Venice July 1617 for 2 lire" in Italian, as well as "I came to Naples from Venice" in English.[32] Further marginalia indicate that Jeffrey then gave it to a female friend or relative. In another example, "D. Juan Gaspar Zorrila de S. Mta de el consejo de S.M." signed a 1673 French itinerary, suggesting that the royal Spanish counselor relied on the book several decades after its publication.[33]

Reader additions could also be poetic. In a 1553 French book, we find Canto 7 from Ariosto's Orlando Furioso on the first blank page: "He who travels far from his home sees / things, which are far from what he once believed." In a 1568 Spanish itinerary, a reader wrote several Bible verses that addressed death, memory, and law—topics that were never far from the mind of a traveler on the road.[34] Many marks seem to track readers' journeys and show that they relied on the books abroad, sometimes many years after their initial publication. A 1563 copy of Stella and Herba's itinerary shows numerous examples, includes many checked-off intermediary stops along journeys, most likely marked as the traveler reached them (figures 17 and 18). Similarly, Robert Ashley annotated his copy of *Itinerarium Galliae* with his Paris sightseeing notes in 1617.[35] These examples illustrate that itinerary texts had long and dynamic lives, as titles were continually corrected and supplemented by both publishers and readers over decades.

Even before reader contributions, book dedications expressed and reinforced a key element of soft infrastructure: they described administrative relationships that made hard infrastructure possible. The Milanese postal lieutenant Ottavio Codogno printed his itineraries at a pivotal moment in his career trajectory. He dedicated the book to his important patrons: the Spanish postmaster general and the governor of Milan. Under fire from the Spanish visitation, Codogno had defended the dual public-private service of his post office. The book extended Codogno's legal defense back in time, presenting the Tassis postal network as a pinnacle of administrative achievement originating from the alliance among the Tassis family, princes, and businessmen. Furthermore, Codogno took every opportunity in the book to advertise the state posts over his great rivals, the merchant mail and independent procacci. While such freelancers might casually delay or misplace the

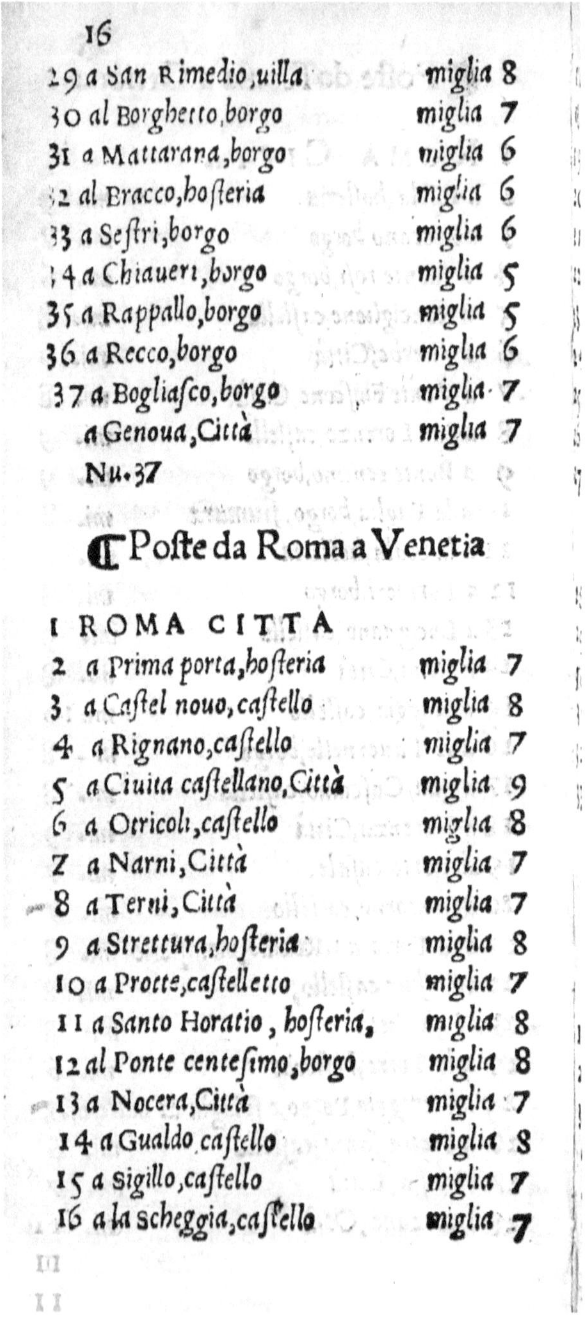

16
29 a San Rimedio, uilla   miglia 8
30 al Borghetto, borgo   miglia 7
31 a Mattarana, borgo   miglia 6
32 al Bracco, hosteria   miglia 6
33 a Sestri, borgo   miglia 6
34 a Chiaueri, borgo   miglia 5
35 a Rappallo, borgo   miglia 5
36 a Recco, borgo   miglia 6
37 a Bogliasco, borgo   miglia 7
   a Genoua, Città   miglia 7
Nu. 37

⁋ Poste da Roma a Venetia

1 ROMA CITTA
2 a Prima porta, hosteria   miglia 7
3 a Castel nouo, castello   miglia 8
4 a Rignano, castello   miglia 7
5 a Ciuita castellano, Città   miglia 9
6 a Otricoli, castello   miglia 8
7 a Narni, Città   miglia 7
8 a Terni, Città   miglia 7
9 a Strettura, hosteria   miglia 8
10 a Protte, castelletto   miglia 7
11 a Santo Horatio, hosteria,   miglia 8
12 al Ponte centesimo, borgo   miglia 8
13 a Nocera, Città   miglia 7
14 a Gualdo, castello   miglia 8
15 a Sigillo, castello   miglia 7
16 a la scheggia, castello   miglia 7

FIGURE 17. Examples of marginalia from the 1563 copy of Cherubino Stella and Giovanni Herba, *L'Itinerario per diverse parte del mondo* (Rome: Valerico Dorico, 1563). An anonymous reader has made check marks next to the cities of Terni and Nocera Umbra on the route from Rome to Venice. Image from Bayerische Staatsbibliothek, München, Rar. 1073.

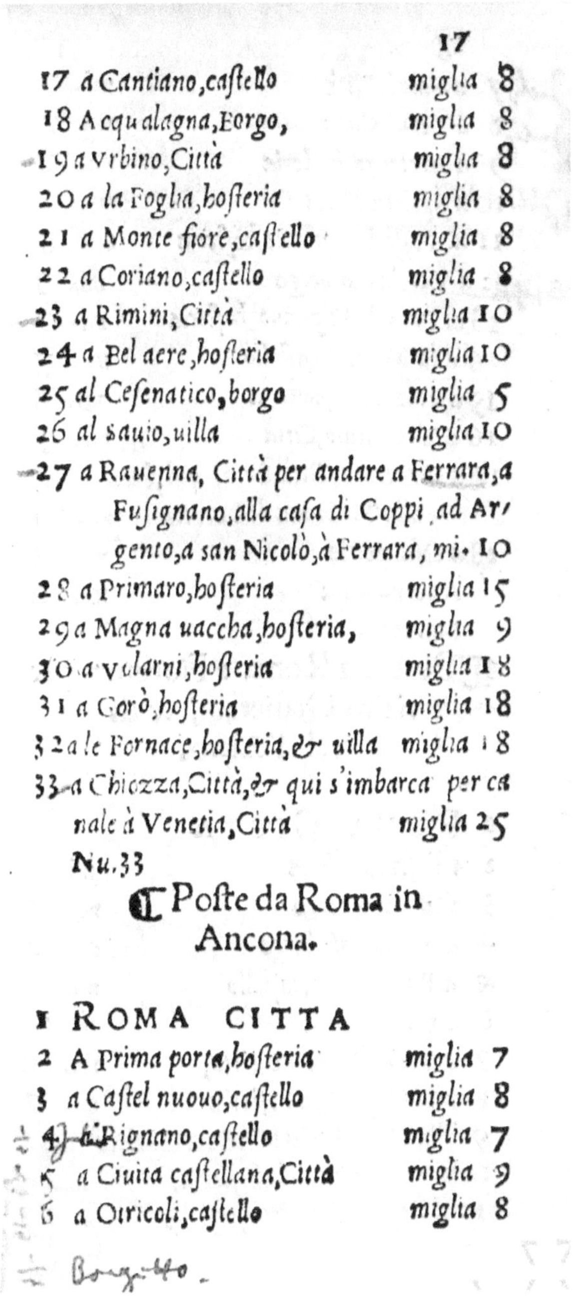

17 a Cantiano, castello   miglia 8
18 A cqualagna, Borgo,   miglia 8
19 a Vrbino, Città   miglia 8
20 a la Foglia, hosteria   miglia 8
21 a Monte fiore, castello   miglia 8
22 a Coriano, castello   miglia 8
23 a Rimini, Città   miglia 10
24 a Bel aere, hosteria   miglia 10
25 al Cesenatico, borgo   miglia 5
26 al sauio, uilla   miglia 10
27 a Rauenna, Città per andare a Ferrara, a Fusignano, alla casa di Coppi, ad Ar/ gento, a san Nicolò, à Ferrara, mi. 10
28 a Primaro, hosteria   miglia 15
29 a Magna uaccha, hosteria,   miglia 9
30 a Volarni, hosteria   miglia 18
31 a Corò, hosteria   miglia 18
32 a le Fornace, hosteria, & uilla   miglia 18
33 a Chiozza, Città, & qui s'imbarca per ca nale à Venetia, Città   miglia 25
Nu. 33

℃ Poste da Roma in Ancona.

1 ROMA CITTA
2 A Prima porta, hosteria   miglia 7
3 a Castel nuouo, castello   miglia 8
4 à Rignano, castello   miglia 7
5 a Ciuita castellana, Città   miglia 9
6 a Otricoli, castello   miglia 8

Borghetto.

FIGURE 18. Additional examples of marginalia from the 1563 copy of *L'Itinerario per diverse parte del mondo*. An anonymous Spanish-speaking reader has underlined cities, indicated where half posts could be found, and added a stop (Borghetto) to the journey from Rome to Ancona. "Julio" (July) appears next to Rignano Flaminio. Image from Bayerische Staatsbibliothek, München, Rar. 1073.

mail, Codogno related his own great efforts to correctly deliver "a pearl worth thirty scudi, which had been sent to jeweler Battista Parisi in Venice, and through inattention, had been posted without the name of the city."[36] His narrative advertised the professionalism of the postal official, as well as Codogno's personal dedication to public service.

Postal itineraries from before the Thirty Years' War laid the groundwork for the post-Westphalian realization of postal travel infrastructure across Europe. Building on the longstanding relationship among postal systems, inns, and horse rentals, subordinate postmasters and postilions advertised postal infrastructure. Yet on a more conceptual level, they also staked the postal official's claim to the geographic, administrative, and even public relations expertise essential to posting people. Itineraries advertised the postal official himself as a personable guide who would offer advice on the best inns, easy river crossings, fine wines, and not-to-be-missed destinations of historical or religious significance. That guidance could be accessed as easily as by stopping by the post house or consulting the book in one's pocket.

The Appeal of the Postilion and Postal Coach

If sixteenth-century travelers had one reason to complain, it was simple extortion. A foreign traveler was at a natural disadvantage abroad, naive to local customs and thus an easy target for scams. Montaigne noted that interpreters and guides worked in concert with innkeepers and other services, splitting their profits. The tourism industry was especially aggressive on the postal route to Rome, where Montaigne observed that landlords sent guides far along the road to promote their services and lead travelers to their door. He fatalistically concluded that it was "impossible to escape being cheated by them in some way or other; for if you keep them to their agreement in one thing, they rob you in another."[37] The human element of the travel infrastructure was by far the most variable in quality.

"Postilion" is the most direct English translation of *postiglione*. Entering the lexicon by the end of the sixteenth century, "postilion" described the outrider or forerunner who accompanied the postal coach. Ottavio Codogno had defined the postal lieutenant as "exercising the entirety of the office in the absence of the postmaster general," but over time, the postilion-as-guide became the public face of the post office.[38] Northern travelers frequently mixed *postiglioni* up with their private counterparts, hackneymen (*vetturini*).[39] Postilions and hackneymen competed with one another by advertising themselves as fonts of local information, from the safest routes to the best entertainment and lodging. Once again, the practice dialogues of *Introduction to the Italian Tongue* (1657) are illustrative. In one, an English traveler complains that despite being promised "a notable hackneyman (*vetturino*), a jester that will make ye burst with laughing every foot," he had found his guide "ill vers'd." The hackneyman had not instructed his client about "Custom-house men, & Waiters," and thus failed to protect him from traps designed for unsuspecting travelers.[40] When confronted with such "blockhead" guides, the next best alternative was to educate oneself. In another dialogue, when asked to cover the cost of the meal and boarding of his hackneyman, the Englishman snaps back, "'Do not thou make me believe this flam, do not I know that the hackney-man is scot-free, wherever he goes?'" Many polities specified a set rate for postilions, but in this case, the Englishman knows that common custom (and collusion) mean that the hackneyman will not shoulder any cost. The suspicion is confirmed when the put-upon hackneyman spits, "'Ye Northerners (*tramontani*) are Romanized (*Romanescati*) to that trick, that there's no good to be done with you,'" lamenting that travelers have grown too experienced to be duped.[41]

With much of Europe speaking the *lingua postale*, postal officials were well positioned to shape the overall politics and economics of mobility in the age of the stagecoach. Partnerships between post offices and coach lines were developing across Europe by the first decades of the seventeenth century. The term "stage" derived from the ancient distance measurement of the *stadia*, and "coach" from the Hungarian *kocsi* ("carriage from Kocs").[42] Together they became the most common English variant: the stagecoach.

From 1650 onward, the postal stagecoach—with its postilion and set routes, rates, and timetables—became the symbol of European travel and tourism. Traditionally, France has held the title of the first public postal travel system: Henry IV (1553-1610) had established a public stage system for travel by 1597, which had fully merged with the official posts by 1602.[43] By the 1620s, chief minister Cardinal Richelieu (1585-1642) had reformed the French postal system to fully integrate the newspaper, travel, and postal infrastructures. Public coach systems had cropped up as far afield as London, where John Taylor's *Carrier's Cosmography*—a compendium like the continental itineraries—listed several coach lines running to and from London.[44]

Yet northern Italy saw key early developments in postal coach travel percolate from the ground up. By the end of the sixteenth century, the busiest routes in northern Italy merited a carriage or "cart" (*carro*), including the routes connecting Milan, Venice, and Rome. Small vehicles pulled by two horses known as the *sedie* or *selle della posta* were common enough to be employed as a literary metaphor by the late sixteenth century.[45] Like other travelers, couriers were inclined to hitch a ride when possible. For instance, a 1601 letter reporting an assault on a Venetian Company courier mentioned "the carriageman (*carozzero*) who carried him" near Salvaterra, outside of Mantua.[46] While coaches offered the advantages of relative comfort and carrying capacity, they were appropriate only for certain roads, such as the relatively flat terrain of the Po Valley. It was not until the eighteenth century that carriages crossed the Alps at locations other than the relatively low-elevation Brenner Pass. Postal coaches continued to hand passengers off to ferries or muleteers and even porters who carried sedan chairs over more challenging terrain.[47]

Northern Italian post offices competed and collaborated with other horse-letters (*nolesini*), carriagemen (*carozzeri*), and bargemen (*barcaroli*). Earlier edicts focused on preventing these agents from smuggling mail or their unauthorized use of postal insignia, but by the beginning of the seventeenth century, postmasters began to assert privileges regarding transporting people as well as mail. A 1599 Venetian edict forbade coachmen from renting horses for travel on postal routes without licensing by the postmaster.[48] The post office in Milan under Lucina Cattanea Tassis (d. 1619) owned two carriages and held privileges related to renting coaches in nearby Pavia.[49] Hackneymen were known to hide letters in the seats, but passengers and heavy baggage were presumably harder to conceal, which didn't stop the carriers from trying. In 1611, Ottavio Codogno complained that coachmen were asking passengers to dismount as they approached the city to evade licensing fees paid to the post office. He indicated that Bologna and Parma had recently issued edicts prohibiting these practices.[50]

Unlike the private carriages on increasingly crowded roads, postal coaches were granted a few unique privileges, even within cities. Given the strict timetables of postal delivery, postal coaches were granted the right to sound the postal horn to signal that private carriages should give way. Eighteenth-century edicts in Milan specified that vehicles stop in place and move to the side when the horn sounded, much as modern vehicles are required to give way to emergency responders. Yet it was widespread disregard that necessitated the edict, especially by "nobles who don't respect the financial penalty and believe that they can keep doing as they have always done." Instead, the Milanese postal lieutenant proposed that a revised edict clarify that "*all* are encompassed by the state."[51] As officers of a public utility, postal officials saw their traffic as superseding even that of an aristocratic elite.

In addition to increased policing of private travel agents, travelers turned to public transportation for the same reasons that modern tourists might: information about times, rates, and itineraries were available and verifiable, even from abroad. Patterned after the international "ordinary" couriers, postal coaches traveled on timetables that were clearly posted and communicated, and of which many printed copies survive. Decades of postal service and communications, from itineraries to posted regulation, successfully sold postal service as uniquely accessible and reliable, especially to foreigners. The turning point toward postal stagecoaches came soon after the end of the Thirty Years' War (1648), when, less than a year later, a postmaster in Kassel applied for a patent to establish a regular post coach (calling it an *ordinari-fahrpost*) between Kassel and Frankfurt.[52] The enterprising Maffeo Tasso (d. 1677), a member of the Venetian Company of Couriers, sought permission to establish carriage systems across northern Italy in 1653.[53] In German territories postal coaches were often called "diligences," which reflected that they were defined primarily by their reliability. By the 1680s, diligences were widely available across Europe and included new rivals to the Tassis, such as Saxony's postal system.[54]

The postal itinerary genre also adapted to reflect the widespread availability of the postal coach. *Burattino's Directions* (1682) and *Practical Travel* (1718) devoted long sections to the arrival and departure times of ordinaries and coaches—vital information for travelers as well as administrators.[55] Even prominent officials who traveled *a vettura* or in personal vehicles relied on postilions by the eighteenth century. In *Practical Travel*, the Venetian postal official Giovanni Maria Vidari wrote from several decades of experience accompanying ambassadors abroad. He routinely negotiated with each of the individual transportation agents, most often the *capo vetturino*—the chief hackneyman. Vidari warned travelers that they would face routine extortion, especially at customs points. He nonetheless asserted that the informed postilion could ensure that previously agreed-upon rates and privileges would be honored. He supported this with day-by-day accounts of his own journeys, demonstrating how he combined modes of travel for the best value. While the Venetian ambassador traveled by post-chaise (*in sedia*) in France, accompanied by a few riders, the remainder of the party traveled by a combination of the diligence and a coach for hire.[56]

Then, as now, customer service was not always easy-going. Relationships were complicated by financial transactions, class differences, and mutual xenophobia. The traveler and novelist Tobias Smollet found that "the hostlers, postilions, and other fellows hanging about the post-houses in Italy are the most greedy, impertinent, and provoking." Samuel Sharp similarly informed a correspondent, "You will never imagine half the disagreeableness that Italian beds, Italian cooks, Italian post-horses, Italian postilions, and Italian nastiness, offer to an Englishman . . . much more to an English woman."[57] Like many service workers, Italian guides relied on tips to supplement their meager wages. Vidari recommended that the traveler tip "in order to be well-served" but indicated that tipping was to the taste of the traveler.[58] Many northerners found tipping to be the height of distastefulness, resenting what they viewed as grifting.[59] Travel tensions could erupt into full brawls. Fights with, between, and among postilions and travelers might be incited by bravado, alcohol, or traffic incidents. Sharp relayed that a fight between postilions on the road between Rome and Naples ended with one stabbing the other to death.[60]

The postilions' growing reputation for short tempers and reckless disregard for authority might be explained by the fact that most were young men. This reputation also seemed to reflect deeper social anxiety regarding the apparent rootlessness of these agents of mobility. Broadsheet ballads like "The Knight Out Rid; or, The Postilion in His Master's Saddle" adopted the postilion for satirical, political, or social commentary.[61] A short serial story, "The History of Tom White, the Postillion" (c. 1795), used the trope of a misbehaving postilion for a morality tale. Enamored by the "smart red jackets and tight boots of the Post-boys," Tom White was determined to drive a post-chaise. He fell in among the "evil company" of the drunk, foul-mouthed, street-racing chaise-boys, only to eventually be redeemed "from an idle post-boy to a respectable farmer."[62] Travelers may have hoped for a seasoned guide and entertaining companion, but the adventurous job also attracted young men with high risk tolerance.

Despite inconveniences such as having to interact with unreliable guides, soft infrastructure had its benefits. As early as the 1580s, Montaigne was especially enamored with a system that he encountered along the route to Rome:

> They charge you five Julios a horse, each post of two miles, and you can hire one at the same rate for two or three posts, or for several days, without putting you to any trouble about the care of the

horse at the end of the journey, for all the landlords here all take charge of one another's horses; and if the one you have hired fails you before it has reached its destination, you are entitled, by the terms of the agreements in all these cases, to replace it by another, at any of the inns on your route.[63]

In addition to its simple convenience, Montaigne was fascinated that such a system could rely on trust alone, granting the rental of an expensive asset to a stranger "altogether unknown to every person there ... the horse is wholly at your mercy, and it entirely depends upon your sense of honesty to leave him at the place you have undertaken to deposit him." In fact, it was a measure of the confidence that providers had in one another to maintain surveillance and insure against abuse.[64]

By the 1680s, the system had been formalized into the little-known financial instrument known as the *polizza di cambiatura*, or roughly, the "relay policy." Upon arrival at their first postal inn, travelers could purchase "a letter of credit addressed to the corresponding innkeeper, to be renewed every two posts where an exchange [i.e., horse relay] is made."[65] The instrument bore a clear relation to the more common "bills of exchange" (*polizza* or *lettere di cambio*), an early credit instrument that proliferated during the period.[66] By the eighteenth century, the practice of *cambiatura* could be found in other parts of Italy.[67] Historians of capitalism have long indicated the importance of credit relations to the development of eighteenth-century commerce. The *cambiatura* models a very early trust-based infrastructure for travel commerce. While coopted and later guaranteed by the state, all evidence indicates that the system arose out of the mutual interest of private and public transportation professionals, much as the postal ordinary had a century earlier.

Traveler accounts indicate that public coaches were spaces where class, gender, status, and nationality mixed. British tourists often first encountered such coaches in France and remarked upon the unique milieu within them. The traveler Peter Heylyn (d. 1662) bemoaned the state of the coach itself, in which travelers were alternately soaked by rain, plastered with dust, and jolted about on poor roads. But for all his complaints, Heylyn marveled at the company: "A man may be sure to be merry in them, were he as certain to be wholesome. This, in which we travelled, contained ten persons, as all of them commonly do; and amongst these ten, one might have found English, Scots, French, Normans, Dutch, and Italians, a jolly medley ... men and women, lords and serving men, scholars and clowns, ladies and chambermaids, priests and lay-men, gentlemen and artificers, people of all sexes and almost all ages." He concluded that "seriously, I think our coach to have been no unfit representation of the Ark."[68] The same was often remarked of postal inns. For all its dangers, public transportation infrastructure exposed travelers to an unmatched variety of society, much as a modern traveler might experience on a long-distance bus or train.

Subsidies and penalties also served to incentivize or limit forms of travel. Moryson recalled paying a tax to the duke of Florence upon hiring a hackneyman to journey to Ponte a Cappiano, "which taxe they say the Duke imposed, to withdraw Merchants from trading that way, leading to Lucca." With his usual frugal eye, Moryson remarked, "Let no man marvel, that these Princes favour the Post-masters and Innkeepers to the prejudice of strangers, because in that respect they extort great rents from them."[69] The Savoyards even contemplated requiring private carriers to bring travelers to the postmaster first to see if he could meet their offered rates. That same set of regulations prevented private carriers from also acting as guides. The state granted that privilege to postmasters exclusively, "in recognition of the service that these postmasters do."[70] This postal system was a utility that served the public, but on behalf of their prince.

Profit in Free Commerce

In addition to the *lingua postale*, the seventeenth century brought another pan-European language: that of political economy. Statesmen from Francis Bacon (d. 1626) to Jean Baptiste de Colbert (d. 1683) advocated for the state to develop national industrial and commercial power. Calling upon Cicero's characterization of finances as the "sinews of war," reformers sought to expand revenue-generating institutions.[71] Postal systems, which operated at one of the first great economies of scale, modeled private-public reinvention. Leaders no longer sought to exclude private or foreign participation in postal service but rather to channel and, most importantly, tax it.

Postal itineraries communicated the new institutional role of the post by reframing its history as the origins of the fiscal state. Early itinerary authors such as Ottavio Codogno emphasized the driving need for princes to communicate with their armies. Exemplary stories focused on couriers overcoming great obstacles to travel with the greatest speed and reliability. By contrast, in 1683, Giuseppe Miselli presented a new (and somewhat forced) view of their origins: "The head courier was called the prefect of taxes (*prefetto de fisco*). In later centuries, he was called 'curious' (*curioso*) for the responsibility he bore for the public roads, and his service to the *curia*, to whom he brought all news." Instead of a traditional connection to feats of horsemanship and military service, Miselli tied couriership to the day-to-day operations of a state fiscal system.[72]

At the same time, as late as 1585, postmasters expressed disbelief that the state could standardize postage, let alone tax it.[73] They believed that such interventions would drive customers into the eager arms of merchant carriers and foreign couriers. By the beginning of the seventeenth century, offices across the Tassis postal systems nonetheless published standardized rates that included a tax on letters. By law, the printed placard was hung on the door of the post office and above any marketplace bench. Both the Tassis and Venetian systems expressed the standardization and prosecution of violators as a means of protecting travelers and correspondents from precisely the kinds of extortions lamented by Montaigne. That transparency also manifested in the postage mark—a predecessor to the modern stamp. Officials introduced ink stamps (*bolli*) indicating the city of origin on the route between Milan and Venice around the same period.[74] These marks were intended to make the charges and record of payment to customers as well as postmen as clear as possible.[75] New generations of officials pushed for radical transparency as the best competitive strategy to secure the growing clientele of private correspondents.

By the later seventeenth century, the public demanded even further transparency and standardization from this system. Postage complaints proliferated in contemporary correspondence, as letters in the Early Modern Letters Online Union Catalog reveal. In 1679, the Dutch author Nicolaas Heinsius decried the Amsterdam city messengers as "poisonous" and "extortionate," asking instead that his correspondent utilize the twice-weekly postal packet boat. In 1728, the Dutch scholar Pieter Burman wrote to the philosopher Jacques-Philippe d'Orville to determine "whether the controllers of the public courier post are extortionate in their charges," and he quoted a price encountered in Dijon.[76] Quibbling about the cost of service nonetheless indicated acceptance of and even high expectations for service. Circumventing postage was a far preferable form of resistance to utilizing unlicensed competitors or assaulting the courier.

Running ordinaries and providing travel services further lodged the postal service—and by extension, the state—in the commercial sphere.

Canny postal officials had always marketed the mutual benefit of such an arrangement, especially regarding state surveillance of and intervention in communications. The post-Westphalian shift was that of rhetoric, away from confessional control and toward mutual so-called conveniences that benefited the prince as well as the public. By 1660, Venice had instituted a public tax on foreign letters received in the city, which initially consisted of a uniform *soldo* per ounce.[77] The Provveditori di Comun's 1662 postal tariffs explained such costs as subsidies of the system, which served "private persons as well as businessmen." As the Venetians formulated their postage rates, they looked to other states for examples, noting how "in foreign states [these measures] add considerable gains to their treasuries."[78] In 1672, control over the French posts was similarly transferred to the Fermé Generale, the state revenue-gathering service.[79] The English and Swedish systems, which originated in the mid-seventeenth century, held that public-private postal systems must be self-funding as a basic premise. Authorities further hoped to generate profit that could be channeled to other arms of governance.[80]

Free commerce was also in the air at Westphalia. The Peace Conferences of Westphalia (1645–1648) brought together representatives from across Europe. Münster and Osnabrück were geographically central but distant backwaters in comparison with the hubs of pan-European commerce and communication. At the request of his envoys, Ferdinand III (1608–1657) wrote to the postmistress general Alexandrine von Rye und Taxis (d. 1666, o. 1628–1645) to shift postal routes from Cologne and establish a post house in Münster.[81] In 1645, Ferdinand ordered that biweekly ordinary couriers travel between the imperial delegation and court as further affirmation of his desire to "get to the bottom of things, about whether the French are serious about peace and with what conditions."[82] The establishment of postal routes symbolized the first step toward repairing diplomatic relations.

At the conferences, the Hanseatic states joined the Swedes as some of the loudest proponents of free commerce. A 1646 manifesto titled "Memorial for Free Trade" demanded that the "free exercise of commerce" be reinstated as it was believed to have existed in 1618. "Without the liberty and security of cities and routes on water and land, the freedom of commerce (along with soul, life, and growth) cannot exist, but rather like the bees are driven away by smoke, flees to foreign free places with notable harm." Along with the removal of customs houses and blockades, the manifesto called for "affordable postage" and guarantees that postal routes would be "unhindered."[83] The fact that a Westphalian rhetoric of free commerce now grouped postal service with safe access to roads and waterways underscored the diversity of stakeholders in communications systems. Ordinary postal service as public service—in the sense of a utility—marked a major transition from the extraordinary couriers of the Renaissance.

Much as postal routes represented good conversation among states, they had come to symbolize the strength of social ties more generally. Postage was not just a tax: it involved the state in a measure of relationships. A book could be deemed "not worth the cost of postage," while letters might be complimented by saying that "no money is better spent than that paid for postage."[84] The English cleric Edmund Elys showed his great admiration for the scholar Thomas Smith when he offered to cover the full postage for any letters that Smith might deign to send him.[85] Despite the common practice in which a recipient paid to receive a letter—much like the twentieth-century collect call—by the eighteenth century, it could be rude to leave one's correspondent responsible for the postage.[86]

While serving both prince and public, postal service was never intended to be a level playing field. Private letters subsidized state letters. Post offices carried public (state) letters "freely franked" (*franca libero*) in return for the state's guarantee of their privileges.[87] The selective extension of free or reduced franking was the carrot to censorship's stick: governments could intervene in society by subsidizing some mail and penalizing other mail, much as they channeled travel. Clergy, for example, often received franking privileges throughout the eighteenth century.[88]

State bureaucracies had also ballooned across the seventeenth century, and by the eighteenth, many more officials claimed franking privileges. English correspondents regularly traded favors so their mail might travel freely franked. Members of Parliament used their signature in place of a postage stamp. This loophole was so widely exploited that William Bishop concluded that "a daily post from Bath is not likely to be granted for 'tis said three parts of the letters from thence are franked."[89] In later centuries, the free or reduced franking of newspapers encouraged a journalism boom in the United States, where putting its citizens into "good conversation" with one another became part and parcel of a nation-building campaign.[90]

In fact, postal service was increasingly approached more as a right than a privilege. In 1659, the English attorney John Hill authored a scathing polemic against state postal monopoly. He described the imported continental practice as impinging on the "liberty and birthright of every Englishman."[91] Hill framed his arguments in terms of English common law but advanced the same argument as any German *Landespost* or Italian cavallari would: that monopoly and the administration of tax-farmers that it enabled were harmful to society. The public deserved the greatest possible access at the lowest price, or a "Penny Post." A few decades later, a former customs house official made the London Penny Post a reality. William Dockwra established a packet service that would carry deliveries several times a day within the city boundaries for the low price of a penny.[92] An advertising pamphlet listed its "conveniences," or the many day-to-day uses of such a system:

- All Gentlemen, Countrey-Chapmen, &c. can give notice of their Arrival to Town.
- Shopkeepers and Tradesmen send for what they want to their Workmen.
- Much time saved in Sollicitation for Money.
- Appointments of Meetings among men of Business.
- Bills dispersed for Publication of any Concern.
- Summons or Tickets convey'd to all parts.
- Brewers Entries safely sent to the Excise-Office.
- Lawyers and Clients mutually correspond.
- Patients send to Doctors, Apothecaries, &c. for what they want.
- ...
- And the Poor Prisoners can now address to their Creditors or Benefactors for one Penny, and save 5 pence to buy them a Dinner.
- Many other Benefits are to be had by this Conveyance, which (though for brevity omitted) the Ingenious will find out.[93]

Letters manifested the relationships that bound together commercial society. Such conveniences had gone from luxuries to essentials within the space of a century. In fact, Dockwra's service competed with the Royal Posts before being absorbed by them. The ensuing legal conflict between the Penny Post and the Royal Posts paralleled similar agents, services, and debates across Europe.[94] Perhaps unsurprisingly, free commerce by way of monopoly remains the contradiction at the heart of utilities even today.

It is true that postal service had been fundamentally reinvented during the late seventeenth and early eighteenth centuries. The reluctant opening of state-sponsored postal routes to private travelers as well as correspondents—advanced, as always, by postal officials and their competitors—had become a foundation of the new fiscal state, alongside other guarantees of free commerce. The same postal officials who produced itineraries conceived of providing expansive public services to private patrons under the auspices of state privileges. The state archives of Turin, Venice, and Milan all preserve "grand plans" submitted to states in the 1620s by postal officials claiming the ability to renew infrastructure and thus make local services not only possible, but profitable.[95] The Thirty Years' War may have delayed implementation, but the speed with which the stagecoach overtook Europe demonstrated the successful exportation of soft infrastructure and the perception of postal networks as the sinews of European society.[96]

By the end of the seventeenth and beginning of the eighteenth century, a vast swath of European society shared familiarity with the language and culture of the post. Administrative techniques that first developed in the transalpine posts had been exported as far as Sweden and England. The result was a truly international lexicon: post, posting, traveling posthaste; by diligence, ordinary, or stagecoach; with postmaster or postilion; paying postage or franking, and so on. The similarities among postal systems invited constant comparison and contrast as travelers were surprised to find differences in the quality and cost of services on their journeys. The postal guide smoothed the way, whether embodied by the postilion or as a post-book in a traveler's pocket.

Print publicized the professional expertise of couriers and officials. This radical transparency was strategic: it advertised with precision the accessibility and predictability of postal infrastructure, especially when contrasted with the extortion and scams to which a traveler otherwise might fall prey. Predictability was in the very name of the postal coach known as the "diligence." Itineraries accompanied and amplified the clear communication of routes and rates in posted placards. They advanced the personal prospects of postmasters like Ottavio Codogno, and later Giuseppe Miselli and Giovanni Maria Vidari, who used their books to advertise state postal commercial activity and their own ability to balance patronage from princes with public commerce. They integrated postal service into the history of the fiscal state, in line with the new interest in political economy.

This free commerce model of postal service of the late seventeenth and early eighteenth centuries introduced many of the tropes associated with postal systems today. It brought the postage stamp, the postman, and an enduring association between postal service and nation-building, from connecting cities to one another to integrating the hinterlands by way of letters and newspapers. Early modern postal systems were primarily concerned with regulating international rather than domestic mail, although the distinction was never clear-cut. Local letter carriers had likely always been employed in some capacity, but they began to make more frequent appearance in post office records as full employees, akin to couriers. Artistic depictions of such letter dispensers (*dispensatori*) appeared alongside the more heroic galloping couriers.[97] By the eighteenth century, political leaders paid new attention to the matter of tying the outskirts to the urban center in new plans for local services. Enlightened despots rebuilt the hubs and aligned the long spokes of empire.

Take, for example, Austrian Milan. The War of Spanish Succession (1701–1714) shifted the duchy of Milan from the Spanish to the Austrian branch of Habsburg rulers. While overseen by the Austrian-appointed general director of the posts, the post office of Milan remained a network of proprietors. The postmaster general was a distant and largely uninvolved figurehead.[98] The postal lieutenant, Giovanni Battista Balbi, earned a sizable salary of 3,300 lire and, as Ottavio Codogno had, oversaw an extensive staff, including fourteen couriers and additional servants, notaries, and lawyers. In addition to the post house, there was a full shop (*bottegha*) at the Piazza dei Mercanti, described as "the office on the Piazza, or where they distribute the letters." That office was run by a different person, called the "head" (*capo*), who oversaw an additional seven staff members who likely acted as letter distributors.[99]

Balbi had grand plans for a more comprehensive local postal service. As it stood, foot messengers received and distributed mail in Milan's inns. His plan listed the messengers by name, the regions they served, and even details about the inns where they distributed letters. A brief excerpt represents the network's thoroughness, as well as its reliance on a wider hospitality industry: messengers for Romagnano, Valsesia, Verallo, Borgo Mangero, Oleggio, Riviera d'Orta, Novara, and Vigevano could be found in the Inn of the Falcon. Additional messengers for Novara, Miasino, and Vigevano lodged at the Inn of the Hat. Those for Caravaggio, Treviglio, Gerra d'Adda, Bergamo, Como, Crema, and the Valtellina lodged at the Inn of the Crown. Messengers for Lodi could be found in the Two Blades, while those of Lindau and Lugano were in the historic postal inn of the Three Kings.[100] Balbi proposed to Milan's new rulers that the post office incorporate these, as well as services to local villages, while explicitly recognizing that "such business" had not preoccupied the office in the past.[101]

Most postal histories take officials at their word that expanding into local coverage fulfilled a cherished public service mandate. That may well have been true, but there was also new hope for the financial profitability of postal services. Private competitors such as the London Penny Post demonstrated the existence of a promising market sector, and population and literacy rates were on the rise. Nonetheless, market takeovers of domestic mail services resembled those of the international ordinaries of earlier decades, in that they could feel disastrous and even tyrannical to the original proprietors. The expansion of the postal service came at the cost of both long-standing and innovative alternative systems of mail-carrying.

Despite the rising rhetoric of "free commerce," postal systems remained tied to competitive international relations. Then, as now, tourists and foreigners were hit by fees and restrictions harder than native residents were. The public coach and Roman *cambiatura* had a reputation for being remarkably egalitarian, but they also enabled travel surveillance. The next chapter will follow these developments into the final bifurcation of the modern postal system into domestic civil service and foreign intelligence operations.

CHAPTER 7

High Towers and Black Chambers
Twin Legends of Postal Service

Postal interference featured prominently in the manifesto that the Swedish king Gustavus Adolphus (d. 1632) issued upon entering the Thirty Years' War (1618–1648). The declaration achieved the widest-known circulation of a pamphlet up to that time, appearing in five languages and twenty-three editions.[1] It alleged that Habsburg agents had seized Gustavus's letters to the prince of Transylvania, and "after they had been opened, and false glosses put upon them, to load His Majesty with the people's hatred, and render him odious everywhere, they were maliciously published; and the courier who carried them was put in prison and treated as a criminal by open and public violence contrary to the law of nations." In this sense, the manifesto advanced the unprecedented claim that letter interception and republication constituted a casus belli.[2]

The Swedish pamphlet explicitly called postal interference a breach of an overarching code of conduct of international relations. The Transylvanian intercept was just one example of the "thousands of secret and open practices and threats made use of by the Spaniards and their partisans."[3] Several such letter interceptions and publications took place over the course of the war, including the publication of entire chancelleries left behind in the aftermath of battle.[4] Intercepting letters and arresting their courier nonetheless contravened the common custom of sanctity for postal service and its agents.

This chapter looks to the later Baroque period as the source of both a legend and a black legend of postal service: whereas the first emphasized the heroism, nobility, and self-sacrifice of postal agents, the second proclaimed their villainy, pettiness, and self-service. Both spins on the history relied on shifting notions of privacy and publicity to make their case, as proponents and critics of state postal service disagreed about for whom and from whom letters should be kept guarded. The private-public function of the post seemed to be at a breaking point: either postmasters served a broad public impartially, guarding letters against such interference, or they only served the jealousy of princes.

We can understand early modern and especially post-Westphalian views on the default publicity or privacy of letters as whether states should have default access to the content of letters sent by state posts—namely, whether postal services should observe secrecy of correspondence, or "official secrecy." Secrecy of correspondence dictates a default privacy, or protection from the state: letters do not concern state authorities until adequately shown to do so. Private and foreign users of postal service often claimed that all users of state postal service should be accorded secrecy of correspondence. Yet official secrecy describes a state's right to undertake surveillance in the interest of national security. Official secrecy is often extended to include the identities of the individuals carrying out this surveillance and their means of doing so. In practice, this means a default "publicity": correspondents must assume that their letters concern the state unless they have ascertained otherwise—or Schrodinger's letter.

Despite subsequent advances in communications technologies, balancing the secrecy of correspondence and official secrecy remains a quandary for modern signals intelligence.[5] Official secrecy dictates the de facto publicity of the private letter, but it also protects the secrecy of intelligence operations. Here, we find a second axis, with official secrecy on one end and the public's right to know on the other. Whereas official secrecy shields intelligence operations from scrutiny, the public's right to know sees the state's desire to shield its operations as corruption and conspiracy. In this view, only full transparency of the state to its citizens or an international audience can prevent evil. Later philosophers such as Jeremy Bentham fully realized these ideas as theory, and yet such dilemmas preoccupied postal officials much earlier, as well as critics who went so far as to claim that state letters should be thrown open to a wider public.[6]

At the core of these debates lay the fact that despite their reliance on the Tassis systems, Protestants and foreign nationals were never entirely comfortable with them. The 1629 Swedish invasion of central Europe and the appointment of Johann von den Birghden as the Swedish postmaster in Frankfurt had briefly established a system capable of challenging Tassis primacy.[7] Protestants were not willing to turn back the clock to the prewar monopolization of state postal service by imperial appointees. In 1658, Brunswick-Lüneburg, Hessen-Kassel, Brandenburg, and Sweden held their own postal conference in Hildesheim, with the goal of cementing an alternative postal union.[8] Postilions, postmasters, and the wider public had advocated for brand renewal for the Tassis international postal system for several decades. The collaboration of new rivals with state mandates meant that the Tassis international postal system needed postwar revitalization, without delay.

Chapter 6 showed how postal guides advertised new transparency to travelers. This chapter addresses how postal systems offered secrecy of correspondence—meaning the protection of letter privacy—to correspondents. Following the example set by their employees and competitors, the Tassis embraced print to advertise their services to Protestant Europe, including Britain. They commissioned cartography and genealogies to depict a family above imputations of espionage and responsible for a legendary postal service. The reinvention of the Tassis family as Thurn und Taxis went hand in hand with the reinvention of postal service as state beneficence for universal utility. This final reinvention of the international posts proved to be a mixed success. While Thurn und Taxis remains German aristocracy today, this final reinvention was, in many ways, the beginning of the end for the Bergamaschi international posts. Europe's postmasters and postmistress generals recast themselves as nobility rather than the descendants of servants to many masters.

Commissioning genealogies and embracing postal cartography memorialized a Tassis legacy as inventors and exporters of the posts. Nobility aided Tassis postmasters and their French counterparts as they moved among the status-conscious circles of the post-Westphalian diplomatic era. In combination with new (recognized, if not always obeyed) limits upon state surveillance, postal propaganda emphasized the nobility of public service. This legacy was itself attuned to the modernizing efforts of absolutist courts.[9] Postal maps and related literature evoked both a neoclassical tradition and a novel focus on infrastructure as a national project intended for a largely domestic usership. New genealogies rewrote the Tassis family's origins as aristocratic, even royal. This was the era of domestication of postal practice, which eventually culminated in a partnership between postal service and the nation-state. Duncan Campbell-Smith characterizes this mythos as "the enduring perception of the Post Office as the friendly face of the state, and of local post offices as one of the last bastions of village life in many areas."[10] The centralization and nationalization of postal infrastructure—of what had been a fundamentally international system—divorced the domestic from the international mails.

This reinvention took place even as postal intelligencing operations reached new levels of sophistication with the advent of the cryptanalysis operation known as the "black chamber," or postal lodge. The late seventeenth through nineteenth centuries was a new age of systematic mail interception and intelligence-gathering operations based in post offices. Official secrecy continued a long vein of *arcana imperii*, or secrets of state, in the governance of postal systems. The black chambers that operated in Vienna and Paris were open secrets among diplomats and even well-versed private correspondents. The result was a Janus-faced postal service: espionage, counterespionage, censorship, and surveillance were known risks, and yet they were gradually displaced from the public eye by the visibility of the postal newspaper, stagecoach, or increasingly the friendly local letter dispenser. From the outset, the invention of modern privacy was intrinsically linked to bureaucratic doublespeak surrounding it.

Black chambers remain largely absent from postal historiography or are treated as a perversion of postal practice therein. They are primarily associated with the interference of powerful (continental) chancellors and secretaries of state in communications infrastructure. Anglo-American postal histories emphasize instead the role of the postal service in building the nation-state and expanding public services. Placing the black chambers in a longer historical trajectory reveals that they were merely the latest guise of postal intelligencing. Signals intelligence operations were rumored to exist in key postal hubs such as Augsburg, Milan, and Turin as early as the 1580s. The international postal ordinaries established in that decade routed all mailbags through a central post house under a single postmaster for purposes of surveillance. Postal officials emphasized to governors the danger of messengers going to and fro as a matter of state security. They explained channeling mail through a central post office as bookkeeping, but it was well known that the practice also aided intelligence gathering. This was precisely why postmasters abroad worked with embassy officials to defend the ambassador's letters from similar incursion—a privileged status that diplomatic pouches retain today.

Whether it was framed as secrecy of correspondence, official secrecy, or the right to know, the mailbag remained at the center of the tug-of-war between the state and civil society. The expansion of mail-carrying to private clients—now increasingly termed the "public" and a "public service"—meant involving many more stakeholders in the state, for whom such debates became very personal. This chapter explores how nobility inflated the importance of postal public service on the one hand, while satirical literature punctured it on the other. The mailbag novel, a subgenre of epistolary literature, used the postal service to mock mutually exclusive expectations. How could you claim secrecy for your letters and yet justify opening another's?

Postal Propaganda: Pamphlets, Genealogies, and Maps

By the mid-seventeenth century, postmaster and postmistress generals were no longer the day-to-day faces of the post house. The Tassis had stepped back from the new incarnation of the postal service as a service industry. They continued to manage public relations for their family brand and their rulers, but they did so through lease-holding lieutenants and new media, including print. They also employed language more consistent with the post-Westphalian culture of international relations, which emphasized highly orchestrated harmony among the European elite.

Participants in the Westphalian Peace Conferences (1645–1648) by and large sought to roll back the changes wrought by decades of war. The notion of an international order composed of largely independent, sovereign nation-states would take several more decades to crystallize.[11] Instead, dynastic politics and composite monarchies remained driving forces in international relations. The Peace Conferences nonetheless brought a new format for international diplomacy: the aristocratic congress. Noble representatives and their bureaucratic staff conducted diplomacy with all the pomp, circumstance, and jostling of any Baroque court. The international conference set the mold for later august assemblies, from the Congress of Vienna (1814–1815) to the Paris Peace Conference (1919–1920).[12]

Postal practice continued to evolve in parallel with diplomacy. The later seventeenth century was also the age of the grand international postal congress and resulting postal union. Whereas earlier postal treaties took place in the post house—haggled among family members—finalizing a French Road was a more aristocratic affair.[13] Representatives of the Spanish Countess of Oñate and Villamediana (d. 1684) and of the imperial Count of Thurn und Taxis (d. 1676) gathered at the house of the French general intendant, Baron de Ligniéres (d. 1668, o. 1651–1668). The conference closely followed the Peace of the Pyrenees (1659), which settled armed conflict between France and Spain. Representatives agreed on new postal relations between France, Spain, and the Netherlands. Mail would travel between Irun (in the Basque region) and Paris in 5 to 5.5 days (6 to 6.5 in winter) and Paris and Brussels in 40 to 42 (48 to 50) hours.[14] The accord guaranteed interlocking postal service like that of the Italian and German roads.

Such new agreements also showed that Tassis brand revitalization was well underway. As early as the spring of 1633, the postmistress general, Alexandrine von Rye und Taxis (1589–1666, o. 1628–1645), had negotiated a treaty with the postmaster of foreign mails, Thomas Witherings (d. 1651, o. 1632–1640), for English mail to travel by the posts of Antwerp and Calais.[15] A surviving inventory of correspondents in the Tassis mailbag attests to the postal service's wide range of clients. It included hard-line Puritan members of Parliament, Charles II's secretary of state, and prominent members of London's merchant community.[16]

In 1660, the imperial branch of the family in Brussels produced an English-language pamphlet. That advertisement survives in two places today: the Thurn und Taxis family archives and the British National Archives. Commissioned by the "Count de la Tour & Tassis, General Hereditary of the Post for his Imperial Majesty," the pamphlet endorsed the expansion of existing service between London, Antwerp, and Brussels. It promised improvement in speed and security "for the benefit of the Merchants, particularly the English."[17] Printed pamphlets like this one were likely aimed at members of Parliament and meant to encourage their approval of a pending agreement between the Tassis postmistress general and the English postmaster general Henry Bishop (d. 1691, o. 1660–1663). The Tassis offered increased frequency of service to ensure that letters to London that had been "four or five days on the way, sometimes longer" would now arrive in just two days and nights, "all this upon the condition that in England they do the like" of dispatching mail to

Flanders twice a week. Commercial advantage held top billing: more frequent mail meant "so much the fresher advises wherein the merchants on this side of the sea, & especially the Hollanders, have hitherto had a great advantage of the English." The speed of news had relative, as well as absolute, value: the pamphlet made the case that the English could not compete with their Dutch rivals without equally fast mail. Not only were the Tassis continuing to bid for Protestant business, but they were also doing so using this language of political economy, and in countries outside their traditional sphere of influence.

Competitive advantage was marketed more explicitly than political surveillance. "Not to speak of the interest of the State," the pamphlet added, almost as an afterthought, "wherein, in point of honor, how far the King of England may think himself concerned."[18] The flipped priority is fascinating when we consider the context of Restoration Britain in which it was received. Charles II (1630-1685) was just establishing his rule after the revolutionary English protectorate. Signals intelligence had played a decisive role in the preceding decades of conflict between British royalists and republicans. Charles and his successor, James II (1633-1701), would continue to monitor conspiracies that stretched across the English Channel.[19] The Tassis campaign took a different tack, however, distancing their postal service from political interference with the mailbag. This was likely a wise move and aligned with the mixed sympathies of their foreign audiences. Winning over new clientele such as the English and maintaining their dominant role required a public relations campaign that portrayed Thurn und Taxis as above the dirty business of espionage.

In fact, the 1660 pamphlet was just the latest salvo in a long-standing campaign to refine and redeem the Tassis brand. When the Countess Rye und Taxis inherited the administration of the Thurn und Taxis imperial postal system from her husband, she also suffered from his public relations headaches. This included the ongoing and highly publicized court battle with the Frankfurt postmaster Johann von den Birghden over his dismissal, featured in chapter 5 of this book. It also encompassed new claims against the imperial post pressed by regional competitors (*Landesposts*) across the Holy Roman Empire and the Netherlands at the Westphalian Peace Conferences. Countess Rye und Taxis nominally held her office on behalf of her minor son (the count of Thurn und Taxis of the 1660 pamphlet), but in a common pattern of widow-postmistresses, she played an active administrative role until her death in 1666.

Soon after the end of the war and the death of her husband, Countess Rye und Taxis commissioned a recent young graduate at Leuven,

Jules Chifflet, to create a finely illustrated genealogy of the family dedicated to her young son.[20] Chifflet and the later genealogist Engelbert Flacchio adopted many aspects of an earlier Neapolitan work, Francesco Zazzera's *Della nobilità dell'Italia* (1628). Zazzera posited the marriage of a "Taccio," count of Valsassina (north of Camerata Cornello), to Milanese nobility, a member of the della Torre family. Chifflet further added that the Tassis descended from a Hungarian king, "Taxis," located far back in antiquity.[21] Zazzera and Chifflet worked with both the Tassis family and their agents to gather evidence of their noble descent and a family tradition of public service. Relying on both Zazzera and Chifflet as references, the postmaster general Lamoral II Tassis (d. 1677) received imperial approval for the adoption of the name Thurn (German for *Torre*, meaning "tower") und Taxis in 1649/1650.[22] It was a key step toward securing a seat for the postmaster and postmistress generals among the elite post-Westphalian diplomatic order.

Offering commercial competitive advantage was one public relations tactic, but so was this reframing of the Tassis family history. Scandals of past decades had rendered Tassis postal services distasteful to a foreign, Protestant audience. Critics especially resented what they viewed as postal officials' partisan interference in the mail. Emphasizing the family's history of imperial service solidified its contemporary credentials by recasting celebration of Habsburg symbology as family pride, even when such symbols had clear contemporary political implications for the character of a post-Westphalian European order.

The lavishly engraved illustrations of Chifflet's *Les marques d'honneur de la maison de Tassis* (1645) evoked Baroque neoclassicism (figure 19), but Chifflet and especially Flacchio also drew upon a medieval, crusading past. The Lombard progenitor Taxis had allegedly married his two daughters to two della Torre brothers out of admiration for their chivalry and peacekeeping. Flacchio described them as "two young Frenchmen of royal blood . . . who lived civilly in the [Valle Sassina] and who conducted themselves so well that they were loved by all." The della Torre family combatted an undisputed enemy, the "infamous heretics called *Fratticelli*, the Anabaptists of Munster," as well as "purging the crimes of some Milanese who had been infected with such disorders."[23] Despite the crusading rhetoric, emphasizing the pious loyalty of the Tassis over their national allegiances made for a more ecumenical history in post-Westphalian Europe.

Claiming unfailing loyalty to the Catholic faith also provided a history consistent with the new interreliance of Bourbon and Habsburg

FIGURE 19. An elaborate allegorical image from Jules Chifflet, *Les marques d'honneur de la maison de Tassis* (1645). The badger (*tasso*), double-headed Habsburg eagle, and tower (della Torre) are featured liberally, while the fantastical neoclassical design speaks to the Roman legacy inherited by the Tassis family. Image from Bayerische Staatsbibliothek, München, 2 Geneal. 38.

postal systems. European diplomatic communications trended French in the decades to come. Countess Rye und Taxis kept much of her correspondence in French and appeared to struggle with Italian. Both Chifflet's and Flacchio's genealogies were published in French.[24] Their target audience was a Francophone cosmopolitan elite from Brussels to Paris and even London.

In making their case for the nobility of the Tassis, the genealogists largely dropped any reference to banking, trade, or even postal service.

Zazzera postulated that the Tassis family prefigured, rather than derived from, the postal tradition: the inclusion of a horn derived from the ample game in their home valley (including badgers, or *tassi*), "although many err in believing that they took the horn as fathers of the posts."[25] Hunting evoked a more aristocratic activity than did couriers riding in relay. For more recent generations, Zazzera noted every Tassis family member who was the ambassador for various notables, especially "Il Colonnello" Giovanni Battista Tassis (d. 1588), who had died in battle.[26] Chifflet and Flacchio placed an even greater emphasis on military and ambassadorial service, and Flacchio especially highlighted the marriage alliances that had further linked the Tassis to nobility and even royalty across Europe. Commissioned by the Brussels-based branch of the family, the books devoted relatively little space to family branches that remained in Italy. In this respect, the campaign continued the century-long rivalry for the singular patrimony of the imperial postmaster general.

How was this public relations campaign received? We see some successes, notably represented in the postal itinerary genre. Take, for example, the comparison between *New Itinerary of the Posts of the World* (1608) and *Burattino's Directions* (1682). In *New Itinerary*, Ottavio Codogno described an ideal postal official primarily in terms of his administrative acumen and prudence. In *Burattino's Directions*, Giuseppe Miselli described the ideal postmaster as "illustrious through clarity of blood," in addition to being "practiced in foreign places and tongues, and well-informed as to politics and the state."[27] While Miselli's own background was in the papal post, he admired above all "the Lord Barons Tassis, who possess the advantage of centuries of enjoyment of the prerogatives of their position, the inheritance of their most illustrious family, made so in return for the best service rendered to the Emperors and Austrian Princes in regulating, building, and enriching that wonderful invention of the Post throughout the Empire, Spain, Italy, the Netherlands, and Burgundy."[28] He finished this high praise by referencing Zazzera's account of the family's long-held noble status. Whereas Codogno had repeatedly emphasized the Tassis family's service to both prince and public, Miselli's account stressed that the elite social standing of the postal service matched that of its most famous patrons.[29]

The greatest evidence of international reception is emulation. The Tassis continued to set an example for postmastership as far abroad as England, where leaders anxiously sought equal social footing on the international stage to remain commercially competitive. The first English postmaster general with whom the Countess Rye und Taxis worked in 1633 had been Thomas Witherings, who was previously a mercer by trade. In calling for Witherings's removal in 1640, the English secretary of state claimed that the noble foreign postmasters were disinclined to deal with the low-born Witherings. Witherings's successor, the postmaster general Henry Bishop, was the second son of a baronet, and therefore somewhat closer in social standing to his continental counterparts.[30] From Bishop's appointment onward, postmaster generals were forbidden from taking part in foreign trade, despite the origins of foreign mail service with the Guild of Merchant Adventurers and the Stranger's Post.[31]

Canonization of family lore was also a natural extension of the legal defenses that the Tassis had mounted for decades. From their first publications into the nineteenth century, Zazzera and Chifflet's genealogies were a touchstone in the defense of the Tassis family monopoly. The Biblioteca Civica Angelo Mai in Bergamo holds a representative collection called the Raccolta Tassiana.[32] A manuscript note on one collection of documents reads "against those who argue that the municipal messengers do not oppose the nobility." A long-standing rivalry between merchant messengers, or cavallari, and the Tassis could now be reframed as commoners challenging their social betters. The preserved legal cases feature elaborate printed family trees alongside the usual notarial evidence.[33] Genealogies were valuable, admissible evidence in the legal struggle to control the posts.

To the pamphlet, genealogies, and family trees, we can add a final propagandizing genre: postal cartography. Michele Tassis (d. 1711), a descendant of the Tassis family of Milan, sponsored the first postal map of Italy in 1695, Giacomo Cantelli's *L'Italia con le sue poste* (figure 20).[34] Like the genealogies, the map promoted the historical accomplishments of the family and their strong association with Habsburg power in Italy. The cartouche featuring two riders declared the maps' patron as the "corriero maggiore in perpetuity of His Catholic Majesty." Much as the inventor of the boat had "united the most divided provinces with a piece of wood," so should the people "applaud with grateful voices your Most Excellent House, from which the introduction of the post they have reaped the benefit of becoming a *Patria commune*." Several centuries before the realization of a national unity, the mapmaker advanced the claim that the Tassis, as inventors of the posts, had brought cultural unity to Italy's politically divided landscape.

The administrative units of the 1690s and beyond were nation-states, borders, and grand roads. The organization of printed postal itineraries was comparatively chaotic, but there seems to have been a strong contemporaneous trend to organize space in more national terms after the 1680s, most likely influenced by these maps.[35] Creators consolidated

FIGURE 20. Giacomo Cantelli, *L'Italia con le sue poste* (1695). The cartouche features a passenger traveling by post, accompanied by a postilion wielding a whip. The text lauds the service provided to Italy by the Tassis family. Map from David Rumsey Map Collection, David Rumsey Map Center, Stanford University Libraries.

smaller routes or left them out entirely. Cantelli focused attention on the Brenner Pass postal route—the administration of which was a point of pride for the Tassis of Milan and Venice, as well as the Tassis-Bordogna of Trento. By comparison to the small, ephemeral itineraries with their handwritten notes, the Cantelli map was an elegant engraving. A copy printed on fabric held at the British Library seems like a luxurious souvenir brought back by a Grand Tourist, a diplomatic gift, or the latest innovation in the pocketable post-book, but with an elite owner in mind.[36] Such postal maps preceded the golden age of grand state-sponsored cartography projects, but they also advanced similarly nationalistic goals and marked a distinct shift from the catch-as-catch-can publication of itineraries.

Postal maps tied together a history of establishing postal systems with the modernizing projects of the late Baroque and early Enlightenment states. We can look to the 1660 English-language pamphlet as evidence of a commerce-oriented ecumenicism, whereas genealogies illustrated the nobility of public service. Maps monumentalized the postal service, but they also—significantly—portrayed postal infrastructure as a form of territorial sovereignty. Similar arguments have long been advanced about roadbuilding and road-mapping projects in France and Britain, or the US Postal Service.³⁷

The Cantelli map was intended to celebrate the Tassis legacy, but it soon came to symbolize the changing of the guard. Rationalized depiction of postal systems preceded and accompanied many administrative efforts toward centralization and renewal. The Treaty of Utrecht (1714) gave possession of Mantua, Milan, Sardinia, Naples, and Sicily to the Austrian Habsburgs. Emperor Charles VI (1685-1740) sought to create a unified postal service throughout his expanded domain as early as 1718. By 1722, he had awarded the Austrian von Paar family new monopoly rights.³⁸ By 1747, Empress Maria Theresa (1717-1780) seized the Tyrolean posts from the Taxis-Bordogna family branch and the Italian posts soon after, subordinating them to the general post office of Vienna. She appointed an imperial postmaster of Italy, and by 1751, new campaigns to reform and consolidate the Italian posts were well underway.³⁹ The cartouches of later postal maps no longer celebrated the postmasters, by and large; instead, they lauded the rulers who had commissioned both the postal systems and cartography. Campaigns to render public-private postal service synonymous with state power had come to their natural resolution. Like roads or taxes, rulers now lay direct claim to their postal services as a mark of territorial sovereignty.

Official Secrecy: The State's Hidden Face

Toward the end of the Thirty Years' War, postal officials themselves applied an increasingly commercial rather than political logic to information security. Even the aging imperial postmaster of Venice, Ferdinando Tassis (d. 1648), became increasingly opposed to interfering with the mail. In 1643, he sent a dispatch note to the postmistress general's lieutenant:

> This week the Dutch and German merchants called me before the Doge to complain that they are dismayed by the packages arriving opened from Augsburg and even more so those that come from Cologne. They send letters to Amsterdam by a different road which takes an additional eight days, by which they have experienced some business losses. They seek another option because the

opening of packages of another is a barbarous thing and not to be practiced in any part of the world. . . . I beg your Honor to tell me how this has come to pass and what I might do, as I have a bad feeling about this matter, for my part.[40]

Tassis received a standard response that the letters had to be opened in order to be correctly sorted and priced. Ferdinando was not satisfied, expressing his opinion: "This seems badly conceived, and I have made a complaint to His Majesty and await a response from the Countess [Rye und Taxis], because the breaking of merchant's seals and those of others goes against every conscience and duty." The surviving letter of complaint employed similarly strong language, calling the breaking of seals "a barbarous and strange thing."[41]

Since antiquity, merchants had employed wax seals as a means of quality control over goods. Seals marked ownership and attested to the untampered nature of the goods within. Composed of beeswax, resin, tallow, or shellac, letter seals served a similar purpose for letter writers by the seventeenth century. Pressing the hot wax with a signet, such as on a ring or fob, authenticated the sender. An intact seal had been used to indicate the authority of state or notarized documents, but the sixteenth and seventeenth centuries saw its increasing use to indicate the privacy of correspondence.[42] The seal served as material evidence of a new cultural expectation, as did the occasional additional expense of utilizing a blank sheet of paper to provide an envelope. The recent rediscovery of the Brienne trove, a chest of around 2,600 undelivered letters in the Hague dating to between 1689 and 1706, illuminated another practice, called "letter-locking." Through intricate folding and occasional additions of wax or thread, a letter could be transformed into its own secure container. Researchers of the Brienne trove have categorized several such locks in terms of their relative security, even identifying a select few as potentially self-destructing in the event of tampering. In general, however, the locking served a similar purpose to the seal: providing a means of authentication and the ability to identify tampering quickly.[43]

The postmistress general and her lieutenant justified opening mail as an accounting practice. The English ambassador Sir Balthazar Gerbier (1592–1663) was nonetheless convinced that the postmistress was systematically copying, deciphering, and forwarding mail as well as opening it. He even wrote a treatise for his successor on how to circumvent the postmistress's operations in Brussels.[44] Gerbier echoed and amplified the Tassis postmasters' complaints in describing the opening of mail as even a type of sexual violation.[45] In fact, postal subterfuge served both espionage and counterespionage purposes. Nadine Akkerman has found, for example, that the postmistress helped to carry the correspondence of the queen of Bohemia, Elizabeth Stuart, thus avoiding surveillance by her brother, the king of England.[46]

Akkerman credits the postmistress general with making the Taxis postal system cross-confessional as well as international.[47] In fact, postal officials along the German and Swiss roads had long carried Protestant mail, although perhaps not always to its intended destination. Whereas the prewar years of Counter-Reformation had delineated trustworthiness along the lines of national and religious identity, by the mid-seventeenth century, the entire framework had shifted. With the cessation of open conflict and an increasing intellectual movement toward freedom of commerce, the Tassis pivoted once again. Postmasters along the German and Swiss roads shied away from the appearance of impropriety. Impartiality, speed, and security had come to characterize the ideal postmaster, who served the state by serving its cosmopolitan businessmen.[48] At the same time, the postmistress was defending against renewed appeals by Birghden for recompense; Birghden astutely continued to direct popular pressure against the Tassis by publishing pamphlets proclaiming their wrongdoing.[49]

The Tassis family's internal correspondence should also always be read considering intrafirm jostling. In forwarding his client's complaints, the middle-aged Ferdinando may have been expressing his own resentment toward the young postmistress general, a Tassis by marriage. Yet in his decades of serving powerful businessmen, Ferdinando had risen within Venetian society. He had cultivated relationships with his German and Dutch clients and felt personally embarrassed by the perceived impropriety. Letter interception earned him no favors among his religiously and nationally diverse clientele. Faced with new competitors and enjoying new titles, the Tassis paid new attention to the impact of such interference on public opinion with regard to personal and family reputation.[50]

The fact remained that the post office was the heart of seventeenth-century European intelligence agencies. The term "black chamber" describes the systematic interception, decryption, and extraction of intelligence from postal systems. It originates as a direct translation from the French *cabinet noire*, sometimes translated as "black room" or "dark chamber." The appellation was rarely used by contemporaries, who referred obliquely to the "secret of the post."[51] Black chambers were the original signals intelligence offices, meaning that their constituting purpose was to extract politically sensitive information from letters. Still, the relative scarcity of scholarship on the origins of the black chamber reflects the sparseness of primary sources. Black chambers are concealed from both the public eye and archival records. In keeping with the principle of official secrecy, states denied the existence of intelligence operations tied to the postal systems. Historians have accordingly attributed the advent of "systematic letter espionage" to France in the second half of the seventeenth century. In an essay addressing the origins of black chamber operations, the historian of the Dutch Republic, Karl de Leeuw, calls the War of Spanish Succession (1702–1713) the "watershed" for Habsburg efforts, asserting "the whole practice of using information, based on covertly intercepted messages, was well established after the turn of the century, but not earlier." However, this periodization often relies on proof of the standardized employment of professional, full-time cryptanalysts.[52]

The material evolutions of the letter make it clear, by contrast, that correspondents expected systematic interception far earlier than the documented proof of systematic operations would suggest. For instance, the letter network of the English scholar Thomas Smith (1638–1710) spanned much of the continent in the 1670s. A librarian friend of Smith's residing in Florence asked that the well-connected scholar convey a message: "please inform all his friends if they write to him to make no mention of the R.C. [Roman Catholic] Church, for letters are opened by both the Inquisition and the Post House." The same correspondent reiterated the warning later that year when writing from Rome. A foreign Protestant was able to keep regular correspondence from the heart of the Catholic world, but at some risk. The threat of letter interception between France and England—which saw a prohibition of trade that year—also led to dwindling correspondence across Smith's network. He admitted to taking a guarded approach in his own letters, "lest they bring him into bad odor with the government." The thwarted scholar wrote of his "hopes for a future when men will be less stupid."[53] By the end of the century, the "secret of the post"—that is, the opening and inspection of letters for intelligence purposes—was hardly secret to Europe's cosmopolitan elite. Letter writers also occasionally expressed their suspicion. The prolific correspondent Marie de Rabutin-Chantal, Madame de Sévigné (1626–1696), for example, preemptively scolded the interceptor in the text of her letter to "at least take the trouble to put [the letters] back in their envelopes."[54]

By the beginning of the eighteenth century, postmaster generals had monitored correspondence on behalf of their employers for more than a century. But while past generations had published intercepted letters and bragged of broken ciphers, the postal systems of later decades sought to distance themselves from this legacy. Postal officials could not deliver the revenue-generating machines that they promised without courting usership, especially foreign clientele. Fiscal-minded states equally wanted commercial clients to subsidize their freely franked mail.[55] To succeed against their new competitors, international posts needed to be the most trusted option. Outwardly, then, interference—at least in domestic correspondence—did not happen. States passed new legislation giving legal backing to the principle of secrecy of correspondence. In 1711, the English passed legislation requiring the post office to obtain a warrant for opening letters.[56] Reflecting the influence of such thinking, the 1792 Post Office Act in the new United States of America set high penalties for postal officials who interfered with the mail, up to and including death.[57]

Yet this was bureaucratic doublespeak, the logic of which depended upon a key distinction: domestic mail would be treated differently from international mail. The logic of official secrecy continued to allow the state to act against the potential of "foreign threat." The decision to break a letter's seal depended upon its origin and destination, as well as the citizen-subject status of the correspondents. The division of international from domestic mail mirrored a new bureaucratic division more broadly: even today, most nations maintain separate agencies for domestic or international intelligence gathering.[58] Privacy of communications is not enjoyed by all by default.

The goal of letter-locking, seals, and even the latest adaptation, the envelope, was not to prevent interception, but rather to make the correspondents aware that interference had taken place. This was, in a sense, a material practice of the public's right to know: letter closures forced the state to admit to the secret of the post. States adapted in response. Samuel Morland bragged of bringing a "Spanish method" to the British post office to seamlessly remove and reapply seals. He later submitted a proposal to prototype a machine that would execute the method.[59] Louis XIV's secretary of war, François Michel Le Tellier, the marquis de Louvois (1641–1691), reportedly used quicksilver to remove a seal intact. National security was not the only motive for such actions. The published memoir of a lady's maid to the king's chief mistress (*maîtresse-en-titre*) recounts in detail how post office clerks worked to open mail: "Six or seven clerks of the post office picked out the letters they were ordered to break open and took the impression of the seals with a ball of quicksilver. Then they put each letter, with the seal downwards, over a glass of hot water, which melted the wax without injuring the paper. It was then opened, the desired matter extracted, and it was sealed again, by means of the impression." The lieutenant of police and the postmaster general supposedly reveled in sharing the "ludicrous stories and love affairs" that appeared in the letters.[60] There was no such thing as depersonalized surveillance.

These most famous sources about intelligence practices are often retrospective and semifictionalized, making periodizing the development of the black chamber even more difficult. The best-known centralized operations date to the late eighteenth and early nineteenth centuries, such as the Vienna Geheime Ziffernkanzlei. Smaller-scale black chambers were often referred to as "post lodges" (*Postloge*). Employing deft "bone knives" and novel methods of steaming open letters and forging seals, the interceptors worked with postmasters to minimize delay of mail delivery and thus avoid raising suspicion.[61] Vito Salierno finds that there was an Austrian operation in Milan by 1707, while an equivalent can be found for the Saxon posts at Celle as early as the 1690s.[62] The cases of letter interception discussed in previous chapters give every indication that these operations were underway by the beginning of the seventeenth century in Frankfurt, Augsburg, and Nuremberg.[63] Every early modern reinvention of the postal service to date had begun first with postal officials. The postmaster-in-residence, the international ordinaries, and infrastructure for tourism: each was practiced on the ground long before it was given formal recognition. It seems only natural that the same would be true for the black chamber.

While it is difficult to give precise dates, we can safely conclude that systematic signals intelligence was well underway long before the eighteenth century. The novelty of later decades was not the practice or professionalization of interception, but rather the veil of official secrecy. Technologies of letter interception evolved to be subtler, perpetuating the notion of postal service as uninterrupted. The distinction of international from domestic mail services maintained the image of the state's friendly face toward native subjects. But authoritarian regimes throughout history have used ambiguity to powerful effect. If you can never know when the state is watching, you must assume that it always is.

The Mailbag Novel and a Public Right to Know

By the later Baroque and early Enlightenment periods, postal service had many faces. One was the postal service of itinerary books, printed newspapers, and even travel journals. This postal service was more transparent and personable than ever. From the postilion who guided travelers to the courier who brought the letter to your town, or even the dispenser who came to your door, the professional staff of the post office embodied the state's friendly, familiar face.

Familiarity, however, can also breed contempt. New genres of literature explored the ambivalence and ambiguities of state involvement in communications. Secret histories, and especially epistolary novels, demonstrate a popular fascination with the contents of the mailbag. Satirists exploited the public-private mailbag for carnivalesque inversions of power.[64] Rather than recognizing communications agents and systems as being above the fray, such authors depicted them as both the victims and instigators of conflict. "Mailbag novels," as I term them, consisted of letters allegedly found in a single mailbag, usually violently wrested from the messenger.[65] Rather than weaving letters together into singular, diachronic narrative (like most epistolary novels), mailbag novels reveled in chaotic conjuncture. At their most radical, these novels even advanced a preliminary notion of a public right to know.[66] If the state could read private letters, why couldn't the public read state correspondence?

Ferrante Pallavicino (1615–1644)—a prolific author of satirical, political, and occasionally pornographic publications—produced the best-known mailbag novel, *The Courier Waylaid* (*Il corriero svaligiato*), in 1641. The seventh son of a minor Italian noble, Pallavicino belonged to a cosmopolitan milieu.[67] He and Ottavio Codogno shared a geopolitical context on either side of the Thirty Years' War, but they had very different takes on the role of official secrecy. When he wrote *The Courier Waylaid*, Pallavicino was already on the lam because of his scandalous publications. He remained just steps ahead of censors in northern Italy and Germany. He traveled alongside couriers, very likely hearing firsthand and secondhand tales of highway robberies that may have inspired the novel's premise.[68] While his novel is often discussed as the first of its type, Pallavicino may have drawn inspiration from earlier mailbag novels. The earliest example that I have identified is Nicholas Breton's *A Poste with a Mad Packet of Letters* (1602). The English author, who had strong ties to a local Italian community and had previously translated Italian works, may also have drawn upon earlier examples, which are now unknown.⁶⁹ On the whole, however, the mailbag novel came into its own in the later seventeenth century, following Pallavicino's example. Italian novels included *Il postiglione* (1666) and *Degli avanzi delle poste* (1677). Similar books in France and England included a reworking of *The Courier Waylaid* by Charles Gildon, *The Post-Boy Robbed of His Bag* (1692).⁷⁰

The Courier Waylaid has a convoluted frame story of conspiracy, surveillance, and resulting paranoia in northern Italy. Pallavicino depicts a world in which all parties watch one another via mail interception. The (fictional) publisher, Gironfaccio Spironcini, explains to the reader that the letters within the novel were taken from the ordinary courier of Milan. A German baron seized the messenger when he unwisely wandered off course. The baron discarded the letters that did not interest him, which were then reassembled by various court wits (*ingegni vivaci*) into the novel. These wits supplied additional letters and, the fictional publisher states, a fictional account of another court and waylaid courier, obscuring their crime. In the second concocted scenario, the letters were seized instead by an Italian prince seeking to spy on the Spanish governor of Milan.⁷¹

The Courier Waylaid's labyrinthine premise reflects a popular Baroque fascination with truth, secrecy, and the human capacity for simulation and dissimulation.⁷² After parsing these layers of deception—no doubt confusing contemporary censors—the basic frame-within-a-frame bears remarkable similarity to the espionage operations recounted in chapter 4. There, the Venetian resident in Milan claimed that the governor of Milan worked with the post office to spy on the letters of the Spanish ambassador in Venice. In *The Courier Waylaid*, the letters were either taken by a German baron, "Hochenberg" (perhaps a play on "Habsburg") or an Italian prince who wished to spy on the Spanish governor of Milan. Much like the German, Italian, and Spanish actors who populate "Spironcini's" world, even nominal allies kept tabs on one another by peeking in the mailbag.

Libertines like Pallavicino delighted in lampooning the grand claims of northern Italy's political and religious institutions.⁷³ Northern Italy frequently set French, Spanish, Italian, papal, and imperial interests at odds with one another and among their own ranks. Debates about privacy and publicity in postal service involved every user. Pallavicino's readers also sought to send letters, traffic goods, and communicate personal matters without the threat of robbery or interference. Pallavicino even jokingly suggested that readers who sent packages by the post put the book down, as the following discussion might be "too painful."⁷⁴

The chaotic reality often betrayed the rhetoric of a professional and impenetrable system advertised by Codogno, among others.

Mailbag authors dramatically depicted how a human element would always compromise systems, beginning with blaming the unwary courier for his own predicament. The assailants, after all, "only took what suited their intent, in this interest of politics."[75] Breton also blamed his courier's "lacke of heed, to let fall a Packet of Idle Papers."[76] Given the inevitability of interference, sharing the mailbag more widely—including the letters of so-called superiors—could only benefit the public. By reading letters, people would realize the true, petty nature of society and dispel the climate of secrecy and fear created by institutional surveillance. Tricks, traps, and elaborate backstories were more common than brute force. The mailbag novel reversed the logic of the postal itineraries, implying that the secrecy of the mailbag prevented, rather than aided, public service.[77]

The letters assembled in *The Courier Waylaid* vary widely in tone and from edition to edition. The first edition contained thirteen letters that were viciously polemical: the writers included an executioner seeking a soon-to-be-vacated office in Rome, a Jesuit priest confessing the misdeeds of his order, and anonymous writers railing against the censorship of books, Spanish tyranny in Italy, and sodomy in the monasteries. The wits provided minimal commentary, usually echoing the points made within the letters. Mailbag novels resembled the "news from Parnassus" genre, in which gods from the Greek pantheon or allegorical figures debated current events. That genre also originated in Pallavicino's Venice and confronted the hypocrisy of church and state.[78] Despite sharp barbs, mailbag novels conjured a fantasy world in which letters led to plenty of mockery, but not executions.

A 1646 edition of *The Courier Waylaid* retained the original thirteen and included another thirty-seven letters, with expanded commentary. The novel now included many letters from secretaries, merchants, scholars, and lovers, both young and mature. In short, it included the full range of everyday behavior that might end up in a mailbag. The amorous, misogynistic, mundane, and absurd diluted the religious and political polemic. Many of these additions heightened the verisimilitude, including the viceroy of Naples's order for glasses, a creditor's debt dispute, and a receipt for a cardinal's shipment of soap.[79] These also provided the wits with metaphors to milk for further satire.[80] This edition aligned more with the appeal of mailbag novels to readers who did not seek to know the secrets of church and state, but rather to experience the mailbag as a mirror of society. As a later novelist, Antonio Lupis, put it, the mailbag was "a universal table, at which the woman, the cavalier, the theologian, and the lover may all dine."[81] The mailbag novels were thus capacious containers that shrunk, expanded, and were reworked to appeal to readers.

The success of the mailbag novel as a genre hinged upon common knowledge of postal culture. In many cases, humor arose from the contrast with an ideal postal service. For example, the gullible wandering courier, the pomposity of the correspondents, and the jocularity with which the court wits broke seals clearly strayed from the ideal depicted by postal propaganda. In one of *Courier*'s letters, a writer told a fantastical story of how a snail arrived as a courier for the king of Transylvania, carrying "a valise full of shadows and chimeras," perhaps a reference to the phenomenon of fake war news.[82] The wits addressed the "cryptic" style of one secretary's requests in another letter: "It is from some great man," added the marquis, "because like princes, he uses signs in order to not be understood, like ciphers. . . . Perhaps whoever was to receive this letter was a pharmacist, who would have found aromatics to discover his ambitious designs."[83] Here, the humor depended on the contemporary use of invisible ink and chemicals to reveal them. Gildon similarly referenced a "letter in figures," hinting that "one of the Company having found a *Key* for it, but too late to have it inserted, the whole being printed off," and promised instead that one might find "letters of a very *surprizing nature*, and many that discover abundance of secret Intrigues" in future editions.[84] Ciphers, invisible inks, and "fake news" were familiar enough to be joking matters to readers.

Pallavicino's mailbag represented postal culture as an essential structure for contemporary civility, but the news hunger that it both stirred and fed was shared across lines of gender, class, and status. A letter relates how an old man, driven by paranoia, sought to steal the mail to prevent his enemies from discussing him. In reading about his trial, the wits mock the man, agreeing with the judge's verdict of insanity. The irony of their own waylaying of the courier, ordered by their paranoid patron, is completely lost on all but the author and reader.[85] The desire to know that which was secret, or believed to be secret, defied rational explanation.

Whether fictional or real, intelligence was a dangerous game. Papal representatives demanded, for instance, that the author Ferrante Pallavicino be executed for his obscene and libelous corpora. Unsure of his allies, he later fled Venice to relatives in Bergamo. In fact, the future imperial postmaster of Venice, Ottavio Tassis (d. 1691) and his brother,

Ruggero, were distantly related to the unfortunate Pallavicino. After the author's betrayal and arrest in France, the Tassis waged a letter-writing campaign to secure his release.[86] Pallavicino was nonetheless executed in Avignon in March of 1644.[87]

We end this journey by jumping ahead to another fugitive story in the 1840s, a fateful decade for social revolutions across Europe. Italian nationalists fought the Austrian-Hungarian Habsburg Empire in northern Italy. Continental exiles, including Giuseppe Mazzini (1805–1872), took refuge in the relatively liberal United Kingdom. Mazzini nonetheless began to suspect that the British Post Office was monitoring his correspondence. He tested his theory by placing seeds, hair, and sand in his envelopes and observing whether they were still there when the letters arrived. Mazzini's suspicions were soon confirmed. He turned to a radical member of Parliament, who brought the matter to the parliamentary floor in June 1844. Enraged parliamentarians demanded a full inquiry into the black chamber operating in the London post office. As it turned out, Austrian-Hungarian intelligence services had asked the English to monitor the revolutionary-in-exile. Parliament passed new regulations demanding and enforcing secrecy of correspondence.[88]

An editorial appeared shortly thereafter in the *Westminster Review*, titled "Mazzini and the Ethics of Politicians." The piece notably accompanied several others about the technological revolution of the day: the railways. In contrast to its praise for the railways, roads, and British press as advances of civilization, the journal condemned the post office, calling it "PETTY LARCENY," "*Fraud, Forgery, and Felony*" (emphasis in the original).[89] It decried that "the vices of the rulers of a people inevitably become national vices. The position occupied by a minister is more exposed to observation than that of any other human being. Every action is watched, every word is chronicled."[90] Satirists could not have written a better juxtaposition of the ideals governing postal service with the darker politics that it in fact served on the world stage.

The "Post Office Scandal" of 1844, also called "the Mazzini affair," showed that despite new presumptions of secrecy of correspondence, the hidden face of the state was alive and well. The literary scholar James Purdon identifies it as the first appearance of the term "official secrecy" in parliamentary debates employed to defend the post office's intelligencing role.[91] Authorities claimed that the office distinguished between British citizens and foreign nationals but asked for public trust in the bureaucratic professionalism of the office. The revelation that letter monitoring was regularly practiced upon Irish letters, especially by the Lords Lieutenant, undermined such arguments. The author of the *Westminster Review* op-ed found cold comfort in the knowledge that postal intelligencing had been a common practice during the previous three hundred years. He argued that the logic of official secrecy boiled down to a power of precedence and to the old Machiavellian chestnut, "the ends justify the means."[92] Ultimately, public opinion sided with these critics, and within two months of the debacle, the administration disbanded the Secret Department of the Post Office and pensioned off its longtime cryptanalysts.[93]

The Mazzini affair, like other turning points in Anglo-American postal history, takes on new significance when considered in a longer European context. Arguments against surveillance and for the public right to know developed from ideas first advanced in the decades surrounding the Thirty Years' War. Parliamentarians decried letter interference as "repugnant to every principle of the British constitution," but they specifically emphasized its harm to British commerce.[94] Such ideas had been introduced nearly two centuries earlier by postal lieutenants, among others. Secrecy of correspondence was essential for maintaining the business of the cosmopolitan commercial community. The same logic shaped protections enshrined in new laws in the young United States: early regulation of secrecy of correspondence seeking "primarily to improve trust in the post so as to facilitate the circulation of high-value commercial correspondence became a cornerstone of U.S. communications policy—and a precedent for the present-day liberal norm of communicative privacy."[95] From Codogno's *negotianti* to colonial entrepreneurs, the financial success of the postal service—and by extension, the nation-state—came to rely upon the merchant's unbroken seal.

Print offered new ways to communicate to a wider public, but it did not revolutionize postal services. Postal officials were fundamentally public facing across the early modern period, even before their adoption of print. The earliest appointments of postmasters underwent public scrutiny and debate, and postal officials' correspondence shows increasing sensitivity to their public reputation—especially among wealthy, private patrons—alongside the rise of commercial service and print publication. Postmasters like Simone Tassis of Milan and Ruggero Tassis of Venice were information managers in this sense, as well as the administrators of a communications infrastructure. Regardless of its true political power, public opinion mattered to state-building agents.[96]

Public outrage, however, might lead only to public disavowal. Several decades after the explosive public reaction to the Mazzini affair, those in the know admitted that letter interference was still "more usual than is generally supposed."[97] At the conclusion of World War I, the United States dabbled in its own "Black Chamber" operation. The Cipher Bureau chief Herbert Yardley borrowed the name for the title of his 1931 memoir.[98] That operation had been shuttered by 1929. The secretary of state, Henry Stimson, reportedly declared that "gentlemen do not read each other's mail."[99] The quote well represents the public face of post-Westphalian international relations, which took for granted the existence of a shared code of honor among the international elite that included the presumption of secrecy of correspondence.

The neoclassical postal service has perhaps held the greatest traction in historical memory, but it was one of many historical guises. The postal service might be the postal official, who was too refined to open letters but not above collecting a tidy profit. It might be embodied by the familiar mail carrier, dispensing letters to inns and cafés. It was the increasingly nationalistic symbols of guaranteed diligence in public service, from the postal horn to the postage stamp. Postal service was also the responsibility of the staff of the black chambers, who worked late into the night, carefully unsealing and resealing letters to monitor correspondents and surveil dissent. The seventeenth century gave birth to public representations of the post that predominate even in the modern day. Apart from cyclical scandals over letter interference, state postal services largely succeeded in balancing the monumental, the mundane, and the murky.

While seventeenth-century postal officials would not have employed the term "official secrecy," it well represents the political doublespeak that surrounded the development of black chambers. Intelligence gathering via letter interception remained a core component of postmastership and postal service. Later incidents such as the Mazzini affair depicted such interference incidents as highly anomalous departures from dedication to transparent public service. Even today, the ramifications of communications companies collecting, storing, and selling personal data (especially in cooperation with governments) remain poorly understood or regulated. Violations are often characterized as the bleeding of politics into public service; however, the history of communications technologies has always been about intelligence gathering as well as state-building.

Conclusion
Reinventing Revolutions

A sixteenth- or seventeenth-century individual, plucked out of his or her own time, would find the contemporary world fundamentally foreign. At the same time, an early modern postmaster or postmistress might find many aspects of modern postal service shockingly familiar. Most national postal systems still rely on a politically appointed postmaster general. Postal services handle mail, but also the logistics of collection and distribution more broadly, from taxes to passports and newspapers. They serve both governments and private clients. Current headlines (much like the *avvisi* of a prior age) feature corruption scandals, political interference in the mail, and debate over the sources of funding for postal systems. The postal service has taken on new functions with the advent of new transportation technologies, but it always has, from stagecoaches to railroads and autonomous vehicles.

The term "revolution" can indicate the wheel of fate that topples a king, but it can also refer to a full orbit, such as that of a planet that circles the sun in predictable, repeating patterns. "Revolution" took on new meaning in the seventeenth century as "a way of describing the tortuous but ultimately triumphant chain of ruptures, reversals, and political upheavals."[1] Early modern writers understood that they lived in revolutionary times, as evidenced by the prevalence of "the world turned upside down" trope across art and literature.² Mail services altered the horizon of possibility in the age of empires. Postal networks radicalized the impact of text on early modern international relations and popular politics, much as the internet has transformed computing in an age of globalization. What, then, can the early modern communications revolution tell us about such revolutions across time, including in our own moment?

There are general patterns that contextualize how any communications revolution looks, feels, and moves. These rhythms do not depend, by and large, on the specifics of the technologies, but rather on their role in social systems. Three such patterns carry us from Codogno's world of the post into our own age. The first is the constant reinvention of both what communications technologies can be and whom they might serve. The second is the shifting status of technocrats, especially in relation to statecraft and international relations. Third are the respective boundaries of public and private knowledge and the importance of intelligencing to shaping the structures and practices of communication.

Scope and Scale of Service

Communications infrastructure is expensive. Establishing postal way stations, provisioning stables, and training and paying staff all required an enormous financial outlay. Much like war-making, the spending power of rulers and the government contractors they employed necessarily facilitated this investment. As a result, the right to send mail or travel by post was initially a jealously guarded privilege. Governments disallowed private interference that might compromise the speed and security of the mail and, in the case of brigandage, punished it with increasing severity.

The expansion of governing and diplomatic institutions extended the licit use of postal systems. While quantitative records remain difficult to compare across time, state archives alone contain hundreds of thousands of letters exchanged among rulers, councils, governors, and ambassadors. The sixteenth and seventeenth centuries marked an overall historical trend toward the creation of an enormous apparatus of state. The coincidence of information war with the social crises of the late sixteenth century drove rulers toward further dependence upon state-sponsored posts as essential personnel for managing vast composite monarchies.

Crises both test and renew infrastructures. The postal wars and years of plague, brigandage, and bankruptcy that followed invigorated investment in postal systems, but the greatest initiative to expand postal service to private mail came from postal officials themselves. Financial necessity (and self-interest, or even avarice) drove the shift from reliance on state-paid extraordinary service toward subsidized ordinary postal service. The 1612 prosecution of the postmistress of Milan and her lieutenant discussed in chapter 4 demonstrated that states initially viewed this commercial orientation as signaling corruption. The mid-seventeenth-century shift toward welcoming more businesslike aspects to postal services was in part grudging recognition and in part the result of successful lobbying by postal officials.

The arguments that postal officials made to keep and extend monopolistic privileges changed with the political theory de jure. Justifications of postal monopoly began with the Counter-Reformation control of communications, as well as the intelligencing benefit offered to states. Couriers and other messengers, such as the cavallari of the Venetian terraferma, petitioned states based on legal precedence and the preservation of their livelihoods. Office leasing added new pressure to these petitions: leaseholders were more likely to ask forgiveness than permission for implementing innovations geared toward increasing the commercial viability of postal service.

It was not until the close of the Thirty Years' War that the rhetoric of "free commerce" gained traction at higher levels of government, but these ideas were already at play among postal lieutenants of the 1620s. Free commerce and ideological ecumenicalism characterized the writing of up-and-comer postal lieutenants, including Ottavio Codogno. Even dyed-in-the-wool intelligencers like the imperial postmasters of Venice were newly conscious of their public reputations among a cosmopolitan elite. The reinvention of the Tassis family as Thurn und Taxis was one of many rhetorical moves to distance postal service from the espionage and counterespionage of prior decades. Another was to reframe the origins of postal service as part of the fiscal rather than political apparatus of state. And a final move was to emphasize the distinction between domestic and foreign mail services, which continues even today. All in all, the business of postal service modeled the political economic cultivation of both revenue and public service.

Traditional postal historiography undeniably portrays the postal revolution as a triumph: a system intended for an elite became the foundation of a mobile civil society. The birth of the printed newspaper was a further populist victory, made possible by the regular arrival of news and distribution of news publications. This is a remarkably standard narrative across national postal historiographies. It shows the fingerprints of the nineteenth-century age of nation building, but the essential form was in place by the close of the early modern period.

In fact, every incarnation of a communications system has undergone several centuries of invention, adaptation, and reinvention. The many functions of the postal service—from international couriership to ordinary messengership to local letter dispensing, and even to ferrying travelers—derived from aggressive market interventions, with a set of justifications that mirrored the political culture of the time. Postal monopoly was never a true monopoly in this sense—it arguably moved too quickly—but it was invariably monopolistic in its goals. Excluding alternative providers remained a constant concern and even a prerequisite to postal expansion. And the first step toward legislation to restrict the activities of miscellaneous messengers was to sow distrust of the dangers and harm such messengers might wreak among policymakers. This offers, in many ways, the darker side of the triumphalist narrative of postal public service: trust in the postal carrier followed, rather than preceded, cultivated distrust of any alternative.[3]

Postal Officials as Technocrats

The story of Europe's transnational postal services is also the story of the Bergamaschi—indeed, of a mere handful of families from the Valle Brembana. Living at the geographic, economic, and political intersection of empires meant acting as brokers. The Bergamaschi could be imperial, Lombard, or Venetian all at once. The Tassis were one of several such families whose names appear and reappear across generations of couriers. Such early training in brokerage led the Bergamaschi to wield an undeniably disproportionate influence on Europe's communications revolution.

The fate of the Tassis diverged from their brethren at the end of the fifteenth century, when they landed the first lucrative contracts to act as postmasters to the Habsburg dynasty of imperial and Spanish rulers. Tassis postal systems were deeply entangled with international relations from the outset. The Italian Wars brought Europe's great dynasties to vie for power in the Italian peninsula. Monarchs, armies, and messengers crossed the Alps with frequency. These were international routes that necessitated passing through many jurisdictions and so required postal officials to work with many different authorities. The new *cursus honorum* saw Tassis family members rise from messengers to administrators, and even become ambassadors. But Italian imperials still walked a dangerous path. Particularly traumatic incidents included the expulsion of the Sandri branch of the family from the Venetian Company of Couriers, the arrest and exile of Janetto Tassis, and the arrest and torture of Giovan Antonio Tassis in Rome.

The advent of the corriero maggiore meant reconfiguring centuries-long traditions of messengership into new administrative hierarchies. The Tassis, whose name became nearly synonymous with this office, combined the traits of a family firm with state officeholding. Contemporaries recognized the power of this position and the Tassis also advertised it through their elite marriages, new knighthoods and fiefdoms, and patronage of art, literature, and cartography. Postmastership brought social and financial mobility, but it relied upon maintaining a strong social network. Outsiders, such as the deputized postmaster Francesco Tassignano in Milan or the newcomer corriero maggiore Ludovico Fioravante in Venice, struggled to gain a foothold. The power of the Bergamaschi cartel lay in exclusive access to a network girded by social solidarities.

New information technologies yield new terminology, and yet older terms also take fundamentally new meanings. The significance of the maestro delle poste changed with the delegation of foreign postmasters to reside abroad. The institutionalization of resident ambassadors was itself relatively novel in the sixteenth century.[4] From Rome to Venice, post houses forced larger discussions about extraterritoriality, information sovereignty, and communications monopoly. Diplomatic letters naturally emphasize the role of official representatives and embassies, but we also see the power and personality of individual postal officials. The papal postmaster Mattia Gherardi drove the postal wars of the 1550s to 1570s, sometimes in agreement with political leaders, but often in conflict with them.

Postal officials showed great agency in determining the who, where, when, and why of postal services across time. Resulting ley lines of communication had a wider impact than the postal service alone: they shaped the domestic and foreign policies of early modern states. Sometimes their impact was feeding an insatiable hunger for information: governors, diplomats, and businesspeople came to depend upon the state-sponsored posts to meet their demand for news on a weekly or even daily basis. By 1575–1576, rulers and governors were unwilling to interrupt the flow of news even during plague. Spying cavallari, gossiping postilions, and postmasters-turned-newswriters also fed the wider popular demand for intelligence from abroad.

Contemporaries may not have used the term "technocrat," but it offers the best description of how and why postal administrators exercised their powers. Postmasters and couriers drove new treaties, unions, and laws by influencing governing bodies. This was the case for the Italian Road when the Venetian Company of Couriers worked with the Spanish postmaster of Milan to formulate a communications condominium in northern Italy. Petitions from couriers and proposed legislation from postmasters shaped policy, defining contraband letters and other crimes against the state. From the cisalpine to the transalpine routes, postal infrastructure had a long-term impact on travel and exchange, further amplified by its advertisement in new genres of print publication, such as itineraries and travel journals.

Given all of this, why have postal officials remained largely anonymous in history? The answer lies in part with the sources that we use to tell the story of communication. When it works best, infrastructure is invisible: its customs and modes become so universal that they are taken for granted and commented upon only in moments of breakdown, as historians of travel have long known. Even at abysmal survival rates, letters themselves are easily the most plentiful sources for early modern history. Couriers and postal officials are simply rarely named in letters outside of diplomatic incidents or other scandals.

The mythos of postal service provides further answers. Political activity on the part of the postmaster always brings discomfort. Much like the self-interest or multiple allegiances of diplomats, the personal involvement of messengers undermines their role as avatars for correspondents. It throws into doubt the letter as a direct transcription of the sender's voice. Faced with new challenges, state postal services deliberately deemphasized the partisan history of postal service in policymaking. They favored instead a kind of neoclassical ecumenicalism. This was the friendly face of the state, further achieved by the substitution of the postilion for the socially and geographically removed postmaster general. Even the general's martial origins were erased with time, rewritten to reflect the sheer variety of functions overseen by one state appointee. The "diligence of the courier" became a turn of phrase, much as the postal stagecoach took on the name of the "diligence" coach in many parts of Europe. Speed, security, and reliability defined ideal services, with aspects like the black chamber relegated to the margins of their history.

Anonymity served other goals. From the eighteenth century onward, the postal service has traditionally fit neatly within the models of bureaucratization sketched by Max Weber.[5] Depersonalization of the postmaster mirrored that of all bureaucrats. The office of the postmaster distributed—some might even say "evaded"—individuality, much in the way that modern corporate structures do. It became harder to hold any individual officeholder liable for failures in the system. The impartial bureaucrat became curiously divorced from policy and its impact, especially social upheaval.[6]

That legacy resonates in how we discuss a digital information revolution today. Much like the postal system, the internet often exists in regulatory limbo, as legislation fails to keep up with the rapid pace of change. In the United States, internet services are grouped with other utilities provided by semipublic, semiprivate service providers. Silicon Valley technocracy enacts an undeniable influence on domestic and foreign politics. Much as the Tassis did, "Big Tech" mediates between commercial society and political power.[7] The impact is nonetheless described as both unprecedented and unpredictable by journalists and policymakers alike. In the first decades of the twenty-first century, social media took on a near-mystical, depersonalized power, not unlike that of the madness of the mailbag.[8] Grappling with such a revolutionary social impact often obscures the point that information technologies and systems are shaped by the deeply personal choices, allegiances, and enmities of the individuals who build and manage them. Reintegrating the day-to-day agents of infrastructure—not just its inventors—draws attention to the social transformations rather the big technological breaks in communications.

Public and Private Knowledge

We add power back into the history of communications by reading it as a history of both intelligence and technological revolution. Postal officials traded in politically sensitive information as a profession. The espionage, counterespionage, surveillance, and other interventions of postmasters and mistresses into the mailbag show that postal routes were far from dormant channels. Letters that traveled by post were designated as public or private, and each variation determined intelligencing as well as administrative practices.

Northern Italians of the sixteenth and seventeenth centuries used a variety of terms to describe the concepts that we now associate with the term "privacy." Chief among them was *segretezza*, more commonly translated as the English "secrecy." Postal officials trafficked in official secrets from an early date, but secrets gain much of their value from the in-groups and out-groups that they help to create.[9] The Carafa, the Venetian ambassadors in Milan, and satirists like Ferrante Pallavicino sought to disrupt secret channels as a means of challenging the conspiracies they supported. To protect secrets, it was often necessary to hide their very existence. For instance, Count Fuentes used secret charges (*gastos segretos*) to evade observation, but Spanish visitors feared that this also evaded accountability and perhaps worked against personal political rivals.

Some groups could not be trusted to traffic in secrets, and powerful postal officials used this fear of unfettered communications to their advantage. Distrust was ever-present in the family firm infrastructure as members competed for honors and influence, often at a long distance from the courts that provided them. Familial distrust threatened total system breakdown at several points, including when the cousins Ruggero of Milan and Venice turned to new allies. However, distrust of the innovative foreigner often won out, conveniently edging out rival leaseholders and, eventually, postal lieutenants like Johann von den Birghden. "Foreign" was nonetheless a capacious and flexible category, and postmasters often wielded it against local groups like merchants, who were potential abettors to dissent, rebellion, or invasion.

Another permutation of "private" in the Italian was *particolare*, which described things that did not pertain to state business. The modern legal understanding of privacy carries this idea into terms such as "private business" or "private parties." *Lettere particolari* were described as such because they did not directly serve the needs of governing authorities, and so were not charged to the state, as opposed to the *lettere pubbliche*. Even this seemingly straightforward definition quickly broke down, as contemporary postal records reveal. Were the letters sent between two administrators who were also brothers public or private? What about the funds carried for the Fuggers, Welsers, or *negotianti* of Genoa? Were letters public or private when states sent secrets through merchant factors to avoid foreign interference?

The English term "privacy" transformed in these same key decades to mean matters that *should not* preoccupy the state.[10] In Shakespeare's *Troilus and Cressida* (1602), Achilles hides his emotions, saying "of this my privacy, I have strong reasons." His companion, Ulysses, begs to differ: "But 'gainst your privacy / The reasons are more potent and heroical."

Ulysses continues: "The providence that's in a watchful state / keeps place with thought and almost, like the gods, / do thoughts unveil in their dumb cradles."[11] Contrary to Achilles's assertion of privacy, Ulysses asserts that the love that Achilles bears for Priam's daughter is a matter of state. An individual's conscience cannot be separated from the acts that they might take: that assumption drove over a century of religious warfare in Europe.[12] Such sentiments of both private violation and public right echoed those of contemporary correspondents, authors, and politicians regarding the mail.

The central dilemma remains essentially the same for modern intelligence services: How do you determine what constitutes a threat to the state worthy of incurring feelings of violation in civil society? Public disapprobation has always defined the boundary of privacy, but through reactive rather than proactive policing. Many modern intelligence agencies practice the same division that postal officials made between "native" and "foreign" actors, with the latter constituting an increased threat meriting decreased rights.[13] Yet if we take anything away from the "us versus them" rhetoric of past centuries, it should be how contextual and shifting these distinctions are. Ultimately, the wide-net approach of black chambers and letter interception eroded the protections of all groups, as well as the trust of users. The same issues that preoccupied the Tassis as businesspeople challenge technocracy today. Communications technocrats frequently part ways with governments when it comes to the issue of eroding consumer trust.[14]

Published secrets become revelations, and then records. Ottavio Codogno certainly advocated that postmasters avoid gaining a reputation as gossips in order to protect private as much as public clients, but postal officials had always trafficked in strategically publicizing knowledge, much as the postmaster Simone Tassis controlled the imperial narrative in Italy. Codogno did as well, both as an intelligencer and the author of a celebrated book. The northern Enlightenment would in turn tie the notion of public knowledge, and even public record, to the ideals of democracy. Jeremy Bentham even framed it as a counterinsurgency principle when he wrote, "Publicity is the fittest law for securing the public confidence ... without publicity, no good is permanent: under the auspices of publicity, no evil can continue."[15] Pallavicino and the other authors of mailbag novels endorsed a similar idea by ripping away control of the mailbag.

The best takeaways are simple ones. First, context determines privacy and publicity, and a communications system, by its nature, translates information across contexts. Postal services remain at the center of debates about publicity and privacy because they give an abstracted debate a very material form, whether in the shape of the assaulted messenger or the unsealed letter. Second, postal history shows us the folly of assuming universal ethics and norms when it comes to protecting correspondence or the means of its conveyance. A "gentleman's code" rarely holds up against the power and profit of trading in secrets.

Glossary

The following are terms referring to offices, types of messengers, types of mail, and travel modes as used in this volume. Postal terminology was often adapted and reapplied, causing considerable confusion even at the time.

Officials

Corriero maggiore: "Postmaster general"; a state appointee acting as postmaster or postmistress and overseeing a hierarchy of subordinates.

Maestro delle poste: "Postmaster"; responsible for staffing and maintaining a postal infrastructure, meaning regularly spaced way stations for messengers in relay. I use the term "postmaster-in-residence" to describe when such an official is stationed abroad, such as the imperial postmasters and postmistresses who resided in places like Rome and Venice.

Postiglione: "Postilion"; among many other responsibilities, a postilion was responsible for acting as a guide and travel companion to couriers and notables traveling by post.

Postino, postiere: "Postman"; general-purpose terms referring to the staff of the post office. The term appears more commonly from the eighteenth century onward.

Messengers

Cavallaro: Municipal messenger licensed to carry letters and funds between local governments and capital cities.

Corriere: "Courier"; for the sake of clarity, I have reserved the use of this term to describe individuals belonging to state-licensed corporate bodies and primarily responsible for carrying letters and money, as opposed to more general-purpose "carriers."

Distributore: "Distributor"; a person responsible for running an additional distribution bench in the marketplace or making home deliveries.

Ordinario: "Ordinary"; a messenger traveling on a set route and regulated timetable. While merchant ordinaries predated postal ordinaries, by the seventeenth century the term was often used to refer to postal ordinaries.

Pedone/fante: A messenger traveling on foot.

Portalettere: "Letter carrier"; generally responsible for door-to-door delivery. The term is often used to refer to unlicensed carriers, by comparison to municipal messengers and postal couriers.

Procaccio: A single-route carrier; procacci might hold state-granted privileges, as was the case for the Florentine procaccio to and from Venice. However, their primary clients were merchants. Procacci might travel by any mode but generally did so only by day.

Staffetta: A postal messenger traveling by horse in relay; see "*a staffetta*."

Straordinaro: "Extraordinary"; an ad hoc messenger traveling by post, see "*a posta*."

Vetturino/nolesino: "Hackney"; a private carrier providing travel services by horse or coach.

Letters

Lettere particolari: "Private letters"; refers to all correspondence not categorized as *lettere pubbliche*, and postage of letters charged to individuals rather than the state.

Lettere pubbliche: "Public letters"; refers to correspondence of state officials, and postage of letters charged to state treasuries or freely franked as a condition of state-backed mail-carrying privileges.

Travel Modes

A cambiatura: "Changing"; this term refers to changing horses every thirty or forty miles (roughly every ten posts).

A giornata: "By day"; that is, resting at night.

A posta: "By post"; this term means utilizing postal way stations.

A staffetta: "In relay"; traveling at a gallop or trot and changing horses at every way station while accompanied by the postilion.

Cavalcata: An alternative form of relay to *a staffetta*, at a reduced cost and taking roughly twice as long.

In diligenza: "Diligently"; refers to traveling by day and night and changing horses at every postal way station. By the mid-seventeenth century, the term *diligenza* might also refer to the postal coach.

Abbreviations

ADB	Allgemeine Deutsche Biographie (Online)
ADN	Archives départementales du Nord
AGS	Archivo General de Simancas
	Consejo Real de Castilla (CRC)
	Consejo de Estado (Estado)
	Consejo de Italia (Italia)
	Patronato Real (PR)
	Secretarías Provinciales (SP)
	Visitas de Italia (Visitas)
ASBg	Archivio di Stato di Bergamo
ASBr	Archivio di Stato di Brescia
	Atti dei deputati (Deputati)
	Atti notarili (Notarili)
ASC	Archivio Storico Civico di Milano
	Famiglie
	Materie, Finanze
	Materie, Poste
ASDMi	Archivio Storico Diocesano di Milano
ASF	Archivio di Stato di Firenze
	Mediceo del Principato (Mediceo)
ASMi	Archivio di Stato di Milano
	Atti di Governo (AG)
	Carteggio delle cancellerie dello Stato (Carteggio)
	Dispacci Reali (Dispacci)
	Registri delle cancellerie dello Stato (Registri)
	Miscellanea Storica (MS)
	Notarile
ASR	Archivio di Stato di Rimini
ASTo	Archivio di Stato di Torino
	Materie economiche (ME)
	Materie politiche (MP)

ABBREVIATIONS

ASV	Archivio Apostolico Vaticano (formerly Archivio Segreto Vaticano)
ASVe	Archivio di Stato di Venezia
	Compagnia dei Corrieri (Corrieri)*
	Capi del consiglio di dieci (CCX)
	Consiglio di dieci (CX)
	Consiglio di dieci, Deliberazioni, Parti secreti (CX, Deliberazioni)
	Consiglio di dieci, Processi (CX, Processi)
	Consiglio di dieci, Registri, Parti secreti (CX, Registri)
	Inquisitori di Stato (IS)
ASVer	Archivio di Stato di Verona
	Processi, Uffici pubblici, Cavallari e portalettere (Cavallari)
BAM	Biblioteca Civico Angelo Mai (Bergamo)
	Raccolta tassiana (Tass.)
BDG	Banchedati Gonzaga (Online)
BL	British Library
BNE	Biblioteca Nacional de España
BNF	Bibliothèque nationale de France
BSB	Bayerische Staatsbibliothek
Corr.	Biblioteca del Museo Correr
DBE	Diccionario Biográfico Electrónico (Online)
DBI	Dizionario Biografico Italiano (Online)
FTTZA	Fürst Thurn und Taxis Hofbibliothek und Zentralarchiv
	Haus- und Familiensachen (HFS)
	Postakten (PA)
	Posturkunden (PU)
Herzog.	Herzog August Bibliothek Wolfenbüttel
MAP	Medici Archive Project (Online)
Marc.	Biblioteca Nazionale Marciana
ODNB	Oxford Dictionary of National Biography (Online)
Querr.	Biblioteca della Fondazione Querini Stampalia
RB	Real Biblioteca
SP	British State Papers (Online)
TLA	Tiroler Landesarchiv
	Adelsarchiv, Taxis-Bordogna (TB)

---

*This collection is divided into two series, the first of which is distinguished by the use of Roman numerals (i.e., ASVe, *Corrieri*, IV).

Notes

Introduction

1. Ottavio Codogno, *Nuovo itinerario delle poste per tutto il mondo* (Milan: Girolamo Bordoni, 1608); Ottavio Codogno, *Compendio delle poste* (Milan: Gio. Battista Bidelli, 1623).

2. Codogno, *Nuovo itinerario*, 1–2.

3. Francesco Senatore, *Uno mundo de carta: Forme e strutture della diplomazia Sforzesca* (Naples: Liguori, 1999).

4. Codogno, *Nuovo itinerario*, 6–7.

5. For a more recent take on the "coevolution" of paper and practice, see Paul Marcus Dover, "The Impacts of Paper's Abundance, 1450–1650: An Episode in Coevolution," in *Paper Stories—Paper and Book History in Early Modern Europe*, ed. Silvia Hufnagel, Þórunn Sigurðardóttir, and Davíð Ólafsson (Berlin: De Gruyter, 2023), 47–72.

6. Christina Corsi, *Le strutture di servizio del cursus publicus in Italia: Ricerche topografiche ed evidenze archeologiche* (Oxford: J. and E. Hedges and Hadrian, 2000); Anne Kolb, *Transport und Nachrichtentransfer im römischen Reich* (Berlin: Akademie Verlag, 2000).

7. Giorgio Chittolini, "The 'Private,' the 'Public,' and the State," in *The Origins of the State in Italy, 1300–1600*, ed. Julius Kirshner (Chicago: University of Chicago Press, 1996), 34–61.

8. Schiera calls upon scholars to "re-evaluate the role of communication in the doctrinal-disciplinary aspect of the state." Pierangelo Schiera, "Legitimacy, Discipline, and Institutions: Three Necessary Conditions for the Birth of the Modern State," in *The Origins of the State in Italy, 1300–1600*, ed. Julius Kirshner (Chicago: University of Chicago Press, 1996), 31.

9. A cohesive school of academic work emerged in pre–World War I Germany, built from the Thurn und Taxis family archives (Fürst Thurn und Taxis Zentralarchiv, FTTZA) in Regensburg, Germany, and guided by the archive director Joseph Rübsam (1854–1927). In 1991, the Museo dei Tasso e della Storia Postale in Camerata Cornello joined FTTZA. The museum and the Aldo Cechi Institute of Postal History in Prato (est. 1982) began ambitious conference and publication programs that continue today, and to which I am indebted.

10. The thirteenth-century Venetian Marco Polo described the postal system of the Mongols, providing one of the earliest mentions of a postal system in postclassical literature. On the theory of a Eurasian origins of postal systems,

see Didier Gazagnadou, *The Diffusion of a Postal Relay System in Premodern Eurasia* (Paris: Klime, 2016).

11. Codogno noted that Theodoric the Great (d. 526 CE) and Ludwig the Pious (d. 840 CE) appointed both a secular and a clerical administrator to the office of imperial foreign dispatches. See Enrico Melillo, *Le poste italiane nel medioevo* (Rome: Desclée, Lefebvre e C. Editori, 1904), 26.

12. This can be compared to the fastest recorded speeds of three days to Milan and seven to Naples in the late Middle Ages. Armando Serra, "Corrieri e postieri sull'itinerario Venezia-Rome nel Cinquecento e dopo," *Archivio per la storia postale* 3, no. 7-9 (January–December 2001): 6.

13. Filippo de Vivo, *Information and Communication in Venice: Rethinking Early Modern Politics* (Oxford: Oxford University Press, 2007).

14. Until recently, postal service was largely absent from historiographical debate surrounding the impact of print revolution. Elizabeth Eisenstein, *The Printing Press as an Agent of Change: Communications and Cultural Transformations in Early-Modern Europe* (Cambridge: Cambridge University Press, 1980); Marshall McLuhan, *The Gutenberg Galaxy: The Making of Typographic Man* (Toronto: University of Toronto Press, 1962); Jürgen Habermas, *The Structural Transformation of the Public Sphere: An Inquiry into a Category of Bourgeois Society* (Cambridge, MA: MIT Press, 1989).

15. Paul Marcus Dover, *The Information Revolution in Early Modern Europe* (Cambridge: Cambridge University Press, 2021).

16. Randolph C. Head, *Making Archives in Early Modern Europe: Proof, Information and Political Record-Keeping, 1400-1700* (Cambridge: Cambridge University Press, 2019).

17. Hélène Merlin-Kajman, "'Privé' and 'Particulier' (and Other Words) in Seventeenth-Century France," in *Early Modern Privacy: Sources and Approaches*, ed. Michaël Green, Lars Cyril Nørgaard, and Mette Birkedal Bruun (Leiden, Netherlands: Brill, 2022), 79-104.

18. Thomas Max Safley, *Family Firms and Merchant Capitalism in Early Modern Europe* (New York: Routledge, 2020); Joanna Milstein, *The Gondi Family: Strategy and Survival in Early Modern France* (New York: Routledge, 2016). Thank you to my Cornell University Press reviewers for these references.

19. Richard Harding and Sergio Solbes Ferri, eds., *The Contractor State and Its Implications, 1659-1815* (Las Palmas de Gran Canaria, Spain: Universidad de Las Palmas de Gran Canaria, 2012); David Parrott, *The Business of War: Military Enterprise and Military Revolution in Early Modern Europe* (Cambridge: Cambridge University Press, 2012).

20. Henry Kamen, *Empire: How Spain Became a World Power, 1492-1763* (New York: HarperCollins, 2003); Rupali Mishra, *A Business of State: Commerce, Politics, and the Birth of the East Indian Company* (Cambridge, MA: Harvard University Press, 2018). Scholars similarly indicate political absolutism's reliance on collaboration from venal officeholders, although this scholarship tends to focus on the ruling elite. See William Beik, "The Absolutism of Louis XIV as Social Collaboration," *Past & Present* 188, no. 1 (August 2005): 195-224.

21. On confessionalization, see Heinz Schilling, "Confessional Europe," in *Handbook of European History 1400-1600: Late Middle Ages, Renaissance, and*

Reformation, vol. 2: Visions, Programs, and Outcomes, ed. Thomas A. Brady Jr., Heiko A. Oberman, and James D. Tracy (Grand Rapids, MI: William B. Eerdmans, 1995), 641-681. For a more recent retrospective, see Helmut Puff, "Belief in the Reformation Era: Reflections on the State of Confessionalization," *Central European History* 51, no. 1 (2018): 46-52.

22. Jacob Burkhardt, *Die Kultur der Renaissance in Italien* (Leipzig, Germany: E. A. Seeman, 1868).

23. Eric Cochrane, *Florence in the Forgotten Centuries, 1527–1800: A History of Florence and the Florentines in the Age of the Grand Dukes* (Chicago: University of Chicago Press, 1973). For a more recent revision, see Edward Muir, "Italy in the No Longer Forgotten Centuries," *I Tatti Studies in the Italian Renaissance* 16, no. 1/2 (2013): 5-11.

24. Donald Queller, *The Office of Ambassador* (Princeton, NJ: Princeton University Press, 1967), 5.

25. Tommaso Garzoni, *La piazza universale di tutte le professioni del mondo, e nobili et ignobili* (Venice: Gio. Battista Somascho, 1585).

26. Fernando Rea, *Le poste a Bergamo* (Bergamo, Italy: Società Editrice Bergamasca, 1976), 7.

27. Melillo, *Le poste italiane*, 45; Martina Hacke, "Aspekte des mittelalterlichen Botenwesens: Die Botenorganisation der Universität von Paris und anderer Institutionen in Spätmittelalter," *Mittelalter: Perspektiven Media? Vestischer Forschung: Zeitschrift des Mediavistenverbandes* 1, no. 11 (June 2006): 132-149.

28. Dover, *The Information Revolution*, 46-47. The rough wage estimates are based on Paolo Malanima, *L'economia italiana: Dalla crescita medievale alla crescita contemporanea* (Bologna, Italy: Società editrice il Mulino, 2002), as made available by Leticia Arroyo Abad, "Italy—North, 1285-1850," in *Global Price and Incomes Database* (University of California, Davis: 2015), https://gpih.ucdavis.edu/Datafilelist.htm. On the role of paper, see Silvia Hufnagel, Þórunn Sigurðardóttir, and Davíð Ólafsson, eds., *Paper Stories—Paper and Book History in Early Modern Europe* (Berlin: De Gruyter, 2023); Daniel Bellingradt and Anna Reynolds, eds., *The Paper Trade in Early Modern Europe: Practices, Materials, Networks* (Leiden, Netherlands: Brill, 2021).

29. The Florentine nobleman Rinaldo degli Albizzi saw many such merchant couriers when he traveled in the fifteenth century. Cesare Guasti, ed., *Commissioni di Rinaldo degli Albizzi per il comune di Firenze* (Florence: M. Cellini, 1867); Giorgio Migliavacca, "The Globetrotting Scarselle: The Italian Merchant Mail of the 1200s and 1300s," *Fil–Italia* 40, no. 4 (Autumn 2014): 206-207.

30. Richard Goldthwaite, *The Economy of Renaissance Florence* (Baltimore: Johns Hopkins University Press, 2009), 94-96.

31. Francesco Datini, *Le lettere di Francesco Datini alla moglie Margherita (1385–1410)*, ed. Elena Cecchi (Prato, Italy: Società pratese di Storia Patria, 1990); Federigo Melis, *Aspetti della vita economica medievale: Studi nell'Archivio Datini di Prato* (Florence: Leo S. Olschki, 1962). The same was true for the prolific Paston family of England a few decades later. Norman Davis, ed., *Paston Letters* (Oxford: Clarendon, 1958).

32. Federico Chabod, "Alcune questioni di terminologia: Stato, nazione, patria nel linguaggio del Cinquecento," in *Scritti sul Rinascimento* (Turin, Italy: Einaudi, 1967), 625-661.

33. See generally the essays within Julius Kirshner, ed., *The Origins of the Italian State in Italy, 1300–1600* (Chicago: Chicago University Press, 1996).

34. Francesco Sforza, Galeazzo's predecessor, described the system in 1461. Paul Marcus Dover, "Ambassadors as Travelers in Italy in the Second Half of the Fifteenth Century," in *Travel and Conflict in the Early Modern World*, ed. Gábor Gelléri and Rachel Willie (New York: Routledge, 2022), 147–166. Thanks to the editors and author for sharing an advance copy.

35. Paolo Vollmeier, *Bolli prefilatelici di Milano dalle origini al 1850* (Padua, Italy: A. Ausilio, 1976). Envelopes carried in safe-conduct processions could bear a similar noose. Luca Scholz, *Borders and Freedom of Movement in the Holy Roman Empire* (Oxford: Oxford University Press, 2020), 66.

36. Letter from Galeazzo Sforza to Nicodemo Trenchedini (July 29–30, 1471), in Lorenzo de' Medici, *Lettere*, vol. 1, ed. Riccardo Fubini, Nicolai Rubinstein, F. W. Kent, et al. (Florence: Giunti-Barbèra, 1977), 318; Clemente Fedele and Marco Gallenga, *"Per servizio di nostro signore": Strade, corrieri, e poste dei papi dal medioevo al 1870* (Prato, Italy; Modena, Italy: Mucchi, 1988), 47, 79. In 1519, a courier brought Charles V news of the election of the ruler's former tutor as pope, traveling from Rome to Brussels in just twelve days. Geoffrey Parker, *Emperor: A New Life of Charles V* (New Haven, CT: Yale University Press, 2019), 383.

37. The "Canzona dei corrieri" or "canto dei corrieri" was one of a set of songs performed in the mid-sixteenth century and associated with various professions. Alessandro Granzini, *Canti carnascialeschi: Trionfi, carri e mascherate* (Milan: Casa Editrice Sonzogno, 1883), 257–258; Rachel Midura, "Italian Messengers and Couriers," in *Routledge Resources Online: The Renaissance World* (June 18, 2023), https://doi.org/10.4324/9780367347093-RERW103-1. A 1516 postal contract between the Tassis family of postmasters and Holy Roman Emperor Charles V set the time of a journey from Rome to Brussels as between 10½ and 12 days, depending on the season. Contract (March 1, 1501), in Martin Volker Albus Dallmeier, ed., *Quellen zur Geschichte des Europaischen Postwesens, 1501–1806*, vol. 2, no. 3 (Kallmünz, Germany: Lassleben, 1977), 4–5. Historians have often calculated the speed of couriers based on newsletter and correspondence collections, such as the isometric maps of time-distance from Venice in Fernand Braudel, *The Mediterranean and the Mediterranean World in the Age of Philip II* (Berkeley: University of California Press, 1995), 365–368. For a novel physiological approach to riding couriers, see Alberto Minetti, "Efficiency of Equine Express Postal Systems," *Nature: Brief Communications* 426, no. 6968 (2003): 785–786.

38. The body of scholarship on the Habsburg family is vast, but for a good overview, see Mia Rodríguez-Salgado, *The Changing Face of Empire: Charles V, Philip II, and Habsburg Authority, 1551–1559* (Cambridge: Cambridge University Press, 1988).

39. Wolfgang Behringer, *Thurn und Taxis: Die Geschichte ihrer Post und ihrer Unternehmen* (Munich: Piper, 1990). See also Wolfgang Behringer, *Im Zeichen des Merkur: Reichspost und Kommunikationsrevolution in der Frühen Neuzeit* (Göttingen, Germany: Vandenhoeck & Ruprecht, 2003).

40. See, for example, the discussion of the Tuscan papal postmaster Mattia Gherardi in chapter 2 of this book.

41. On the French posts, see Alexander Tessier, *La poste, servante et actrice des relations internationales (XVIe–XIXe siècle)* (Brussels: Peter Lang, 2016); John Rule and Ben Trotter, *A World of Paper: Louis XIV, Colbert de Torcy, and the Rise of the Information State* (Montreal, Canada: McGill-Queen's University Press, 2014); Eugène Vaillé, *Histoire generale des postes françaises* (Paris: Presses universitaires de France, 1949-1955). On the British posts, see James Daybell and Andrew Gordon, eds., *Cultures of Correspondence in Early Modern Britain* (Philadelphia: University of Pennsylvania Press, 2016); Lindsay O'Neill, *The Opened Letter: Networking in the Early Modern British World* (Philadelphia: University of Pennsylvania Press, 2015); Duncan Campbell-Smith, *Masters of the Post: The Authorized History of the Royal Mail* (London: Allen Lane, 2011).

42. On the Spanish Atlantic, see Sylvia Sellers Garcia, *Distance and Documents at the Spanish Empire's Periphery* (Stanford, CA: Stanford University Press, 2014). On the eastern Mediterranean, see Bruno Crevato-Selvaggi, "Tra Parigi e Constantinopoli: Una via postale rivoluzionaria attraverso Sebenico in Dalmazia," *Archivio per la storia postale* 43, no. 14 (September–December 2021): 31-54; Eric Dursteler, "Power and Information: The Venetian Postal System in the Early Modern Eastern Mediterranean," in *From Florence to the Mediterranean and Beyond: Essays in Honour of Antony Molho*, ed. Diogo Ramada Curto and Niki Koniordos (Florence: L. S. Olski, 2009), 601-623.

43. Despite the similarity to the Italian term for horses (*cavalli*), *tabellari* or "cavallari" did not technically designate messengers on horseback. As with "messenger," from the Latin *missum*, or message, the term is derived from the item being carried—in this case, tablets. See "Tabellarius," in *A Latin Dictionary*, ed. Charlton T. Lewis and Charles Short (Oxford: Clarendon, 1879). Accessed via the Perseus Digital Library, at https://www.perseus.tufts.edu/hopper/text?doc=Perseus:text:1999.04.0059:entry=tabellarius.

44. Luigi Dedé, "Il servizio postale fra Brescia e Venezia durante il dominio veneto," in *Commentari dell'Ateneo di Brescia per l'anno 1986* (Brescia, Italy: Tipolito Fratelli Geroldi, 1987), 157-198.

45. Goldthwaite, *The Economy of Renaissance Florence*, 95.

46. On the related distinction between information and knowledge, see Peter Burke, *A Social History of Knowledge: From Gutenberg to Diderot* (Cambridge: Polity, 2000).

47. Drelichman and Voth explain the popularity of contingent lending to Philip II (present in 270 of 393 identified contracts) as resulting from the verifiability of news: "Commercial gazettes all over Europe carried detail on the value of treasure brought from the Indies; a major determinant of the king's fiscal position became public knowledge almost instantly." Mauricio Drelichman and Hans-Joachim Voth, *Lending to the Borrower from Hell: Debt, Taxes, and Default in the Age of Philip II* (Princeton, NJ: Princeton University Press, 2016), 233. In fact, the speed of different channels and the dangers of preferential service, especially for the Genoese, were a major source of conflict, which I discuss further in chapter 4 of this book.

48. This was allegedly spoken by Dr. François Quesnay with reference to French postal surveillance, quoted in Amy M. Sacker, ed., *Memoirs of the Courts of Louis XV and XVI: Being Secret Memoirs of Madame Du Hausset Lady's Maid to Madame*

De Pompadour and of the Princess Lamballe (Boston: L. C. Page, 1899). Accessed via Project Gutenberg, https://www.gutenberg.org/ebooks/3883 (unpaginated).

49. The letter is undated, but it likely originates from the struggles with merchants faced by Ruggero Tassis of Milan between 1566 and 1582 and discussed in chapter 3 of this book. See also Archivio di Stato di Milano (ASMi), *Miscellanea Storica (MS)*, 43.

50. See chapter 1 of this volume for more on the use of the term "information war" in international relations. On information war and the relationship between state and civil society, see Paul Virilio, *Speed and Politics: An Essay on Dromology*, trans. Mark Polizzotti (Cambridge, MA: MIT Press, 2006).

51. Jon R. Snyder, *Dissimulation and the Culture of Secrecy in Early Modern Europe* (Berkeley: University of California Press, 2012); James H. Johnson, *Venice Incognito: Masks in the Serene Republic* (Berkeley: University of California Press, 2011); Fernando R. de la Flor, *Pasiones Frías: Secreto y disimulación en al Barroco hispano* (Madrid: Marcial Pons, 2005).

52. Safley, *Family Firms*, 20.

53. "Guardare a chi uno fida le lettere. Così, Guardate a chi voi fidare le vostre lettere," in Lorenzo Franciosini, *Vocabolario italiano e spagnolo* (Rome: Ruffinelli & Manni, 1620), 305.

1. The Tassis Family Firm

1. The play premiered in Venice in 1746. Carlo Goldoni, *Il servitore di due padroni*, ed. Valentina Gallo (Venice: Marsilio Editori, 2011).

2. Rosa Salzberg makes a similar point in *The Renaissance on the Road: Mobility, Migration and Cultural Exchange* (Cambridge: Cambridge University Press, 2023).

3. Renata Ago and Benedetta Borello, eds., *Famiglie: Circolazione di beni, circuiti di affetti in età moderna* (Rome: Viella Libreria Editrice, 2008).

4. Elena Bonora, *Aspettando l'Imperatore: Principi italiani tra il papa e Carlo V* (Turin, Italy: Einaudi, 2014).

5. The *Journal of Information Warfare* is produced by, and largely for, the cyberdefense industry. The term "information war" has gained wider prominence associated with twenty-first-century Russian disinformation campaigns. See, for example, Richard Stengel, *Information Wars: How We Lost the Global Battle against Disinformation and What We Can Do about It* (New York: Atlantic Monthly, 2019).

6. André J. Krischer and Hillard von Thiessen, "Diplomacy in a Global Early Modernity: The Ambiguity of Sovereignty," *International History Review* 41, no. 5 (2019): 1100–1107.

7. Thomas Max Safley, *Family Firms and Merchant Capitalism in Early Modern Europe* (New York: Routledge, 2020), 37; Mark Casson, "The Economics of the Family Firm: An Analysis of the Dynastic Motive," *Scandinavian Economic History Review* 47, no. 1 (1999): 10–23.

8. Tarcisio Bottani, "Tasso di Valle Brembana: I Signori delle poste d'Europa," in *I Signori delle Alpi, Famiglie e poteri tra le montagne d'Europa*, ed. Luca Giarelli (Tricase, Italy: Self-published, 2015), 179–195. See also Tarcisio Bottani and

Adriano Cattani, eds., *Cornello e i Tasso* (Bergamo, Italy: Museo dei Tasso e della Storia Postale and Corponove, 2010).

9. Bottani, "Tasso di Valle Brembana."

10. Many copies of this document dating to December 30, 1305, survive in the archives of the company, which are now held in the Archivio di Stato di Venezia.

11. The composition of the voting bench (*banco*) altered over time, but generally five or six members served in elected positions, headed by the gastaldo.

12. This document also exists in many copies and dates to October 30, 1490. Bonaventura Foppolo, "La Mariegola della Compagnia dei Corrieri Veneti," in *Le poste dei Tasso, un'impresa in Europa: Contributi in occasione della mostra I Tasso, l'evoluzione delle poste . . . 28 aprile–3 giugno 1984*, ed. Tarcisio Bottani (Bergamo, Italy: Comune di Bergamo, 1984), 13–45. See also Tarcisio Bottani and Wanda Taufer, eds., *Mariegola della Compagnia dei Corrieri della Serenissima Signoria* (Bergamo, Italy: Museo dei Tasso e della Storia Postale and Corponove, 2001).

13. The company was temporarily forced from this location after the fire and instead operated out of Sant'Aponal. It returned by 1520. Bottani and Taufer, *Mariegola*, 28.

14. On Venetian guild culture, see, generally, Richard MacKenny, *Venice as the Polity of Mercy: Guilds, Confraternities, and the Social Order, c. 1250–c. 1650* (Toronto: University of Toronto Press, 2019).

15. See *capitolo* (chapter) 11 in Bottani and Taufer, *Mariegola*, 78.

16. The precise number of members in the Venetian Company varied over time, as shown by various capitoli of the *Mariegola*. The forty couriers in 1489 (capitoli 1 and 17) became thirty-one by the mid-sixteenth century by order of the Provveditori di Comun (capitoli 55-59) and thirty-two by the end of the century (capitolo 112). Bottani and Taufer, *Mariegola*, 75, 79, 90–92, 133-134. In 1439, the Roman couriers were also encouraged to reduce their numbers, Archivio Apostolico Vaticano (ASV), Arm. LIII, 13, c. 284v, in *Mariegola*. Early measures like the instructions given to couriers in 1355 and a later controversy over the regulation of livery demonstrate a similar standardization of the profession of couriership. See, generally, Clemente Fedele and Marco Gallenga, *"Per servizio di nostro signore": Strade, corrieri, e poste dei papi dal medioevo al 1870* (Modena, Italy: Mucchi, 1988), and Margaret Meserve, *Papal Bull: Print, Politics, and Propaganda in Renaissance Rome* (Baltimore: Johns Hopkins University Press, 2021), 32.

17. See capitolo 6 in Bottani and Taufer, *Mariegola*, 77.

18. See, for example, the rights granted to the merchants of Milan in Venice in Ettore Verga, *La Camera dei mercanti di Milano nei secoli passati* (Milan: Allegretti, 1914), 164.

19. Bottani and Taufer, *Mariegola*, 22.

20. Klaus Beyrer, "Botenwesen," in *Enzyklopädie der Neuzeit* (Leiden, Netherlands: Brill, 2014), columns 361–366.

21. Wolfgang Behringer, *Im Zeichen des Merkur: Reichsport und Kommunikationsrevolution in der Frühen Neuzeit* (Göttingen, Germany: Vandenhoeck & Ruprecht, 2003), 53–60. Fedele and Gallenga, *Per servizio*, 35. The records for Visconti postal practice were hard-hit by the archival losses in the 1440s. Paul Marcus

Dover, "Deciphering the Diplomatic Archives of Fifteenth-Century Italy," *Archival Science* 7 (2007): 301.

22. Andrea Gamberini, "Milan and Lombardy in the Era of the Visconti and Sforza," in *A Companion to Late Medieval and Early Modern Milan: The Distinctive Features of an Italian State*, ed. Andrea Gamberini (Leiden, Netherlands: Brill, 2015), 19–45. See also Caterina Santoro, *Gli offici del Comune di Milano e del dominio visconteo sforzesco (1216–1515)* (Milan: A. Giuffrè, 1968).

23. Bottani, "Tasso di Valle Brembana," 180–181.

24. In 1463, Cristoforo Tassis received the title of *magister cursorum venetorum* in Rome and payments from the Camera Apostolica. Archivio Segreto Vaticano, *Camera Apostolica, Introitus et Exitus*, 455; Archivio di Stato di Roma, *Camerale I, Mandati*, 847–851 in Bottani, "Tasso di Valle Brembana," 182–183. See, generally, Fedele and Gallenga, *Per servizio*.

25. It remains difficult to identify the correct Ruggero. Tarcisio Bottani, *Francesco Tasso e la nascita delle poste d'Europa nel Rinascimento* (Bergamo, Italy: Museo dei Tasso e della Storia Postale and Corponove, 2017), 3–25.

26. This is based on the supposition that Janetto Tassis was the same "Janetto da Bergamo" who had received payment as a papal courier in Rome. Bottani, *Francesco Tasso*, 3–25.

27. Payments to "Johann Dachs" also appear in the *Tiroler Raitbuchern* from Innsbruck. Stadtbibliothek Memmingen, *Memminger Stadtchronike*, Inv.n.2.2.20. Bottani, *Francesco Tasso*, 29; Bottani, "Tasso di Valle Brembrana," 185. See also Wolfgang Behringer, *Thurn und Taxis: Die Geschichte ihrer Post und ihrer Unternehmen* (Munich: Piper, 1990), 26–30.

28. The French system employed similar terminology, although Rule and Trotter refer to the use of "postmaster" as a mistranslation of *maître de poste*. John Rule and Ben Trotter, *A World of Paper: Louis XIV, Colbert de Torcy, and the Rise of the Information State* (Montreal, Canada: McGill-Queen's University Press, 2014), 213.

29. See, for example, a 1517 edict that accords Giovan Battista Tassis rights as the "*maistre de nous postes et couriers*." Edict (November 30, 1517) in Martin Volker Albus Dallmeier, ed., *Quellen zur Geschichte des Europaischen Postwesens, 1501–1806*, vol. 2, no. 6 (Kallmünz, Germany: Lassleben, 1977), 6.

30. Pay records at the Archives départementales du Nord (ADN) show the early involvement of Davide Tassis (d. 1538) and Giovanni Battista Tassis (d. 1541), among others. These are transcribed and treated in greater depth in Giorgio Migliavacca and Tarcisio Bottani, *Simone Tasso e le poste di Milano nel Rinascimento* (Bergamo, Italy: Museo dei Tasso e della Storia Postale and Corponove, 2007).

31. Edict (March 11, 1490). See Behringer, *Thurn und Taxis*, 26–30. Christoph Schorer, *Memminger Chronik oder Kurtze Erzählung vieler denkwürdiger Sachen* (Ulm, Germany: Kühnen, 1660), 51. Bottani, *Francesco Tasso*, 30.

32. In 1508, Janetto Tassis described himself as having served as "*magistro dei corrieri e poste* with my brothers and nephews for 20 years." Fürst Thurn und Taxis Hofbibliothek und Zentralarchiv (FTTZA), *Taxis Bergamo Urkunden* 27, n. 5. Privilege of Francesco Tassis (March 1, 1501) in ADN, b. 2.178. See also Dallmeier, *Quellen*, vol. 2, no. 1, 3. Dallmeier's transcription instead refers to Francesco as "*capitaine et maistre des nos postes*."

33. Postal Contract of Philip I (January 18, 1505), in FTTZA, *PU*, 1. See also Dallmeier, *Quellen*, vol. 2, no. 2, 3.

34. See, generally, David Parrott, *The Business of War: Military Enterprise and Military Revolution in Early Modern Europe* (Cambridge: Cambridge University Press, 2012).

35. Bonaventura Foppolo, "La parabola del ramo veneziano dei Tasso da Cornello a Venezia," in *I Tasso e le poste d'Europa*, ed. Tarcisio Bottani (Bergamo, Italy: Corponove, 2012), 27-48. A petition for pay in 1502 survives in the Tiroler Landesarchiv (TLA), *Maximiliana*, XIV, 206 and is transcribed in Bottani, *Francesco Tassis*, 32.

36. TLA, *Geschäft von Hof*, 1505-1507, in Erika Kustatscher, *Die Innsbrucker Linie der Thurn und Taxis: Die Post in Tirol und den Vorlanden (1490-1769)* (Innsbruck, Austria: Universitätsverlag Wagner, 2018), 19-20. Behringer, *Thurn und Taxis*, 44. On the Istrian holdings, see Girolamo Figini, *I Tasso e i feudi di Rachele e Barbana nell'Istria* (Bergamo, Italy: Fagnani & Galeazzi, 1895).

37. For a close reading of the tapestry's symbolism, see the "Wall Tapestry— The Legend of Our Lady of the Sablon" visiting aid provided by the Brussels City Museum; available online at http://www.brusselscitymuseum.brussels/documents/view/wall-tapestry-the-legend-of-our-lady-of-the-sablonpdf?id=157. Max Piendl, *Wandteppiche des Hauses Thurn und Taxis* (Munich: Hirmer, 1967). See also Max Piendl, *Beiträge zur Geschichte Kunst und Kulturpflege im Hause Thurn und Taxis* (Kallmünz, Germany: Lassleben, 1978).

38. Gianni Molinari, "Villa Celadina, aspetti descrittivi," in *I Tasso e le poste*, ed. Bottani, 135-140; Gabriele Medolago, "Villa Celadini e le dimore tassiane in Bergamo: Primi risultati di una ricerca," in *I Tasso e le poste*, ed. Bottani, 141-164.

39. See, generally, Bonora, *Aspettando l'Imperatore*.

40. The failure of the Tassis bank occasioned much dismay and gossip among its Venetian investors, as recorded by the Venetian diarist Marin Sanudo. The fugitive banker, Lorenzo Tassis, was brought to the Castel Sant'Angelo on rumors that he had committed several homicides. By January, Sanudo recorded merely that "the creditors of Lorenzo di Taxis have been brought to an agreement." See the entries of November 1518 through February 1519 in Marino Sanudo, *I diarii di Marino Sanuto*, ed. Rinaldo Fulin, et al., vol. 26 (Venice: F. Visentini, 1889), columns 216-219, 233-234, 243-244, 251-252, 285, 359, 485-486. On the moral repugnancy of bankruptcy, see, generally, Safley, *Family Firms*.

41. Entry of May 30, 1526, in Sanudo, *Diarii*, vol. 41 (1894), columns 290-292.

42. Ago and Borello, eds., *Famiglie*, 10.

43. Decree (May 31, 1512). Bruno Caizzi, *Dalla posta dei re alla posta di tutti: Territorio e comunicazioni in Italia dal XVI secolo all'Unità* (Milan: Franco Angeli, 1993), 19.

44. Charles V mentioned the conflict among the Tassis in a letter to his wife transcribed in *Annales de las ordenanzas*, 8. The deception is referenced by an archival note from 1726. Migliavacca and Bottani, *Simone Tasso*, 107.

45. They shared this problem with other expatriated Italian dynasties that were active in both politics and commerce, such as the Gondi of France. See, generally, Joanna Milstein, *The Gondi Family: Strategy and Survival in Early Modern France* (New York: Routledge, 2016).

46. See, generally, Ago and Borello, eds., *Famiglie*.

47. Tarcisio Bottani, Gianfranco Lazzarini, et al., *Genealogia Tasso* (Bergamo, Italy: Santini Pubblicità, July 2007), https://www.museodeitasso.com/export/sites/default/documenti/albero-genealogico-casato-tasso.pdf.

48. This echoes the unofficial Habsburg motto, *Bella gerant alii, tu felix Austria nube*. Both seventeenth-century genealogists Jules Chifflet and Francesco Zazzera provide much of the documentation cited in later works, discussed in greater detail in chapter 7 of this book. Elisabetta Tassis, sister to Simone, married Bono Bordogna in 1509. Postmistress Marquessa Victoria Zapata Tassis of Sicily (d. 1635), granddaughter to Simone, went on to serve as postmistress in her widowhood (o. 1612-1634).

49. On the Zapatas, see Vincenzo Fardella de Quernfort, "Documenti tassiani in Sicilia: La nascita della Regia Correria di Sicilia," in *I Tasso e le poste d'Europa*, ed. Bottani, 125-134.

50. Behringer, *Thurn und Taxis*, 479.

51. Migliavacca and Bottani, *Simone Tasso*, 169. For more on postmistress-widows, see chapter 4 of this book.

52. Katia Occhi, "Exploiting the Alps: Wood Supplies and Waterways in Early Modern Europe," *Annali dell'Istituto storico italo-germanico in Trento* 46, no. 2 (2020): 36.

53. See, generally, A. Le Glay, ed., *Correspondance de l'empereur Maximilien Ier et de Marguerite d'Autriche . . . de 1507 à 1519* (Paris: J. Renouard, 1839).

54. Translated and included in James van der Linden, "The Thurn und Taxis Postal Administration in the Spanish Netherlands from 1492 to 1713: A Postal Historical Survey," in *I Tasso le poste d'Europa*, ed. Bottani, 291.

55. See capitolo 32 in Bottani and Taufer, *Mariegola*, 83. For an overview of the incident, see Bonaventura Foppolo, "La Mariegola della Compagnia dei Corrieri," in *Mariegola*, ed. Bottani and Taufer, 19. See also Tarcisio Bottani, *I Tasso e le poste pontificie, sec. XV-XVI* (Bergamo, Italy: Corponove, 2000), 117-118.

56. See capitolo 33 in Bottani and Taufer, *Mariegola*, 84.

57. The legal battle to regain control of the fiefdoms outlived Janetto, stretching into the 1530s. Tarcisio Bottani, "I testamenti di Ruggero, Janetto, e Leonardo Tasso," in *I Tasso e le poste d'Europa*, ed. Bottani, 14-15. See, generally, Figini, *I Tasso e i feudi*.

58. This is often quite literal: the Tassis correspondence demonstrates proficiency in many of the languages associated with the Habsburg realms.

59. Margaret Jacobs finds that the perception and policing of the threat of cosmopolitanism may involve authorities, but they often originate in popular xenophobia. Margaret Jacobs, *Strangers Nowhere in the World: The Rise of Cosmopolitanism in Early Modern Europe* (Philadelphia: University of Pennsylvania Press, 2006), 17-18. J. H. Elliot, "A Europe of Composite Monarchies," *Past and Present* 137 (November 1992): 48-71. H. G. Koenigsberger, "Dominium Regale or Dominium Politicum et Regale: Monarchies and Parliaments in Early Modern Europe," in *Politicians and Virtuosi: Essays in Early Modern History*, ed. H. G. Koenigsberger (London: Hambledon, 1986), 1-25.

60. See Geoffrey Parker, *Emperor: A New Life of Charles V* (New Haven, CT: Yale University Press, 2019), 82-83. Edict (August 28, 1518), in Dirección General de

Correos y Telégrafos, *Anales de las ordenanzas de correos de España* (Madrid: Victor Saiz, 1879), 3–5. See also Dallmeier, *Quellen*, vol. 2, no. 8, 8–9.

61. Sanudo, *Diarii*, vol. 29 (1890), column 262.

62. Entries of December 1519 through March 1520 in Sanudo, *Diarii*, vol. 27 (1890), columns 218, 338, 341, 385–386. Many members of the Gamba family can be found in the Venetian Company rolls.

63. Both agreements are mentioned in the entries of September 1521 in Sanudo, *Diarii*, vol. 31 (1891), columns 376, 419–420.

64. Entries of February 18 and 19, 1524, in Sanudo, *Diarii*, vols. 35 (1892) and 36 (1903), columns 447, 453. Literally "trumpet," the term *trombetta* may also refer to an eponymous messenger, or "trumpeter."

65. That did not mean that they were always reliable: Sanudo wrote with disgust about a courier spreading the false news that the new pope had died in Barcelona. Entry of June 3, 1533, in Sanudo, *Diarii*, vol. 33 (1892), column 276.

66. Entry of September 6, 1525, in Sanudo, *Diarii*, vol. 39 (1894), column 402.

67. Entry of November 1525 in Sanudo, *Diarii*, vol. 40 (1894), column 229.

68. Bonora, *Aspettando l'Imperatore*, 16.

69. María José Bertomeu Masiá, ed., *La guerra secreta de Carlos V contra el Papa— La cuestión de Parma y Piacenza en la correspondencia del cardenal Granvela* (Valencia, Spain: Publicacions de la Universitat de València, 2009). Maria Antonietta Visceglia, "'Farsi imperiale': Faide familiari e identità politiche a Roma nel primo Cinquecento," in *L'Italia di Carlo V: Guerra, religione e politica nel primo Cinquecento*, ed. Francesca Cantù and Maria Antonietta Visceglia (Rome: Viella, 2003), 477–508.

70. The earliest appearance in Archivo General de Simancas (AGS) appears to be a Spanish-language copy of the privilege of Simone Tassis of March 15, 1518, in AGS, 128. See *Annales de las ordenanzas de correos*, 3. The first instance recorded by Martin Dallmeier's transcriptions does not occur until 1595, in an agreement between the Milanese office and Leonardo von Tassis. In the index, Dallmeier merely translates the term into the German *Postmeister*. Dallmeier, *Quellen*, vol. 2, no. 95, 46–47.

71. This chapter builds upon an excellent biography, Migliavacca and Bottani, *Simone Tasso*.

72. Carlo de Lellis, *Discorsi delle famiglie nobili del Regno di Napoli, parte I* (Naples: Honorio Safio, 1654), 423. Migliavacca and Bottani, *Simone Tasso*, 43.

73. Migliavacca and Bottani, *Simone Tasso*, 40–59.

74. [Simon de Taxis] to [Spinelly] (December 10, 1515), Cotton Vitellius B/II f.187, accessed via British State Papers Online (SP) MC4300581277. Louis Maroton to Francis de Taxis, Master of the Posts, SP 1/4 f.86, SPO MC4300380244; Francis Taxis to Sir Bryan Tucke, postmaster in England (March 23, 1516), Cotton Galba B/IV, f.49, SPO MC4318890128.

75. Francis de Taxis to the Council (January 3, 1513), Cotton Galba B/III f.68, SPO MC4318890039.

76. Letter from Sir Robert Wingfield (July 10, 1515), in *Letters and Papers, Foreign and Domestic, of the Reign of Henry VIII*, ed. J. S. Brewer, vol. 2, part I: 1515–1516 (London: Longman, Roberts & Green, 1864), n. 684. For more on the role of cryptography, see chapter 2 of this book.

77. "Ultima Nova ex Italia" and Letter of Thomas Spinelly to Henry VIII (July 8, 1512), SP 1/2 f.147–151, in *Letters and Papers, Foreign and Domestic, of the Reign of Henry VIII*, ed. J. S. Brewer and R. H. Brodie, vol. 1, part I: 1509–1513 (London: His Majesty's Stationery Office, 1920), SPO MC4300201328 & MC4300281329. Simone Tassis wrote to Wolsey to pressure the treasurer for payment for the posts between Calais and Brussels. Letter from Simon de Taxis to Wolsey (March 7, 1518) SP 1/16 f.157, in *Letters and Papers, Foreign and Domestic, of the Reign of Henry VIII*, ed. J. S. Brewer, vol. 2, part II: 1517–1518 (London: Longman, Roberts & Green, 1864), SPO MC4300601271.

78. Bottani and Cattani, eds., *Cornello e i Tasso*.

79. Letter of Thomas Spinelly to Henry VIII (March 23, 1518), Cotton Vespasian C/I f.127, in *Letters and Papers*, vol. 2, part II, SPO MC4300601294.

80. Migliavacca and Bottani, *Simone Tasso*, 105.

81. Entries of November 4 and 7, 1521, in Sanudo, *Diarii*, vol. 32 (1892), columns 105, 107. See note 64 regarding the ambiguity of the term *trombetta*.

82. Entry of September 1521 in Sanudo, *Diarii*, vol. 31, columns 376, 419–420.

83. See entries of October 1525 in Sanudo, *Diarii*, vol. 40, columns 134, 143.

84. Simone Tassis appears frequently in 1525–1526. See Sanudo, *Diarii*, vol. 40, columns 369, 382, 392–393, 403, 406, 420, 434, 482, 605, 631, 644, 709, 727, 780, 782–783, 840, 881. Sanudo's diary preserves a letter from one "Alosius Taxis" from Milan regarding French intelligence received from Lyon. Letter of January 8, 1526, in Sanudo, *Diarii*, column 648. "Cristoforo Tasso, Bergamasco," can be tentatively identified as either a Venetian courier, or less likely, the postal official in Augsburg. Sanudo further indicates that Simone acquired news in Spain from his nephew, Bartolomeo Vitali, who served in his stead when Simone withdrew for his health in 1527. Sanudo, *Diarii*, vol. 40, column 783.

85. Entries of November and December 1525 in Sanudo, *Diarii*, vol. 40, column 369.

86. Entry of October 1523, in Sanudo, *Diarii*, vol. 34 (1892), columns 424–426. On the harassment, see the entry of April 2, 1524, in Sanudo, *Diarii*, vol. 35, columns 151–152.

87. Entry of April 5, 1526, in Sanudo, *Diarii*, vol. 41, column 148.

88. They then forwarded a letter from Simone, indicating, perhaps, the source of the warning. Entries of November 26, 1525, in Sanudo, *Diarii*, vol. 40, columns 368–369.

89. Entry of July 25, 1532, in Sanudo, *Diarii*, vol. 56 (1901), column 639.

90. Entry of June 22, 1526, in Sanudo, *Diarii*, vol. 56, columns 691–693. Another similar incident took place in April. The Venetian spy Zuan Griego ran into several imperial couriers, asking each what news they carried. While the first replied only "bad," the second responded with detailed fears of an impending uprising in Milan. Entry of April 26, 1526, in Sanudo, *Diarii*, vol. 41, column 230. The Venetian Council of Ten secretly mandated the interception of imperial couriers by 1529. Megan Williams, "The Perils of the Post Road: Diplomats, Diplomatic Couriers, and the Informational Fabric of Early Modern Europe," in *Information and Power in History: Towards a Global Approach*, ed. Ida Nijenhuis, M. van Faasen, Ronal Sluijter, Joris Gijsenbergh, and Wim de Jong (Abingdon: Routledge, 2020), 112–113.

91. Entry of January 20, 1526, in Sanudo, *Diarii*, vol. 40, columns 701–702.

92. Entry of October 19, 1519, in Sanudo, *Diarii*, vol. 28 (1890), column 32.

93. Figini, *I Tasso e i feudi*.

94. Milan began the century with a population of around 100,000, which fell midcentury to around 70,000 before reaching 120,000 again by 1600. Jan de Vries, *European Urbanization, 1500-1800* (Cambridge, MA: Harvard University Press, 1984). See also Stefano d'Amico, *Spanish Milan: A City within Empire* (London: Palgrave Macmillan, 2016).

95. Bonora, *Aspettando l'Imperatore*.

96. See, generally, Parker, *Emperor*.

97. Postmasters resemble Italian *condottieri*, and later military contractors who received titles in exchange for the ability to muster and manage troops. See, generally, Parrott, *The Business of War*.

98. Postal ordinance (January 9, 1533) in Archivio di Stato di Milano (ASMi), *Atti di Governo (AG), Finanze*, 933. Transcribed in Migliavacca and Bottani, *Simone Tasso*, 83-84.

99. Payments to Simone Tassis (November 10, 1536) (January 15, 1538), in ASMi, *Registri*, XXII, 1.

100. Paolo Malanima, *L'economia italiana: Dalla crescita medievale alla crescita contemporanea* (Bologna, Italy: Società editrice il Mulino, 2002).

101. ASMi, *Registri*, XXII, 1.

102. See, for example, the letters of Alessandro Landriano (imperial envoy in Parma) to the governor of Milan, Cardinal Marino Caracciolo (September 6, 1536), in ASMi, *Carteggio*, 7.

103. Payments to Pietro Martire Borro and Giovanni Paolo Carrara (May 12, 1537). See various payments in ASMi, *Registri*, XXII, 1.

104. Sarto often wrote directly to Spanish patrons, bypassing Tassis to request reimbursement or privileges. Letter from Giovan Antonio ("detto il Sarto") to Cardinal Caraza (January 9, 1537), in ASMi, *Carteggio*, 20.

105. Letter from Giovan Antonio Vignale ("il Sarto") to Cardinal Caracciolo (December 21, 1536), in ASMi, *Carteggio*, 7.

106. Letter from Giovan Antonio Vignale ("il Sarto") to Cardinal Caracciolo (December 21, 1536), in ASMi, *Carteggio*, 7.

107. Letter from il Sarto to Cardinal Caraza (January 9, 1537), in ASMi, *Carteggio*, 20.

108. Stefano dall'Aglio, *The Duke's Assassin: Exile and Death of Lorenzino de' Medici*, trans. Donald Weinstein (New Haven, CT: Yale University Press, 2015), 10-11. Gene Brucker, *Florence: The Golden Age, 1138-1737* (Berkeley: University of California, 1998), 258.

109. The orders of Governor Antonio de Leyva (March 10, 1536) are transcribed in Emilio Motta, "Un regolamente postale milanese del 1535-1536," *Archivio Storico Lombardo* 33, no. 10 (1906): 425. Simone circulated the 1536 series of instructions of ordinances issued by Charles V, which confirmed Simone Tassis's rights of appointment and salary distribution over all other imperial postmasters in Italy. The governor asked local rectors to sign a document signifying their receipt and obedience. See a signed document of receipt and obedience by the rectors of Cremona (November 19, 1536) in ASMi, *AG, Finanze*, 933. Dallmeier, *Quellen*, vol. 2, no. 15, 11-12.

NOTES TO PAGES 42–44

110. Letter from Francesco Tassignano to Francesco Taverna (Grand Chancellor of Milan) (April 7, 1536), in ASMi, *Carteggio*, 7.

111. "Gian de Steffano detto Capeletto" is listed as vice steward (*vice gastaldo*) of the Venetian Company of Couriers in an entry from August 31, 1537 in Archivio di Stato di Venezia (ASVe), *Corrieri*, 21 and 62. Tassignano further described him as "serving the Cavallaro Benzon." Payments to a "Benzono Cavallaro" appear in the Milanese registry of the same period, often riding to and from Turin. ASMi, *Registri*, 22.

112. Luigi Dedé, "Il servizio postale fra Brescia e Venezia durante il dominio veneto," in *Commentari dell'Ateneo di Brescia per l'anno 1986* (Brescia, Italy: Tipolito Fratelli Geroldi, 1987), 186.

113. Tassignano to Taverna in ASMi, *Carteggio*, 7. Directive from Governor Antonio de Lleyva (June 10, 1536), in *Carteggio*. The struggle to establish mastery in the post house notably coincided with an overall shift in master-servant relations in northern Italy. See Dennis Romano, *Housecraft and Statecraft: Domestic Service in Renaissance Venice* (Baltimore: Johns Hopkins University Press, 1996).

114. Francesco Bonamigo (d. 1492) had played a key role in formalizing the Venetian Company of Couriers in 1489, around the time of the company charter. By 1492, his son took over as *magister cursorum*, as well as a salaried brokerage at the German residence and storehouse (*Fondaco dei Tedeschi*). The Bonamigo sold the office to the de Sancti family, by which point it was more commonly referred to as the corriero maggiore, contemporaneous to the appearance of the term in imperial sources. The de Sancti family passed the office down through several generations before selling it to Ludovico Fioravante (d. 1538). Entries from July 29, 1492, and January 1524 in ASVe, *Compagnia*, I, 1. Foppolo, "La Mariegola della Compagnia dei Corrieri Veneti," in *Mariegola*, ed. Bottani and Taufer, 28.

115. See Bottani and Taufer, *Mariegola*, 30.

116. Foppolo, "La Mariegola della Compagnia dei Corrieri Veneti," in *Le poste dei Tasso*, ed. Bottani, 51–86.

117. On Venetian social divisions of the sixteenth century, see James S. Grubb, "Elite Citizens," in *Venice Reconsidered: The History and Civilization of an Italian City-State, 1297–1797*, ed. John Jeffries Martin and Dennis Romano (Baltimore: Johns Hopkins University Press, 2000), 339–364.

118. Entry (January 6, 1521), in Sanudo, *Diarii*, vol. 29, column 560. The entry that connects these biographic threads is January 3, 1521, in Sanudo, *Diarri*, vol. 29, column 560. Fioravante had carried letters to and from France that had been crucial for a Venetian decision regarding French alliance. Entry (April 17, 1515), in Sanudo, *Diarii*, vol. 20, column 126. See also Patricia H. Labalme and Laura Sanguineti White, eds., *Venice, città excelentisisima: Selections from the Renaissance Diaries of Marin Sanudo*, trans. Linda L. Carroll (Baltimore: Johns Hopkins University Press, 2008), 140–142.

119. Ioanna Iordanou, *Venice's Secret Service: Organising Intelligence in the Renaissance* (Oxford: Oxford University Press, 2019), 162.

120. "Ordine al Maestro di Venetia" (December 16, 1538), in ASVe, *Corrieri*, 21. Decision against Lodovico Fioravante in favor of Bernardin da Janetto (April 8, 1538) in *Corrieri*.

121. See capitolo 78 (September 26, 1538), in Bottani and Taufer, *Mariegola*, 100.
122. ASVe, *Corrieri*, IV.
123. It is difficult to say whether this was an earlier practice, but it seems unlikely given a lack of documentation.
124. The complicated nature of Codogno's office belied this definition: he frequently shared the title of corriero maggiore with a Tassis widow-postmistress, her minor sons, and their Spanish noble patron, as later chapters of this book will explore. Ottavio Codogno, *Nuovo itinerario delle poste per tutto il mondo* (Milan: Girolamo Bordoni, 1608), 31.
125. Convention of February 9, 1542, ASMi, *Notarile*, cart. 10985, transcribed in Marco Gerosa, "Personaggi della posta dello Stato di Milano tra Simone e Ruggero Tasso," in *I Tasso e le poste d'Europa*, ed. Bottani, 81–92.
126. Archivio Storico Civico di Milano (ASC), *Famiglie*, 184; ASMi, *AG, Finanze*, 933. Additional related documents are in ASMi, *Carteggio*, 150; ASMi, *MS*, 41. Precise dates are often absent, but the events mentioned tie the documents to the early 1550s.
127. ASC, *Famiglie*, 184; ASMi, *AG, Finanze*, 933.

2. The Arrest of a Postmaster

1. The captain's report on the interception, Giovan Antonio's wrappers, and the details regarding the courier survive in the assorted documents within "Autos hechos en Roma relativos a los preliminares de la guerra entre Felipe II y Paulo IV" (1556) in Archivo General de Simancas (AGS), *Patronato Real (PR)*, 17, 49.
2. Letter from Bernardo Navagero to the Venetian Senate (July 9, 1556) in Bernardo Navagero, *Bernardo Navagero: Dispacci al Senato dal 7 settembre 1555 al 6 novembre 1557*, ed. Daniele Bernardo Santarelli (November 11, 2011), accessed at http://www.storiadivenezia.net/sito/testi/Navagero2.pdf; Pietro Nores, "Storia della guerra degli spagnoli contro Papa Paolo IV," *Archivio Storico italiano* 12 (1847): 346.
3. Angelo Massarelli, "Diarium VII," *Concilium Tridentinum: Diariorum, actorum, epistularum, tractatuum: Nova collectio*, vol. 7 (Freiburg im Breisgau, Germany: Herder, 1901), 292–293. Charles V would fully abdicate as Spanish monarch and Holy Roman emperor in August 1556. I have adopted the term "Spanish-imperial" for the summer of 1556, but Charles's heirs, Philip II of Spain and Ferdinand of Austria, Holy Roman emperor, maintained separate diplomatic representatives in Rome.
4. Nores, "Storia della guerra," 347.
5. On the homes and role of Cardinal Jean du Bellay, see Flaminia Bardati, "Between the King and the Pope: French Cardinals in Rome (1495–1560)," *Urban History* 37, no. 3 (2010): 419–433.
6. Letter from Bernardo Navagero to the Venetian Senate (July 14, 1556), in Navagero, *Bernardo Navagero*, 182.
7. See, for example, Cornel Zwierlein, *Discorso und Lex Dei: Die Entstehung neuer Denkrahmen im 16. Jahrhundert und die Wahrnehmung der französischen Religionskriege in Italien und Deutschland* (Göttingen, Germany: Vandenhoeck & Ruprecht, 2006), 264.

8. Elena Bonora, *Aspettando l'Imperatore: Principi italiani tra il papa e Carlo V* (Turin, Italy: Einaudi, 2014). See also José Ignacio Tellechea Idìgoras, "Felipe II y los Carafa: Noticias y sucesos de una difìcil relacìon," *Scriptorium Victoriense* 55, no. 1-2 (January 2008): 5-100.

9. See, for example, copies in the manuscripts of the Strozzi family held at the Folger Shakespeare Library, W.b.132, vol. 130.

10. Linda Frey and Marsha Frey, "Diplomatic Immunity/Privilege," in *The Encyclopedia of Diplomacy*, ed. G. Martel (New York: John Wiley, 2018), 1-10. Accessed via Wiley Online Library at https://doi.org/10.1002/9781118885154.dipl0410.

11. Maïa Pal, "Early Modern Extraterritoriality, Diplomacy, and the Transition to Capitalism," in *The Extraterritoriality of Law: History, Theory, Politics*, ed. Daniel S. Margolies, Umut Özsu, Maïa Pal, and Nntina Tzouvala (London: Routledge, 2019), 69-86. Classic accounts include Garrett Mattingly, *Renaissance Diplomacy* (London: Jonathan Cape, 1955), and Edward Robert Adair, *The Extraterritoriality of Ambassadors in the Sixteenth and Seventeenth Centuries* (London: Longmans, 1929).

12. Juraj Kittler adopts the same terminology in his work on conflict between the Venetian Company of Couriers and Rome. Juraj Kittler, "Renaissance Postal Wars: A Fight over the Lucrative Mail Connection between Rome and Venice," in *Second Convegno Internazionale Storia Postale. Sguardi multidisciplinary, sguardi diacronici*, ed. Bruno Crevato-Selvaggi and Raffaella Gerola (Prato, Italy: Istituto di studi storici postali Aldo Cechi, forthcoming).

13. Radim Polčák and Dan Jerker B. Svantesson, *Information Sovereignty* (Cheltenham: Edward Elgar, 2017).

14. See, generally, Hannah Marcus, *Forbidden Knowledge: Medicine, Science, and Censorship in Early Modern Italy* (Chicago: University of Chicago Press, 2020); Paul F. Grendler, *The Roman Inquisition and the Venetian Press, 1540–1605* (Princeton, NJ: Princeton University Press, 1977).

15. Contemporary terminology did not clearly distinguish a postmaster in his native city from a postmaster stationed abroad. In Italian, both appeared as either "master of couriers" (maestro dei corrieri) or "master of posts" (maestro delle poste), often interchangeably. In theory, the master of couriers oversaw the personnel, while the master of posts oversaw the physical and jurisdictional infrastructure, offering licenses and horses as needed. Either might serve their prince in a home city or be appointed to reside abroad. In practice, however, these distinctions were collapsed under the Tassis corriero maggiore, as discussed in chapter 1 of this book.

16. Frey and Frey, "Diplomatic Immunity/Privilege," 2.

17. Innkeepers often handled the collection and distribution of mail for their compatriots in Rome before the sixteenth century. Municipal messengers and merchant trading nations carried mail for both residents and expatriates. Wilhelm Beck, "Ursprung und Ende der fremden Posten in Rom," *Archiv für das Post- und Fernmeldewesen*, no. 1-7 (1959): 564-588.

18. The contract was given to distant relative Pellegrino Tassis, acting on behalf of Giovanni Baptista and Maffeo Tassis. Beck, "Ursprung und Ende," 571.

19. Papal bull (November 27, 1513) in Archivio Segreto Vaticano (ASV), Arm. XXIX, 72, c. 35. On the Vantaggio family and the Florentine *scarselle*, see Antonio di Bartolomeo del Vantaggio (d. 1480) in Richard Goldthwaite, *The Economy of Renaissance Florence* (Baltimore: Johns Hopkins University Press, 2009), 95. Clemente Fedele and Marco Gallenga, *"Per servizio di nostro signore": Strade, corrieri, e poste dei papi dal medioevo al 1870* (Modena, Italy: Mucchi, 1988), 52-55.

20. Giorgio Migliavacca and Tarcisio Bottani, *Simone Tasso e le poste di Milano nel Rinascimento* (Bergamo, Italy: Museo dei Tasso e della Storia Postale and Corponove, 2007), 72-74. Papal bull (December 21, 1523) ("Pro Maffeo fu Giovanni da Bergamo"), in ASV, Arm. XL, 5, c. 40-40v. See also Fedele and Gallenga, *Per servizio*, 52-55.

21. On the papal monarchy, see Peter Partner, *Renaissance Rome, 1500–1559: A Portrait of a Society* (Berkeley: University of California Press, 1976).

22. Elizabeth Cohen and Thomas Cohen, eds., *Words and Deeds in Renaissance Rome: Trials before the Papal Magistrates* (Toronto: University of Toronto Press, 1993).

23. Elections of Pellegrino Gamba (March 12, 1533) and Angelo Longo (December 26, 1556), in Archivio di Stato di Venezia (ASVe), *Compagnia dei Corrieri (Corrieri)*, 62. Bonaventura Foppolo, "La Mariegola della Compagnia dei Corrieri Veneti," in *Le poste dei Tasso, un'impresa in Europa: Contributi in occasione della mostra I Tasso, l'evoluzione delle poste . . . 28 aprile–3 giugno 1984*, ed. Tarcisio Bottani (Bergamo, Italy: Comune di Bergamo, 1984), 21-22. On gambling, see capitolo 99 in Tarcisio Bottani and Wanda Taufer, eds., *Mariegola della Compagnia dei Corrieri della Serenissima Signoria* (Bergamo, Italy: Museo dei Tasso e della Storia Postale and Corponove, 2001), 113-119.

24. The nickname roughly translates as "the lame," suggesting an injured or disabled leg. On the relationship between the imperial postmaster and diplomatic circles in Rome in the 1520s and 1530s, see Megan Williams, "The Perils of the Post Road: Diplomats, Diplomatic Couriers, and the Informational Fabric of Early Modern Europe," in *Information and Power in History: Towards a Global Approach*, ed. Ida Nijenhuis, M. van Faasen, Ronal Sluijter, Joris Gijsenbergh, and Wim de Jong (Abingdon: Routledge, 2020), 105-121.

25. Letter from Simone Tassis (February 11, 1547), photographed in Júlia Benavent, "Lettere dei Tasso a Madrid: Biblioteca Nacional de España e Real Biblioteca," in *I Tasso e le poste d'Europa*, ed. Tarcisio Bottani (Bergamo, Italy: Corponove, 2012), 238.

26. This presumably refers to the ducal and Spanish/imperial postmasterships of Milan. Letter of Simone Tassis to Granvelle (September 4, 1555), Real Biblioteca (RB) II 2271, ff.120r–121r in Júlia Benavent and Bruno Crevato-Selvaggi, eds., *La corrispondenza della famiglia Tasso con Antoine Perrenot de Granvelle* (Prato, Italy: Istituto di studi storici postali Aldo Cecchi, 2023), 161-162. Thanks to the editors for sharing an advance copy. For more on the tensions between Simone and Giovanni Baptista, Giovan Antonio's father, see chapter 1 of this book.

27. See letters of Cardinal Cristoforo Madruzzo from April and May 1556, including a letter from Mattia Gherardi on October 23, 1556. Cristoforo

Madruzzo, *L'epistolario del cardinale Cristoforo Madruzzo presso l'Archivio di Stato di Innsbruck*, ed. A. Galante (Trieste, Italy: Caprin, 1910).

28. These gifts alone would have been worth between 200–300 Florentine lire, or the equivalent of around eight months of wages for skilled labor. Paolo Malanima, *L'economia italiana: Dalla crescita medievale alla crescita contemporanea* (Bologna, Italy: Società editrice il Mulino, 2002), as made available by Leticia Arroyo Abad, "Italy–North, 1285–1850," in *Global Price and Incomes Database*, University of California, Davis, 2015, https://gpih.ucdavis.edu/Datafilelist.htm. All Tuscan correspondence was accessed via the Medici Archive Project BIA (Building Interactive Archives) database unless otherwise noted. Letter from Cosimo I de Medici to Pedro Alvarez de Toledo (Marques de Villafranca) (September 14, 1543), in Archivio di Stato di Firenze (ASF), *Mediceo*, vol. 5, f. 318. Letter from Pier Francesco Riccio to Cristiano Pagni (November 13, 1544), in ASF, *Mediceo*, vol. 1169, f. 512. Unknown to Lorenzo di Andrea Pagni (July? 1545), in ASF, *Mediceo*, vol. 1171, f. 503. Unknown to Cosimo de Medici (January 7, 1549), in ASF, *Mediceo*, vol. 617, f. 666.

29. On the use of gifts by Venetians abroad, see Ioanna Iordanou, "Bribes and Gifts," in *Venice's Secret Service: Organising Intelligence in the Renaissance* (Oxford: Oxford University Press, 2019), 208–212. In 1532, the representative of Ferdinand of Habsburg in Rome complained that generous tips to the papal postmaster had failed to ensure prompt service. Williams, "The Perils of the Post Road," 116.

30. Various letters from 1552 and 1554 are preserved in AGS, *Consejo de Estado (Estado)*, 1382, 1384. Max Lossen, ed., *Briefe von Andreas Masius und seinen Freunden 1538 bis 1573* (Leipzig, Germany: Alphons Dürr, 1886). See further letters in Fürst Thurn und Taxis Hofbibliothek und Zentralarchiv (FTTZA), *HFS*, 114.

31. Andreas Masius's brother, Jakob, had married Giovan Antonio Tassis's half sister, Adelheid von Taxis. Letter from Andreas Masius to the duke of Cleves (March 5, 1549) and (April 5, 1549) in Lossen, *Briefe von Andreas Masius*, 35–38, 39–42. On the news culture of Rome, see Mario Infelise, "Roman Avvisi: Information and Politics in the Seventeenth Century," in *Court and Politics in Papal Rome, 1492–1700*, ed. Gianvittorio Signorotto and Maria Antonietta Visceglia (Cambridge: Cambridge University Press, 2002), 212–228.

32. Bonora attributes a pivotal role to Gian Pietro Carafa in worsening imperial-papal relations in the 1540s, even prior to his election as pope. See Bonora, *Aspettando l'Imperatore*, 243–244.

33. Letter from Navagero to the Senate (October 5, 1555), in Navagero, *Bernardo Navagero*, 6–7; Letter from Navagero to the Senate (October 9, 1555), in Navagero, *Bernardo Navagero*, 8–10.

34. Letter from Giovan Antonio Tassis to Andrea Masius (October 21, 1555), in Lossen, *Briefe von Andreas Masius*, 221–223.

35. Letter from Navagero to the Senate (December 7, 1555), in Navagero, *Bernardo Navagero*, 42–44. Letter from Navagero to the Senate (February 8, 1556), in Navagero, *Bernardo Navagero*, 80–82.

36. The French representative in Rome was Jean de Saint-Marcel of Avanson (d. 1564), but the bishop of Paris, Cardinal Jean du Bellay (d. 1560), played an

important mediating role, hosting the July 14 gathering. Michel François, "Le rôle du cardinal François de Tournon dans la politique française en Italie de janvier à juillet 1556," *Mèlanges d'archèologie et d'histoire* 50 (1933): 293-333.

37. Felice Colonna escaped from the city only through bribery, sparking an all-out woman-hunt. Letters from Navagero to the Senate (January 11, 1556), in Navagero, *Bernardo Navagero*, 62-64; February 29, 1556, in Navagero, *Bernardo Navagero*, 92-93; January 18, 1556, in Navagero, *Bernardo Navagero*, 69-71; March 14, 1556, Navagero, *Bernardo Navagero*, 99-100.

38. Evidently, the imperial ambassador was so offended—presumably because he had not been entrusted with this information—that friends had to talk him out of turning on the duke of Alba. Letter from Navagero to the Senate (May 9, 1556), in Navagero, *Bernardo Navagero*, 138-139; May 23, 1556, in Navagero, *Bernardo Navagero*, 145-148; June 6, 1556, in Navagero, *Bernardo Navagero*, 152-154; June 27, 1556, in Navagero, *Bernardo Navagero*, 164-166. Letters being smuggled in clothing was not uncommon, as one such account of a Venetian spy in Pera demonstrates in Iordanou, *Venice's Secret Service*, 184.

39. "Sommario della confessione di Gio. Ant.o Tasso Mastro di Poste dell'Imperatore," in ASV, *Ottoboniani latini*, 2348. Thanks to Clemente Fedele.

40. "Autos hechos en Roma" (1556), in AGS, *PR*, 17, 49.

41. Letter of Simone Tassis to Granvelle (March 16, 1557), RB II 2272, f. 243r. Later letters recognized the new knowledge of Giovan Antonio's suffering and took a decidedly mollifying tone, suggesting that his allegations had not been well received (May 29, 1557), RB II 2264, f.149r, in Benavent and Crevato-Selvaggi, *La corrispondenza della famiglia Tasso*, 167-169.

42. As Williams writes about the 1530s, "The diplomats' united front extended to lodging together, assisting each other in audiences, sharing information, and facilitating regular recourse to fast, discreet imperial couriers and to 'ordinary' as well as 'extraordinary' posts departing Rome—from the Taxis family's papal or imperial post to that of imperialist cardinals or curialists." Williams, "The Perils of the Post Road," 112.

43. From the third interrogation of Giovan Antonio Tassis (July 9, 1556), in AGS, *PR*, 17, 49, f. 358-363.

44. From the third interrogation of Giovan Antonio Tassis (July 9, 1556), in AGS, *PR*, 17, 49, f. 358-363.

45. David Kahn, *The Codebreakers: The Story of Secret Writing* (New York: Scribner, 1996), 115. See also J. P. Devos, *Les chiffres de Philippe II (1555–1598) et du despacho universal durant le XVIIe Siècle* (Brussels: Palais des académies, 1950).

46. Kahn, *The Codebreakers*.

47. From 1555 forward, members of the Argenti family served as the papal cipher secretary. Aloys Meister, *Die Geheimschrift im Dienste der Päpstlichen Kurie von ihren Anfängen bis zum Ende des XVI. Jahrhunderts* (Paderborn, Germany: F. Schöningh, 1906).

48. Mambrin Roseo, *Compendio dell'istoria del regno di Napoli* (Venice: B. Barezzi, 1591). ASVe, *Consiglio di dieci (CX), Deliberazioni secrete*, f. 8 (July 27, 1552), in Iordanou, *Venice's Secret Service*, 141.

49. Roseo, *Compendio*. Interrogation of Hippolito Capilupi (July 11, 1556), in AGS, *PR*, 17, 49, f. 358-363. Like Tassis, Capilupi's confession also survives

as a manuscript summary in Biblioteca Apostolica Vaticana, Barb. Lat. 5674, ff. 126-127. The Capilupi family had made much of its fortunes from service to the Gonzaga family in Mantua. Ippolito was offered his freedom if he deciphered the letters, but he rejected the offer, remaining imprisoned for thirteen months instead. Giovanni Battista Intra, *Di Ippolito Capilupi e del suo tempo* (Milan: Tipografia Bortolotti dei Fratelli Rivara, 1893), 76-142. Thanks to Juraj Kittler.

50. Jon R. Snyder, *Dissimulation and the Culture of Secrecy in Early Modern Europe* (Berkeley: University of California Press, 2012), 6.

51. Sforza Pallavicino, *Istoria del Concilio di Trento, Libro XIII* (Rome: Angelo Bernabò dal Verme, 1656), 75.

52. Nores, "Storia della guerra," 70-71.

53. Pallavicino, *Istoria*, 75-76.

54. Carlo Bromato, *Vita di Paolo IV* (Ravenna, Italy: Antonmaria Landi, 1753), 309-311.

55. Geoffrey Parker, *Imprudent King: A New Life of Philip II* (New Haven, CT: Yale University Press, 2014), 51.

56. See, for example, copies in both the English State Papers originally included in a letter of Peter Vannes to Sir William Petre (September 7, 1556), British State Papers (Online) (SP) 69/9 f.49. SPO MCU310800533.

57. Letter from Resident Giangaliazzo to Cosimo I de Medici (October 24, 1556), in the footnote of Nores, "Storia della guerra," 71. Letter from Bernardo Navagero to the Venetian Senate (November 3, 1556), in Navagero, *Bernardo Navagero*, 296-297.

58. "Vale. Romae in carcere die XXI. Maji 1557. Tuus Taxius." Letter from Giovan Antonio Tassis to Masius (May 21, 1557), in Lossen, *Briefe von Andreas Masius*, 290-291. See also FTTHZA, *HFS*, 114.

59. Letter from Navagero to the Senate (September 5, 1557), in Navagero, *Bernardo Navagero*, 223-235. A translation of Navagero's letter in the Calendar of the English State Papers mistakenly states that it said that Garcilaso and Tassis had already been put to death.

60. Letter from Andreas Masius to the duke of Cleves (October 20, 1557), in Lossen, *Briefe von Andreas Masius*, 299-300. This mistake has been repeated by most later authors, including in Beck, "Ursprung und Ende."

61. Letter of Sir Edward Carne to Queen Mary (October 30, 1557), SP 69/11 f.90. SPO MCU4310800681.

62. Navagero's last identified mention appears in his letter to the Senate (October 30, 1557), in Navagero, *Bernardo Navagero*, 590-592. Privilege of Giovan Antonio Taxis as postmaster in Rome (August 1558), in Martin Volker Albus Dallmeier, ed., *Quellen zur Geschichte des Europaischen Postwesens, 1501-1806*, vol. 2, no. 33 (Kallmünz, Germany: Lassleben, 1977), 19.

63. Gio. Battista Sorrer, *Idea del perfetto ambasciadore* (Venice: Gio. Giorgio Hertz, 1654), 296-298.

64. Mattingly, *Renaissance Diplomacy*, 247-248.

65. Frey and Frey point out the sacred status of messengers and heralds worldwide was underscored by visible emblems. Frey and Frey, "Diplomatic Immunity/Privilege," 1.

66. Pallavicino, *Istoria*, 75, 78.

67. Nores, "Storia della guerra," 100.

68. On papal propaganda, see Margaret Meserve, *Papal Bull: Print, Politics, and Propaganda in Renaissance Rome* (Baltimore: Johns Hopkins University Press, 2021).

69. See, for example, the edict of April 2, 1539, that marked the cessation of Sandro privileges in favor of Gherardi "di San Casciano," transcribed in Tarcisio Bottani, *I Tasso e le poste pontificie, sec. XV–XVI* (Bergamo, Italy: Corponove, 2000), 101–104.

70. Tarcisio Bottani, "Tasso di Valle Brembana: I Signori delle poste d'Europa," in *I Signori delle Alpi, Famiglie e poteri tra le montagne d'Europa*, ed. Luca Giarelli (Tricase, Italy: Self-published, 2015), 183.

71. Letter from Giovanni di Filippo dell'Antella to Cosimo I de Medici (October 9, 1540), in ASF, *Mediceo*, v.3263, fo. 243. Letter to the Venetian ambassador in Rome and letter from Commissari to Maestro delle Poste (February 24, 1539/1540), in ASVe, *Corrieri*, 37. Letter to the community of Rimini from Matteo da San Casciano (November 24, 1543), in Archivio di Stato di Rimini (ASRi), *Comunale*, Ap 734. In Fedele and Gallenga, *Per servizio*, 58. See also "Dichiarazione di Ben. Geronimo Simonetto" (December 19, 1585), in ASVe, *Corrieri*, 59. Decree establishing Roma-Bologna postal ordinary (February 25, 1551) in ASV, Arm. XXXIX, 58, c. 37. See also Fedele and Gallenga, *Per servizio*, 59.

72. Bull of Paul III (May 18, 1544), in ASVe, *Corrieri*, 37. See also the later modifications issued (October 19, 1549) and (May 20 and 23, 1550), referenced in "Nota delli Brevia dati al Illustrissimo Signor Ambasciatore," in ASVe, *Corrieri*, 61.

73. Letter from Roman consistory to the Venetian ambassador (July 16, 1544), in ASVe, *Corrieri*, 62. Letter (December 20, 1550), in *Nunziature di Venezia: Secoli XVI–XVIII*, ed. Franco Gaeta, vol. 5 (Rome: Istituto Storico italiano per l'Età Moderna e Contemporanea, 1967), 188–189. See also Fedele and Gallenga, *Per servizio*, 10.

74. From the first interrogation of Giovan Antonio Tassis (July 7, 1556), in AGS, *PR*, 17, 49.

75. I have not yet been able to identify the woman or her brother from Viterbo. Letter of Simone Tassis to Granvelle (March 16, 1557), RB II 2272, f. 243r.

76. Navagero's reference to this courier as a "procaccio" likely derived from the Roman practice of calling the Roman-Neapolitan ordinary by this term. Letter from Navagero to the Senate (November 8, 1557), in Navagero, *Bernardo Navagero*, 7–8.

77. Letter from Navagero to the Senate (November 8, 1557), in Navagero, *Bernardo Navagero*, 7–8.

78. Letter from Navagero to the Senate (November 13, 1557), in Navagero, *Bernardo Navagero*, 13.

79. See ASVe, *Corrieri*, 37.

80. Patent of Mattia Gherardi (April 22, 1566), in ASVe, *Corrieri*, 37.

81. On the role of nunci, and especially papal relations with Spain, see Maria Antoinetta Visceglia, *Roma papale e Spagna: Diplomatici, nobili e religiosi tra due corti* (Rome: Bulzoni, 2010).

82. Letter from Michele Bonelli to Giovanni Antonio Facchinetti (October 5, 1566), in Aldo Stella, ed. *Nunziature di Venezia: Secoli XVI–XVIII*, vol. 8 (Rome: Istituto Storico italiano per l'Età Moderna e Contemporanea, 1963), 117; Letter from Giovanni Antonio Facchinetti to Michele Bonelli (October 12, 1566), in Stella, *Nunziature di Venezia*, vol. 8, 119–121.

83. On Milan-Venice connections, see chapter 4 of this book. Many documents related to the Florentine portalettere in Venice survive in the Archivio di Stato di Firenze. See, generally, Sergio Chieppi, *I servizi postali dei Medici dal 1500 al 1737* (Arezzo, Italy: Servizio editoriale fiesolano, 1997).

84. Prohibition of foreign couriers by the Provveditori di Comun (July 10, 1539), in Museo Correr, Mss. Cl. IV. 165 and Archivio di Stato di Verona (ASVer), *Processi, Uffici pubblici, Cavallari e portalettere (Cavallari)*, 119.1826. See also Bottani and Taufer, *Mariegola*, 41.

85. Venetian couriers were frequently reminded to carry mail for the foreign diplomats of Rome, both as a professional courtesy and as a strategic intelligence-gathering opportunity. Williams, "The Perils of the Post Road," 113.

86. Letters from Facchinetti to Bonelli (October 12, 1566), in Stella, *Nunziature di Venezia*, vol. 8, 119–121; and July 9, 1568, in Stella, *Nunziature di Venezia*, vol. 8, 406–407.

87. Letters from Paolo Tiepolo to the Venetian Senate (July 2, 1568) and (July 17, 1568), in ASVe, *Senato, Dispacci*, 3.

88. Letters from Facchinetti to Bonelli (June 12, 1568), in Stella, *Nunziature di Venezia*, vol. 8, 304–396; August 10, 1568, in Stella, *Nunziature di Venezia*, vol. 8, 426; August 14, 1568, in Stella, *Nunziature di Venezia*, vol. 8, 426–427.

89. Letter from Gironimo Simonetti and Company to the Venetian ambassador and Company of Couriers in Rome (April 24, 1568), in ASVe, *Corrieri*, 37.

90. Letters from Facchinetti to Bonelli (August 18, 1568), in Stella, *Nunziature di Venezia*, vol. 8, 427–428; August 25, 1568, in Stella, *Nunziature di Venezia*, vol. 8, 430–431. A letter from Paolo Tiepolo seems to indicate that Lomboni was also a family member of Mattia Gherardi. Letter of Paolo Tiepolo to the Venetian Senate (July 17, 1568) in ASVe, *Senato, Dispacci*, 3.

91. Letter from Facchinetti to Bonelli (August 28, 1568), in Stella, *Nunziature di Venezia*, vol. 8, 432. An example of the short notice survives in the Museo Correr in MS. Cic. 3588. Letter to the Senate on behalf of Venetian Company (1568) in ASVe, *Corrieri*, 37. Paolo Tiepolo included a manuscript transcription of the ban in his dispatches, (October 6, 1568), in ASVe, *Senato, Dispacci*, 3.

92. Letter from Facchinetti to Bonelli (February 19, 1569), in Stella, *Nunziature di Venezia*, vol. 8, 501–502.

93. See attachment of October 19, 1570, in Aldo Stella, ed., *Nunziature di Venezia: Secoli XVI–XVIII*, vol. 9 (Rome: Istituto Storico italiano per l'Età Moderna e Contemporanea, 1972), 374–375.

94. Letter from Bonelli to Facchinetti (March 12, 1569), Stella, *Nunziature di Venezia*, vol. 8, 509–510. Letter from Facchinetti to Girolamo Rusticucci (October 21, 1570), in Stella, *Nunziature di Venezia*, vol. 9, 373–374.

95. Entry (September 20, 1569), in ASVe, *Corrieri*, 37; "Modula di Capitoli mandata a Roma per M. Cristoforo Rotta" (April 22, 1569), in ASVe, *Corrieri*, 61; entry (June 12, 1572), in ASVe, *Corrieri*, 21. See also ASVe, *Corrieri*, 37.

96. The camerlengo was Cardinal Luigi Cornaro (d. 1584, o. 1570-1584). Letter to the Venetian ambassador in Rome (July 3, 1572), in ASVe, *Corrieri*, 37.

97. "Memoriale dei Corrieri di Venetia," in ASVe, *Corrieri*, 37.

98. "Privilegio di Papa Gregorio Decimoterzo" (November 22, 1572), in *Documenti dell'istituzione fatta dalla compagnia de' corrieri Veneti delli due viaggi di Roma e Milano e poste* (Venice: Perlini, 1790), 33-35.

99. Entry (September 28, 1577), in ASVe, *Corrieri*, 37. The company also explored working around the papal posts. In the case of Bologna, they instead delegated two members of their order to negotiate directly with the local cavallari. They came to an agreement in July 1578 for the Bolognese cavallari to carry the mail to and from Venice. Entry (July 5, 1578), in ASVe, *Corrieri*, 62.

100. Papal bull of Sixtus V (May 22, 1585), in ASVe, *Corrieri*, 37.

101. Francesco Zazzera, *Della nobiltà dell'Italia* (Naples: Ottavio Boltrano, 1628).

102. "Discorso sopra l'unione delle Poste," in Biblioteca Corsiana Roma, MS Cod. 703, cc. 85-92 a c. 90v. In Fedele and Gallenga, *Per servizio*, 89.

3. Deadly Letters

1. Colin Rose, *Renaissance of Violence: Homicide in Early Modern Italy* (Cambridge: Cambridge University Press, 2019); Geoffrey Parker, *Global Crisis: War, Climate Change and Catastrophe in the Seventeenth Century* (New Haven, CT: Yale University Press, 2017).

2. Ottavio Codogno, *Nuovo itinerario delle poste per tutto il mondo* (Milan: Girolamo Bordoni, 1608), 6-7.

3. See, for example, Francesca Trivellato, *The Familiarity of Strangers: The Sephardic Diaspora, Livorno, and Cross-Cultural Trade in the Early Modern Period* (New Haven, CT: Yale University Press, 2009).

4. Andrew Pettegree, *Reformation and the Culture of Persuasion* (Cambridge: Cambridge University Press, 2005); Robert W. Scribner, *For the Sake of Simple Folk: Popular Propaganda for the German Reformation* (Oxford: Oxford University Press, 1994).

5. Letter from Antonio Mazza to the Venetian Council of Ten (March 30, 1563), quoted in Domenico Maselli, *Saggi di storia ereticale lombarda al tempo di S. Carlo* (Naples: Società Editrice Napoletana, 1979), 33.

6. Letter from Giovanni Ricci, Cardinal of Pisa, to Cardinal Borromeo (September 4, 1568) and Letter from the Cardinal of Pisa to Cardinal Borromeo (May 14, 1575), in Maselli, *Saggi di storia ereticale*, 162, 171. See, generally, Rachel Midura, "Policing in Print: Social Control in Spanish and Borromean Milan (1535-1584)," in *Print and Power in Early Modern Europe (1500-1800)*, ed. Helmer Helmers, Nina Lamal, and Jamie Cumby (Leiden, Netherlands: Brill, 2021), 21-46.

7. Juraj Kittler, "Capitalism and Communication: The Rise of Commercial Courier Networks in the Context of the Champagne Fairs," *Capitalism: A Journal of History and Economics* 4, no. 1 (Winter 2023): 109-152.

8. A 1436 series of negotiated conventions appear in Ettore Verga, *La Camera dei mercanti di Milano nei secoli passati* (Milan: Allegretti, 1914), 164.

9. On the role of merchants as heretical networks inside and outside Italy, see Diego Pirillo, *The Refugee-Diplomat: Venice, England, and the Reformation* (Ithaca, NY: Cornell University Press, 2018).

10. "Chi corre in posta, con la morte scherza." The phrase may also have connoted a reckless speed, like the English "Live fast, die young." Orlando Pescetti, *Proverbi italiani* (Verona, Italy: Compagnia degli Aspiranti, 1603), 196.

11. John Florio, *Queen Anna's New World of Words, or a Dictionarie of the Italian and English Tongues* (London: Melch, Bradwood, Edward Blount and William Pazret, 1611), 543. Early sixteenth-century references were more likely to use *assasinamento*, which described homicide accompanied by robbery. Rose, *Renaissance of Violence*, 35.

12. The most famous appearance of this is in Ferrante Pallavicino's satirical novel, *The Courier Waylaid (Il corriero svaligiato)*, a remarkable work discussed in chapter 7 of this book.

13. Peter Laven, "Banditry and Lawlessness in the Venetian Terraferma in the Late Cinquecento," in *Crime, Society, and the Law in Renaissance Italy*, ed. Trevor Dean and Kate Lowe (Cambridge: Cambridge University Press, 1994), 221–248. The classic work is Eric Hobsbawm, *Bandits* (London: Weidenfeld & Nicolson, 1969).

14. See, generally, Rose, *Renaissance of Violence*.

15. This is true in the United States, for example, where it is prosecuted as a felony. See 18 U.S. Code § 1708.

16. Further discussion of the Tassis relationship with the Fuggers and Welsers can be found in chapter 5 of this book.

17. Marco Gerosa, "Personaggi della posta dello Stato di Milano tra Simone e Ruggero Tasso," in *I Tasso e le poste d'Europa*, ed. Tarcisio Bottani (Bergamo, Italy: Corponove, 2012), 81–92.

18. Letter from Giovanni Antonio Facchinetti to Michele Bonelli (July 24–26, 1568), in Aldo Stella, ed., *Nunziature di Venezia: Secoli XVI–XVIII*, vol. 8 (Rome: Istituto Storico italiano per l'Età Moderna e Contemporanea, 1963), 417–418.

19. In this case, the brothers, "Hieronimo and Ulysses Falconi," were taken into custody, and some of the gold was recovered. Letter from Calistan Bartolomeo to Guglielmo Gonzaga (May 2, 1587), Banchedati Gonzaga (Online) (BDG) 3716. Many of the goods likely came from the Jewish jeweler Solomon da Hostiglia, who traveled with the courier. David de Cervi, a famous Jewish agent for the Mantuan court, likely had this and other incidents in mind when he wrote to the Milanese government in August 1599, requesting protection for himself and his servant due to the "spies and assassins" that frequented the road and received permission to carry a beretta gun. Letter from David Cervi of Mantua (August 26, 1599), in Archivio di Stato di Milano (ASMi), *Carteggio delle cancellerie dello Stato (Carteggio)*, 349.

20. Letter from Aurelio Pomponazzi to Donati Marcello (October 12, 1585) BDG 6828. Writing again in 1591, Pomponazzi declined to send several pens to the Count of Ponzano for the same reason (January 12, 1591), BDG 5538.

21. Letter to the Gonzaga court from Girardi Gregorio in Cremona (September 7, 1589), BDG 7146.

22. The precise dating and name of the assaulted courier (Gio. Paulo Pagliaro) are preserved because of the notification coming from the postmaster of Cremona, Geronimo Cipelleto. See letter (July 24, 1601), in ASMi, *Carteggio*, 359. Further detail is provided by a letter from Mario Corradi to Pedro Enríquez de Acevedo, Count of Fuentes (August 4, 1601), in ASMi, *Carteggio*.

23. Letter from Vincenzo Gonzaga to Annobale Chieppio (August 1, 1601), BDG 9907.

24. Members of the Longho/Longhi family are present on the membership rolls of both the cavallari of Verona and the Venetian Company of Couriers, but any familial relation remains speculative.

25. The full account derives from the letters of Manuel del Pozo (January 20 and 26, 1604), in ASMi, *Carteggio*, 369.

26. Edict (September 28, 1602), in *Compendio di tutte le gride e ordini pubblicati nella Città e Stato di Milano* (Milan: Giovanni Battista Malatesta, 1612).

27. The soldiers had initially come under suspicion for trying to fence the fine stolen goods, which included "several handmade collars," "several works of Flanders," and "a silver cloth embroidered with an image of Charles Borromeo and the four Evangelists," in Bergamo. Report to the rectors of Bergamo (March 14, 1612), in Archivio di Stato di Venezia (ASVe), *Consiglio di dieci (CX), Criminale*, 40.

28. Corradi to the Count of Fuentes (August 4, 1601), in ASMi, *Carteggio*, 359.

29. Colin Rose finds that homicides generally peaked in summer and autumn. Rose, *Renaissance of Violence*, 94.

30. Ottavio Codogno noted the fairs of Hostia (August 10–31) and Madonna delle Gratie (August 15–18). Ottavio Codogno, *Compendio delle poste* (Milan: Gio. Battista Bidelli, 1623), 502. He also emphasized the pressure for speed and volume of correspondence placed on the post by businessmen at the fairs throughout the book. On the determinative role of fairs on late medieval courier systems, see Kittler, "Capitalism and Communication."

31. Laven, "Banditry and Lawlessness," 236. On the antibanditry campaigns of this period, see, generally, Stuart Carroll, *Enmity and Violence in Early Modern Europe* (Cambridge: Cambridge University Press, 2023).

32. Letter from Antonio Pauluzzi (September 29, 1604), in ASVe, *Senato, Dispacci*, 28. As in most studies of crime, it is difficult to parse a real increase in banditry from a law-and-order campaign of prosecution. See, generally, Guido Ruggiero, *Violence in Early Renaissance Venice* (New Brunswick, NJ: Rutgers University Press, 1980).

33. Letters of the Capi del Consiglio di X to the Podestà of Citadella (April 11, 1601) and to the Secretary in Milan (July 17, 1601), in ASVe, *CX, Registri (Consiglio di dieci, Registri, Parti secreti)*, 14. Thanks to Ioanna Iordanou.

34. As of July, the extradition to Bergamo appeared to have been successful. See also a letter from the Capi del Consiglio di X (January 23, 1601/2), ASVe, *CCX*, 17. For more on the Italian-Venetian postal ordinary, see chapter 4 of this book.

35. This included attempting to require all barbers to cut hair short so that faces would be visible. Printed edict (June 5, 1604) included in the letters of the Venetian resident of Milan, ASVe, *Senato, Dispacci*, 28. An earlier version dating to July 16, 1601, appears in the Milanese *Compendio delle gride*.

36. Letter from the Count of Fuentes (September 23, 1604), in ASMi, *Registri delle cancellerie dello Stato (Registri)*, 16, 10.

37. Edict (March 19, 1604, and April 1, 1605), in *Compendio delle gride*.

38. Letter from Codogno (January 1604), in ASMi, *Miscellanea*, 43.

39. Marco Gerosa, *La famiglia Tasso e le poste nello Stato di Milano in età spagnola (1556-1650)* (Bergamo, Italy: Corponove, 2019), 31.

40. "Supplica che non sia innovata cosa alcuna circa le Poste" (July 10, 1620), in ASVe, *Compagnia dei corrieri*, I, 1.

41. Letter of February 3, 1568, in ASMi, *Carteggio*, 276.

42. Letter of November 9, 1599, in ASMi, *Carteggio*, 351.

43. Count of Fuentes's edict to this effect (March 10, 1605) appears in the Venetian diplomatic resident's letters. ASVe, *Senato, Dispacci*, 29.

44. In discussing eighteenth-century Lombardy, Sophus Reinert goes further, describing how "wars on banditry were acute symptoms of, and vehicles for, the gradual territorialization of commercial society, of what we today would call 'marketization.'" Sophus Reinert, *The Academy of Fisticuffs: Political Economy and Commercial Society in Enlightenment Italy* (Cambridge, MA: Harvard University Press, 2018), 23.

45. Marina Inì, "Materiality, Quarantine and Contagion in the Early Modern Mediterranean," *Social History of Medicine* 34, no. 4 (2021): 1161-1184; Alex Bamji, "Health Passes, Print and Public Health in Early Modern Europe," *Social History of Medicine* 32, no. 3 (August 2019): 441-464. On recent findings in bioarcheology, see Monica Green, "The Four Black Deaths," *American Historical Review* 125, no. 5 (December 2020): 1601-1631.

46. G. Lazzari, G. Colavizza, F. Bortoluzzi, et al., "A Digital Reconstruction of the 1630-1631 Large Plague Outbreak in Venice," *Nature: Scientific Reports* 10, no. 17849 (2020), https://doi.org/10.1038/s41598-020-74775-6; Samuel Cohn, *Cultures of Plague: Medical Thinking at the End of the Renaissance* (Oxford: Oxford University Press, 2011).

47. Luigi Dedé, for example, describes the "nearly total suspension of both state and private epistolary exchanges." Luigi Dedé, "Il servizio postale fra Brescia e Venezia durante il dominio veneto," in *Commentari dell'Ateneo di Brescia per l'anno 1986* (Brescia, Italy: Tipolito Fratelli Geroldi, 1987), 170. For the alternative view, see Wouter Kreuze, "Temporal Philology: Reconstructing Patterns of Avvisi Creation and Distribution with Travel Times," *Magazén* 3, no. 1 (2022): 11-38.

48. The courier was often detained at Cassano, located between Milan and Bergamo. Letter from Ottaviano Marzi to the Venetian Senate (October 31, 1575), in ASVe, *Senato, Dispacci*, 4.

49. Venetian edict (November 6, 1575), in Karl Friedrich Meyer, *Disinfected Mail* (Holton, KS: Gossip Print, 1962), 11.

50. Letter from Paolo Tiepolo to the Venetian Senate (June 30, 1576), in ASVe, *Senato, Dispacci*, 12.

51. One courier, Francesco Puintino, was bathed in vinegar before being allowed to cross the border into Milanese territory near Brescia in December 1575. ASMi, *Carteggio*, 295, in Gerosa, *La famiglia Tasso*, 35-36.

52. By the eighteenth century, letters could be slit, punctured, burned, and doused by the time they reached the recipient—many measures that continued

through the nineteenth-century epidemics of yellow fever. Alicia Ault, "Mail Handlers Used to Poke Holes in Envelopes to Battle Germs and Viruses," *Smithsonian Magazine* (June 2, 2020), https://www.smithsonianmag.com/smithsonian-institution/mail-handlers-used-poke-holes-envelopes-battle-germs-and-viruses-180975020/. See, generally, Meyer, *Disinfected Mail*.

53. Letter from Ottaviano Marzi to the Senate (October 31, 1575), in ASVe, *Senato, Dispacci*, 4.

54. Avviso from Rome (November 11, 1575), Archivio di Stato di Firenze (ASF), *Mediceo del Principato (Mediceo)*, vol. 4026, fo. 475, Medici Archiv Project (MAP) 26277.

55. Avviso from Rome (November 16, 1575), ASF, *Mediceo*, vol. 4026, fo. 491, MAP 26283.

56. Avviso from Rome (November 22, 1579), ASF, *Mediceo*, vol. 4026, fo. 740. MAP 28623.

57. Unsigned letter to the Venetian State Inquisitors (June 15, 1620), in ASVe, *Inquisitori di Stato (IS)*, 610. A note on the back of "letters incoming June 10 from London, Antwerp, and Augsburg" reveals the informant as a prior of the lazaretto. ASVe, *IS*, 1214. Losses at the lazaretto could also be more tangible than intelligence: in 1617, the imperial postmaster Ferdinando Tassis lamented the disappearance of some thirty pearls during disinfection outside Venice. Letter from Ferdinando Tassis to the Postmaster General (February 17, 1617), in Fürst Thurn und Taxis Hofbibliothek und Zentralarchiv (FTTZA), *Postakten (PA)*, 1227. Rachel Midura, "'They Hide from Me, Like the Devil from the Cross': Transalpine Postal Routes as Intelligence Work, 1555–1645," *History: The Journal of the Historical Association* 108, no. 381 (2023): 315.

58. Archivio di Stato di Turino (ASTo), *Sezione corte, Materia politiche per rapporto all'estero, Corti Estere, Venezia*, 2.

59. Athanasius Kircher described very similar difficulties in 1657 and discussed mail disinfection methods in a later treatise. Athanasius Kircher, *Scrutinium physico-medicum contagiosae luis, qui pestis dicatur* (Rome: Giacomo Mascardi, 1658), 154, cited in Paula Findlen, "Microscopic Musings: Athanasius Kircher and the Roman Plague of 1656–57," *Harvard Library Bulletin*, https://nrs.harvard.edu/URN-3:HUL.INSTREPOS:37370849.

60. "Galileo's First Deposition (April 12, 1633)," in Galilei Galileo, *The Essential Galileo*, ed. Maurice A. Finocchiaro (Indianapolis: Hackett, 2008), 276–282. Thanks to Laura Smoller. On Galileo's correspondence and experience of censorship, see Paula Findlen and Hannah Marcus, "Deciphering Galileo: Communication and Secrecy before and after the Trial," *Renaissance Quarterly* 72, no. 3 (Fall 2019): 953–995; and Paula Findlen and Hannah Marcus, "The Breakdown of Galileo's Roman Network: Crisis and Community, ca. 1633," *Social Studies of Science* 47, no. 3 (2017): 326–352.

61. A record from Verona shows that authorities punished the cavallaro Nicolai da Porto for traveling in violation of restricted service. Ex Actis (July 24, 1576), in Archivio di Stato di Verona (ASVer), *Processi, Uffici pubblici, Cavallari e portalettere (Cavallari)*, 122.646.

62. See, for example, the letter from Paolo Tiepolo to the Venetian Senate (May 1576), in ASVe, *Senato, Dispacci*, 12.

63. When Trento was rumored to be hit by plague, an imperial postilion went by another road, packing food for himself and his horse to minimize stops. Letter from Ferdinando Tassis in Venice (August 22, 1636), in FTTZA, PA, 5403.

64. Ex Actis (October 1623), in ASVer, Cavallari, 120.1272.

65. Much of the documentation regarding recovery from the plague years, including a list of associated expenses, can be found in ASVe, *Compagnia dei Corrieri (Corrieri)*, 66.

66. Filippo Tassis (1574–1603), the eldest son of Lucina Cattanea, murdered a man in a tavern brawl and fled to the family's property in Friuli in 1592. His younger brothers, Vittorio (1581–1606) and Ottavio (d. c. 1632), followed his example in 1601. Filippo and Vittorio did not return to Milan before their deaths, but Ottavio won a reprieve through military service, eventually marrying a Milanese noblewoman. Gerosa, *La famiglia Tasso*, 166–170. The eldest son of Postmistress Lucia Ropele Bordogna of Trento was also involved in at least one duel, much to the family's dismay. Testimony of Giacomo Farizzelle (July 10, 1690), in Tiroler Landesarchiv (TLA), *Adelsarchiv, Taxis-Bordogna (TB)*, 11, 10.

67. See, for example, an edict issued September 27, 1576, in ASMi, *Registri*, 16, 2.

68. Letter to Cardinal Charles Borromeo (June 5, 1568), in Biblioteca Civico Angelo Mai (Bergamo) (BAM), P3 inf., fo. 80. Kevin Stevens, "Printers, Publishers, and Booksellers in Counter-Reformation Milan: A Documentary Study" (PhD diss., University of Wisconsin, 1992), 222–223.

69. See also the bandit known as Giovanni Battista Martinengo, discussed earlier in this chapter.

70. The earliest known agreement dated to 1436, but I have been unable to locate the original document in the Archivio storico civico of Milan. The terms of the 1525 document were renewed with few changes in 1551, 1559, and 1596. Verga, *La Camera dei Mercanti*, 164–168.

71. The Venetian diplomatic resident, Bonifacio Antelmi (o. 1580–1587), did not distinguish between payments intended for the Spanish or imperial Tassis postmasters, although the majority can be inferred as destined for the Spanish postmaster of Milan based on the recipient location.

72. Bollino is identified as such in an anonymous, undated letter complaining about the unlicensed activities of the merchant mail carriers in ASMi, *Atti di Governo (AG), Miscellanea Storica*, 43.

73. The possibility remains that he may have chosen one or the other, depending on the sensitivity of the contents, but determining that would require a more in-depth analysis.

74. Midura, "Policing in Print," 21–46.

75. On the religious climate of Milan, see Wietse de Boer, *The Conquest of the Soul: Confession, Discipline, and Public Order in Counter-Reformation Milan* (Leiden, Netherlands: Brill, 2001). Maselli, *Saggi di storia ereticale*. On foreign relations, see Federico Chabod, *Storia di Milano nell'epoca di Carlo V* (Turin, Italy: Einaudi, 1961).

76. Reprinted copy of edict (August 29, 1578), in ASMi, *Atti di Governo (AG), Finanze*, 933.

77. The letter is undated, but it likely originates from the struggles of Ruggero Tassis of Milan between 1566 and 1582. ASMi, *Miscellanea Storica (MS)*, 43. Midura, "'They Hide from Me,'" 311.

78. Letter from Governor Don Sancho de Padilla (January 26, 1582), in Archivo General de Simancas (AGS), *Consejo de Estado (Estado)*, 1257, fo. 59. Midura, "'They Hide from Me,'" 311.

79. Letter from Governor Don Sancho de Padilla (January 26, 1582), in AGS, *Estado*, 1257, fo. 59. Midura, "'They Hide from Me,'" 311.

80. Letter from Governor Don Sancho de Padilla (January 26, 1582), in AGS, *Estado*, 1257, fo. 59. Midura, "'They Hide from Me,'" 311.

81. Gianvittorio Signorotto, "Stabilità politica e trame antispagnole nella Milano del Seicento," in *Complots et conjurations dans l'Europe moderne*, ed. Yves-Marie Bercé and Elena Fasano Guarini (Rome: École française de Rome, 1996): 721-745.

82. "Memoriale della Università dei mercanti di Milano contro il Tasso Corriero Maggiore" (December 5, 1580) and addition (November 28, 1580), in ASMi, *AG, Finanze*, 933.

83. Padua, Vicenza, and Verona each had an early foot messenger established to connect them to Venice and to one another. All three cities were in a key region for the channeling of goods and people to Trent, and across the Brenner Pass to Innsbruck and Augsburg. Similarly, border cities like Cremona, located along the route to the Papal States, had a strong local municipal messenger system. See especially ASMi, *Carteggio*, 288, 294, and 315, cited in Gerosa, *La famiglia Tassis*, 31. Fernando Rea, *Le poste di Bergamo* (Bergamo, Italy: Società Editrice Bergamasca, 1976). On similar central European struggles, see, generally, Wolfgang Behringer, *Im Zeichen des Merkur: Reichsport und Kommunikationsrevolution in der Frühen Neuzeit* (Göttingen, Germany: Vandenhoeck & Ruprecht, 2003).

84. Marco Gerosa writes that "cavallari" was simply the Venetian term used instead of "procacci" as utilized in Spanish territories. Yet sources like the council of Verona and Ottavio Codogno, who use both terms, complicate this distinction. Gerosa, *La famiglia Tassis*, 33. In early Tuscan sources, Kittler finds that the term "procaccio" refers to "all nonmembers' mail carried by the courier in addition to the contents of his sealed *scarsella*," as well as "extra mail solicited by the courier and the innkeeper-postmaster to generate additional revenues then shared between them based on a certain agreed-upon ratio." Kittler, "Capitalism and Communication," 128.

85. "Supplica della Compagnia dei Corrieri" (1582), in ASVe, *Corrieri*, 35.

86. "Memoriale della Università dei mercanti di Milano contro il Tasso Corriero Maggiore" (December 5, 1580) and addition (November 28, 1580), in ASMi, *AG, Finanze*, 933. Midura, "'They Hide from Me,'" 312-313.

87. "Per la difficoltà con [i] Corrieri da Mantova" (December 23, 1588), in ASVe, *Corrieri*, 36.

88. "Scrittura contro i Corrieri di Mantova" (1584), in ASVe, *Corrieri*, 36.

89. ASMi, *Notarile*, 17136, in Gerosa, *La famiglia Tassis*, 54-55.

90. "Decreto senato per l'istituzione staffette da noi proposta al Principe" (September 29, 1584), in ASVe, *Corrieri*, I, 1.

91. "Proclama simile di Vicenza" (July 18,1582), in ASVe, *Corrieri*, 23.

92. Ducal edict (June 2, 1582), in ASVe, *Corrieri*, 22.

93. The first record of the cavallari of Verona and their privileges dates to 1405, the same year that the city capitulated to Venice. By 1545, surviving records suggest a similar makeup to that of the Venetian Company. ASVer, *Cavallari*, no. 27, 701. In 1546, four such cavallari were active in Vicenza, while numbers in Padua and Verona were closer to thirty. Archivio Civico di Vicenza, *Atti del Consiglio*, lib. I, c. 87 in A. Ciscato, "I portalettere in Padova nel cinquecento," *Bolletino del Museo civico di Padova* 3 (1901): 32–39.

94. Supplication on behalf of cavallari of Verona (May 28, 1583), in ASVer, *Cavallari*, 121.647. As late as 1556, the Venetian state recognized the rights of the Brescians to carry out thrice-weekly service with Venice. The agreement is referenced in a later decision regarding livery. "Pro Tabellaris Civitis per non nullis impensis" (January 22, 1558), in Archivio Storico Civico di Brescia, *Atti dei Deputati & Provvisioni*, 544.

95. See, generally, the essays in Julius Kirshner, ed., *The Origins of the Italian State in Italy, 1300–1600* (Chicago: Chicago University Press, 1996).

96. Presentation by the Son of Piero da Porto, Cavallaro (October 10, 1583), in ASVer, *Cavallari*, 121.691.

97. Testimony of Piero da Porto (July 19, 1584), in ASVer, *Cavallari*, 121.691.

98. This may be the same Bartolomeo Benzon who worked as a courier in the Venetian Company around the same date.

99. Inventory (October 10, 1583), in ASVer, *Cavallari*, 121.691.

100. Documents from the 1580s and 1590s show that the Verona cavallari continued to carry public (state) letters to and from Venice for 3 soldi and 12 denari per journey, and as often as every other day. ASVe, *Corrieri*, 23.

4. The Postmistress and the Spy

1. On the earlier persistence of Padan patterns, see Luca Zenobi, *Borders and the Politics of Space in Late Medieval Italy: Milan, Venice, and Their Territories* (Oxford: Oxford University Press, 2023).

2. Mauricio Drelichman and Hans-Joachim Voth, *Lending to the Borrower from Hell: Debt, Taxes, and Default in the Age of Philip II* (Princeton, NJ: Princeton University Press, 2016), 78.

3. The German and Swiss Roads (discussed in chapter 5) parallel Geoffrey Parker's "Spanish Road," which describes the network of routes that ferried arms and armies between Habsburg Italy and the Netherlands. I similarly adopt the term to mirror the Italian *via*, describing a general way rather than specifying a paved surface. Geoffrey Parker, *The Army of Flanders and the Spanish Road* (Cambridge: Cambridge University Press, 2004).

4. "Decreto Senato sopra progetto nostro per l'introduzione di un ordinario per Milano" (January 27, 1582), in Archivio di Stato di Venezia (ASVe), *Compagnia dei Corrieri (Corrieri)*, 35.

5. Roger Knight and Martin Willcox, *Sustaining the Fleet: War, the British Navy and the Contractor State* (Woodbridge, UK: Boydell, 2010).

6. Richard Harding and Sergio Solbes Ferri, eds., *The Contractor State and Its Implications, 1659–1815* (Las Palmas de Gran Canaria, Spain: Universidad de Las Palmas de Gran Canaria, 2012), 13.

7. See the brief literature overview in the introduction of this book.

8. Thomas Dandelet and John Marino, eds., *Spain in Italy, Politics, Society, and Religion 1500-1700* (Leiden, Netherlands: Brill, 2006).

9. Thomas Max Safley, *Family Firms and Merchant Capitalism in Early Modern Europe* (New York: Routledge, 2020).

10. The finances of the office are well summarized in a printed pamphlet, likely dating to the later seventeenth century: "Breve information, & dichiarazione delle cause che muovono i corrieri che servono a S. Maestà nel presente stato di Milano," in Archivio di Stato di Milano (ASMi), *Atti di Governo (AG), Finanze*, 933.

11. On the period following Charles's abdication and relations between the Habsburg branches, see Mia Rodríguez-Salgado, *The Changing Face of Empire: Charles V, Philip II, and Habsburg Authority, 1551-1559* (Cambridge: Cambridge University Press, 1988).

12. Seraphin Taxis (d. 1582, o. 1569-1582), the imperial postmaster of Augsburg, replaced the Spanish postmaster Cristoforo de Montenegro in 1569. Wolfgang Behringer, *Thurn und Taxis: Die Geschichte ihrer Post und ihrer Unternehmen* (Munich: Piper, 1990), 59. See also Wolfgang Behringer, *Im Zeichen des Merkur: Reichspost und Kommunikationsrevolution in der Frühen Neuzeit* (Göttingen, Germany: Vandenhoeck & Ruprecht, 2003), 86.

13. This count includes Simone (d. 1563) and Ruggero Tassis (d. 1588) in Milan; Ruggero Tassis (d. 1583) in Venice; Giovan Antonio Tassis (d. 1580) in Rome; Raimondo Tassis (d. 1579) in Spain; Leonardo Tassis (d. 1612) in Brussels; Giovanni Battista Tassis (d. 1593) in Trento; Elena Bordogna Taxis (d. 1566) in Saint Michael; Maffeo Tasso (d. 1577), Maestro dei Corrieri in the Venetian Company of Couriers; Seraphin Taxis (d. 1582) in Augsburg; Antonio Taxis (d. 1574) in Antwerp; and Innocenzo Tassis (d. 1592) in Füssen.

14. Emperor Charles V appointed Ruggero Tassis to succeed his father in that role in 1539, reaffirmed with the establishment of the post office in 1541. Fürst Thurn und Taxis Hofbibliothek und Zentralarchiv (FTTZA), *Posturkunden (PU)*, 12.

15. Correspondents often referred to the Tassis post house as the "Spanish/Dutch office" due to the importance of the Tassis route to the Spanish Netherlands. Bonvantura Foppolo, "La Mariegola della Compagnia dei Corrieri Veneti," in *Mariegola della Compagnia dei Corrieri della Serenissima Signoria*, ed. Tarcisio Bottani and Wanda Taufer (Bergamo, Italy: Museo dei Tasso e della Storia Postale and Corponove, 2001), 41. Júlia Benavent and Miriam Bucuré, "Introduccion," in *Epistolario inedito entre Ruggero de Tassis y el Cardenal Granvelle (1536-1565)*, ed. Júlia Benavent and Miriam Bucuré (Prato, Italy: Istituto di Studi Storici Postali, 2017), 21-39. Thanks to Júlia Benavent.

16. A street sign in the vicinity today says, "Calle della Posta de Fiandra," although the name is no longer in official use.

17. Letters from Ruggero Tassis to Cardinal Granvelle (October 29, 1547, and November 1, 1547), in Benavent and Bucuré, *Epistolario*, 234-236.

18. Letter from Ruggero Tassis to Cardinal Granvelle (December 4, 1547), in Benavent and Bucuré, *Epistolario*, 81-84. On the related Tridentine posts and Bordogna branch of the family, see Francesca Brunet, *"Per essere quest'ufficio la chiave dell'Italia e Germania...": La famiglia Taxis Bordogna e le comunicazioni postali*

nell'area di Trento e Bolzano (sec. XVI–XVIII) (Bergamo, Italy: Museo dei Tasso e della Storia Postale and Corponove, 2018).

19. Letter from Ruggero Tassis to Antoine Perrenot de Granvelle (September 24, 1547), in Benavent and Bucuré, *Epistolario*, 229–230.

20. Marco Gerosa, *La famiglia Tasso e le poste nello Stato di Milano in età spagnola (1556–1650)* (Bergamo, Italy: Corponove, 2019), 27. Letter from Vito de Dorimbergo (February 12, 1573), in Archivo General de Simancas (AGS), *Consejo de Estado (Estado)*, 1509, fo. 238.

21. A letter from the Spanish ambassador, Guzman de Silva, in Venice summarized the arrangement (June 14, 1571), in AGS, *Estado*, 1329, fo. 64.

22. See, for example, the establishment of a postal ordinary with Lyon in 1560–1561, discussed in ASVe, *Corrieri*, 34. Examples of company representatives being sent abroad to conduct negotiations are located throughout the *capitoli* of the company; see especially ASVe, *Corrieri*, 10. Most documentation on the establishment of the ordinary can be found in *Documenti dell'istituzione fatta dalla compagnia de' corrieri Veneti delli due viaggi di Roma e Milano e poste* (Venice: Perlini, 1790).

23. On the importance of Desenzano, see Clemente Fedele, *Un lago per comunicare: Il Garda e l'Italia nella storia della cultura postale di età moderna* (Salò: Ateneo di Salò, 2024).

24. Copies can be found throughout the Venetian Company archives. See, for example, "Istituzione e parte presa dai corrieri del servizio d'un ordinario per Milano per la via di Mantova e Cremona..." (March 7, 1581), in ASVe, *Corrieri*, 35.

25. For more, see chapter 3 of this book.

26. "Supplicazione per l'instituire del viaggio suddetto per Milano, e Genova" (May 15, 1581), in ASVe, *Corrieri*, 35.

27. The sum recorded by Antelmi is roughly 14,000 soldi, but the conversion remains rough given an artificial conversion rate of 6 lire to 1 scudo. Letter of Bonifacio Antelmi to the Senate (March 16, 1584), in ASVe, *Senato, Dispacci*, 9.

28. The term here may derive from the Spanish for a twentieth of a ream, with three hands perhaps referring to approximately 75 sheets. *Real Academia Española: Diccionario de la lengua española*, 23rd ed., version 23.7; accessed online at https://del.rae.es/mano?m=form&m=form&wq=mano. Thanks to Emma Katherine Bilski and Alex Wingate. Letters were sent to the senate of Genoa, members of the Doria family, and the Venetian consul. Letter from Bonifacio Antelmi to the Senate (March 16, 1584), in ASVe, *Senato, Dispacci*, 9.

29. The Tassis were the only providers to repeatedly carry Venetian letters to and from France or the imperial court at Prague.

30. Letters from Savoy to Verona (and vice versa) constituted twenty entries, or 35 lire. The consul in Genoa and his brother in Bergamo also charged their correspondence and packages to the state (eleven entries, or 13 lire). The final 11 percent of Antelmi's expenses included a miscellany of onetime payments to terraferma cavallari and clerks to deliver mail and judicial proceedings. Letter from Bonifacio Antelmi to the Senate, in ASVe, *Senato, Dispacci*, 9.

31. On the Venetian political situation of this era, see William Bouwsma, *Venice and the Defense of Republican Liberty: Renaissance Values in the Age of the Counter-Reformation* (Berkeley: University of California Press, 1968).

32. See copies of relevant deliberations in ASVe, *Corrieri*, 35. The cavallari of Verona even enlisted a representative in Venice to defend their interests in the drawn-out legal disputes. Act (April 30, 1583), in Archivio di Stato di Verona (ASVer), *Processi, Uffici pubblici, Cavallari e portalettere (Cavallari)*, 27.701.

33. Act (December 6, 1584), in ASVer, *Cavallari*, 27.701.

34. See, for example, the objections raised against an edict circulated in Bologna that encouraged sending transalpine mail through Verona and bypassing the company monopoly. ASVe, *Corrieri*, V. The original edict collected by the couriers is also preserved: Alessandro Bernacci, "Ordinario da Bologna a Verona e Fiandra" (c. 1582), in ASVe, *Corrieri*. "Scrittura contro i corrieri di Mantova" (1584), in ASVe, *Corrieri*, 36. A similar struggle took place in 1564 between the imperial postmaster in Venice and the Venetian Company of Couriers regarding the power of appointment in Castelnuovo del Garda. ASVe, *Corrieri*, 21.

35. "Per la difficoltà con i corrieri da Mantova" (December 23, 1588), in ASVe, *Corrieri*, 36.

36. "Scrittura contro i corrieri di Mantova" (1584), in ASVe, *Corrieri*, 36.

37. ASMi, *Notarile*, 17136, cited in Gerosa, *La famiglia Tasso*, 54–55.

38. See, for example, "Decreto Senato per l'istituzione staffette da noi proposta al principe" (September 29, 1584), in ASVe, *Corrieri*, I.

39. The agreement also specified higher rates for carrying money, as moving currency continued to be a central function of postal service. "Decreto Senato per l'istituzione staffette da noi proposta al principe" (September 29, 1584), in ASVe, *Corrieri*, I.

40. "Decreto Senato per l'istituzione staffette da noi proposta al principe" (September 29, 1584), in ASVe, *Corrieri*, I.

41. Gerosa, *La famiglia Tasso*, 64–69.

42. On the phenomenon of office-leasing in France, see James B. Collins, *The State in Early Modern France* (Cambridge: Cambridge University Press, 1995), and Ralph E. Giesey, "State-Building in Early Modern France: The Role of Royal Officialdom," *Journal of Modern History* 55, no. 2 (June 1983): 191–207. On office-leasing in the Ottoman postal system, see Choon Hwee Koh, "The Mystery of the Missing Horses: How to Uncover an Ottoman Shadow Economy," *Comparative Studies in Society and History* 64, no. 3 (2022): 576–610.

43. See, generally, Drelichman and Voth, *Lending to the Borrower from Hell*.

44. Panizone's predecessor had advanced similar ideas. AGS, *Secretarías Provinciales (SP)*, 2014; ASMi, *Carteggio delle cancellerie dello Stato (Carteggio)*, 323; and in Gerosa, *La famiglia Tasso*, 65–66.

45. "Memoriale dei fratelli Adda" (July 1, 1593), in ASMi, *Carteggio*, 324.

46. Panizone had already proved unable to maintain order among the rebellious couriers. Pay disputes with the ordinary magistrate resulted in several imprisonments in the course of 1594. ASMi, *Carteggio*, 326. See Gerosa, *La famiglia Tasso*, 68–69. Appiano's appointment also appears in AGS, *SP*, 2014, 35.

47. Letter from il Bollino regarding Ercole Appiano (November 1596), in ASVe, *Corrieri*, 61.

48. Anonymous letter regarding the Milanese post office (c. 1596), in ASVe, *Corrieri*, 61.

49. Anonymous letter (c. 1596), in ASVe, *Corrieri*, 61. The merchants of Milan presented similar complaints to Spanish authorities; see "Memoriale dell'Università di mercanti di Milano" (1593), in AGS, *Estado*, 1345.

50. Interestingly, Appiano does not appear by name in the agreement, which specified only the corriero maggiore (March 23, 1596), in Martin Volker Albus Dallmeier, ed., *Quellen zur Geschichte des Europaischen Postwesens, 1501–1806*, vol. 2, no. 95 (Kallmünz, Germany: Lassleben, 1977), 46.

51. Drelichman and Voth, *Lending to the Borrower from Hell*, 12.

52. Drelichman and Voth, *Lending to the Borrower from Hell*, 133, 146.

53. "Consulta sobre lo que Don Juan de Tassis supplica cerca del oficio de correo mayor de Milan" (January 16, 1599), in AGS, *SP*, 2014, f.5. On the sale to the Serra, see a letter from Count Fuentes to the King (October 18, 1604), in ASMi, *Registri delle cancellerie dello Stato (Registri)*, XVI, 10; and a letter from Lucina Cattanea Tassis to Count Fuentes (August 28, 1605), in ASMi, *Carteggio*, 375.

54. Cattanea Tassis bought the lease for 3,700 Spanish reales. ASMi, *Notarile*, 15735. The terms would be renegotiated periodically in subsequent years and during several court battles. See Gerosa, *La famiglia Tasso*, 87–88.

55. Giorgio Migliavacca and Tarcisio Bottani, *Simone Tasso e le poste di Milano nel Rinascimento* (Bergamo, Italy: Museo dei Tasso e della Storia Postale and Corponove, 2007), 165. The authors of *Europa Postale* present a more generous take, describing that Codogno could be attributed "molteplici funzioni e mansioni." Marco Gerosa, "Per una biografia di Ottavio Codogno luogotenente delle poste di Milano e autore di guide postali," in *Europa Postale*, ed. Clemente Fedele, Armando Serra, and Marco Gerosa (Bergamo, Italy: Museo dei Tasso e della Storia Postale, 2014), 235. Gerosa updates his assessment in a book, describing "una proficua collaborazione con la Cattaneo Tasso." Gerosa, *La famiglia Tasso*, 86.

56. The Cattaneo family was also one of the top ten Genovese banking families; however, I have not been able to establish a direct connection. Lucina's maiden name was often rendered in the feminine form (Cattanea), but it also appeared as "Cattagna."

57. While Roman law allowed women greater legal powers, Lombard custom continued to limit participation without a male guardian. Fregulia finds that the principle of *undualdus* (female guardianship) remained a prevalent if inconsistent principle in Milan. Jeanette Fregulia, "Making Their Own Way: Women of Means in Late Renaissance Milan" (PhD diss., University of Nevada, Reno, 2007), 86–88.

58. AGS, *SP*, 2014, also in Gerosa, *La famiglia Tasso*, 4, 84.

59. Giovanni Battista Rebaglio preceded Codogno in this office. Gerosa, *La famigla Tasso*, 85–90.

60. Notarial records of May 8, 1602, September 25, 1603, and October 27, 1604, in ASMi, *Notarile*, 22345. Gerosa, *La famiglia Tasso*, 96–97. On widows, see also Robert Lopez, *Medieval Trade in the Mediterranean World* (New York: Norton, 1967), 180–181.

61. Archivio Storico Diocesano Milano (ASDMi), *Sezione X, Visite pastorali, Santo Stefano in Brolio*, vol. 21, in Gerosa, "Per una biografia di Ottavio Codogno," 236.

62. Entry (January 10, 1623), in ASMi, *Notarile*, 22353 in Gerosa, "Per una biografia di Ottavio Codogno," 238.

63. A document from the time of Ruggero Tassis names these posts as Lodi, Pizzighettone, Cremona, Bonavoglia, San Giacomo Lopio, Marcaria, Castelluccio, Castelnuovo, Volargne, Vò, Rovereto, Binasco, Bastia, Voghera, Alessandria, Felizzano, della Rosa, Vigevano, and Novara. ASMi, *Notarile*, 15807, also in Gerosa, *La famiglia Tasso*, 25.

64. Gerosa, "Per una biografia di Ottavio Codogno," 244.

65. See, for example, a summary of a letter from Ottavio Codogno (July 23, 1607), which begins "dice il corriero maggiore che . . ." In ASMi, *Carteggio*, 384.

66. The same Count Villamediana who leased the office in Milan to Lucina Cattanea Tassis appointed his wife, Doña Maria de Peralta y Muñatones, as procuress of the Castillian posts in his absence when he was sent on a diplomatic mission to England in 1604. In the Swedish postal system, Britta Lundgren finds: "During the period 1637-1722 40 post mistresses were in service as compared with 483 men. In other words, females made up slightly more than 8% of the total." Britta Lundgren, "'Det äro många postmästaränkor som sitta vid tjänsterna efter männen . . .' om postmästaränkor på 1600-talet," *Historisk tidskrift* 107, no. 1 (1987): 23-34. Thanks to Magnus Linnarsson.

67. AGS, *Consejo Real de Castilla (CRC)*, 969, f.37. Maria Antonia Blat, "I fondi Tassis del'Archivio di Simancas," in *I Tasso e le poste pontificie, sec. XV-XVI*, ed. Tarcisio Bottani (Bergamo, Italy: Corponove, 2000), 247-254.

68. Recent scholarship on the role of women in the history of the book is as wide and geographically diverse as its subjects. With regard to Lucina Cattanea's Milan, Jeanette Fregulia explores the case of the active Milanese businesswoman, Caterina Pirogallo, the widow of a bookseller. Fregulia, "Making Their Own Way." See also the widow printer Dorotea Scotto in Milan, introduced in Kevin Stevens, "New Light on Andrea Calvo and the Book Trade in Sixteenth-Century Milan," *La Bibliofilia* 103, no.1 (2001): 48-49. On women in espionage, see Nadine Akkerman, *Invisible Agents: Women and Espionage in Seventeenth-Century Britain* (Oxford: Oxford University Press, 2018).

69. The Venetian Company records also show frequent direct dealings with the postmistress. Cattanea Tassis and the Company reached two major agreements to reconcile their respective debts in July 1604 and June 1606. Both agreements survive in several copies. Agreements between Cattanea Tassis and the Venetian Company (July 17, 1604), in ASVe, *Corrieri*, 35, and (June 8, 1606), in ASVe, *Corrieri*, 51. See also Gerosa, *La famiglia Tasso*, 134-136.

70. On the role of Genovese merchants as provisioners for Spanish forces in the Netherlands, see, generally, Parker, *The Army of Flanders*.

71. Letter from Lucina Cattanea Tassis to Count Fuentes (August 28, 1605), in ASMi, *Carteggio*, 375.

72. The sale was completed gradually in the form of "shares" of the existing office. Letter from the Chamber of Merchants to Count Fuentes (August 12, 1605), in ASMi, *Carteggio*, 375. Letter from Count Fuentes to the Spanish King (October 18, 1604), in ASMi, *Registri*, XVI, 10. Gerosa, *La famiglia Tasso*, 90-93.

73. Dennis Romano, *Housecraft and Statecraft: Domestic Service in Renaissance Venice* (Baltimore: Johns Hopkins University Press, 1996), 14. See also Daniela Frigo,

Il padre di famiglia: Governo della casa e governo civile nella tradizione dell'"economica" tra Cinque e Seicento (Rome: Bulzoni, 1985).

74. Cinzia Lorandini, "Looking beyond the Buddenbrooks Syndrome: The Salvadori Firm of Trento, 1660s-1880s," *Business History* 57 (2015): 1005-1019.

75. These included the posts of Rioseco, Cuenca, Galicia, Aragon, and Siguenza. Otis Green, "Villamediana as Correo Mayor in the Kingdom of Naples," *Hispanic Review* 15, no. 2 (April 1947): 302-306; Isabel Perez Cuenca, "Otras noticias para la reconstrucción biográfica del Conde de Villamediana," in *Actas del Congreso de la Asociación Internacional Siglo de Oro*, ed. María Cruz Gracía de Enterría and Alicia Cordón Mesa (Alcalá de Henares, Spain: Universidad de Alcalá de Henares, 1996), 1211-1222. On the senior Villamediana, see María José Bertomeu Masiá, "Documenti su Juan de Tassis a Simancas," in *I Tasso e le poste*, ed. Tarcisio Bottani (Bergamo, Italy: Corponove, 2012), 255-262.

76. Filippo and Vittorio did not return to Milan before their deaths, but Ottavio earned a reprieve through military service, marrying a Milanese noblewoman, Lucrezia Vimercati. Gerosa, *La famiglia Tasso*, 166-170.

77. The pattern was not unique to the Tassis or imperial system. Postmistress widow Gese Wechel directed the Swedish postal system, working with Bernhard Stein von Steinhausen as *Generikschultz*. While anomalous to the Swedish system ("No one else, before or since, has been *generalriksschultz*"), the position makes more sense when considered in a transnational context. Magnus Linnarsson, "The Development of the Swedish Post Office, c. 1600-1721," in *Connecting the Baltic Area: The Swedish Postal System in the Seventeenth Century*, ed. Heiko Droste (Stockholm: Södertörns högskola, 2011), 39.

78. Gerosa also provides a summary of the charges in *La famiglia Tasso*, 123-124. In 1588, shortly before his death, Ruggero Tassis of Milan faced charges from an earlier visitation, as had his father, Simone, before him in 1560. ASMi, *Uffici*, 16, fo. 737; AGS, *Visitas de Italia (Visitas)*, 288, fo. 53-54, also in Gerosa, *La famiglia Tasso*, 44-46.

79. "Wherever contractors and state performance meet, contemporary political rhetoric almost universally highlights corrupt systems, profiteering and substandard quality." Harding and Ferri, *The Contractor State*, 12.

80. Miguel Ángel Echevarría Bacigalupe, "Pedro Enríquez de Guzmán de Acevedo y Toledo," in *Diccionario Biográfico electrónico* (Online) (DBE).

81. Haro often publicly invoked Frías's support. In a response to an anonymous 1607 polemic condemning Haro, the Council of Italy reaffirmed that Haro was to proceed, "as we do not know of a Visit to the Italian provinces that has not seen similar displeasures and complaints between Viceroys and Visitors...," AGS, *SP*, 1088, cited in Massimo Carlo Giannini, "'Con il zelo di sodisfare all'obligo di re e principe,' Monarchia cattolica a stato di Milano nella visita General di don Felipe Haro (1606-1612)," *Archivio storico lombardo* 120 (1994): 182-183.

82. Cardinal Antoine Perrenot de Granvelle (d. 1586) had previously used a visitation to discredit his rival, the viceroy of Naples, Marc'Antonio Colonna (d. 1584). Raphael Patrick Murillo, "Disciplining Empire: The Visita under the Spanish Hapsburgs, 1516-1700" (PhD diss., University of California, Berkeley, 2018), 106. On the rivalry between the two and Spanish political intrigues of

the period, see, generally, Geoffrey Parker, *Europe in Crisis: 1598-1648* (Oxford: Blackwell, 2001), and Geoffrey Parker, *The Grand Strategy of Philip II* (New Haven, CT: Yale University Press, 1998).

83. In another example, Count Fuentes allegedly ordered the arrest of a bandit "dead or alive," despite Haro's promise of safe conduct for the witness. Giannini, "'Con il zelo,'" 186-189.

84. Letters from 1606 indicate that Count Fuentes was receiving news on a weekly basis, likely with every ordinary courier. In a letter of July 6, 1606, for example, he wrote: "I have not received letters from you with this ordinary, and I hope it is not due to your poor health." FTTZA, *Haus- und Familiensachen (HFS)*, 119.

85. An anonymous accuser maintained that Count Fuentes had spent more than 1.3 million scudi on undocumented expenses over the course of 1600-1607. Giannini shows that more than 880,000 went to pension the duke of Savoy and various Swiss entities, but he was unable to trace another 437,000 in expenses. Later, the Milanese treasurer general, Muzio Parravicino, recounted being threatened with imprisonment if he did not pay secret payments as ordered by the governor's secretary. Many of these payments were also likely payoffs—both regular and onetime—to regional powers intended to maintain the delicate peace. Giannini, "'Con il zelo.'"

86. In addition to their regular dispatches to the senate, the Venetian residents were expected to provide reports to both the Council of Ten and State Inquisitors. See Ioanna Iordanou, *Venice's Secret Service: Organising Intelligence in the Renaissance* (Oxford: Oxford University Press, 2019). Letter from Antonio Pauluzzi with ciphered sections (September 13, 1606), in ASVe, *Capi del consiglio di dieci (CCX), Dispacci*, 17.

87. On the propaganda of the Venetian interdict, see, generally, Filippo de Vivo, *Information and Communication in Venice: Rethinking Early Modern Politics* (Oxford: Oxford University Press, 2007).

88. Letter from Pauluzzi to the Inquisitori di Stato (April 25, 1607), in ASVe, *Inquisitori di Stato (IS)*, 449. I have been unable to identify the Vitale mentioned, but it seems likely to be a relative of Giovanni Antonio Vitali Tassis, first cousin to Ruggero Tassis of Milan, as well as an associate of the Venetian Company of Couriers. Pauluzzi's concerns were not the first time that a Venetian resident feared postal intelligencing in Milan: in 1600, the Council of Ten wrote to Pauluzzi's predecessor, Valerio Antelmi (o. 1597-1602), that "regarding the fraud that you suspect of ministers opening packages and letters: we have never had reason to believe a similar operation, as packages do not appear to be opened ... we council you to investigate in order to determine the truth." Letter to Antelmi from the Council of Ten (December 3, 1600), in ASVe, *Consiglio di dieci (CX), Registri*, 14.

89. AGS, *Visitas*, 400, and in Gerosa, *La famiglia Tasso*, 167. One of the letters also refers to Ottavio as the *gastaldo*, the Venetian role that most closely mapped to that of the postmaster lieutenant of Milan.

90. Between October 1605 and February 1606, the Venetian resident made many payments to the Spanish post office of Milan, ranging from 10 soldi to more than 50 lire to cover multiple months of postage. ASMi, *Notarile*, 22348.

91. Letter to Pauluzzi from Inquisitori di Stato (April 28, 1607), in ASVe, *IS*, 157.

92. In November, Pauluzzi was still tracking who was writing to and from Venice, this time working with the Rectors of Bergamo to investigate a list of persons and report the results to the Council of Ten. Letter (November 25, 1607), in ASVe, *IS*, 157.

93. Letter to the Venetian Senate from Pauluzzi (August 31, 1605), in ASVe, *Senato, Dispacci*, 29. On espionage in Italy, see Iordanou, *Venice's Secret Service*, and Paolo Preto, *I servizi segreti di Venezia* (Milan: Saggiatore, 1994).

94. Letter (May 6, 1607), in ASVe, *Senato, Dispacci*, 29. The Inquisitors expressed great satisfaction at Pauluzzi's findings and encouraged him to continue his probe. Letter from Inquisitori di Stato to Pauluzzi (May 16, 1607), in ASVe, *Senato, Dispacci*.

95. The effort to reroute the postal route through Switzerland instead of Savoy involved Spanish ambassadors, the Spanish postmaster general, Count Fuentes, and the post office of Milan. Villamediana agreed with Count Fuentes about the suitability of the Swiss route through Lucerne, particularly for couriers from Naples. Yet he raised issues with the route henceforth, notably disagreeing with the "list of the lieutenant to the Postmaster of Milan." AGS, *Estado*, 1297. On rerouting the Spanish Road, see Parker, *The Army of Flanders*, 57–69.

96. Letter to Count Fuentes from Ottavio Codogno (June 23, 1603), in ASMi, *AG, Finanze*, 933. Printed edict with manuscript notations (August 12, 1603), in ASMi, *Carteggio*, 372. See also *Grida sopra i svaligiamenti, o assasinamenti de' corrieri* (March 19, 1604), in *Compendio di tutte le gride e ordini publicati nella Città e Stato di Milano* (Milan: Giovanni Battista Malatesta, 1612).

97. Letter to Count Fuentes from Ottavio Codogno (June 23, 1603), in ASMi, *AG, Finanze*, 933.

98. Recommendations for the Office of Coadjutor to the Extraordinary Magistrate (August 17, 1604), in AGS, *SP*, 1798.

99. Letter of Ottavio Codogno (May 20, 1606), in ASMI, *Registri*, S17, 38.

100. Letter of Ottavio Codogno (May 20, 1606), in ASMI, *Registri*, S17, 38. Édouard Rott addresses a similar discovery of a French mole in the governor's household, although there is no clear connection between Gualtieri (alias "Beauceron") and "Quattrocavi." Édouard Rott, *Henri IV: Les Suisses et la haute Italie, la lutte pour les Alpes (1598–1610)* (Paris: E. Plon, 1882), 128–129.

101. As far as I have been able to ascertain, this includes the Venetian archives, raising the possibility that Codogno had invented the story from whole cloth or used an alias.

102. Later that day, when one of Pauluzzi's servants stopped by the post office, he observed a messenger leaving for Venice. The servant questioned whether Pauluzzi had been properly alerted, resulting in the postmaster threatening that the servant "had better leave and not come back, or he would be sorry." Pauluzzi expressed somewhat disingenuous dismay that he had been treated so poorly by Codogno, a man "to whom I have never been remiss in courtesy." Letter to the Venetian Senate from Pauluzzi (May 1, 1607), in ASVe, *Senato, Dispacci*, 31.

103. See, generally, de Vivo, *Information and Communication*.

104. Akkerman, *Invisible Agents*.

105. Letter wrapper signed by Ottavio Codogno (July 23, 1610), in AGS, *Estado*, 1298.

106. Council notes (November 3, 1610), in ASMi, *Carteggio*, 399.

107. The list provides a glimpse into the varied tasks asked of the post. For example, it includes payments for a foot messenger from Turin, several couriers to Spain, the delivery of paper to the secretaries, and the dispatch of a coach to conduct notables to and from Milan. Payments recorded in ASMi, *Registri*, XXII, 50.

108. "Risposta fatta per Donna Lucina Cattanea de Tassis, a cui carica sta l'officio di Corriero maggiore nel Stato di Milano" (August 3, 1611), in AGS, *Visitas*, 268.

109. The payment is unusual, in that payments were always recorded in the name of Lucina Cattanea Tassis or the office of the postmaster prior to that point. Payment recorded July 1, 1611, in ASMi, *Registri*, XXII, 50.

110. Royal letter of commendation (April 4, 1621), in ASMi, *Dispacci reali (Dispacci)*, 57.

111. Codogno successfully negotiated that Villamediana sell his final shares of the office to Ottavio Tassis for 70,750 Spanish ducats. Entry (July 30, 1621), in ASMi, *Notarile*, 70750. By 1622, the Tassis sons had paid only 1,850 lire in restitution to the Spanish crown. ASMi, *Finanza confische*, 2844, and in Gerosa, *La famiglia Tasso*, 129.

112. Gerosa, "Per una biografia di Ottavio Codogno," 247.

113. Deciphered letter from Piero Antonio Marioni to the Venetian Senate (August 21, 1630), in ASVe, *Senato, Dispacci*, 71.

114. The other candidates to whom the resident might refer—such as the Serra, or the Tassis brothers—did not die within this time frame. The resident Venetian postmaster in Milan would have been referred to as the maestro delle poste or maestro dei corrieri, with the term *corriero maggiore* reserved for the head of the local system.

115. Letter from "Ottavio Tassis" [Ottavio Codogno] (March 13, 1607), in AGS, *Visitas*, 400.

116. Appended note (October 18, 1607), in AGS, *Visitas*, 400.

5. Breaking Records

1. Imperial instructions to the postmaster at Trento officially forbade private mail-carrying as late as 1555, for example. Lamoral Taxis-Bordogna and Erhard Riedel, *Zur Geschichte der Freiherren un Graffen Taxis-Bordogna-Valnigra und ihrer Obrist-Erbpostämter zu Bozen, Trient und an der Etsch* (Innsbruck, Austria: Wagner, 1955), 52.

2. Letter from King Philip II to Don Diego de Guzman de Silvia (May 31, 1573), in Archivo General de Simancas (AGS), *Consejo de Estado (Estado)*, 1330, fo. 187. For similar conversations with respect to the imperial post, see Anna Frey-Schlesinger, "Die volkswirtschaftliche Bedeutung der habsburgischen Post im 16. Jahrhundert," *Vierteljahrschrift für Sozial- und Wirtschaftsgeschichte* 15, no. 3/4 (1919): 399–465.

3. For examples, see chapter 3 of this book.

4. The letters are in the collections of the Museumsstiftung Post und Telekommunkation in Frankfurt, inventory number 4.2017.233. Andrew Pettegree, *The Invention of News: How the World Came to Know about Itself* (New Haven, CT: Yale University Press, 2014), 174–175. Another forgotten mail trunk inspired the "Signed, Sealed, Undelivered" project: see Rebekah Ahrendt and David van der Linden, "The Postmasters' Piggy Bank: Experiencing the Accidental Archive," *French Historical Studies* 40, no. 2 (April 2017): 189–213.

5. Howard Hotson and Thomas Wallnig, eds., *Reassembling the Republic of Letters in the Digital Age: Standards, Systems, Scholarship* (Göttingen, Germany: University of Göttingen Press, 2019). Digital projects build on the work of a predigital age: Pierre Sardella produced influential calculations based on the many volumes of diaries of the Venetian Marin Sanudo, who meticulously recorded Venice's receipt of both dispatches and newsletters. Fernand Braudel and Geoffrey Parker replicated and expanded upon those macro-findings, while there are numerous comprehensive studies of single news events or local networks. Geoffrey Parker, *The Grand Strategy of Philip II* (New Haven, CT: Yale University Press, 1998), 50–58; Fernand Braudel, *The Mediterranean and the Mediterranean World in the Age of Philip II*, vol. 1 (Berkeley: University of California Press, 1995), 362–363, 366–367; Pierre Sardella, *Nouvelles et spéculation à Venise au début du XVI siècle* (Paris: Libraire Armand Colin, 1948).

6. Nikolaus Schobesberger, "Mapping the *Fuggerzeitungen*: The Geographical Issues of an Information Network," in *News Networks*, ed. Joad Raymond and Noah Moxham (Leiden, Netherlands: Brill, 2016), 216–240.

7. Jay Caplan, *Postal Culture in Europe 1500–1800* (Oxford: Voltaire Foundation, 2016); Peter Miller, *Peiresc's Mediterranean World* (Cambridge, MA: Harvard University Press, 2015).

8. For a good overview, see Chris Shore and Susan Wright, "Audit Culture Revisited," *Current Anthropology* 56, no. 3 (June 2015): 421–444. Jacob Soll has long emphasized the impact of accounting and archiving in an early modern context. Jacob Soll, "From Note-Taking to Data Banks: Personal and Institutional Information Management in Early Modern Europe," *Intellectual History Review* 20, no. 3 (2010): 355–375.

9. The *Deductio Birghdiana*, addressed to the "impartial reader," attributed Birghden's dismissal to the Tassis postmaster general's "great hatred" of him. The defense routinely contrasted the "dispassionate" approbation and commendations in support of Birghden against the dissimulating Tassis. A printed copy survives in the Bavarian State Libraries, where it has been dated to c. 1636. Johann von den Birghden, *Deductio Birghdiana, Das Ist, Etlicher Hochst-und Hochansehenlicher Chur-Fursten und Herren, Intercessiones, Commendations, von Attestastions* (n.p.: n.p., c. 1636), Augsburg, Staats- und Stadtbibliothek 2 S 44.

10. The historian Wolfgang Behringer, as well as many literary scholars, have described how postal infrastructure shifted conceptions of space-time. Wolfgang Behringer, "Communications Revolutions: A Historiographical Concept," *German History* 24, no. 3 (2006): 333–374.

11. Bruno Caizzi, *Dalla posta dei re alla posta di tutti: Territorio e comunicazioni in Italia dal XVI secolo all'Unità* (Milan: Franco Angeli, 1993).

12. Carolyn Boyes-Watson, "Recordkeeping as a Technology of Power," *Berkeley Journal of Sociology* 39 (1994): 1-32.

13. Codogno enjoined the postal lieutenant to record all the same information upon any courier's arrival. Ottavio Codogno, *Nuovo itinerario delle poste per tutto il mondo* (Milan: Girolamo Bordoni, 1608), 38-39.

14. Supplication of the brothers d'Adda (July 1593), in Archivio di Stato di Milano (ASMi), *Carteggio delle cancellerie dello Stato (Carteggio)*, 324. See Marco Gerosa, *La famiglia Tasso e le poste nello Stato di Milano in età spagnola (1556–1650)* (Bergamo, Italy: Corponove, 2019), 67.

15. Paul Marcus Dover, "Deciphering the Diplomatic Archives of Fifteenth-Century Italy," *Archival Science* 7 (2007): 297-316.

16. Soll, "From Note-Taking to Data Banks."

17. ASMi, *Notarile*, 22348.

18. See, generally, Domenico Sella, *Salari e lavoro nell'edilizia lombarda durante il secolo XVII* (Pavia, Italy: Fusi, 1968).

19. Couriers took issue with this practice, but Codogno and Cattanea Tassis defended it to the visitation as being necessitated by their leaseholder status. "Carichi risultanti dall'atti della Visita generale contro il Corriero Maggiore dello stato di Milano," in AGS, *Visitas de Italia (Visitas)*, 268.

20. Records of diplomatic postings and company elections can be found throughout the archives, but especially in Archivio di Stato di Venezia (ASVe), *Compagnia dei Corrieri (Corrieri)* 10 and 11. Leadership positions here include the steward (*gastaldo*), vice steward (*vice gastaldo*), members of the voting bench (*banco*), and postmastership of the company office in Rome.

21. On the role of servants, see, generally, Dennis Romano, *Housecraft and Statecraft: Domestic Service in Renaissance Venice* (Baltimore: Johns Hopkins University Press, 1996).

22. This was common practice in the Venetian Company of Couriers, shown across the *Corrieri* archives.

23. The ages of the dissatisfied couriers interviewed by the Spanish visitors generally fell between forty and fifty years, of which they had spent ten or twenty years as couriers.

24. Only some of the missions were explicitly noted as *"staffetta,"* but as opposed to the ordinaries, they did not occur in a regular pattern.

25. The remaining expenses consisted of a variety of household goods (wine, flour, candles, and hay for the horses, 3 percent) and scribal and legal fees (associated with edicts, legal cases, and notaries, 1.2 percent).

26. I have tested and confirmed the calculation of 1 postal ounce = approx. 31 grams = approx. 4 letters from Joseph Rübsam, "Postavisi und Postkonto aus den Jahren 1599 bis 1624," *Deutsche Geschichtsblätter* 7, no. 7 (1906): 8-19. Contemporary tariffs, which often put the price of a postal ounce at the price of four single folio sheets, also support this calculation, but it notably does not account for undeclared enclosures (such as coins).

27. AGS, *Visitas*, 268.

28. See Albert Hirschman, *The Passions and the Interests: Political Arguments for Capitalism before Its Triumph* (Princeton, NJ: Princeton University Press, 2013).

29. "Magistrato supplicatione" (May 15, 1581), in ASVe, *Corrieri*, 35. See also "Capitoli accordati a noi da Ruggiero de Tassis..." (1582), in ASVe, *Corrieri*. The Spanish governor had recently ruled in Ruggero of Milan's favor regarding the subordination of Genoa to the Milan office. ASMi, *Notarile*, 17136, in Gerosa, *La famiglia Tasso*, 54–55. Wrangling over the Spanish postmastership of Genoa also generated a wealth of documents; see especially AGS, *Estado*, 1414, 1423.

30. AGS, *Visitas*, 268. See also Gerosa, *La famiglia Tasso*, 123–124.

31. The printed defense issued by Codogno and Cattanea Tassis can also be found in AGS, *Visitas*, 268.

32. Paolo Malanima, *L'economia italiana: Dalla crescita medievale alla crescita contemporanea* (Bologna, Italy: Società editrice il Mulino, 2002).

33. On shifting definitions of corruption in Spanish administration, see, generally, Raphael Patrick Murillo, "Disciplining Empire: The Visita under the Spanish Hapsburgs, 1516–1700" (PhD diss., University of California, Berkeley, 2018).

34. The testimonies can be found in AGS, *Visitas*, 268 and 399.

35. Testimony of Francesco dal Monte (February 7, 1607), in AGS, *Visitas*, 399.

36. Testimony of Giuseppe Pellano ("Giuseppino") (February 9, 1607), in AGS, *Visitas*, 399.

37. Testimony of Dioniseo Gallarato (February 9, 1607), in AGS, *Visitas*, 399.

38. Pellano in AGS, *Visitas*, 399.

39. Gallarato in AGS, *Visitas*, 399.

40. Testimony of Giuseppe de Caravaggio (March 6, 1607), in AGS, *Visitas*, 268.

41. Pellano in AGS, *Visitas*, 399.

42. This accusation appears in several testimonies, but see, particularly, Hieronimo Corte in AGS, *Visitas*, 268. On the importance of Genoese bills of exchange to the rise of pan-European financial markets, see, generally, Francesca Trivellato, *The Promise and Peril of Credit: What a Forgotten Legend about Jews and Finance Tells Us about the Making of European Commercial Society* (Princeton, NJ: Princeton University Press, 2019).

43. Codogno, *Nuovo itinerario*, 22–23. Rachel Midura, "Publishing the Baroque Post: The Postal Itinerary and the Mailbag Novel," in *The Renaissance of Letters: Knowledge and Community in Italy, 1300–1650*, ed. Paula Findlen and Suzanne Sutherland (New York: Routledge, 2020), 259–260.

44. Testimony of Alosius Marinetto in AGS, *Visitas*, 268

45. Testimony of Giovanni Pocapaglia in AGS, *Visitas*, 399.

46. The Bozen merchant Heinrich Kunter sponsored the building of a mule road through the Eisack gorge that made the Brenner passable in 1314, while the Fugger family had contributed to rebuilding portions of it in the sixteenth century. Uwe A. Oster, *Wege über die Alpen: Von der Frühzeit bis heute* (Darmstadt, Germany: Primus, 2006), 35. See also Gudrun Schnekenburger, *Über die Alpen: Menschen, Wege, Waren* (Stuttgart: Archäologisches Landesmuseum Baden-Württemberg, 2002), 48–49, 83; Rachel Midura, "'They Hide from Me, Like the Devil from the Cross': Transalpine Postal Routes as Intelligence Work, 1555–1645," *History: The Journal of the Historical Association* 108, no. 381 (2023): 308.

47. Several excellent works address different branches of the Tassis family along the German Road, including Francesca Brunet, *"Per essere quest'ufficio la*

chiave dell'Italia e Germania...": La famiglia Taxis Bordogna e le comunicazioni postali nell'area di Trento e Bolzano (sec. XVI–XVIII) (Bergamo, Italy: Museo dei Tasso e della Storia Postale and Corponove, 2018); Erika Kustatscher, *Die Innsbrucker Linie der Thurn und Taxis: Die Post in Tirol und den Vorlanden (1490–1769)* (Innsbruck, Austria: Universitätsverlag Wagner, 2018); Brigitte Mazohl-Wallnig, "Österreichisch-italienische Postgeschichte im 18. und 19. Jahrhundert. Werkstattbericht," *Jahrbuch der Österreichischen Gesellschaft zur Erforschung des 18. Jahrhunderts* 7, no. 8 (1992/93): 7-25.

48. Wolfgang Behringer, *Thurn und Taxis: Die Geschichte ihrer Post und ihrer Unternehmen* (Munich: Piper, 1990), 36.

49. Joseph Rübsam, "Taxis, Anton von," in *Allgemeine Deutsche Biographie* (Online) (ADB) 37 (1894), S. 482, https://wrww.deutsche-biographie.de/pnd138592489.html#adbcontent. The office passed down through Seraphin Tassis (d. 1582) and his descendants (June 4, 1543, and December 22, 1543), in Martin Volker Albus Dallmeier, ed., *Quellen zur Geschichte des Europaischen Postwesens, 1501–1806*, vol. 2, no. 17-18 (Kallmünz, Germany: Lassleben, 1977), 12. Martin Volker Albus Dallmeier and Fürstliches Marstallmuseum (Regensburg), *500 Jahre Post Thurn und Taxis: Ausstellung Anläßlich der 500jährigen Wiederkehr der Anfänge der Post in Mitteleuropa 1490–1990: Fürstliches Marstallmuseum Regensburg, Emmeramsplatz, 5 12. Mai bis 29. Juli 1990* (Neusäss, Germany: Kieser, 1990), 29-30. See also Behringer, *Thurn und Taxis*, 47; Schobesberger, "Mapping the *Fuggerzeitungen*."

50. Dallmeier and Marstallmuseum (Regensburg), *500 Jahre Post*, 25; Wolfgang Behringer, "Fugger und Taxis: Der Anteil Augsburger Kaufleute an der Entstehung des europäischen Kommunikationssystems," in *Augsburger Handelshäuser im Wandel des historischen Urteils*, ed. Johannes Burkhardt (Berlin: Akademie Verlag, 1996), 241-248. The *Fuggerzeitungen*, or *Fugger Newsletters*, consist of over 16,000 newsletters assembled by the family and their agents in Augsburg from 1568 to 1605, many of which traveled along the Tassis postal routes.

51. The post house outside the city walls is depicted in the Lucas Kilian engraving *Augsburg Posthaus* (c. 1616).

52. These dispatch notes were sent by Ferdinando Tassis to his second cousin, Lamoral I Tassis (d. 1624), in Prague at the court of Holy Roman Emperor Rudolph. The records continue into 1611, and Behringer notes increasing traffic over that time. Behringer, *Thurn und Taxis*, 79-82. Unless otherwise stated, Lamoral I or his staff were the recipients of all the following correspondence from Ferdinando and Octavio Tassis from this collection.

53. Fürst Thurn und Taxis Hofbibliothek und Zentralarchiv (FTTZA), *Haus- und Familiensachen (HFS)*, 117. These cities, along with Rome and Venice, were notably the same ones that a recent study utilizing newly cataloged metadata identified as being the most important within the *Fuggerzeitungen* (www.univie.ac.at/fuggerzeitungen/en/).

54. FTTZA, *HFS*, 117.

55. Accessed February 1, 2023, at http://emlo.bodleian.ox.ac.uk/forms/advanced?dat_to_year=1609&dat_to_day=31&dat_to_month=1&dat_from_day=1&dat_from_year=1607&dat_from_month=12.

56. Joseph Rübsam, "Taxis, Octavio von," in ADB 37 (1894), S. 520-521, https://www.deutsche-biographie.de/pnd130008877.html#adbcontent.

Behringer, "Fugger und Taxis," 247. Octavio Tassis of Augsburg appears in FTTZA, *Postakten (PA)*, 1234, 3001; *PU*, 59, 61; *HFS*, 118–120.

57. Isabella Tassis (c. 1534–1614), Octavio's mother, was the daughter of Simone Tassis of Milan. She ran the Augsburg office as a widow-postmistress following the death of Seraphin, her husband, in 1582, much as Lucina Cattanea Tassis did in Milan. Isabella appeared frequently in Octavio's letters, as did his sister Ginevra Tassis (also written Genoveva Taxis, c. 1560–1628), who married the postmaster general Lamoral Tassis and resided in Brussels.

58. Letter from Octavio Tassis (June 9, 1604), in FTTZA, *PA*, 3001.

59. Mark Granovetter, "The Strength of Weak Ties," *American Journal of Sociology* 78, no. 6 (May 1973): 1360–1380.

60. Letter from Octavio Tassis (July 20, 1605), in FTTZA, *PA*, 1214.

61. Ferdinando sent paintings and books north from Venice to his Antwerp- and Brussels-based colleagues. In other cases, the Tassis traded medical ingredients, foodstuffs, and even scientific instruments: the Venetian Tassis helped the postmaster general to secure a telescope manufactured by Galileo Galilei's preferred artisans. Letter from Ferdinando and Davide Tassis in Venice accompanying a painting by Hans Rottenhamer (d. 1625) (March 18, 1601), in FTZZA, *PA*, 653. Other letters accompanied a copy of Giorgio Vasari's *Lives of the Artists* (1550) and a volume of poetry by Lucrezia Marinella (d. 1653). Letter from Ferdinando Tassis and Davide Tassis to Lamoral Tassis (December 7, 1603, and September 30, 1605), in FTTZA, *HFS*, 117. On the telescope, see letters from Ferdinando Tassis (June 4, July 5, and August 13, 1610); in FTTZA, *HFS*, 118. Massimo Bucciantini, Michele Camerota, and Franco Giudicie, eds., *Galileo's Telescope: A European Story*, trans. Catherine Bolton (Cambridge, MA: Harvard University Press, 2015).

62. Francesca Trivellato, *The Familiarity of Strangers: The Sephardic Diaspora, Livorno, and Cross-Cultural Trade in the Early Modern Period* (New Haven, CT: Yale University Press, 2009).

63. Letter from Ferdinando Tassis (September 13, 1609), in FTTZA, *HFS*, 117.

64. This is the equivalent of approximately 6,000 Milanese lire. Letters from Ferdinando Tassis (February 19 and April 16, 1610), in FTTZA, *HFS*, 118. On couriers facing suspicion for their own robberies, see chapter 3 of this book. Midura, "'They Hide from Me,'" 312.

65. ASMi, *Miscellanea storica (MS)*, 41 and 42.

66. Letter from Ferdinando Tassis (July 14, 1623), in FTTZA, *PA*, 5403. See also ASVe, *Corrieri*, III.

67. Octavio Tassis faced similar questioning in Augsburg: "The ordinary came so late that I had nothing to say to the merchants [here], nor those of Nuremberg..." Letter from Octavio Tassis (September 3, 1620), in FTTZA, *PA*, 1214.

68. On a clock carried for the Fuggers, see letters of Octavio Tassis (August 22 and August 25, 1618), in FTTZA, *PA*, 1214.

69. Letter from Octavio Tassis (April 4, 1623), in FTTZA, *PA*, 1214.

70. Letter from Octavio Tassis (April 12, 1623), in FTTZA, *PA*, 1214. Midura, "'They Hide from Me,'" 316.

71. Rübsam, "Postavisi und Postkonto," 8–19. On *avvisi*, see, generally, Mario Infelise, *Prima dei giornali: Alle origini della pubblica informazione* (Rome: Laterza, 2002).

72. Pelegrin de Tassis, *Neue Zeyttung von Rom / Kay. Mayestat Postmayster zy Rom / Pelegrin de Tassis* (n.p.: n.p., 1527).

73. The newspaper did not regularly carry a title until 1628. For a table of possible production numbers and surviving editions, see Heinz Kremer, *Johann von den Birghden, 1582-1645: Kaiserlicher und königlich-schwedischer Postmeister zu Frankfurt am Main* (Bremen, Germany: Edition Lumière, 2005), 538. Midura, "'They Hide from Me,'" 316.

74. Pettegree, *The Invention of News*, 185.

75. Birghden's newspaper was preceded by nonpostal examples in the Netherlands and other parts of Germany, such as Abraham Verhoeven's *Nieuwe Tydinghe* (Antwerp: Verhoeven, 1605), and Johann Carolus's Strasbourg *Relation: Aller Fürnemmen, und gedenckwürdigen Historien: So sich hin und wider in Hoch und Nieder Teutschland, auch in Franckreich, Italien, Schott und Engelland* (Strassburg, Germany: n.p., 1605). Pettegree, *The Invention of News*, 182-185. Paul Arblaster, *From Ghent to Aix: How They Brought the News in the Habsburg Netherlands, 1550-1700* (Leiden, Netherlands: Brill, 2014), 122-171.

76. See chapter 1 of this book, and Midura, "'They Hide from Me,'" 316.

77. Recipients of Birghden's newspaper via their chancellors and secretaries included "[Friedrich V.], [Ernst von Manssfeld], [Christian von] Halberstadt, Prinz Morizen [von Oranien], Markgrafen [Georg-Friedrich] zu Baden [-Durchlach], Landgrafen Morizen du Hessen-[Kassel]. Korrespondenz-protokoll von [Sachsen-] Anhalt," in Dallmeier, *Quellen*, vol. 2, no. 208, 96. See also FTTZA, *PU*, 98.

78. Dallmeier, *Quellen*, vol. 2, no. 208, 96. Midura, "'They Hide from Me,'" 319.

79. The reason for this resentment is not clear. Kremer suggests that in addition to religious intolerance, Leonardo may have been jealous of Birghden's rising star. Kremer, *Johann von den Birghden*, 287. See also Bernhard Faulhaber, *Geschichte des Postwesens Frankfurt am Main* (Frankfurt: Völckers, 1883). Midura, "'They Hide from Me,'" 316.

80. Nicholas Terpstra, *Religious Refugees in the Early Modern World: An Alternative History of the Reformation* (Cambridge: Cambridge University Press, 2015).

81. Letter of Octavio Tassis (February 9, 1608), in FTTZA, *PA*, 3001.

82. Early in his career, Henot played a crucial role in negotiating an end to strikes that paralyzed the imperial postal system. The strike leader Giuseppe Calepio—a Bergamasco himself, related to the Tassis family by marriage—collaborated with Dutch protestants to build a rival system linking Italy, France, and the Netherlands. An imperial commission estimated that the upheaval cost the post nearly 10,000 imperial florins in 1587 alone, the equivalent of nearly 40,000 Milan lire. Behringer, *Thurn und Taxis*, 58-59, 65.

83. A consortium of Augsburg, Nuremberg, and Frankfurt merchants guaranteed postmasters' salaries several years in advance. Behringer, *Thurn und Taxis*, 72.

84. Engelbert Goller, *Jakob Henot, Postmeister von Cöln: Ein Beitrag zur Geschichte der Sogenannten Postreformation um die Wende des XVI. Jahrhunderts* (Bonn, Germany: Carl Georgi, 1910); Leonhard Ennen, "Henot, Hartger," in ADB 11 (1880), 782, https://www.deutschebiographie.de/pnd133246655.html#adbcontent.

85. Chapter 4 in Goller, *Jakob Henot*, 63-92.

86. See letters in FTTZA, *PA*, 1214 and 3001.

87. Letter from Octavio Tassis (August 24, 1610, December 17, 1603, and July 9, 1604), in FTTZA, *PA*, 1214.

88. Letter from Octavio Tassis (June 9, 1604), in FTTZA, *PA*, 1214.

89. Ennen, "Henot, Hartger," in ADB. See also Gerd Schwerhoff, "Hexenverfolgung in einer frühneuzeitlichen Großstadt—das Beispiel der Reichsstadt Köln," in *Hexenverfolgung im Rheinland Ergebnisse neuerer Lokal- und Regionalstudien*, ed. Thomas Becker and Stephan Lennartz (Bergisch Gladbach, Germany: Thomas-Morus-Akademie Bensberg, 1996), 13–56.

90. Octavio Tassis in Augsburg to Leonardo II Tassis (January 16, 1625), in FTTZA, *PA*, 1234. Midura, "'They Hide from Me,'" 318.

91. Dallmeier and Marstallmuseum (Regensburg), *500 Jahre Post*, 3. See also related documents in FTTZA, *PA*, 1234. Midura, "'They Hide from Me,'" 318.

92. Kremer, *Johann von den Birghden*, 304–313.

93. Both the Swedish king, Gustavus Adolphus, and the "Winter King," Frederick V of Palatinate, were present in Frankfurt in December of that year. Frederick resided in the post house. Faulhaber, *Geschichte*, 54. On the Swedish postal system, see Heiko Droste, ed., *Connecting the Baltic Area: The Swedish Postal System in the Seventeenth Century* (Stockholm: Södertörn University, 2011). Heiko Droste, "Sending a Letter between Amsterdam and Stockholm: A Matter of Trust and Precautions," in *Your Humble Servant: Agents in Early Modern Europe*, ed. Hans Cool, Marika Keblusek, and Badeloch Noldus (Hilversum, Netherlands: Verloren, 2006), 135–148.

94. Letter from David Fray to Leonardo II Tassis (January 7, 1632), in FTTZA, *PA*, 1214. Midura, "'They Hide from Me,'" 320.

95. Letter from David Fray to Leonardo II Tassis (January 7, 1632), in FTTZA, *PA*, 1214. Midura, "'They Hide from Me,'" 320.

96. Letter from Leonardo Tassis to Baron Questemberg (March 20, 1628), in FTTZA, *PA*, 6100.

97. Birghden's printed defense, including letters of advocacy from several prominent noblemen, remains the definitive collection of sources. On the destruction of the original sources at the Frankfurt archives, see Kremer, *Johann von den Birghden*, 3. Midura, "'They Hide from Me,'" 321.

98. Scholars of tolerance have long looked to the Netherlands as pioneering innovative social arrangements accounting for religious diversity. See Benjamin Kaplan, *Reformation and the Practice of Toleration: Dutch Religious History in the Early Modern Era* (Leiden, Netherlands: Brill, 2019).

99. In October 1627, Birghden indicated that he had produced 450 copies of the newspaper, while in 1628, Vrints distributed 778 copies. Kremer suggests that Birghden may have deliberately underreported his distribution. Kremer, *Johann von den Birghden*, 155. Midura, "'They Hide from Me,'" 319.

100. Codogno, *Nuovo itinerario*, 6–7.

6. The Sinews of Society

1. Peter Heylyn, *A Full Relation of Two Journeys* (London: Printed by E. Cotes for Henry Seile, 1656), 13; Richard Lassels, *The Voyage of Italy* (Paris: Simon Wilson, 1670), 259.

2. The editors make a similar point in "Movement and Mobility in the Early Modern World: An Introduction," in *Connected Mobilities in the Early Modern World: The Practice and Experience of Movement*, ed. Rosa Salzberg and Paul Nelles (Amsterdam: Amsterdam University Press, 2023), 7–38.

3. Oliver Landolt, "Mobilität und Verkehr im europäischen Spätmittelalter. Mit besonderer Berücksichtigung der Verkehrspolitik innerhalb der Eidgenossenschaft," *Historische Zeitschrift* 40 (2006): 489–510.

4. One author called postilions "diabolical" on account of their fits of early modern road rage. Thomas Coryate, *Coryate's Crudities* (London: William Stanby, 1611).

5. See, for example, the growing popularity of the term in the title of printed broadsheets across the seventeenth century, such as the "Munsterischer Postillion" (Hohenems, 1619).

6. Gerrit Verhoeven, "Wading through the Mire: Mobility on the Grand Tour," in *Connected Mobilities*, ed. Salzberg and Nelles, 63–85; Sarah Goldsmith, Rosemary Sweet, and Gerrit Verhoeven, eds., *Beyond the Grand Tour: Northern Metropolises and Early Modern Travel Behaviour* (New York: Routledge, 2017).

7. While a royal post had existed since the beginning of the sixteenth century, the appointment of Thomas Witherings as head of the posts began a new period of reform and expansion. Howard Robinson, *The British Post Office: A History* (Princeton, NJ: Princeton University Press, 1948), 28. The agreement between Daniel O'Neill (d. 1664) and Thurn und Taxis can be found in Martin Volker Albus Dallmeier, ed., *Quellen zur Geschichte des Europaischen Postwesens, 1501–1806*, vol. 2, no. 334–337 (Kallmünz, Germany: Lassleben, 1977), 149–151.

8. On the role of infrastructure in political economic debates, see Sophus Reinert, *The Academy of Fisticuffs: Political Economy and Commercial Society in Enlightenment Italy* (Cambridge, MA: Harvard University Press, 2018); Jo Guldi, *Roads to Power: Britain Invents the Infrastructure State* (Cambridge, MA: Harvard University Press, 2012).

9. John Evelyn, *Memoirs of John Evelyn, Comprising His Diary, from 1641 to 1705-6*, ed. W. Bray (London: Henry Colburn, 1827), 153. The translation from Italian is my own.

10. Many of the subordinate postmasters who paid leases to the post office of Milan were innkeepers. The courier Giuseppino named the following to the Spanish visitation: "Giovanni who runs the Inn of the Falcon in Pavia, Antonio Maria who runs the inn of the White Cross in Pavia on the *Strada Nova*." Testimony of Giuseppe Pellano (February 9, 1607) in Archivo General de Simancas (AGS), *Visitas de Italia (Visitas)*, 399. On inns handling mail in Rome, see Wilhelm Beck, "Ursprung und Ende der fremden Posten in Rom," *Archiv für das Post- und Fernmeldewesen*, no. 1–7 (1959): 564–588.

11. Venetian and Milanese postmasters reportedly rented horses to any traveler, although this was a violation of the terms of their privileges, which limited them to providing horses for the couriers. See particularly Archivio di Stato di Venezia (ASVe), *Compagnia dei Corrieri (Corrieri)*, 37 and AGS, *Visitas*, 268. For a similar case in the Ottoman Empire, see Choon Hwee Koh, "The Mystery of the Missing Horses: How to Uncover an Ottoman Shadow Economy," *Comparative Studies in Society and History* 64, no. 3 (2022): 576–610.

12. The procaccio between Rome and Naples was a rigorously timed armed caravan for this reason. For a traveler's description, see Fynes Moryson, *An Itinerary Written by Fynes Moryson* (London: John Beale, 1617), 105.

13. Megan Williams, "The Perils of the Post Road: Diplomats, Diplomatic Couriers, and the Informational Fabric of Early Modern Europe," in *Information and Power in History: Towards a Global Approach*, ed. Ida Nijenhuis, M. van Faasen, Ronal Sluijter, Joris Gijsenbergh, and Wim de Jong (Abingdon: Routledge, 2020), 105–121. On the history of the passport, see, generally, Valentin Groebner, *Who Are You? Identification, Deception, and Surveillance in Early Modern Europe* (Princeton, NJ: Princeton University Press, 2007).

14. Emperor Ferdinand himself preferred to stay in a postal inn in Markdorf en route to and from Italy. Michel de Montaigne, *A Diary of the Journey of Michael de Montaigne into Italy, through Switzerland and Germany, in the Years 1580 and 1581*, trans. William Hazlitt (New York: Hurd and Houghton, 1866), 540.

15. Montaigne, *Diary*, 552.

16. Stefano d'Amico, *Spanish Milan: A City within Empire* (London: Palgrave Macmillan, 2016), 21.

17. See, for example, instructions given to the Savoyard postmaster general Andrea Pelegrino (June 23, 1629), in Archivio di Stato di Torino (ASTo), *Sezione reunite, Poste*, 1. The same regulation stipulated penalties for unlicensed rentals of horses and carriages.

18. See chapter 5 of this book.

19. Marco Gerosa, *La famiglia Tasso e le poste nello Stato di Milano in età spagnola (1556–1650)* (Bergamo, Italy: Corponove, 2019), 104.

20. Coryate, *Coryate's Crudities*; Moryson, *An Itinerary*.

21. Montaigne, *Diary*, 541.

22. *The Marvels of Rome*, or *Mirabilia Urbis Romae*, circulated widely in the twelfth century, while the Aymeric Picaud's account of the path of Saint James appears as the fifth book of the *Codex Calixtinus*, likely dating to around 1140. By 1585, Italian-language editions of the *Marvels of Rome* regularly advertised the addition of "the posts of Italy" or the "principal posts." Rachel Midura, "Itinerating Europe: Early Modern Spatial Networks in Printed Itineraries, 1545–1700," *Journal of Social History* 54, no. 4 (2021): 35.

23. A digitized copy held at the Bavarian State Library was mistakenly dated to the 1550s prior to 2024; however, publishers by the name of Nava were active at the beginning and end of the seventeenth century. Thanks to Clemente Fedele.

24. *Le poste, necessarie a corrieri & viandanti, per l'Italia, Francia, Spagna, & Alemagna con le fiere che si fanno per il mondo* (Brescia, Italy: Damiano Turlano and Ioanne Battista Bozola, 1562); Cherubino di Stella and Giovanni da l'Herba, *L'Itinerario per diverse parte del mondo* (Rome: Valerico Dorico, 1563); *Poste diverse d'Italia, Alemagna, Spagna, e Francia* (Milan: n.p., c. 1620s–1700).

25. "Il Forastiero discorre con un camerata italiano per viaggo / A Stranger discourses with an Italian Comrade upon the way," in Giovanni Torriano, *Della lingua Toscana-Romana, or, An Introduction to the Italian Tongue* . . . (London: J. Martin and J. Allestrye, 1657), 140. Other examples include "Il forastiero

smarrita la strada discorre con un contadino ricercandolo di quella / A stranger having lost his way speaks with a husbandman enquiring about it" and "Il Forestiero pattuisce con un capo vetturino Italiano interono al nollo di cavalli / A stranger bargains with an Italian head-hacknyman about horse-hire." Both the Italian and English translation are taken directly from Midura, "Itinerating Europe," 6.

26. Franciscus Schottus's book appeared under multiple titles and in multiple languages: *Itinerari Italiae* (Antwerp, Belgium: Jan Moretus, 1600); *Itinerarium nobiliorum Italiae regionum* (Vicenza, Italy: Girolamo Giovannini, 1600); *Itinerario: Overo nova descrittione de' viaggi principali d'Italia* (Vicenza, Italy: Pietro Bertelli, 1610); and Edmund Warcupp, *Italy, in its original glory, ruine and revival, being an exact survey of the whole geography, and history of that famous country*... (London: Sara Griffin, for Henry Twyford and Thomas Dring and John Place, 1660); Andrea Palladio, *Le cose maravigliose dell'alma città di Roma... con le poste d'Italia* (Rome: Giovanni Osmarino Gigliotto, 1585). The posts first appeared in Franciscus Schottus, *Itinerario* (Venice: Francesco Bolzetta, 1610), as well as in later editions produced by Bolzetta's heirs. Franciscus Schottus, *Itinerari Italiae* (Antwerp, Belgium: Ioannem Moretum, 1600); Franciscus Schottus, *Itinerarium nobiliorum Italiae regionum* (Vicenza, Italy: Girolamo Giovannini, 1600); Franciscus Schottus, *Itinerario overo nova descrittione*... (Vicenza, Italy: Petrum Bertellium, 1610).

27. Gail explicitly designated five postal routes, including Augsburg to Antwerp and several outward from Vienna. Jörg Gail, *Ein neüwes nützliches Raißbuechlin der fürnemesten Land unnd StettWerk* (Augsburg, Germany: Valentin Otmar, 1563); Hermann Wolpert, *Schrifttum über das Deutsche Postwesen* (Munich: Ges. zur Erforschung der Postgeschichte in Bayern, 1937); Herbert Krüger, "Jörg Gails Augsburger's Raißbüchlin aus dem Jahre 1563," *Archiv für Deutsche Postgeschichte* 1, no. 11 (1969): 10–17.

28. Only one of the routes by Mayr was specified as a postal route (*postweg*): an alternative journey from Dresden to Prague, and then by post to Vienna and beyond. Georg Mayr, *Wegbüchlin: Die furnemesten Weg unnd gebreuchlichsten Strassen durch ganz Teutschland, Hungern, Bohhem, Polen, Luttaro, Schroeden, Dennmarck* (Augsburg, Germany: Georg Mayr, 1576); Daniel Witzenberger, *Ein Naw Reyse Büchlein* (Dresden: Gimel Bergen, 1578); "Von Dresden ein ander Weg nach Prag/und den Postweg gegen Wien/und ferner den Postweg von Wien gegen Rascha in Zips/und Zagmar," in Mayr, *Wegbüchlin*.

29. Richard Verstegan, *The Post of the World* (London: Richard Rowlands, 1576); James Wadsworth, *The European Mercury: Describing the Highwayes and Stages from Place to Place*... (London: John Raworth for Henry Twyford, 1641).

30. See, generally, Midura, "Itinerating Europe."

31. Histories of travel, like histories of correspondence, have naturally tended to focus on the cosmopolitan members of the Republic of Letters, who left behind personal archives and publications. Margaret Jacobs, *Strangers Nowhere in the World: The Rise of Cosmopolitanism in Early Modern Europe* (Philadelphia: University of Pennsylvania Press, 2006); Jeremy Black, *Italy and the Grand Tour* (New Haven, CT: Yale University Press, 2003); Jeremy Black, *The British and the Grand Tour* (London: Croom Helm, 1985).

32. The English inscription includes a longer love poem. Franciscus Schottus, *Itinerario: Overo nova descrittione de' viaggi principali d'Italia* (Vicenza, Italy: Francesco Bolzetta, 1615), Biblioteca Nacional de España (BNE), Perg. 3/77287, viewed online at http://bdh.bne.es/bnesearch/detalle/bdh0000247015.

33. This likely was Juan Gaspar Zorrilla de San Martín (1672–1735), who became a member of the Council of Castile in 1733. Francisco Andújar Castillo, "Juan Gaspar Zorrilla de San Martín," in *Diccionario Biográfico Electrónico* (Online) (*DBE*), http://dbe.rah.es/biografias/35532/juan-gaspar-zorrilla-de-san-martin.

34. "Chi va lontan da la sua patria, vede / Cose, da quel che già credea, lontane . . . ," Charles Estienne, *La guide des chemins de France* (Paris: Charles Estienne, 1553); Bayerische Staatsbibliothek (BSB) Gall.g.279, viewed online at https://mdz-nbn-resolving.de/urn:nbn:de:bvb:12-bsb10177440-5; "Memor esto iudici mei: sic enim erit & tuum: mihi heri, & tibi hodie," in Alonso de Meneses, *Memorial ō abecedario de los mas principales caminos de España* (Toledo, Spain: Juan de Ayala, 1568); Herzog August Bibliothek Wolfenbuttel Gi 247, viewed online at http://n2t.net/ark:/87925/drs1.iberian.14697.

35. Astrid Kelser, Jennifer K. Nelson, and Renae Satterley, "A Transcription and Translation of Sloane MS. 2131, Robert Ashley's (1561–1641) Vita: With Additional Biographical Details," *Electronic British Library Journal* (2021), Article 10, https://doi.org/10.23636/j7af-2714. Thanks to Renae Satterley.

36. Ottavio Codogno, *Nuovo itinerario delle poste per tutto il mondo* (Milan: Girolamo Bordoni, 1608), 38; Rachel Midura, "Publishing the Baroque Post: The Postal Itinerary and the Mailbag Novel," in *The Renaissance of Letters: Knowledge and Community in Italy, 1300–1650*, ed. Paula Findlen and Suzanne Sutherland (New York: Routledge, 2020): 256–271.

37. At least the inns along this route were "of the best description, owing to its being the high post-road." Montaigne, *Diary*, 363.

38. See, for example, the *Oxford English Dictionary*: "1. A guide or forerunner for the post, or for a messenger, etc." and "postilion, n.," OED Online. December 2022 (accessed February 8, 2023), https://doi.org/10.1093/OED/1068049333. Codogno, *Nuovo itinerario*, 32.

39. Clemente Fedele describes that the terms *postiglione* and *vetturino della posta* were synonymous. Clemente Fedele, *Un lago per comunicare: Il Garda e l'Italia nella storia della cultura postale di età moderna* (Salò: Ateneo di Salò, 2024).

40. Torriano, *Della lingua Toscana-Romana*, 31.

41. Torriano, *Della lingua Toscana-Romana*, 59.

42. Wolfgang Behringer, *Im Zeichen des Merkur: Reichspost und Kommunikationsrevolution in der Frühen Neuzeit* (Göttingen, Germany: Vandenhoeck & Ruprecht, 2003), 438.

43. By March 1597, routes were expanded to all French territory, except Brittany. E. John B. Allen, "The Royal Posts of France in the Fifteenth and Sixteenth Century," *Postal History Journal* 15 (1971): 13–17.

44. John Taylor, *The Carriers Cosmographie* (London: A. G., 1637).

45. The author compared a skilled conversationalist matching his topic to his audience to how a postal coach could be hitched to any horse. Stefano

Guazzo, *La civil conversation del signor Stefano Guazzo* (Venice: Altobello Salicato, 1580). *Sedie della posta* were used by the Venetian-Rome ordinary by 1591 and the journey cost around 8 julians per post, or approximately 276 julians, not counting additional fees such as those paid for crossing water. Adriano Cattani and Bonaventura Foppolo, "La Compagnia dei Corrieri Veneti un'impresa bergamasca a Venezia dal 1400 al 1800," in *Le poste dei Tasso: Da Cornello all'Europa* (Bergamo, Italy: Corponove, 2021), 21-41.

46. Letters from Geronimo Cipelleto. See a letter (July 24, 1601) and Marrio Corradi (August 4, 1601) in Archivio di Stato di Milano (ASMi), *Carteggio delle cancellerie dello Stato (Carteggio)*, 359. Clemente Fedele and Marco Gallenga, *"Per servizio di nostro signore": Strade, corrieri, e poste dei papi dal medioevo al 1870* (Modena, Italy: Mucchi, 1988), 174.

47. A Turin postal regulation stipulated that carriers not overcharge guests of "larger stature." "Per il passaggio delle sedie, e carrozze dalla Novalesa a Lanneburgo, e da Lanneburgo alla Novalesa" (c. 1723), in ASTo, *Sezione riunite, Finanze, Poste*, 2.

48. Edict (June 3, 1599), in ASVe, *Corrieri*, 88.

49. See ASMi, *Notarile*, 22349, in Gerosa, *La famiglia Tasso*, 104.

50. Letter from Ottavio Codogno (July 8, 1611), in ASMi, *Finanze*, 933.

51. Giovanni Battista Balbi, "Pianta o regolamento del officio delle poste," (1726), in ASMi, *Finanze*, 933.

52. Behringer, *Im Zeichen*, 438.

53. ASVe, *Corrieri*, 48. See also Luigi Dedé, "Il servizio postale fra Brescia e Venezia durante il dominio veneto," in *Commentari dell'Ateneo di Brescia per l'anno 1986* (Brescia, Italy: Tipolito Fratelli Geroldi, 1987), 157-198. Maffeo Tasso acted as a Venetian courier for much of his life. He acquired a substantial personal fortune and purchased several individual licenses for running *vetturini* services, seemingly with a goal of consolidation. Fernando Rea, *Le poste a Bergamo* (Bergamo, Italy: Società Editrice Bergamasca, 1976).

54. Behringer, *Im Zeichen*, 450. There were also several proposals for unified travel and postal systems in Savoy. See, for example, "Propositione per il stabilimento di una cambiatura" (1698), in ASTo, *Finanze, Poste*, 1.

55. Giuseppe Miselli, *Il Burattino veridico* (Rome: Michel'Ercole, 1682); Giovanni Maria Vidari, *Il viaggio in pratica* (Naples: Francesco Ricciardo, 1718).

56. Vidari, *Il viaggio*, 295.

57. Tobias Smollet, *Travels through France and Italy* (London: R. Baldwin, 1766), 76. Letter of October 1765 in Samuel Sharp, *Letters from Italy* (London: R. Cave, 1766), 43.

58. Vidari, *Il viaggio*, 12.

59. "An Admonition to Gentlemen Who Pass the Alps, and Make the Tour of Italy," in Sharp, *Letters*, 311.

60. Letter of January 1766, in Sharp, *Letters*, 126-128.

61. "The Knight Out Rid; or, The Postilion in His Master's Saddle, a New Ballad" (London: R. Amey, c. 1730). Earlier examples include Charles Bonaventure de Longueval, "Postillion" (Antwerp, 1621), and "Jüdischer Postillion von Franckfurt nach Prag und Westphalen" (Frankfurt, c. 1675).

62. "The History of Tom White, the Postillion" (c. 1795), 2, 14.

63. Montaigne, *Diary*, 363.

64. Montaigne, *Diary*, 363.

65. Miselli, *Burattino*, 180.

66. Francesca Trivellato, *The Promise and Peril of Credit: What a Forgotten Legend about Jews and Finance Tells Us about the Making of European Commercial Society* (Princeton, NJ: Princeton University Press, 2019).

67. *Il viaggiatore moderno* (Basano, Italy: Giuseppe Remondini, 1794), 11. British travelers struggled to distinguish the differences. Samuel Sharp, writing in the 1760s, described the *cambiatura* as roughly equivalent to the Venetian *bolletone*: "Both the Cambiatura and the Bolletino, are orders to the post-masters to furnish horses at the low price; but I was never called upon to shew them at any of the post-houses." Sharp, *Letters*, 310.

68. Heylyn, *A Full Relation*, 27-28.

69. Moryson, *An Itinerary*, 164, 97.

70. "Privilegi del Conte di Casalborgone, Baldessare Masserati" (September 2, 1633), in ASTo, *Sezione riunite, Poste*, 1.

71. The saying originated from Cicero's "Fifth Philippic" (44 CE). On political economic thought, see, generally, Reinert, *The Academy of Fisticuffs*; Istvan Hont, *Jealousy of Trade: International Competition and the Nation-State in Historical Perspective* (Cambridge, MA: Belknap, 2005); John Brewer, *The Sinews of Power: War, Money, and the English State, 1688–1883* (Cambridge, MA: Harvard University Press, 1990).

72. Miselli, *Burattino*, 135. See also Vidari, *Il viaggio*, 16. Miselli and Vidari utilized Codogno's book, as follows: "in doing so I observed that Codogno had put things differently in his itinerary than how they are done today." Vidari, *Il viaggio*, 21.

73. Behringer, *Im Zeichen*, 86-88.

74. Appendix of Adriano Cattani, *Le comunicazioni postali nella Repubblica di Venezia* (Padua, Italy: Editrice Elzeviro, 2018).

75. A 1708 ordinance required that "every postmaster write the cost of a letter in Arabic numerals on the blank side without abbreviation," ensuring that postal officials not employ a code unknown to the layman. Paolo Vollmeier, *Repubblica di Venezia: Catalogo documentato (con storia postale)* (Castagnola, Switzerland: Alfaprint, 2003), 17.

76. Letter from Pieter Burman to Jacques-Philippe d'Orville (January 26, 1728), the Bodleian Card Catalogue on Early Modern Letters Online, ed. Howard Hotson and Miranda Lewis, emlo.bodleian.ox.ac.uk/w/8644.

77. Decree (April 1, 1661) in ASVe, *Corrieri*, IX, 26.

78. Copy of Senate Decree (March 5, 1701). The decision supported the reenforcement of the 1661 tariffs. The archival note summarizes several related decisions made over the next few years, particularly related to its enforcement on the foreign posts of Venice. ASVe, *Corrieri*, 1, IX, and 26. Milan adopted a similar fee in 1675. ASMi, *Atti di Governo (AG), Finanze*, 933.

79. Nikolaus Schobesberger, et al., "European Postal Networks," in *News Networks*, ed. Joad Raymond and Noah Moxham (Leiden, Netherlands: Brill, 2016), 36.

80. English rulers expected the post to yield "an annual cash windfall," which conveniently did not require relying on Parliament. Duncan Campbell-Smith, *Masters of the Post: The Authorized History of the Royal Mail* (London: Allen Lane, 2011), 39. Similarly in the Swedish system, "by 1643 ordinance: the postage paid for private letters was meant to finance the rest of the postal organization." Magnus Linnarsson, "The Development of the Swedish Post, c. 1600–1721," in *Connecting the Baltic Area: The Swedish Postal System in the Seventeenth Century*, ed. Heiko Droste (Stockholm: Södertörns högskola, 2011), 39.

81. Johann Baptiste Krane to Ferdinand III (June 5, 1643), in *Acta Pacis Westphalicae II A 1: Die kaiserlichen Korrespondenzen, Band 1: 1643–1644*, ed. Elfriede Merla (Münster Westfalen: Aschendorffsche Verlagsbuchhandlung, 1964), 28. Ferdinand III (Vienna) to Krane (June 17, 1643), in *Acta Pacis Westphalicae III D 1: Stadtmünsterische Akten und Vermischtes*, ed. Helmut Lahrkamp, 41–42. All documents from Acta Pacis Westphalicae, taken from APW Digital Edition at https://apw.digitale-sammlungen.de/apweinf/static.html?lang=en. Ludwig Kalmus, *Weltgeschichte der Post mit Besonderer Berücksichtigung des Deutschen Sprachgebietes* (Vienna: A. F. Göth, 1937), 251. See also Fürst Thurn und Taxis Hofbibliothek und Zentralarchiv (FTTZA), *Postakten (PA)*, 653.

82. Ferdinand III (Linz) to Graf Johann Ludwig von Nassau-Hadamar and Isaak Volmar (September 30, 1645), in *Acta Pacis Westphalicae II A 2: Die kaiserlichen Korrespondenzen, Band 2: 1644–1645*, ed. Wilhelm Engels, 497–501.

83. Hansestädte to Stadt Münster (March 19, 1646), in *Acta Pacis Westphalicae III D 1: Stadtmünsterische Akten und Vermischtes*, ed. Helmut Lahrkamp, 136–137.

84. Letter of Thomas Smith to Dr. Edward Chamberlayne (May 25, 1684), in the Bodleian Card Catalogue, *EMLO*.

85. Letter of Edmund Elys to Thomas Smith (April 26, 1702), in the Bodleian Card Catalogue, *EMLO*.

86. Letter of Barnabas Oley to Francis Turner (November 24, 1685), in the Bodleian Card Catalogue, *EMLO*.

87. For example, Tassis family correspondence shows that serving the peace congresses of Westphalia was costly because of the rerouting, but also because little to no postage was collected from the state representatives. Wilhelm Fleitman, "Postverbindungen für den Westfälischen Friedenskongress 1643 bis 1648," *Archiv für Deutsche Postgeschichte* 1 (1972): 10.

88. See the letter from the Reverend James Harries to the Reverend Arthur Charlet (February 10, 1718), in the Bodleian Card Catalogue, *EMLO*. As early as 1553, the devout Spanish postmaster Maffeo Tassis (d. c. 1536) had requested that Postmaster Giovan Antonio Tassis (d. 1580) in Rome carry Jesuit letters as freely franked in recognition of the value of their mission.

89. This means that the post office could not hope to profit from extending a service that had to be offered gratis. Letter from William Bishop to the Reverend Arthur Charlett (July 14, 1713), in the Bodleian Card Catalogue, *EMLO*.

90. "In fact, one of the first and principal functions of the state consists precisely in providing a structure and apparatus capable of building and maintaining the consensus and participation of citizen-subjects." Pierangelo Schiera, "Legitimacy, Discipline, and Institutions: Three Necessary Conditions

for the Birth of the Modern State," in *The Origins of the State in Italy, 1300–1600*, ed. Julius Kirshner (Chicago: Chicago University Press, 1996), 14. In fact, the postal reformer Jacob Henot (d. 1625) considered the question of free franking of newspapers in a report on imperial postal standardization as early as 1588. Behringer, *Im Zeichen*, 315. On the postal system and nation-building, see Cameron Blevins, *Paper Trails: The U.S. Post and the Making of the American West* (Oxford: Oxford University Press, 2021); David Henkin, *The Postal Age: The Emergence of Modern Communications in Nineteenth-Century America* (Chicago: University of Chicago Press, 2006); Richard R. John, *Spreading the News: The American Postal System from Franklin to Morse* (Cambridge, MA: Harvard University Press, 1998).

91. Hill's complaint arose from the postal route that he had run between London and York, which was declared unlawful in 1653. John Hill, *A Penny Post: or, a Vindication of the Liberty and Birthright of Every English-Man* (London: n.p., 1659).

92. ". . . delivery of letters and parcels not exceeding 1 lb in weight, or any sum of money, or parcels of not more than £10 in value. In the suburbs there were four deliveries daily at a charge of 2d. for delivery within a given 10 mile radius," in Joan Day, "Dockwra [Dockwray], William (bap. 1635, d. 1716)," in *Oxford Dictionary of National Biography*, September 23, 2004; accessed October 7, 2022. Campbell-Smith, *Masters of the Post*, 59–61.

93. Hill, *A Penny Post*.

94. See, for example, a contemporaneous case in the Swedish system from 1658 to 1661: Linnarsson, "The Development of the Swedish Post," 41.

95. In Venice, a 1620 plan submitted by a "secret person," as well as a 1621 letter from secretary Ottavio Medici—who was also one of Venice's top cryptographers—laid out comprehensive plans for reform. ASVe, *Corrieri*, 20. On Ottavio Medici and cryptography in Venice, see Ioanna Iordanou, *Venice's Secret Service: Organising Intelligence in the Renaissance* (Oxford: Oxford University Press, 2019), 152–155. Mandricardo Benzoni, named "Deputy of the Government of Posts Throughout the Terraferma States," shaped discussion and also wrote an itinerary that seemed intended for publication, modeled after that of Ottavio Codogno. "Itinerario di Viaggi, 1629," in ASVe, *Corrieri*, 32. Benzoni belonged to a family that had been active in the Venetian Company of Couriers for at least a century, dating to the appearance of a "Hieronimus Benzoni" in 1519. ASVe, *Corrieri*, 21.

96. In Venice, for example, the 1775 reform efforts still largely replicated principles first put forward in 1624 and preserved in the archives of the Venetian Company. "Relazioni istoriche delle dispute e vertenze seguite sulla proposizione postale" (1775), Corr. MS Cicogna 3588 (originally 1426). Pietro Rigobon, *Di Nicolò e Francesco Donà: Veneziane del settecento e dei loro studi storici e politici* (Venice: Istituto Veneto di Arti Grafiche, 1910), 19. Other examples produced in the late eighteenth century include Corr. MS Cicogna 2512 and 2532.

97. See, for example, the Bolognese "Portalettere," in Annibale Carracci, *Diverse figure* (1646) and the German "Der Neueu Allamodische Postbot" (1650), in Rheinisches Bildarchiv RBA 156321.

98. Appointment of Pietro Luigi Capece, Marquis of Roffrano (December 27, 1708), in ASMi, *Finanze*, 933.

99. Giovanni Battista Balbi, "Pianta o regolamento del officio delle poste" (1726), in ASMi, *Finanze*, 933. Gerosa notes the earlier presence of letter distributors under Ruggero Tassis in *La famiglia Tasso*, 37–39.

100. Balbi, "Pianta o regolamento."

101. Balbi, "Pianta o regolamento."

7. High Towers and Black Chambers

1. Geoffrey Parker, *The Thirty Years' War* (New York: Military Heritage, 1988), 121.

2. "The Official Explanation: The Swedish Manifesto, 1630," in *The Thirty Years War: A Sourcebook*, ed. Peter Wilson (London: Palgrave Macmillan, 2010), 123; Rachel Midura, "'They Hide from Me, Like the Devil from the Cross': Transalpine Postal Routes as Intelligence Work, 1555–1645," *History: The Journal of the Historical Association* 108, no. 381 (2023): 304–305.

3. "The Swedish Manifesto," 122; Midura, "'They Hide from Me,'" 304–305.

4. Wilhelm Jocher, *Secreta principis anhaltini cancellaria* (1621); Ludwig Camerarius, *Der Röm: Spanischen Cantzley Nachtrab* (1624); Ludwig Camerarius, *Mysterium iniquitatis, eiusque ver apocalypsis, sive secreta secretorum turco-papistica secreta* (1622). For an overview of the genre, see Noel Malcolm, *Reason of State, Propaganda, and the Thirty Years' War* (Oxford: Oxford University Press, 2007).

5. See Amy Zegart, *Spies, Lies, and Algorithms: The History and Future of American Intelligence* (Princeton, NJ: Princeton University Press, 2022).

6. Jeremy Bentham, "Of Publicity," in *The Works of Jeremy Bentham*, ed. John Bowring (London: W. Tait, Simpkin, and Marshall, 1843). See also Jeremy Bentham, Catherine Pease-Watkin, and Philip Schofield, eds., *The Collected Works of Jeremy Bentham: On the Liberty of the Press, and Public Discussion, and Other Legal and Political Writings for Spain and Portugal* (Oxford: Oxford University Press, 2012). I look especially to David Vincent, *The Culture of Secrecy: Britain 1832–1998* (Oxford: Oxford University Press, 1998).

7. Heiko Droste, "Sending a Letter between Amsterdam and Stockholm: A Matter of Trust and Precautions," in *Your Humble Servant: Agents in Early Modern Europe*, ed. Hans Cool, Marika Keblusek, and Badeloch Noldus (Hilversum, Netherlands: Verloren, 2006), 135–148.

8. Wolfgang Behringer, *Thurn und Taxis: Die Geschichte ihrer Post und ihrer Unternehmen* (Munich: Piper, 1990), 95–101.

9. I look to the characterization of late seventeenth-century absolutist modernization offered by Alan Houston and Steven Pincus, eds., *A Nation Transformed: England after the Restoration* (Cambridge: Cambridge University Press, 2001).

10. Duncan Campbell-Smith, *Masters of the Post: The Authorized History of the Royal Mail* (London: Allen Lane, 2011), xxvii.

11. Andreas Osiander, "Sovereignty, International Relations, and the Westphalian Myth," *International Organization* 55, no. 2 (Spring 2001): 251–287.

The sociologist Immanuel Wallerstein describes the "long" sixteenth century as the first of three turning points in the construction of the modern world system. Westphalia largely formalized preexisting Italian developments. Immanuel Maurice Wallerstein, *The Essential Wallerstein* (New York: New Press, 2000).

12. See, generally, Derek Croxton, *The Last Christian Peace: The Congress of Westphalia as a Baroque Event* (New York: Palgrave Macmillan, 2013).

13. Spanish couriers had crossed France between Madrid and royal possessions in Italy and Flanders, but the journey was frequently disrupted. Codogno's guide presented two possible options, one by sea and one by land, called "the shortest, when the French permit passage." Ottavio Codogno, *Nuovo itinerario delle poste per tutto il mondo* (Milan: Girolamo Bordoni, 1608), 151–152.

14. Treaty between Octavio Cassiano (Spanish Post), Alexander Roelans (Imperial Post), and Jerome de Nouveau (French Post) (December 15, 1660), in Martin Volker Albus Dallmeier, ed., *Quellen zur Geschichte des Europaischen Postwesens, 1501–1806*, vol. 2, no. 325 (Kallmünz, Germany: Lassleben, 1977), 142. While the treaty bridged a noteworthy political divide, it largely affirmed prewar terms. See Joseph Rübsam, "Ein internationale Postvertrag aus dem Jahre 1660," *Union Postale* 20 (1895): 146–156.

15. Witherings shared this title with William Frizzell and occasionally contested overlapping responsibilities with the postmaster generals, the Barons Stanhope. One historian attributes the "the birth of the postal service" to Witherings's 1635 plan for settling service among London, Edinburgh, Holyhead, and Plymouth. C. R. Clear, *Thomas Witherings and the Birth of the Postal Service* (London: Eyre and Spottiswoode, 1935). Kevin Sharpe, "Thomas Witherings and the Reform of the Foreign Posts, 1632-40," *Historical Research* 57, no. 136 (November 1984): 155. See, generally, J. Wilson Hyde, *The Post in Grant and Farm* (London: Adam & Charles Black, 1894).

16. "Lettres arrives d'Italie" (November 1, 1661), in Fürst Thurn und Taxis Hofbibliothek und Zentralarchiv (FTTZA), *Postakten (PA)*, 4843. Correspondents included the secretary, Sir Edward Nicholas, merchants Thomas Hill and Eliab Harvey, and a member of parliament, Sir Nathanial Barnardiston, among others. The surviving letter book for Thomas Hill provides further confirmation of his and Harvey's correspondence by post with the Lucchese Giuseppe Baldinotti, among others. June Palmer, *The Letter Book of Thomas Hill, 1660-1661: Westcountry Mercantile Affairs and the Wider World* (Exeter: Devon and Cornwall Record Society, 2008), 79.

17. FTTZA, *PA*, 4843. The copy (there dated tentatively to 1637) can also be found on British State Papers Online. See "Printed Bill," in *Calendar of State Papers, Domestic Series*, vol. 12: December 1637–August 1638, 51, SPO ID MC4324900337.

18. "Printed Bill."

19. See, generally, Rachel Weil, *A Plague of Informers: Conspiracy and Political Trust in William III's England* (New Haven, CT: Yale University Press, 2014); Alan Marshall, *Intelligence and Espionage in the Reign of Charles II, 1660–1685* (Cambridge: Cambridge University Press, 2003).

20. On the art commissioned for the book as well as its family legends, see, generally, Cristelle Baskins, *Hafsids and Habsburgs in the Early Modern Mediterranean: Facing Tunis* (Cham, Switzerland: Palgrave Macmillan, 2022).

21. Jules Chifflet, *Les marques d'honneur de la Maison de Tassis* (Antwerp: Balthasar Moretus, 1645), 18; Engelbert Flacchio, *Genealogie de la très-illustre, très-ancienne et autrefois souveraine maison de la Tour, où quantité d'autres familles trouveront leur extraction & parentage* (Brussels: Antoine Claudinot, 1709); Francesco Zazzera, *Della nobilità dell'Italia* (Naples: Ottavio Boltrano, 1628). See also Alonso López de Haro, *Nobiliario geneaologico de los reyes y titulose de España* (Madrid: La Viuda de Fernando Correa de Montenegro, 1622), which incorporated many elements from Zazzera. On the strategic use of fantastical genealogies by Italian nobility, see Roberto Bizzocchi, *Genealogie incredibili: scritti di storia nell'Europa moderna* (Bologna: Il Mulino, 2009).

22. Behringer, *Thurn und Taxis*, 205. Ferdinando Tassis also remained invested in family genealogy, corresponding with Postmaster Jacob Roelans in Antwerp, who was gathering information for Chifflet. Letter from Ferdinand Tassis to Lamoral Tassis (May 6, 1644), in FTTZA, *HFS*, 118. Franz Werner Taxis of the Innsbruck line earned similar approval in 1662. Gabriele Medolago, "Cenni sulle origini della famiglia Tasso," in *Le poste dei Tasso: Da Cornello all'Europa*, ed. Tarcisio Bottani (Bergamo, Italy: Corponove, 2021), 12-13.

23. Flacchio, *Genealogie*, 10.

24. While Rye und Taxis worked primarily in French, in January 1645, she instructed a lieutenant to translate an agreement into Italian before it was sent to the imperial court, as the language was "not to the taste of the court." Rye und Taxis to Hoeswinkel (January 1, 1645) in FTTZA, *PA*, 2152. See Wilhelm Fleitman, "Postverbindungen für den Westfälischen Friedenskongress 1643 bis 1648," *Archiv für Deutsche Postgeschichte* 1 (1972): 3-48.

25. Zazzera, *Della nobilità* (unpaginated).

26. See especially chapters 11-15 on Jean Baptiste (Giovanni Baptista) Tassis in Chifflet, *Les Marques d'honneur*, 100-120. Joseph Rübsam, *Johann Baptista von Taxis, ein Staatsmann und Militär unter Philipp II und Philipp III Nebst einem Exkurs Aus der Urzeit der Taxis'schen Posten, 1505-1520* (Freiburg, Germany: Herder, 1889).

27. Giovanni Maria Vidari, *Il viaggio in prattica* (Naples: Francesco Ricciardo, 1718), 17.

28. Giuseppe Miselli, *Il Burratino veridico* (Rome: Michel'Ercole, 1682), 137. Vidari updated the language to praise the Austrian-appointed Italian postmaster general, the Marquis di Rofrano (d. 1724), in place of the Tassis, likely due to the new Bourbon rule of Spain brought by the War of Spanish Succession (1701-1714). "All'Illustrissimo Signorere d. Prospero de Rosa . . ." in Vidari, *Il viaggio in pratica*. For more on both itineraries and their authors, see Armando Serra, "'Monopolio naturale': Di autori postali nella produzione di guide italiane d'Europa, fonti storico-postali tra cinque e ottocento," *Archivio per la storia postale: Comunicazioni e società*, no. 14-15 (Prato, Italy: Istituto di studi storici postali, 2003): 40-51.

29. Codogno, *Nuovo itinerario*.

30. Sharpe, "Thomas Witherings." Linnarsson describes a similar tactic in the Swedish context: "Queen Christina gave the Post Office in fief to baron Wilhelm Taube, most likely as a reward for his services to the Crown. The official motive for this move, which expressly contravened von Beijer's instructions, was to lend the Post Office respect and authority." Magnus Linnarsson,

"The Development of the Swedish Post Office, c. 1600–1721," in *Connecting the Baltic Area: The Swedish Postal System in the Seventeenth Century*, ed. Heiko Droste (Stockholm: Södertörns högskola, 2011), 40.

31. Sharpe, "Thomas Witherings." See also Mark Brayshay, "Conveying Correspondence: Early Modern Letter Bearers, Carriers, and Posts," in *Cultures of Correspondence in Early Modern Britain*, ed. James Daybell and Andrew Gordon (Philadelphia: University of Pennsylvania Press, 2016): 48–66.

32. Anna Maria Lastrucci, ed., *La raccolta tassiana della Biblioteca civica 'A. Mai' di Bergamo* (Bergamo, Italy: Banca Piccolo Credito, 1960).

33. Biblioteca Civico Angelo Mai (Bergamo) (BAM), *Raccolta Tassiana (Tass)*, D.7.11. On the competitors in Bergamo, see Giampiero Tiraboschi, "Lucca et Nicolo Comenduni: I corrier della magnifica Comunità di Bergamo nel Cinquecento," in *Ataneo Scienze, Lettere ed Arti di Bergamo* (2020), https://ateneobergamo.it/lucca-et-nicolo-comenduni-2/. Thanks to Christopher Carlsmith.

34. The first known postal map is Nicolas Sanson, *Carte Geographicque des Postes qui traversent la France* (Paris: Tavernier, 1632).

35. See, generally, Rachel Midura, "Itinerating Europe: Early Modern Spatial Networks in Printed Itineraries, 1545–1700," *Journal of Social History* 54, no. 4 (2021): 1545–1700.

36. British Library, 20580.(1.). The State Archives have preserved another example of a map of Milan printed on taffeta in 1734. Archivio di Stato di Torino (ASTo), *Sezione Corte, Materie politiche (MP), Scritture relative alle corti stranieri, Milano*, 1.

37. There is an ample body of literature on the creation of modern cartography as state propaganda, see particularly J. B. Harley, *The New Nature of Maps: Essays in the History of Cartography*, ed. Paul Laxton (Baltimore: Johns Hopkins University Press, 2001); chapter 3 in Cameron Blevins, *Paper Trails: The U.S. Post and the Making of the American West* (Oxford: Oxford University Press, 2021), 53–74.

38. "Editto cesareo toccante il nuovo regolamento delle poste," Archivio di Stato di Milano (ASMi), *Atti di Governo (AG), Finanze*, 933. See also Bruno Caizzi, *Dalla posta dei re alla posta di tutti: Territorio e comunicazioni in Italia dal XVI secolo all'Unità* (Milan: Franco Angeli, 1993), 85. On the Paar, see Nevio Basezzi, "I Paar, de Parre ai confini dell'Europa. La storia postale europea tra Tasso e Paar," *Quaderni Brembani* 11 (2013): 94–101.

39. The Bors family was associated with the imperial post of Roermond for several generations. Jakob von Bors contributed to the production of an elaborate postal map in the mid-eighteenth century as imperial postal commissioner: Franz J. Heger, *Neue und vollständige Postkarte durch ganz Deutschland und durch die angränzende Theile der benachbarten Länder / zusammen getragen und ausgefertiget von Franz Joseph Heger = Nouvelle carte geographique des postes d'Allemagne et des provinces limitrophes* (Nuremberg, Germany: Homaennischen Erben, 1764).

40. Letter from Ferdinando Tassis (May 1643), in FTTZA, *PA*, 5090. Midura, "'They Hide from Me,'" 323.

41. Letter from Ferdinando Tassis (May 1643), in FTTZA, *PA*, 5090. Midura, "'They Hide from Me,'" 323.

42. This can be contrasted to the earlier use of a letter seal or signature to serve as authentication of the sender, placed without regard for ensuring

the letter's closure. Marian Rothstein, "What Lies between the Public and the Secret?," in *Early Modern Privacy*, ed. Michael Green, Lars Cyril Nørgaard, and Mette Birkedal Bruun (Leiden, Netherlands: Brill, 2022), 434.

43. Rebekah Ahrendt and David van der Linden, "The Postmasters' Piggy Bank: Experiencing the Accidental Archive," *French Historical Studies* 40, no. 2 (April 2017): 189-213. The frequent loss of material context during archival preservation complicates the history of material practices of letter-writing. For this reason, most such publications have been by literary scholars, as the letter and practices of sealing became an increasingly popular metaphor. Projects such as *Signed, Sealed, Undelivered* (Brienne.org) at the Brienne Museum are adding significantly to our understanding of seals and letterlocking. J. Dambrogio, A. Ghassaei, D. S. Smith, et al., "Unlocking History through Automated Virtual Unfolding of Sealed Documents Imaged by X-ray Microtomography," *Nature Communications* 12, no. 1184 (2021), https://doi.org/10.1038/s41467-021-21326-w.

44. Nadine Akkerman, "The Postmistress, the Diplomat, and a Black Chamber? Alexandrine of Taxis, Sir Balthazar Gerbier and the Power of Postal Control," in *Diplomacy and Early Modern Culture*, ed. Robyn Adams and Rosanna Cox (New York: Palgrave Macmillan, 2011), 172-188. On later concern for Taxis interference, see Matthias Polig, "'Le maître de cette poste est notre plus grand ennemi': Postal Service and Espionage during the War of Spanish Succession," in *Spies, Espionage, and Secret Diplomacy in the Early Modern Period*, ed. Guido Braun and Susanne Lachenicht (Stuttgart: Kohlhammer, 2021), 105-123; Midura, "'They Hide from Me,'" 325.

45. Akkerman, "The Postmistress," 176.

46. Akkerman, "The Postmistress."

47. Akkerman, "The Postmistress."

48. Midura, "'They Hide from Me,'" 325.

49. Johann von den Birghden, *Allerunterthanigst Verwantwort/und Ablehnung auff der Fraw Gravin von Taxis* (n.p.: n.p., 1640).

50. Midura, "'They Hide from Me,'" 312.

51. On French espionage, see, generally, Lucian Bély, *Espions et ambassadeurs au temps de Louis XIV* (Paris: Fayard, 1990), and Eugène Vaillé, *Histoire generale des postes françaises* (Paris: Presses universitaires de France, 1949-1955). Vaillé observed that the French cabinet acquired new fixity under the superintendent of the posts, Jerôme Nouveau, and the French minister Cardinal Mazarin. The same is true for the Austrian variant, the *Geheimen Ziffernkanzlei*, for which Franz Stix found "no document has survived about it," although officials recalled in 1822 that it had been in operation for several generations. Franz Stix, "Zur Geschichte und Organisation der Wiener Geheimen Ziffernkanzlei," *Institut für österreichische Geschichtsforschung, Mitteilungen* 51 (1937): 131-160.

52. The eighteenth century also brings a critical mass of documentation for identifying individual operations, although well-known cases of partnerships between secretaries of state and official cryptanalysts appear much earlier. See, generally, David Kahn, *The Codebreakers: The Story of Secret Writing* (New York: Scribner, 1996); Polig, "Postal Service and Espionage."

53. Letter from John Younger to Dr. Thomas Smith (December 29, 1674); Letter from Thomas Smith to Unknown (marked "G.H.E.") (May 9, 1691), in the Bodleian Card Catalogue on *EMLO*, emlo.bodleian.ox.ac.uk/w/54391 and emlo.bodleian.ox.ac.uk/w/44192.

54. Christopher Andrew, *The Secret World: A History of Intelligence* (New Haven, CT: Yale University Press, 2019), 243, 248. On Madame de Sévigné's own complicated relationship with privacy and publicity, see Hélène Merlin-Kajman, "'Privé' and 'Particulier' (and Other Words) in Seventeenth-Century France," in *Early Modern Privacy*, ed. Green, et al., 79–104.

55. See chapter 6 on franking privileges.

56. "Between 1712 and 1778, ninety warrants were issued for opening of letters—and one warrant could open the letters of multiple people." Lindsay O'Neill, *The Opened Letter: Networking in the Early Modern British World* (Philadelphia: University of Pennsylvania Press, 2015), 211.

57. Efrat Nechushtai, "Making Messages Private: The Formation of Postal Privacy and Its Relevance for Digital Surveillance," *Information & Culture: A Journal of History* 54, no. 2 (2019): 133–158.

58. This intelligence notably does not always necessitate opening the letter. Ruth and Sebastian Ahnert draw a similar connection regarding Tudor letter networks. They quote the former director of the US National Security Agency, General Michael Hayden: "We kill people based on metadata." Ruth Ahnert and Sebastian E. Ahnert, "Metadata, Surveillance and the Tudor State," *History Workshop Journal* 87, no. 1 (2019): 27–51.

59. *An Act for the Setting of the Postage of England, Scotland, and Ireland at the Parliament Begun at Westminster the 17th Day of September, Anno Domini 1656* (London: Henry Hills and John Field, 1656); Samuel Morland, *A New Method of Cryptography* ([London]: n.p., 1666); Samuel Morland, "Samuel Morland [to Shrewsbury], June 18, 1689 (with enclosure and note in Shrewsbury's hand)," in *Historical Manuscripts Commission, Report on the Manuscripts of the Duke of Buccleuch* (London: His Majesty's Stationery Office, 1903): 48–51.

60. *The Private Memoirs of Madame du Hausset; Lady's Maid to Madame de Pompadour* (London: E. Wilson, 1827), 6. On the culture of surveillance and censorship in the ancien régime, see the many works by the historian Robert Darnton.

61. Siegfried Grillmeyer, "Briefgeheimnis oder Staatsräson? Die Schwarzen Kabinette der Thurn und Taxis: Ein Betrag zur Adeslgeschichte," *Verhandlungen des Historischen Vereins für Oberpfalz und Regensburg* 147 (2007): 205–220.

62. Vito Salierno, "Il 'Gabinetto nero' della Milano del settecento: Censura, delazioni, spionaggio," *La Martinella di Milano* 28, no. 5-6 (1974): 174–178. Andrew, *The Secret World*, 255.

63. Letters from Emperor Leopold I demonstrate that individual postmasters were commissioned to monitor letters at post offices such as those at Hamburg and Nuremberg, especially the correspondence of the Swedish crown. Grillmeyer especially looks to the correspondence of the postmaster of Nuremberg, Giovanni Abondio (Baron Somigliano). Grillmeyer, "Briefgeheimnis oder Staatsräson?"

64. Michel Bakhtin, *Rabelais and His World* (Cambridge, MA: MIT Press, 1968). Popular "love letter" collections opened a titillating, if largely fictionalized,

window into the lives of women. Jeannine Basso, *Le genre epistolaire en langue Italienne (1538-1662)* (Nancy, France: Presses Universitaires de Nancy, 1990).

65. See, generally, Rachel Midura, "Publishing the Baroque Post: The Postal Itinerary and the Mailbag Novel," in *The Renaissance of Letters: Knowledge and Community in Italy, 1300–1650*, ed. Paula Findlen and Suzanne Sutherland (New York: Routledge, 2020), 256–271.

66. Anglo-American legal and sociological scholarship on a public right to know has centered on commercial environmental regulation, as well as foreign and domestic policy documentation. See especially the Freedom of Information Act, 5 U.S.C. § 552 (1996).

67. Pallavicino worked as a secretary for Giovanni Francesco Loredan (1607–1661), with whom he took part in Venetian libertine literary circles. Mario Infelise, "Pallavicino, Ferrante," in *Dizionario Biografico degli Italiani* (Online) *(DBI)*, vol. 80 (2014), http://www.treccani.it/enciclopedia/ferrante-pallavicino_%28Dizionario-Biografico%29/.

68. Infelise, "Pallavicino, Ferrante."

69. Nicholas Breton, *A Poste with a Mad Packet of Letters* (London: John Smethicke, 1602). A biographer even speculates that Breton spent time in Italy. Michael Brennan, "Breton [Britton], Nicholas," September 23, 2004, in *Oxford Dictionary of National Biography* (Online) *(ODNB)*, https://doi.org/10.1093/ref:odnb/3341.

70. Pallavicino has also been attributed the authorship of a second mailbag novel, *Mercurio postiglione* ([Amsterdam?]: n.p., 1667), although there is little evidence of this beyond stylistic similarity to his other work. See also Antonio Lupis, *Il postiglione* (Venice: Abondo Menafoglio, 1674); Carlo Celano, *Degli avanzi delle poste* (Venice: Giacomo Zinia, 1677); Charles Gildon, *The Post-Boy Robbed of His Bag* (London: John Dunton, 1692). Also see Albert N. Mancini, "Intorno alle traduzioni in inglese di opere di Ferrante Pallavicino: 'Il corriero svaligiato/The Post-boy rob'd of his mail,'" *Italica* 88, no. 3 (Autumn 2011): 465–482. *Mercurio* was also translated into French and German as *Le Mercure postillon, de l'un à l'autre monde* (Liège, Belgium: Claude Guibert, 1667), and Gabriel Zschirmer, *Der auff der Post angehaltene Mercurius* (Meissen, Germany: n.p., 1668). See, generally, Midura, "Publishing the Baroque Post."

71. Unless otherwise noted, excerpts have been taken from Ferrante Pallavicino, "Il corriero svaligiato," in *Il corriero svaligiato con la Lettera dalla prigionia, aggiuntavi La semplicità ingannata di suor Arcangela Tarabotti*, ed. Armando Marchi (Parma, Italy: Università di Parma, 1984). "A chi legge," in Pallavicino, *Il corriero svaligiato*.

72. See, generally, Jon R. Snyder, *Dissimulation and the Culture of Secrecy in Early Modern Europe* (Berkeley: University of California Press, 2012), and Fernando R. de la Flor, *Pasiones Frías: Secreto y disimulación en al Barroco hispano* (Madrid: Marcial Pons, 2005).

73. See, generally, James H. Johnson, *Venice Incognito: Masks in the Serene Republic* (Berkeley: University of California Press, 2011); Edward Muir, *The Culture Wars of the Late Renaissance: Skeptics, Libertines and Opera* (Cambridge, MA: Harvard University Press, 2007).

74. "A chi legge"; Midura, "Publishing the Baroque Post," 263.

75. "A chi legge."

76. "Gentle Reader," in *Poste*, Breton.

77. Midura, "Publishing the Baroque Post," 262-263.

78. See especially Trajano Boccalini, *Ragguagli di Parnasso e scritti minor*, ed. Luigi Firpo, 3 vols. (Bari, Italy: Laterza, 1948). Some examples of mailbag novels like *Mercurio* (1667) staged their wits in heaven, Olympus, or Parnassus. Momus, a god of rumor, satire, and mockery, upstaged the tighter-lipped deities, such as Harpocrates. Snyder, *Dissimulation*, 10-13.

79. "Lettera d'uno che invia due dozine d'occhiali al Vice Re di Napoli," in *Il corriero svaligiato*, Pallavicino, 21-23; "Lettera d'un balordo lasciato da un mercante alla cura de' suoi negozi," in *Il corriero svaligiato*, Pallavicino, 78-81; "Lettera di chi manda balle per lavar macchie ad un Cardinale," in *Il corriero svaligiato*, Pallavicino, 38-39; Midura, "Publishing the Baroque Post," 265.

80. The additions were occasionally distributed under the separate title of *Continuazione del corriero svaligiato* and seemed to respond to the popularity of these more quotidian elements. The unusual publication history of *Corriero*, rife with variations and false imprints, makes traditional citation difficult. Several editions were attributed to the pseudonymous Spironcini and were likely produced in Geneva; many carried a false location of Villafranca.

81. "A chi vuol leggere," in Lupis, *Il postiglione*.

82. "Lettera di spropositi a proposito," in *Il corriero svaligiato*, Pallavicino, 39-41.

83. "Lettera alla Repubblica di S. Marino," in *Il corriero svaligiato*, Pallavicino, 16-18. Also see Midura, "Publishing the Baroque Post," 266. On the intelligencing role of pharmacists, see Filippo de Vivo, "Pharmacies as Centres of Communication in Early Modern Venice," *Renaissance Studies* 21, no. 4 (September 2007): 505-521.

84. "The Bookseller's Advertisement to the Reader," in Gildon, *The Post-Boy*.

85. "Lettera contro d'un tale vecchi," in *Il corriero svaligiato*, Pallavicino, 70-72. Also see Midura, "Publishing the Baroque Post," 266.

86. Bonaventura Foppolo, "I maestri della posta imperial a Venezia" in *Le Poste dei Tasso: Da Cornello all'Europa* (Bergamo, Italy: Museo dei Tasso e della Storia Postale and Corponove, 2021), 194.

87. Infelise, "Pallavicino, Ferrante"; Midura, "Publishing the Baroque Post," 267.

88. Vincent, *The Culture of Secrecy*, 1-9.

89. "Mazzini and the Ethics of Politicians," in Vincent, *The Culture of Secrecy*, 225, 229.

90. "Mazzini and the Ethics of Politicians," in Vincent, *The Culture of Secrecy*, 225, 229.

91. James Purdon, "Secret Agents, Official Secrets: Joseph Conrad and the Security of the Mail," *Review of English Studies* 65, no. 269 (April 2014): 302-320.

92. Purdon, "Secret Agents."

93. Vincent, *The Culture of Secrecy*, 2.

94. Vincent, *The Culture of Secrecy*, 1.

95. Nechushtai, "Making Messages Private," 135.

96. See, generally, Nina Lamal, Jamie Cumby, and Helmer J. Helmers, eds., *Print and Power in Early Modern Europe (1500-1800)* (Leiden, Netherlands: Brill, 2020).

97. Spencer Walpole, the source of this quote, would later be secretary of the post office. S. Walpole, ed., *A History of England*, vol. 5 (London: Longmans, 1879-1886), 378-379. Purdon, "Secret Agents," 311.

98. Herbert O. Yardley, *America's Black Chamber* (New York: Bobbs-Merrill, 1931).

99. For more on Yardley and Stimson, see generally David Kahn, *The Reader of Gentlemen's Mail: Herbert O. Yardley and the Birth of American Codebreaking* (New Haven, CT: Yale University Press, 2004).

Conclusion

1. David Como, "God's Revolutions: England, Europe, and the Concept of Revolution in the Mid-Seventeenth Century," in *Scripting Revolutions: A Historical Approach to the Comparative Study of Revolutions*, ed. Keith Baker and Dan Edelstein (Stanford, CA: Stanford University Press, 2015), 41-56.

2. See Christopher Hill, *The World Turned Upside Down: Radical Ideas during the English Revolution* (London: Penguin, 1984).

3. Ryan Ellis raises a similar point regarding modern debates on infrastructure regulation in the United States, namely, "The threat of terrorism was a useful and powerful political resource." Ryan Ellis, *Letters, Power Lines, and Other Dangerous Things: The Politics of Infrastructure Security* (Cambridge, MA: MIT Press, 2020), 6.

4. See, generally, Catherine Fletcher, *Diplomacy in Renaissance Rome: The Rise of the Resident Ambassador* (Cambridge: Cambridge University Press, 2015).

5. Max Weber, *Economy and Society: A New Translation*, trans. Keith Tribe (Cambridge, MA: Harvard University Press, 2019).

6. David Vincent, *The Culture of Secrecy: Britain 1832-1998* (Oxford: Oxford University Press, 1998), 29.

7. Adam Segal, "Bridging the Cyberspace Gap: Washington and Silicon Valley," *Prism* 7, no. 2 (2017): 66-77.

8. Discussions often used the term "Web 2.0" to describe the prevalence of user-driven content. W. L. Hosch, "Web 2.0," in *Encyclopedia Britannica*, September 8, 2017, https://www.britannica.com/topic/Web-20.

9. Georg Simmel, "The Sociology of Secrecy and of Secret Societies," *American Journal of Sociology* 11, no. 4 (1906): 441-498.

10. "privacy, n." *OED Online*, Oxford University Press (June 2022), at https://www-oed-com/view/Entry/151596?redirectedFrom=privacy.

11. William Shakespeare, *Troilus and Cressida*, act 3, scene 3.

12. Benjamin Kaplan, *Divided by Faith: Religious Conflict and the Practice of Toleration in Early Modern Europe* (Cambridge, MA: Harvard University Press, 2010).

13. Amy Zegart, *Spies, Lies, and Algorithms: The History and Future of American Intelligence* (Princeton, NJ: Princeton University Press, 2022), 83.

14. Zegart, *Spies, Lies, and Algorithms*, 9.

15. Jeremy Bentham, "Of Publicity," in *The Works of Jeremy Bentham*, ed. John Bowring (London: W. Tait, Simpkin, and Marshall, 1843), 310; chapter 4, in Vincent, *The Culture of Secrecy*, 132-184.

BIBLIOGRAPHY

Printed Primary Sources

Acta Pacis Westphalicae. Serien I–III. 48 vols. Münster, Germany: Verlagsbuchhandlung, 1965–2013.
An Act for the Setting of the Postage of England, Scotland, and Ireland at the Parliament Begun at Westminster the 17th Day of September, Anno Domini 1656. London: Henry Hills and John Field, 1656.
Bentham, Jeremy. *The Works of Jeremy Bentham.* Edited by John Bowring. London: W. Tait, Simpkin, and Marshall, 1843.
Boccalini, Trajano. *Ragguagli di Parnasso e scritti minori.* Edited by Luigi Firpo. Bari, Italy: Laterza, 1948.
Bonaventure de Longueval, Charles. *Postillion.* Antwerp: n.p., 1621.
Breton, Nicholas. *A Poste with a Mad Packet of Letters.* London: John Smethicke, 1602.
Brewer J. S., ed. *Letters and Papers, Foreign and Domestic, of the Reign of Henry VIII: Preserved in the Public Record Office the British Museum and Elsewhere in England.* 2 vols. Cambridge: Cambridge University Press, 2015.
Bromato, Carlo. *Vita di Paolo IV.* Ravenna, Italy: Antonmaria Landi, 1753.
Camerarius, Ludwig. *Der Röm: Spanischen Cantzley Nachtrab.* n.p.: n.p., 1624.
Camerarius, Ludwig. *Mysterium iniquitatis, eiusque ver apocalypsis, sive secreta secretorum turco-papistica secreta.* Justinopoli [Amsterdam?]: n.p., 1622.
Carolus, Johann. *Relation: Aller Fürnemmen, und gedenckwürdigen Historien: So sich hin und wider in Hoch und Nieder Teutschland, auch in Franckreich, Italien, Schott und Engelland.* Strassburg, Germany: n.p., 1605.
Carracci, Annibale. *Diverse figure al numero di ottanta, disegnate di penna nell'hore di ricreatione, intagliate in rame e cavate dagli originali da Simone Giulino, stampatore parigino.* Rome: Ludovico Grignani, 1646.
Celano, Carlo. *Degli avanzi delle poste.* Venice: Giacomo Zinia, 1677.
Chifflet, Jules. *Les marques d'honneur de la Maison de Tassis.* Antwerp: Balthasar Moretus, 1645.
Codogno, Ottavio. *Compendio delle poste.* Milan: Gio. Battista Bidelli, 1623.
Codogno, Ottavio. *Nuovo itinerario delle poste per tutto il mondo.* Milan: Girolamo Bordoni, 1608.
Compendio di tutte le gride e ordini pubblicati nella Città e Stato di Milano. Milan: Giovanni Battista Malatesta, 1612.
Concilium Tridentinum: Diariorum, actorum, epistolarum, tractatuum: Nova collectio. 13 vols. Freiburg im Breisgau, Germany: Herder, 1950–2001.

BIBLIOGRAPHY

Coryate, Thomas. *Coryate's Crudities*. London: William Stanby, 1611.

Datini, Francesco. *Le lettere di Francesco Datini alla moglie Margherita (1385–1410)*. Edited by Elena Cecchi. Prato, Italy: Società pratese di Storia Patria, 1990.

de Haro, Alonso López. *Nobiliario geneaologico de los reyes y titulose de España*. Madrid: La Viuda de Fernando Correa de Montenegro, 1622.

de Lellis, Carlo. *Discorsi delle famiglie nobili del Regno di Napoli*. Naples: Honorio Safio, 1654.

de' Medici, Lorenzo. *Lettere*. Edited by Riccardo Fubini, Nicolai Rubinstein, F. W. Kent, et al. 18 vols. Florence: Giunti-Barbèra, 1977.

de Meneses, Alonso. *Memorial ō abecedario de los mas principales caminos de España*. Toledo, Spain: Juan de Ayala, 1553.

de Tassis, Pelegrin. *Neue Zeyttung von Rom / Kay. Mayestat Postmayster zy Rom / Pelegrin de Tassis*. n.p.: n.p., 1527.

Dirección General de Correos y Telégrafos. *Anales de las ordenanzas de correos de España*. Madrid: Victor Saiz, 1879.

Di Stella, Cherubino, and Giovanni da l'Herba. *L'Itinerario per diverse parte del mondo*. Rome: Valerico Dorico, 1563.

Documenti dell'istituzione fatta dalla compagnia de' corrieri Veneti delli due viaggi di Roma e Milano e poste. Venice: Perlini, 1790.

Estienne, Charles. *La guide des chemins de France*. Paris: Charles Estienne, 1553.

Evelyn, John. *Memoirs of John Evelyn, Comprising His Diary, from 1641 to 1705–6*. Edited by W. Bray. London: Henry Colburn, 1827.

Flacchio, Engelbert. *Genealogie de la très-illustre, très-ancienne et autrefois souveraine maison de la Tour, où quantité d'autres familles trouveront leur extraction & parentage*. Brussels: Antoine Claudinot, 1709.

Florio, John. *Queen Anna's New World of Words, or a Dictionarie of the Italian and English Tongues*. London: Melch, Bradwood, Edward Blount and William Pazret, 1611.

Franciosini, Lorenzo. *Vocabolario italiano e spagnolo*. Rome: Ruffinelli & Manni, 1620.

Gaeta, Franco ed. *Nunziature di Venezia: Secoli XVI–XVIII*. Volume 5. Rome: Istituto Storico italiano per l'Età Moderna e Contemporanea, 1967.

Gail, Jörg. *Ein neüwes nützliches Raißbuechlin der fürnemesten Land und StettWerk*. Augsburg, Germany: Valentin Otmar, 1563.

Galileo, Galilei. *The Essential Galileo*. Edited by Maurice A. Finocchiaro. Indianapolis: Hackett, 2008.

Garzoni, Tommaso. *La piazza universale di tutte le professioni del mondo, e nobili et ignobili*. Venice: Gio. Battista Somascho, 1585.

Gildon, Charles. *The Post-Boy Robbed of His Bag*. London: John Dunton, 1692.

Goldoni, Carlo. *Il servitore di due padroni*. Edited by Valentina Gallo. Venice: Marsilio Editori, 2011.

Guasti, Cesare, ed. *Commissioni di Rinaldo degli Albizzi per il comune di Firenze*. Florence: M. Cellini, 1867.

Guazzo, Stefano. *La civil conversation del signor Stefano Guazzo*. Venice: Altobello Salicato, 1580.

BIBLIOGRAPHY

Heger, Franz J. *Neue und vollständige Postkarte durch ganz Deutschland und durch die angränzende Theile der benachbarten Länder / zusammen getragen und ausgefertiget von Franz Joseph Heger = Nouvelle carte geographique des postes d'Allemagne et des provinces limitrophes.* Nuremberg, Germany: Homaennischen Erben, 1764.

Heylyn, Peter. *A Full Relation of Two Journeys.* London: Printed by E. Cotes for Henry Seile, 1656.

Hill, John. *A Penny Post: or, a Vindication of the Liberty and Birthright of Every English-Man.* London: n.p., 1659.

Historical Manuscripts Commission, Report on the Manuscripts of the Duke of Buccleuch. London: His Majesty's Stationery Office, 1903.

Jocher, Wilhelm. *Secreta principis anhaltini cancellaria.* n.p.: n.p., 1621.

Jüdischer Postillion von Franckfurt nach Prag und Westphalen. n.p.: n.p., 1675.

Kircher, Athanasius. *Scrutinium physico-medicum contagiosae luis, qui pestis dicatur.* Rome: Giacomo Mascardi, 1658.

Lassels, Richard. *The Voyage of Italy.* Paris: Simon Wilson, 1670.

Le Glay, A., ed. *Correspondance de l'empereur Maximilien Ier et de Marguerite d'Autriche... de 1507 à 1519.* Paris: J. Renouard, 1839.

Le Mercure postillon, de l'un à l'autre monde. Liège, Belgium: Claude Guibert, 1667.

Le poste, necessarie a corrieri & viandanti, per l'Italia, Francia, Spagna, & Alemagna con le fiere che si fanno per il mondo. Brescia, Italy: Damiano Turlano and Ioanne Battista Bozola, 1562.

Lossen, Max, ed. *Briefe von Andreas Masius und seinen Freunden 1538 bis 1573.* Leipzig, Germany: Alphons Dürr, 1886.

Lupis, Antonio. *Il postiglione.* Venice: Abondo Menafoglio, 1674.

Madruzzo, Cristoforo. *L'epistolario del cardinale Cristoforo Madruzzo presso l'Archivio di Stato di Innsbruck.* Edited by A. Galante. Trieste, Italy: Caprin, 1910.

Mayr, Georg. *Wegbüchlin: Die furnemesten Weg unnd gebreuchlichsten Strassen durch ganz Teutschland, Hungern, Bohhem, Polen, Luttaro, Schroeden, Dennmarck.* Augsburg, Germany: Georg Mayr, 1576.

Mercurio postiglione. [Amsterdam?]: n.p., 1667.

Miselli, Giuseppe. *Il Burattino veridico.* Rome: Michel'Ercole, 1682.

More, Hannah. *The History of Tom White, the Postillion.* London: n.p., c. 1795.

Morland, Samuel. *A New Method of Cryptography.* [London]: n.p., 1666.

Moryson, Fynes. *An Itinerary Written by Fynes Moryson.* London: John Beale, 1617.

Münsterischer Postillion: das ist wahrhafftige newe Zeitung von dem lang gewünschten Frieden in Teutschland. Hohenems, Austria: n.p., 1619.

Navagero, Bernardo. *Bernardo Navagero: Dispacci al Senato dal 7 settembre 1555 al 6 novembre 1557.* Edited by Daniele Bernardo Santarelli, November 11, 2011. http://www.storiadivenezia.net/sito/testi/Navagero2.pdf.

Palladio, Andrea. *Le cose maravigliose dell'alma città di Roma... con le poste d'Italia.* Rome: Giovanni Osmarino Gigliotto, 1585.

Pallavicino, Ferrante. *Il corriero svaligiato.* Nuremberg: Hans Jacob Stoer, 1641.

Pallavicino, Ferrante. *Il corriero svaligiato con la Lettera dalla prigionia, aggiuntavi La semplicità ingannata di suor Arcangela Tarabotti.* Edited by Armando Marchi. Parma, Italy: Università di Parma, 1984.

Pallavicino, Sforza. *Istoria del Concilio di Trento*. Rome: Angelo Bernabò dal Verme, 1656.
Palmer, June. *The Letter Book of Thomas Hill, 1660–1661: Westcountry Mercantile Affairs and the Wider World*. Exeter: Devon and Cornwall Record Society, 2008.
Pease-Watkin, Catherine, and Philip Schofield, eds. *The Collected Works of Jeremy Bentham: On the Liberty of the Press, and Public Discussion, and Other Legal and Political Writings for Spain and Portugal*. Oxford: Oxford University Press, 2012.
Pescetti, Orlando. *Proverbi italiani*. Verona, Italy: Compagnia degli Aspiranti, 1603.
Poste diverse d'Italia, Alemagna, Spagna, e Francia. Milan: n.p., c. 1620s–1700.
Roseo, Mambrin. *Compendio dell'istoria del regno di Napoli*. Venice: B. Barezzi, 1591.
Sacker, Amy M., ed. *Memoirs of the Courts of Louis XV and XVI: Being Secret Memoirs of Madame Du Hausset Lady's Maid to Madame De Pompadour and of the Princess Lamballe*. Boston: L. C. Page, 1899.
Sanson, Nicolas. *Carte Geographique des Postes qui traversent la France*. Paris: Tavernier, 1632.
Sanudo, Marino. *I diarii di Marino Sanuto*. Edited by Rinaldo Fulin, et al. Venice: F. Visentini, 1889.
Schorer, Christoph. *Memminger Chronik oder Kurtze Erzehlung vieler denkwurdiger Sachen*. Ulm, Germany: Kühnen, 1660.
Schottus, Franciscus. *Itinerari Italiae*. Antwerp, Belgium: Jan Moretus, 1600.
Schottus, Franciscus. *Itinerario*. Venice: Francesco Bolzetta, 1610.
Schottus, Franciscus. *Itinerario: Overo nova descrittione de' viaggi principali d'Italia*. Vicenza, Italy: Francesco Bolzetta, 1615.
Schottus, Franciscus. *Itinerario: Overo nova descrittione de' viaggi principali d'Italia*. Vicenza, Italy: Pietro Bertelli, 1610.
Schottus, Franciscus. *Itinerarium nobiliorum Italiae regionum*. Vicenza, Italy: Girolamo Giovannini, 1600.
Sharp, Samuel. *Letters from Italy*. London: R. Cave, 1766.
Smollet, Tobias. *Travels through France and Italy*. London: R. Baldwin, 1766.
Sorrer, Gio. Battista. *Idea del perfetto ambasciadore*. Venice: Gio. Giorgio Hertz, 1654.
Stella, Aldo, ed. *Nunziature di Venezia: Secoli XVI–XVIII*. Volumes 8 and 9. Rome: Istituto Storico italiano per l'Età Moderna e Contemporanea, 1963-1972.
Taylor, John. *The Carriers Cosmographie*. London: A. G., 1637.
The Knight out rid; or, The postilion in his master's saddle, a new ballad. Occasioned by a baronet's lady, being caught in bed with her postillion. London: R. Amey, 1730.
The Private Memoirs of Madame du Hausset; Lady's Maid to Madame de Pompadour. London: E. Wilson, 1827.
Torriano, Giovanni. *Della lingua Toscana-Romana, or, An Introduction to the Italian Tongue*... London: J. Martin and J. Allestrye, 1657.
Verhoeven, Abraham. *Nieuwe Tydinghe*. Antwerp: Verhoeven, 1605.
Verstegan, Richard. *The Post of the World*. London: Richard Rowlands, 1576.
Vidari, Giovanni Maria. *Il viaggio in pratica*. Naples: Francesco Ricciardo, 1718.
von den Birghden, Johann. *Allerunterthanigst Verwantwort/und Ablehnung auff der Fraw Gravin von Taxis*. n.p.: n.p., 1640.

von den Birghden, Johann. *Deductio Birghdiana, Das Ist, Etlicher Hochst-und Hochansehenlicher Chur-Fursten und Herren, Intercessiones, Commendations, von Attestations.* n.p.: n.p., c. 1636.
Wadsworth, James. *The European Mercury: Describing the Highwayes and Stages from Place to Place* ... London: John Raworth for Henry Twyford, 1641.
Warcupp, Edmund. *Italy, in its original glory, ruine and revival, being an exact survey of the whole geography, and history of that famous country* ... London: Sarah Griffin, for Henry Twyford and Thomas Dring and John Place, 1660.
Wilson, Peter, ed. *The Thirty Years War: A Sourcebook.* London: Palgrave Macmillan, 2010.
Witzenberger, Daniel. *Ein Naw Reyse Büchlein.* Dresden: Gimel Bergen, 1578.
Zazzera, Francesco. *Della nobilità dell'Italia.* Naples: Ottavio Boltrano, 1628.
Zschirmer, Gabriel. *Der auff der Post angehaltene Mercurius.* Meissen, Germany: n.p., 1668.

Secondary Sources

Abad, Leticia Arroyo. "Italy—North, 1285–1850." In *Global Price and Incomes Database.* University of California, Davis, 2015. https://gpih.ucdavis.edu/Datafilelist.htm.
Adair, Edward Robert. *The Extraterritoriality of Ambassadors in the Sixteenth and Seventeenth Centuries.* London: Longmans, 1929.
Ago, Renata, and Benedetta Borello, eds. *Famiglie: Circolazione di beni, circuiti di affetti in età moderna.* Rome: Viella Libreria Editrice, 2008.
Ahnert, Ruth, and Sebastian E. Ahnert. "Metadata, Surveillance and the Tudor State." *History Workshop Journal* 87, no. 1 (2019): 27–51.
Ahrendt, Rebekah, and David van der Linden. "The Postmasters' Piggy Bank: Experiencing the Accidental Archive." *French Historical Studies* 40, no. 2 (April 2017): 189–213.
Akkerman, Nadine. *Invisible Agents: Women and Espionage in Seventeenth-Century Britain.* Oxford: Oxford University Press, 2018.
Akkerman, Nadine. "The Postmistress, the Diplomat, and a Black Chamber? Alexandrine of Taxis, Sir Balthazar Gerbier and the Power of Postal Control." In *Diplomacy and Early Modern Culture.* Edited by Robyn Adams and Rosanna Cox, 172–188. New York: Palgrave Macmillan, 2011.
Allen, E. John B. "The Royal Posts of France in the Fifteenth and Sixteenth Century." *Postal History Journal* 15 (1971): 13–17.
Andrew, Christopher. *The Secret World: A History of Intelligence.* New Haven, CT: Yale University Press, 2019.
Andújar Castillo, Francisco. "Juan Gaspar Zorrilla de San Martín." In *Diccionario Biográfico electrónico.* https://dbe.rah.es/biografias/35532/juan-gaspar-zorrilla-de-san-martin.
Ángel Echevarría Bacigalupe, Miguel. "Pedro Enríquez de Guzmán de Acevedo y Toledo." In *Diccionario Biográfico electrónico.* https://dbe.rah.es/biografias/15646/pedro-enriquez-de-guzman-de-acevedo-y-toledo.

BIBLIOGRAPHY

Arblaster, Paul. *From Ghent to Aix: How They Brought the News in the Habsburg Netherlands, 1550–1700*. Leiden, Netherlands: Brill, 2014.

Ault, Alicia. "Mail Handlers Used to Poke Holes in Envelopes to Battle Germs and Viruses." *Smithsonian Magazine*. June 2, 2020. https://www.smithsonianmag.com/smithsonian-institution/mail-handlers-used-poke-holes-envelopes-battle-germs-and-viruses-180975020/.

Bakhtin, Michel. *Rabelais and His World*. Cambridge, MA: MIT Press, 1968.

Bamji, Alex. "Health Passes, Print and Public Health in Early Modern Europe." *Social History of Medicine* 32, no. 3 (August 2019): 441–464.

Bardati, Flaminia. "Between the King and the Pope: French Cardinals in Rome (1495–1560)." *Urban History* 37, no. 3 (2010): 419–433.

Basezzi, Nevio. "I Paar, de Parre ai confini dell'Europa. La storia postale europea tra Tasso e Paar." *Quaderni Brembani* 11 (2013): 94–101.

Baskins, Cristelle. *Hafsids and Habsburgs in the Early Modern Mediterranean: Facing Tunis*. Cham, Switzerland: Palgrave Macmillan, 2022.

Basso, Jeannine. *Le genre epistolaire en langue Italienne (1538–1662)*. Nancy, France: Presses Universitaires de Nancy, 1990.

Beck, Wilhelm. "Ursprung und Ende der fremden Posten in Rom." *Archiv für das Post- und Fernmeldewesen*, no. 1–7 (1959): 564–588.

Behringer, Wolfgang. "Communications Revolutions: A Historiographical Concept." *German History* 24, no. 3 (2006): 333–374.

Behringer, Wolfgang. "Fugger und Taxis: Der Anteil Augsburger Kaufleute an der Entstehung des europäischen Kommunikationssystems." In *Augsburger Handelshäuser im Wandel des historischen Urteils*. Edited by Johannes Burkhardt, 241–248. Berlin: Akademie Verlag, 1996.

Behringer, Wolfgang. *Im Zeichen des Merkur: Reichsport und Kommunikationsrevolution in der Frühen Neuzeit*. Göttingen, Germany: Vandenhoeck & Ruprecht, 2003.

Behringer, Wolfgang. *Thurn und Taxis: Die Geschichte ihrer Post und ihrer Unternehmen*. Munich: Piper, 1990.

Beik, William. "The Absolutism of Louis XIV as Social Collaboration." *Past & Present* 188, no. 1 (August 2005): 195–224.

Bellingradt, Daniel, and Anna Reynolds, eds. *The Paper Trade in Early Modern Europe: Practices, Materials, Networks*. Leiden, Netherlands: Brill, 2021.

Bély, Lucian. *Espions et ambassadeurs au temps de Louis XIV*. Paris: Fayard, 1990.

Benavent, Júlia. "Lettere dei Tasso a Madrid: Biblioteca Nacional de España e Real Biblioteca." In *I Tasso e le poste d'Europa*. Edited by Tarcisio Bottani, 237–244. Bergamo, Italy: Corponove, 2012.

Benavent, Júlia, and Miriam Bucuré. "Introduccion." In *Epistolario inedito entre Ruggero de Tassis y el Cardenal Granvelle (1536–1565)*. Edited by Júlia Benavent and Miriam Bucuré, 21–40. Prato, Italy: Istituto di Studi Storici Postali, 2017.

Benavent, Júlia, and Bruno Crevato-Selvaggi, eds. *La corrispondenza della famiglia Tasso con Antoine Perrenot de Granvelle*. Prato, Italy: Istituto di studi storici postali Aldo Cecchi, 2023.

Beyrer, Klaus. "Botenwesen." In *Enzyklopädie der Neuzeit*, columns 361–366. Leiden, Netherlands: Brill, 2014.

Bizzocchi, Roberto. *Genealogie incredibili: scritti di storia nell'Europa moderna*. Bologna, Italy: Il Mulino, 2009.
Black, Jeremy. *Italy and the Grand Tour*. New Haven, CT: Yale University Press, 2003.
Black, Jeremy. *The British and the Grand Tour*. London: Croom Helm, 1985.
Blat, Maria Antonia. "I fondi Tassis del'Archivio di Simancas." In *I Tasso e le poste pontificie, sec. XV–XVI*, ed. Tarcisio Bottani, 247–254. Bergamo, Italy: Corponove, 2000.
Blevins, Cameron. *Paper Trails: The U.S. Post and the Making of the American West*. Oxford: Oxford University Press, 2021.
Bonora, Elena. *Aspettando l'Imperatore: Principi italiani tra il papa e Carlo V*. Turin, Italy: Einaudi, 2014.
Bottani, Tarcisio. *Francesco Tasso e la nascita delle poste d'Europa nel Rinascimento*. Bergamo, Italy: Museo dei Tasso e della Storia Postale and Corponove, 2017.
Bottani, Tarcisio. *I Tasso e le poste pontificie, sec. XV–XVI*. Bergamo, Italy: Corponove, 2000.
Bottani, Tarcisio. "I testamenti di Ruggero, Janetto, e Leonardo Tasso." In *I Tasso e le poste d'Europa*. Edited by Tarcisio Bottani, 13–16. Bergamo, Italy: Corponove, 2012.
Bottani, Tarcisio, ed. *Le poste dei Tasso: Da Cornelio all'Europa*. Bergamo, Italy: Corponove, 2021.
Bottani, Tarcisio. "Tasso di Valle Brembana: I Signori delle poste d'Europa." In *I Signori delle Alpi, Famiglie e poteri tra le montagne d'Europa*. Edited by Luca Giarelli, 179–195. Tricase, Italy: Self-published, 2015.
Bottani, Tarcisio, and Adriano Cattani, eds. *Cornello e i Tasso*. Bergamo, Italy: Museo dei Tasso e della Storia Postale and Corponove, 2010.
Bottani, Tarcisio, Gianfranco Lazzarini, et al. *Genealogia Tasso*. Bergamo, Italy: Santini Pubblicità, July 2007. https://www.museodeitasso.com/export/sites/default/documenti/albero-genealogico-casato-tasso.pdf.
Bottani, Tarcisio, and Wanda Taufer, eds. *Mariegola della Compagnia dei Corrieri della Serenissima Signoria*. Bergamo, Italy: Museo dei Tasso e della Storia Postale and Corponove, 2001.
Bouwsma, William. *Venice and the Defense of Republican Liberty: Renaissance Values in the Age of the Counter-Reformation*. Berkeley: University of California Press, 1968.
Boyes-Watson, Carolyn. "Recordkeeping as a Technology of Power." *Berkeley Journal of Sociology* 39 (1994): 1–32.
Braudel, Fernand. *The Mediterranean and the Mediterranean World in the Age of Philip II*. 2 vols. Berkeley: University of California Press, 1995.
Brayshay, Mark. "Conveying Correspondence: Early Modern Letter Bearers, Carriers, and Posts." In *Cultures of Correspondence in Early Modern Britain*. Edited by James Daybell and Andrew Gordon, 48–66. Philadelphia: University of Pennsylvania Press, 2016.
Brennan, Michael. "Breton [Britton], Nicholas." September 23, 2004. In *Oxford Dictionary of National Biography*. https://doi.org/10.1093/ref:odnb/3341.
Brewer, John. *The Sinews of Power: War, Money, and the English State 1688–1883*. Cambridge, MA: Harvard University Press, 1990.

Brucker, Gene. *Florence: The Golden Age, 1138–1737*. Berkeley: University of California, 1998.
Brunet, Francesca. *"Per essere quest'ufficio la chiave dell'Italia e Germania . . .": La famiglia Taxis Bordogna e le comunicazioni postali nell'area di Trento e Bolzano (sec. XVI–XVIII)*. Bergamo, Italy: Museo dei Tasso e della Storia Postale and Corponove, 2018.
Bucciantini, Massimo, Michele Camerota, and Franco Giudicie, eds. *Galileo's Telescope: A European Story*. Translated by Catherine Bolton. Cambridge, MA: Harvard University Press, 2015.
Burke, Peter. *A Social History of Knowledge: From Gutenberg to Diderot*. Cambridge: Polity, 2000.
Burkhardt, Jacob. *Die Kultur der Renaissance in Italien*. Leipzig, Germany: E. A. Seeman, 1868.
Caizzi, Bruno. *Dalla posta dei re alla posta di tutti: Territorio e comunicazioni in Italia dal XVI secolo all'Unità*. Milan: Franco Angeli, 1993.
Campbell-Smith, Duncan. *Masters of the Post: The Authorized History of the Royal Mail*. London: Allen Lane, 2011.
Caplan, Jay. *Postal Culture in Europe 1500–1800*. Oxford: Voltaire Foundation, 2016.
Carroll, Stuart. *Enmity and Violence in Early Modern Europe*. Cambridge: Cambridge University Press, 2023.
Casson, Mark. "The Economics of the Family Firm: An Analysis of the Dynastic Motive." *Scandinavian Economic History Review* 47, no. 1 (1999): 10–23.
Cattani, Adriano. *Le comunicazioni postali nella Repubblica di Venezia*. Padua, Italy: Editrice Elzeviro, 2018.
Chabod, Federico. "Alcune questioni di terminologia: Stato, nazione, patria nel linguaggio del Cinquecento." In *Scritti sul Rinascimento*, 625–661. Turin, Italy: Einaudi, 1967.
Chabod, Federico. *Scritti sul Rinascimento*. Turin, Italy: Einaudi, 1967.
Chabod, Federico. *Storia di Milano nell'epoca di Carlo V*. Turin, Italy: Einaudi, 1961.
Chieppi, Sergio. *I servizi postali dei Medici dal 1500 al 1737*. Arezzo, Italy: Servizio editoriale fiesolano, 1997.
Chittolini, Giorgio. "The 'Private,' the 'Public,' and the State." In *The Origins of the State in Italy, 1300–1600*. Edited by Julius Kirshner, 34–61. Chicago: University of Chicago Press, 1996.
Ciscato, A. "I portalettere in Padova nel cinquecento." *Bolletino del Museo civico di Padova* 3 (1901): 32–39.
Clear, C. R. *Thomas Witherings and the Birth of the Postal Service*. London: Eyre and Spottiswoode, 1935.
Cochrane, Eric. *Florence in the Forgotten Centuries, 1527–1800: A History of Florence and the Florentines in the Age of the Grand Dukes*. Chicago: University of Chicago Press, 1973.
Cohen, Elizabeth, and Thomas Cohen, eds. *Words and Deeds in Renaissance Rome: Trials before the Papal Magistrates*. Toronto: University of Toronto Press, 1993.
Cohn, Samuel. *Cultures of Plague: Medical Thinking at the End of the Renaissance*. Oxford: Oxford University Press, 2011.
Collins, James B. *The State in Early Modern France*. Cambridge: Cambridge University Press, 1995.

Como, David. "God's Revolutions: England, Europe, and the Concept of Revolution in the Mid-Seventeenth Century." In *Scripting Revolutions: A Historical Approach to the Comparative Study of Revolutions*. Edited by Keith Baker and Dan Edelstein, 41–56. Stanford, CA: Stanford University Press, 2015.

Corsi, Christina. *Le strutture di servizio del cursus publicus in Italia: Ricerche topografiche ed evidenze archeologiche*. Oxford: J. and E. Hedges and Hadrian, 2000.

Crevato-Selvaggi, Bruno. "Tra Parigi e Constantinopoli: Una via postale rivoluzionaria attraverso Sebenico in Dalmazia." *Archivio per la storia postale* 43, no. 14 (September–December 2021): 31–54.

Croxton, Derek. *The Last Christian Peace: The Congress of Westphalia as a Baroque Event*. New York: Palgrave Macmillan, 2013.

dall'Aglio, Stefano. *The Duke's Assassin: Exile and Death of Lorenzino de' Medici*. Translated by Donald Weinstein. New Haven, CT: Yale University Press, 2015.

Dallmeier, Martin Volker Albus, ed. *Quellen zur Geschichte des Europaischen Postwesens, 1501–1806*. 2 vols. Kallmünz, Germany: Lassleben, 1977.

Dallmeier, Martin Volker Albus, and Fürstliches Marstallmuseum (Regensburg). *500 Jahre Post Thurn und Taxis: Ausstellung Anläßlich der 500jährigen Wiederkehr der Anfänge der Post in Mitteleuropa 1490–1990: Fürstliches Marstallmuseum Regensburg, Emmeramsplatz, 5 12. Mai bis 29. Juli 1990*. Neusäss, Germany: Kieser, 1990.

Dambrogio, J., A. Ghassaei, D. S. Smith, et al. "Unlocking History through Automated Virtual Unfolding of Sealed Documents Imaged by X-ray Microtomography." *Nature Communications* 12, no. 1184 (2021). https://doi.org/10.1038/s41467-021-21326-w.

d'Amico, Stefano. *Spanish Milan: A City within Empire*. London: Palgrave Macmillan, 2016.

Dandelet, Thomas, and John Marino, eds. *Spain in Italy, Politics, Society, and Religion 1500–1700*. Leiden, Netherlands: Brill, 2006.

Davis, Norman, ed. *Paston Letters*. Oxford: Clarendon, 1958.

Day, Joan. "Dockwra [Dockwray], William." July 21, 2002. In *Oxford Dictionary of National Biography*. https://doi.org/10.1093/ref:odnb/7724.

Daybell, James, and Andrew Gordon, eds. *Cultures of Correspondence in Early Modern Britain*. Philadelphia: University of Pennsylvania Press, 2016.

de Boer, Wietse. *The Conquest of the Soul: Confession, Discipline, and Public Order in Counter-Reformation Milan*. Leiden, Netherlands: Brill, 2001.

Dedé, Luigi. "Il servizio postale fra Brescia e Venezia durante il dominio veneto." In *Commentari dell'Ateneo di Brescia per l'anno 1986*, 157–198. Brescia, Italy: Tipolito Fratelli Geroldi, 1987.

de la Flor, Fernando R. *Pasiones Frías: Secreto y disimulación en al Barroco hispano*. Madrid: Marcial Pons, 2005.

de Montaigne, Michel. *A Diary of the Journey of Michael de Montaigne into Italy, through Switzerland and Germany, in the Years 1580 and 1581*. Translated by William Hazlitt. New York: Hurd and Houghton, 1866.

de Vivo, Filippo. *Information and Communication in Venice: Rethinking Early Modern Politics*. Oxford: Oxford University Press, 2007.

de Vivo, Filippo. "Pharmacies as Centres of Communication in Early Modern Venice." *Renaissance Studies* 21, no. 4 (September 2007): 505–521.

Devos, J. P. *Les chiffres de Philippe II (1555–1598) et du despacho universal durant le XVIIe Siècle*. Brussels: Palais des académies, 1950.

de Vries, Jan. *European Urbanization, 1500–1800*. Cambridge, MA: Harvard University Press, 1984.

Dover, Paul Marcus. "Ambassadors as Travelers in Italy in the Second Half of the Fifteenth Century." In *Travel and Conflict in the Early Modern World*. Edited by Gábor Gelléri and Rachel Willie, 147–166. New York: Routledge, 2022.

Dover, Paul Marcus. "Deciphering the Diplomatic Archives of Fifteenth-Century Italy." *Archival Science* 7 (2007): 297–316.

Dover, Paul Marcus. "The Impacts of Paper's Abundance, 1450–1650: An Episode in Coevolution." In *Paper Stories—Paper and Book History in Early Modern Europe*. Edited by Silvia Hufnagel, Þórunn Sigurðardóttir, and Davíð Ólafsson, 47–72. Berlin: De Gruyter, 2023.

Dover, Paul Marcus. *The Information Revolution in Early Modern Europe*. Cambridge: Cambridge University Press, 2021.

Drelichman, Mauricio, and Hans-Joachim Voth. *Lending to the Borrower from Hell: Debt, Taxes, and Default in the Age of Philip II*. Princeton, NJ: Princeton University Press, 2016.

Droste, Heiko, ed. *Connecting the Baltic Area: The Swedish Postal System in the Seventeenth Century*. Stockholm: Södertörn University, 2011.

Droste, Heiko. "Sending a Letter between Amsterdam and Stockholm: A Matter of Trust and Precautions." In *Your Humble Servant: Agents in Early Modern Europe*. Edited by Hans Cool, Marika Keblusek, and Badeloch Noldus, 135–148. Hilversum, Netherlands: Verloren, 2006.

Dursteler, Eric. "Power and Information: The Venetian Postal System in the Early Modern Eastern Mediterranean." In *From Florence to the Mediterranean and Beyond: Essays in Honour of Antony Molho*. Edited by Diogo Ramada Curto and Niki Koniordos, 601–623. Florence: L. S. Olski, 2009.

Eisenstein, Elizabeth. *The Printing Press as an Agent of Change: Communications and Cultural Transformations in Early-Modern Europe*. Cambridge: Cambridge University Press, 1980.

Elliot, J. H. "A Europe of Composite Monarchies." *Past and Present* 137 (November 1992): 48–71.

Ellis, Ryan. *Letters, Power Lines, and Other Dangerous Things: The Politics of Infrastructure Security*. Cambridge, MA: MIT Press, 2020.

Ennen, Leonhard. "Henot, Hartger." 1880. In *Allgemeine Deutsche Biographie (ADB)* 11. https://www.deutsche-biographie.de/pnd133246655.html#adbcontent.

Fardella de Quernfort, Vincenzo. "Documenti tassiani in Sicilia: La nascita della Regia Correria di Sicilia." In *I Tasso e le poste d'Europa*. Edited by Tarcisio Bottani, 125–134. Bergamo, Italy: Corponove, 2012.

Faulhaber, Bernhard. *Geschichte des Postwesens Frankfurt am Main*. Frankfurt: Völckers, 1883.

Fedele, Clemente. *Un lago per comunicare: Il Garda e l'Italia nella storia della cultura postale di età moderna*. Salò: Ateneo di Salò, 2024.

Fedele, Clemente, and Marco Gallenga. *"Per servizio di nostro signore": Strade, corrieri, e poste dei papi dal medioevo al 1870*. Modena, Italy: Mucchi, 1988.

Figini, Girolamo. *I Tasso e i feudi di Rachele e Barbana nell'Istria*. Bergamo, Italy: Fagnani & Galeazzi, 1895.

Findlen, Paula. "Microscopic Musings: Athanasius Kircher and the Roman Plague of 1656-57." *Harvard Library Bulletin*. https://nrs.harvard.edu/URN-3:HUL.INSTREPOS:37370849.

Findlen, Paula, and Hannah Marcus. "Deciphering Galileo: Communication and Secrecy before and after the Trial." *Renaissance Quarterly* 72, no. 3 (Fall 2019): 953-995.

Findlen, Paula, and Hannah Marcus. "The Breakdown of Galileo's Roman Network: Crisis and Community, ca. 1633." *Social Studies of Science* 47, no. 3 (2017): 326-352.

Fleitman, Wilhelm. "Postverbindungen für den Westfälischen Friedenskongress 1643 bis 1648." *Archiv für Deutsche Postgeschichte* 1 (1972): 3-48.

Fletcher, Catherine. *Diplomacy in Renaissance Rome: The Rise of the Resident Ambassador*. Cambridge: Cambridge University Press, 2015.

Foppolo, Bonaventura. "La Mariegola della Compagnia dei Corrieri Veneti." In *Le poste dei Tasso, un'impresa in Europa: Contributi in occasione della mostra I Tasso, l'evoluzione delle poste ... 28 aprile-3 giugno 1984*. Edited by Tarcisio Bottani, 13-45. Bergamo, Italy: Comune di Bergamo, 1984.

Foppolo, Bonaventura. "La Mariegola della Compagnia dei Corrieri Veneti." In *Mariegola della Compagnia dei Corrieri della Serenissima Signoria*. Edited by Tarcisio Bottani and Wanda Taufer. Bergamo, Italy: Museo dei Tasso e della Storia Postale and Corponove, 2001.

Foppolo, Bonaventura. "I maestri della posta imperiale a Venezia." In *Le Poste dei Tasso: Da Cornello all'Europa*. Bergamo, Italy: Museo dei Tasso e della Storia Postale and Corponove, 2021.

Foppolo, Bonaventura. "La parabola del ramo veneziano dei Tasso da Cornello a Venezia." In *I Tasso e le poste d'Europa*. Edited by Tarcisio Bottani, 27-48. Bergamo, Italy: Corponove, 2012.

François, Michel. "Le rôle du cardinal François de Tournon dans la politique française en Italie de janvier à juillet 1556." *Mèlanges d'archèologie et d'histoire* 50 (1933): 293-333.

Fregulia, Jeanette. "Making Their Own Way: Women of Means in Late Renaissance Milan." PhD diss., University of Nevada, Reno, 2007.

Frey, Linda, and Marsha Frey. "Diplomatic Immunity/Privilege," In *The Encyclopedia of Diplomacy*. Edited by G. Martel, 1-10. New York: John Wiley, 2018. Accessed via Wiley Online Library at https://doi.org/10.1002/9781118885154.dipl0410.

Frey-Schlesinger, Anna. "Die volkswirtschaftliche Bedeutung der habsburgischen Post im 16. Jahrhundert." *Vierteljahrschrift für Sozial- und Wirtschaftsgeschichte* 15, no. 3/4 (1919): 399-465.

Frigo, Daniela. *Il padre di famiglia: Governo della casa e governo civile nella tradizione dell'"economica" tra Cinque e Seicento*. Rome: Bulzoni, 1985.

Gamberini, Andrea. "Milan and Lombardy in the Era of the Visconti and Sforza." In *A Companion to Late Medieval and Early Modern Milan: The Distinctive Features of an Italian State*. Edited by Andrea Gamberini, 19–45. Leiden, Netherlands: Brill, 2015.

Gazagnadou, Didier. *The Diffusion of a Postal Relay System in Premodern Eurasia*. Paris: Klime, 2016.

Gerosa, Marco. *La famiglia Tasso e le poste nello Stato di Milano in età spagnola (1556–1650)*. Bergamo, Italy: Corponove, 2019.

Gerosa, Marco. "Personaggi della posta dello Stato di Milano tra Simone e Ruggero Tasso." In *I Tasso e le poste d'Europa*. Edited by Tarcisio Bottani, 81–92. Bergamo, Italy: Corponove, 2012.

Gerosa, Marco. "Per una biografia di Ottavio Codogno luogotenente delle poste di Milano e autore di guide postali." In *Europa Postale*. Edited by Clemente Fedele, Armando Serra, and Marco Gerosa, 231–250. Bergamo, Italy: Museo dei Tasso e della Storia Postale, 2014.

Giannini, Massimo Carlo. "'Con il zelo di sodisfare all'obligo di re e principe,' Monarchia cattolica a stato di Milano nella visita General di don Felipe Haro (1606-1612)." *Archivio storico lombardo* 120 (1994): 165-207.

Giesey, Ralph E. "State-Building in Early Modern France: The Role of Royal Officialdom." *Journal of Modern History* 55, no. 2 (June 1983): 191-207.

Goldsmith, Sarah, Rosemary Sweet, and Gerrit Verhoeven, eds. *Beyond the Grand Tour: Northern Metropolises and Early Modern Travel Behaviour*. New York: Routledge, 2017.

Goldthwaite, Richard. *The Economy of Renaissance Florence*. Baltimore: Johns Hopkins University Press, 2009.

Goller, Engelbert. *Jakob Henot, Postmeister von Cöln: Ein Beitrag zur Geschichte der Sogenannten Postreformation um die Wende des XVI. Jahrhunderts*. Bonn, Germany: Carl Georgi, 1910.

Granovetter, Mark. "The Strength of Weak Ties." *American Journal of Sociology* 78, no. 6 (May 1973): 1360-1380.

Granzini, Alessandro. *Canti carnascialeschi: Trionfi, carri e mascherate*. Milan: Casa Editrice Sonzogno, 1883.

Green, Monica. "The Four Black Deaths." *American Historical Review* 125, no. 5 (December 2020): 1601-1631.

Green, Otis. "Villamediana as Correo Mayor in the Kingdom of Naples." *Hispanic Review* 15, no. 2 (April 1947): 302-306.

Grendler, Paul F. *The Roman Inquisition and the Venetian Press, 1540–1605*. Princeton, NJ: Princeton University Press, 1977.

Grillmeyer, Siegfried. "Briefgeheimnis oder Staatsräson? Die Schwarzen Kabinette der Thurn und Taxis: Ein Betrag zur Adeslgeschichte." *Verhandlungen des Historischen Vereins für Oberpfalz und Regensburg* 147 (2007): 205-220.

Groebner, Valentin. *Who Are You? Identification, Deception, and Surveillance in Early Modern Europe*. Princeton, NJ: Princeton University Press, 2007.

Grubb, James S. "Elite Citizens." In *Venice Reconsidered: The History and Civilization of an Italian City-State, 1297–1797*. Edited by John Jeffries Martin and Dennis Romano, 339–364. Baltimore: Johns Hopkins University Press, 2000.

Guldi, Jo. *Roads to Power: Britain Invents the Infrastructure State*. Cambridge, MA: Harvard University Press, 2012.

Habermas, Jürgen. *The Structural Transformation of the Public Sphere: An Inquiry into a Category of Bourgeois Society*. Cambridge, MA: MIT Press, 1989.

Hacke, Martina. "Aspekte des mittelalterlichen Botenwesens: Die Botenorganisation der Universität von Paris und anderer Institutionen in Spätmittelalter." *Mittelalter: Perspektiven Media? Vestischer Forschung: Zeitschrift des Mediavistenverbandes* 1, no. 11 (June 2006): 132–149.

Harding, Richard, and Sergio Solbes Ferri, eds. *The Contractor State and Its Implications, 1659–1815*. Las Palmas de Gran Canaria, Spain: Universidad de Las Palmas de Gran Canaria, 2012.

Harley, J. B. *The New Nature of Maps: Essays in the History of Cartography*. Edited by Paul Laxton. Baltimore: Johns Hopkins University Press, 2001.

Head, Randolph C. *Making Archives in Early Modern Europe: Proof, Information and Political Record-Keeping, 1400–1700*. Cambridge: Cambridge University Press, 2019.

Henkin, David. *The Postal Age: The Emergence of Modern Communications in Nineteenth-Century America*. Chicago: University of Chicago Press, 2006.

Hill, Christopher. *The World Turned Upside Down: Radical Ideas during the English Revolution*. London: Penguin, 1984.

Hirschman, Albert. *The Passions and the Interests: Political Arguments for Capitalism before Its Triumph*. Princeton, NJ: Princeton University Press, 2013.

Hobsbawm, Eric. *Bandits*. London: Weidenfeld & Nicolson, 1969.

Hont, Istvan. *Jealousy of Trade: International Competition and the Nation-State in Historical Perspective*. Cambridge, MA: Belknap, 2005.

Hosch, W. L. "Web 2.0." In *Encyclopedia Britannica*. September 8, 2017. https://www.britannica.com/topic/Web-20.

Hotson, Howard, and Miranda Lewis, eds. "The Bodleian Card Catalogue." In *Early Modern Letters Online*. emlo.bodleian.ox.ac.uk/w/8644.

Hotson, Howard, and Thomas Wallnig, eds. *Reassembling the Republic of Letters in the Digital Age: Standards, Systems, Scholarship*. Göttingen, Germany: University of Göttingen Press, 2019.

Houston, Alan, and Steven Pincus, eds. *A Nation Transformed: England after the Restoration*. Cambridge: Cambridge University Press, 2001.

Hufnagel, Silvia, Þórunn Sigurðardóttir, and Davíð Ólafsson, eds. *Paper Stories—Paper and Book History in Early Modern Europe*. Berlin: De Gruyter, 2023.

Hyde, J. Wilson. *The Post in Grant and Farm*. London: Adam & Charles Black, 1894.

Ignacio Tellechea Idìgoras, José. "Felipe II y los Carafa: Noticias y sucesos de una dificil relacìon." *Scriptorium Victoriense* 55, no. 1–2 (January 2008): 5–100.

Infelise, Mario. "Pallavicino, Ferrante." In *Dizionario Biografico degli Italiani (DBI)*, vol. 80 (2014). http://www.treccani.it/enciclopedia/ferrante-pallavicino_%28Dizionario-Biografico%29/.

Infelise, Mario. *Prima dei giornali: Alle origini della pubblica informazione.* Rome: Laterza, 2002.

Infelise, Mario. "Roman Avvisi: Information and Politics in the Seventeenth Century." In *Court and Politics in Papal Rome, 1492–1700.* Edited by Gianvittorio Signorotto and Maria Antonietta Visceglia, 212–228. Cambridge: Cambridge University Press, 2002.

Inì, Marina. "Materiality, Quarantine and Contagion in the Early Modern Mediterranean." *Social History of Medicine* 34, no. 4 (2021): 1161–1184.

Intra, Giovanni Battista. *Di Ippolito Capilupi e del suo tempo.* Milan: Tipografia Bortolotti dei Fratelli Rivara, 1893.

Iordanou, Ioanna. *Venice's Secret Service: Organising Intelligence in the Renaissance.* Oxford: Oxford University Press, 2019.

Jacobs, Margaret. *Strangers Nowhere in the World: The Rise of Cosmopolitanism in Early Modern Europe.* Philadelphia: University of Pennsylvania Press, 2006.

John, Richard R. *Spreading the News: The American Postal System from Franklin to Morse.* Cambridge, MA: Harvard University Press, 1998.

Johnson, James H. *Venice Incognito: Masks in the Serene Republic.* Berkeley: University of California Press, 2011.

Kahn, David. *The Codebreakers: The Story of Secret Writing.* New York: Scribner, 1996.

Kahn, David. *The Reader of Gentlemen's Mail: Herbert O. Yardley and the Birth of American Codebreaking.* New Haven, CT: Yale University Press, 2004.

Kalmus, Ludwig. *Weltgeschichte der Post mit Besonderer Berücksichtigung des Deutschen Sprachgebietes.* Vienna: A. F. Göth, 1937.

Kamen, Henry. *Empire: How Spain Became a World Power, 1492–1763.* New York: HarperCollins, 2003.

Kaplan, Benjamin. *Divided by Faith: Religious Conflict and the Practice of Toleration in Early Modern Europe.* Cambridge, MA: Harvard University Press, 2010.

Kaplan, Benjamin. *Reformation and the Practice of Toleration: Dutch Religious History in the Early Modern Era.* Leiden, Netherlands: Brill, 2019.

Kelser, Astrid, Jennifer K. Nelson, and Renae Satterley. "A Transcription and Translation of Sloane MS. 2131, Robert Ashley's (1561–1641) Vita: With Additional Biographical Details." *Electronic British Library Journal* (2021), Article 10. https://doi.org/10.23636/j7af-2714.

Kirshner, Julius, ed. *The Origins of the Italian State in Italy, 1300–1600.* Chicago: Chicago University Press, 1996.

Kittler, Juraj. "Capitalism and Communications: The Rise of Commercial Courier Networks in the Context of the Champagne Fairs." *Capitalism: A Journal of History and Economics* 4, no. 1 (Winter 2023): 109–152.

Kittler, Juraj. "Renaissance Postal Wars: A Fight over the Lucrative Mail Connection between Rome and Venice." In *Second Convegno Internazionale Storia Postale. Sguardi multidisciplinary, sguardi diacronici.* Edited by Bruno Crevato-Selvaggi and Raffaella Gerola. Prato, Italy: Istituto di studi storici postali Aldo Cechi, forthcoming.

Knight, Roger, and Martin Willcox. *Sustaining the Fleet: War, the British Navy and the Contractor State*. Woodbridge, UK: Boydell, 2010.

Koenigsberger, H. G., ed. *Politicians and Virtuosi: Essays in Early Modern History*. London: Hambledon, 1986.

Koh, Choon Hwee. "The Mystery of the Missing Horses: How to Uncover an Ottoman Shadow Economy." *Comparative Studies in Society and History* 64, no. 3 (2022): 576-610.

Kolb, Anne. *Transport und Nachrichtentransfer im römischen Reich*. Berlin: Akademie Verlag, 2000.

Kremer, Heinz. *Johann von den Birghden, 1582–1645: Kaiserlicher und königlich-schwedischer Postmeister zu Frankfurt am Main*. Bremen, Germany: Edition Lumière, 2005.

Kreuze, Wouter. "Temporal Philology: Reconstructing Patterns of Avvisi Creation and Distribution with Travel Times." *Magazén* 3, no. 1 (2022): 11-38.

Krischer, André J., and Hillard von Thiessen. "Diplomacy in a Global Early Modernity: The Ambiguity of Sovereignty." *International History Review* 41, no. 5 (2019): 1100-1107.

Krüger, Herbert. "Jörg Gails Augsburger's Raißbüchlin aus dem Jahre 1563." *Archiv für Deutsche Postgeschichte* 1, no. 11 (1969): 10-17.

Kustatscher, Erika. *Die Innsbrucker Linie der Thurn und Taxis: Die Post in Tirol und den Vorlanden (1490–1769)*. Innsbruck, Austria: Universitätsverlag Wagner, 2018.

Labalme, Patricia H., and Laura Sanguineti White, eds. *Venice, città excelentissima: Selections from the Renaissance Diaries of Marin Sanudo*. Translated by Linda L. Carroll. Baltimore: Johns Hopkins University Press, 2008.

Lamal, Nina, Jamie Cumby, and Helmer J. Helmers, eds. *Print and Power in Early Modern Europe (1500–1800)*. Leiden, Netherlands: Brill, 2020.

Landolt, Oliver. "Mobilität und Verkehr im europäischen Spätmittelalter. Mit besonderer Berücksichtigung der Verkehrspolitik innerhalb der Eidgenossenschaft." *Historische Zeitschrift* 40 (2006): 489-510.

Lastrucci, Anna Maria, ed. *La raccolta tassiana della Biblioteca civica 'A. Mai' di Bergamo*. Bergamo, Italy: Banca Piccolo Credito, 1960.

Laven, Peter. "Banditry and Lawlessness in the Venetian Terraferma in the Late Cinquecento." In *Crime, Society, and the Law in Renaissance Italy*. Edited by Trevor Dean and Kate Lowe, 221-248. Cambridge: Cambridge University Press, 1994.

Lazzari, G., G. Colavizza, F. Bortoluzzi, et al. "A Digital Reconstruction of the 1630-1631 Large Plague Outbreak in Venice." *Nature: Scientific Reports* 10, no. 17849 (2020), https://doi.org/10.1038/s41598-020-74775-6.

Lewis, Charlton T., and Charles Short. *A Latin Dictionary*. Oxford: Clarendon, 1879.

Linnarsson, Magnus. "The Development of the Swedish Post Office, c. 1600-1721." In *Connecting the Baltic Area: The Swedish Postal System in the Seventeenth Century*. Edited by Heiko Droste, 25-48. Stockholm: Södertörns högskola, 2011.

Lopez, Robert. *Medieval Trade in the Mediterranean World*. New York: Norton, 1967.

Lorandini, Cinzia. "Looking beyond the Buddenbrooks Syndrome: The Salvadori Firm of Trento, 1660s-1880s." *Business History* 57 (2015): 1005-1019.

Lundgren, Britta. "'Det äro många postmästaränkor som sitta vid tjänsterna efter männen . . .' om postmästaränkor på 1600-talet." *Historisk tidskrift* 107, no. 1 (1987): 23-34.

MacKenny, Richard. *Venice as the Polity of Mercy: Guilds, Confraternities, and the Social Order, c. 1250–c. 1650.* Toronto: University of Toronto Press, 2019.

Malanima, Paolo. *L'economia italiana: Dalla crescita medievale alla crescita contemporanea.* Bologna, Italy: Società editrice il Mulino, 2002.

Malcolm, Noel. *Reason of State, Propaganda, and the Thirty Years' War.* Oxford: Oxford University Press, 2007.

Mancini, Albert N. "Intorno alle traduzioni in inglese di opere di Ferrante Pallavicino: 'Il corriero svaligiato/The Post-boy rob'd of his mail.'" *Italica* 88, no. 3 (Autumn 2011): 465-482.

Marcus, Hannah. *Forbidden Knowledge: Medicine, Science, and Censorship in Early Modern Italy.* Chicago: University of Chicago Press, 2020.

Marshall, Alan. *Intelligence and Espionage in the Reign of Charles II, 1660–1685.* Cambridge: Cambridge University Press, 2003.

Maselli, Domenico. *Saggi di storia ereticale lombarda al tempo di S. Carlo.* Naples: Società Editrice Napoletana, 1979.

Masiá, María José Bertomeu. "Documenti su Juan de Tassis a Simancas." In *I Tasso e le poste.* Edited by Tarcisio Bottani, 255-262. Bergamo, Italy: Corponove, 2012.

Masiá, María José Bertomeu, ed. *La guerra secreta de Carlos V contra el Papa—La cuestión de Parma y Piacenza en la correspondencia del cardenal Granvela.* Valencia, Spain: Publicacions de la Universitat de València, 2009.

Mattingly, Garrett. *Renaissance Diplomacy.* London: Jonathan Cape, 1955.

Mazohl-Wallnig, Brigitte. "Österreichisch-italienische Postgeschichte im 18. und 19. Jahrhundert. Werkstattbericht." *Jahrbuch der Österreichischen Gesellschaft zur Erforschung des 18. Jahrhundert*s 7, no. 8 (1992/93): 7-25.

McLuhan, Marshall. *The Gutenberg Galaxy: The Making of Typographic Man.* Toronto: University of Toronto Press, 1962.

Medolago, Gabriele. "Cenni sulle origini della famiglia Tasso." In *Le poste dei Tasso: Da Cornello all'Europa.* Edited by Tarcisio Bottani, 9-19. Bergamo, Italy: Corponove, 2021.

Medolago, Gabriele. "Villa Celadini e le dimore tassiane in Bergamo: Primi risultati di una ricerca." In *I Tasso e le poste.* Edited by Tarcisio Bottani, 141-164. Bergamo, Italy: Corponove, 2012.

Meister, Aloys. *Die Geheimschrift im Dienste der päpstlichen Kurie von ihren Anfängen bis zum Ende des XVI. Jahrhunderts.* Paderborn, Germany: F. Schöningh, 1906.

Melillo, Enrico. *Le poste italiane nel medioevo.* Rome: Desclée, Lefebvre e C. Editori, 1904.

Melis, Federigo. *Aspetti della vita economica medievale: Studi nell'Archivio Datini di Prato.* Florence: Leo S. Olschki, 1962.

Merlin-Kajman, Hélène. "'Privé' and 'Particulier' (and Other Words) in Seventeenth-Century France." In *Early Modern Privacy: Sources and Approaches.* Edited by Michael Green, Lars Cyril Nørgaard, and Mette Birkedal Bruun, 79-104. Leiden, Netherlands: Brill, 2022.

Meserve, Margaret. *Papal Bull: Print, Politics, and Propaganda in Renaissance Rome.* Baltimore: Johns Hopkins University Press, 2021.

Meyer, Karl Friedrich. *Disinfected Mail.* Holton, KS: Gossip Print, 1962.

Midura, Rachel. "Italian Messengers and Couriers." In *Routledge Resources Online: The Renaissance World.* June 18, 2023. https://doi.org/10.4324/9780367347093-RERW103-1.

Midura, Rachel. "Itinerating Europe: Early Modern Spatial Networks in Printed Itineraries, 1545–1700." *Journal of Social History* 54, no. 4 (2021): 1545–1700.

Midura, Rachel. "Policing in Print: Social Control in Spanish and Borromean Milan (1535–1584)." In *Print and Power in Early Modern Europe (1500–1800).* Edited by Helmer Helmers, Nina Lamal, and Jamie Cumby, 21–46. Leiden, Netherlands: Brill, 2021.

Midura, Rachel. "Publishing the Baroque Post: The Postal Itinerary and the Mail-bag Novel." In *The Renaissance of Letters: Knowledge and Community in Italy, 1300–1650.* Edited by Paula Findlen and Suzanne Sutherland, 256–271. New York: Routledge, 2020.

Midura, Rachel. "'They Hide from Me, Like the Devil from the Cross': Transalpine Postal Routes as Intelligence Work, 1555–1645." *History: The Journal of the Historical Association* 108, no. 381 (2023): 303–327.

Migliavacca, Giorgio. "The Globetrotting Scarselle: The Italian Merchant Mail of the 1200s and 1300s." *Fil-Italia* 40, no. 4 (Autumn 2014): 206–207.

Migliavacca, Giorgio, and Tarcisio Bottani. *Simone Tasso e le poste di Milano nel Rinascimento.* Bergamo, Italy: Museo dei Tasso e della Storia Postale and Corponove, 2007.

Miller, Peter. *Peiresc's Mediterranean World.* Cambridge, MA: Harvard University Press, 2015.

Milstein, Joanna. *The Gondi Family: Strategy and Survival in Early Modern France.* New York: Routledge, 2016.

Minetti, Alberto. "Efficiency of Equine Express Postal Systems." *Nature: Brief Communications* 426, no. 6968 (2003): 785–786.

Mishra, Rupali. *A Business of State: Commerce, Politics, and the Birth of the East Indian Company.* Cambridge, MA: Harvard University Press, 2018.

Molinari, Gianni. "Villa Celadina, aspetti descrittivi." In *I Tasso e le poste.* Edited by Tarcisio Bottani, 135–140. Bergamo, Italy: Corponove, 2012.

Motta, Emilio. "Un regolamente postale milanese del 1535–1536." *Archivio Storico Lombardo* 33, no. 10 (1906): 424–428.

Muir, Edward. "Italy in the No Longer Forgotten Centuries." *I Tatti Studies in the Italian Renaissance* 16, no. 1/2 (2013): 5–11.

Muir, Edward. *The Culture Wars of the Late Renaissance: Skeptics, Libertines and Opera.* Cambridge, MA: Harvard University Press, 2007.

Murillo, Raphael Patrick. "Disciplining Empire: The Visita under the Spanish Hapsburgs, 1516–1700." PhD diss., University of California, Berkeley, 2018.

Nechushtai, Efrat. "Making Messages Private: The Formation of Postal Privacy and Its Relevance for Digital Surveillance." *Information & Culture: A Journal of History* 54, no. 2 (2019): 133–158.

Nores, Pietro. "Storia della guerra degli spagnoli contro Papa Paolo IV." *Archivio Storico italiano* 12 (1847): 1–302.

Occhi, Katia. "Exploiting the Alps: Wood Supplies and Waterways in Early Modern Europe." *Annali dell'Istituto storico italo-germanico in Trento* 46, no. 2 (2020): 33–67.

O'Neill, Lindsay. *The Opened Letter: Networking in the Early Modern British World.* Philadelphia: University of Pennsylvania Press, 2015.

Osiander, Andreas. "Sovereignty, International Relations, and the Westphalian Myth." *International Organization* 55, no. 2 (Spring 2001): 251–287.

Oster, Uwe A. *Wege über die Alpen: Von der Frühzeit bis heute.* Darmstadt, Germany: Primus, 2006.

Pal, Maïa. "Early Modern Extraterritoriality, Diplomacy, and the Transition to Capitalism." In *The Extraterritoriality of Law: History, Theory, Politics.* Edited by Daniel S. Margolies, Umut Özsu, Maïa Pal, and Ntina Tzouvala, 69–86. London: Routledge, 2019.

Parker, Geoffrey. *Emperor: A New Life of Charles V.* New Haven, CT: Yale University Press, 2019.

Parker, Geoffrey. *Europe in Crisis: 1598–1648.* Oxford: Blackwell, 2001.

Parker, Geoffrey. *Global Crisis: War, Climate Change and Catastrophe in the Seventeenth Century.* New Haven, CT: Yale University Press, 2017.

Parker, Geoffrey. *Imprudent King: A New Life of Philip II.* New Haven, CT: Yale University Press, 2014.

Parker, Geoffrey. *The Army of Flanders and the Spanish Road.* Cambridge: Cambridge University Press, 2004.

Parker, Geoffrey. *The Grand Strategy of Philip II.* New Haven, CT: Yale University Press, 1998.

Parker, Geoffrey. *The Thirty Years' War.* New York: Military Heritage, 1988.

Parrott, David. *The Business of War: Military Enterprise and Military Revolution in Early Modern Europe.* Cambridge: Cambridge University Press, 2012.

Partner, Peter. *Renaissance Rome, 1500–1559: A Portrait of a Society.* Berkeley: University of California Press, 1976.

Perez Cuenca, Isabel. "Otras noticias para la reconstrucción biográfica del Conde de Villamediana." In *Actas del Congreso de la Asociación Internacional Siglo de Oro.* Edited by María Cruz Gracía de Enterría and Alicia Cordón Mesa, 1211-1222. Alcalá de Henares, Spain: Universidad de Alcalá de Henares, 1996.

Pettegree, Andrew. *Reformation and the Culture of Persuasion.* Cambridge: Cambridge University Press, 2005.

Pettegree, Andrew. *The Invention of News: How the World Came to Know about Itself.* New Haven, CT: Yale University Press, 2014.

Piendl, Max. *Beiträge zur Geschichte Kunst und Kulturpflege im Hause Thurn und Taxis.* Kallmunz, Germany: Lassleben, 1978.

Piendl, Max. *Wandteppiche des Hauses Thurn und Taxis.* Munich: Hirmer, 1967.

Pirillo, Diego. *The Refugee-Diplomat: Venice, England, and the Reformation.* Ithaca, NY: Cornell University Press, 2018.

Polčák, Radim, and Dan Jerker B. Svantesson. *Information Sovereignty.* Cheltenham: Edward Elgar, 2017.

Polig, Matthias. "'Le maître de cette poste est notre plus grand ennemi': Postal Service and Espionage during the War of Spanish Succession." In *Spies, Espionage, and Secret Diplomacy in the Early Modern Period*. Edited by Guido Braun and Susanne Lachenicht, 105-123. Stuttgart: Kohlhammer, 2021.

Preto, Paolo. *I servizi segreti di Venezia*. Milan: Saggiatore, 1994.

Puff, Helmut. "Belief in the Reformation Era: Reflections on the State of Confessionalization." *Central European History* 51, no. 1 (2018): 46-52.

Purdon, James. "Secret Agents, Official Secrets: Joseph Conrad and the Security of the Mail." *Review of English Studies* 65, no. 269 (April 2014): 302-320.

Queller, Donald. *The Office of Ambassador*. Princeton, NJ: Princeton University Press, 1967.

Raymond, Joad, and Noah Moxham, eds. *News Networks in Early Modern Europe*. Leiden, Netherlands: Brill, 2016.

Rea, Fernando. *Le poste a Bergamo*. Bergamo, Italy: Società Editrice Bergamasca, 1976.

Real Academia Española: Diccionario de la lengua española. 23rd edition, version 23.7 (Online). https://del.rae.es/mano?m=form&m=form&wq=mano.

Reinert, Sophus. *The Academy of Fisticuffs: Political Economy and Commercial Society in Enlightenment Italy*. Cambridge, MA: Harvard University Press, 2018.

Rigobon, Pietro. *Di Nicolò e Francesco Donà: Veneziane del settecento e dei loro studi storici e politici*. Venice: Istituto Veneto di Arti Grafiche, 1910.

Robinson, Howard. *The British Post Office: A History*. Princeton, NJ: Princeton University Press, 1948.

Rodríguez-Salgado, Mia. *The Changing Face of Empire: Charles V, Philip II, and Habsburg Authority, 1551-1559*. Cambridge: Cambridge University Press, 1988.

Romano, Dennis. *Housecraft and Statecraft: Domestic Service in Renaissance Venice*. Baltimore: Johns Hopkins University Press, 1996.

Rose, Colin. *Renaissance of Violence: Homicide in Early Modern Italy*. Cambridge: Cambridge University Press, 2019.

Rothstein, Marian. "What Lies between the Public and the Secret?" In *Early Modern Privacy*. Edited by Michael Green, Lars Cyril Nørgaard, and Mette Birkedal Bruun, 423-437. Leiden, Netherlands: Brill, 2022.

Rott, Édouard. *Henri IV: Les Suisses et la haute Italie, la lutte pour les Alpes (1598-1610)*. Paris: E. Plon, 1882.

Rübsam, Joseph. "Ein internationale Postvertrag aus dem Jahre 1660." *Union Postale* 20 (1895): 146-156.

Rübsam, Joseph. *Johann Baptista von Taxis, ein Staatsmann und Militär unter Philipp II. und Philipp III Nebst einem Exkurs Aus der Urzeit der Taxis'schen Posten, 1505-1520*. Freiburg, Germany: Herder, 1889.

Rübsam, Joseph. "Postavisi und Postkonto aus den Jahren 1599 bis 1624." *Deutsche Geschichtsblätter* 7, no. 7 (1906): 8-19.

Rübsam, Joseph. "Taxis, Anton von." 1894. In *Allgemeine Deutsche Biographie (ADB)* 37. https://www.deutsche-biographie.de/pnd138592489.html#adbcontent.

Rübsam, Joseph. "Taxis, Octavio von." 1894. In *Allgemeine Deutsche Biographie (ADB)* 37. https://www.deutsche-biographie.de/pnd130008877.html#adbcontent.

Ruggiero, Guido. *Violence in Early Renaissance Venice*. New Brunswick, NJ: Rutgers University Press, 1980.
Rule, John, and Ben Trotter. *A World of Paper: Louis XIV, Colbert de Torcy, and the Rise of the Information State*. Montreal, Canada: McGill-Queen's University Press, 2014.
Safley, Thomas Max. *Family Firms and Merchant Capitalism in Early Modern Europe*. New York: Routledge, 2020.
Salierno, Vito. "Il 'Gabinetto nero' della Milano del settecento: Censura, delazioni, spionaggio." *La Martinella di Milano* 28, no. 5-6 (1974): 174-178.
Salzberg, Rosa. *The Renaissance on the Road: Mobility, Migration and Cultural Exchange*. Cambridge: Cambridge University Press, 2023.
Salzberg, Rosa, and Paul Nelles. "Movement and Mobility in the Early Modern World: An Introduction." In *Connected Mobilities in the Early Modern World: The Practice and Experience of Movement*. Edited by Rosa Salzberg and Paul Nelles, 7-38. Amsterdam: Amsterdam University Press, 2023.
Santoro, Caterina. *Gli offici del Comune di Milano e del dominio visconteo sforzesco (1216–1515)*. Milan: A. Giuffrè, 1968.
Sardella, Pierre. *Nouvelles et spéculation à Venise au début du XVI siècle*. Paris: Libraire Armand Colin, 1948.
Schiera, Pierangelo. "Legitimacy, Discipline, and Institutions: Three Necessary Conditions for the Birth of the Modern State." In *The Origins of the State in Italy, 1300–1600*. Edited by Julius Kirshner, 11-33. Chicago: University of Chicago Press, 1996.
Schilling, Heinz. "Confessional Europe." In *Handbook of European History 1400–1600: Late Middle Ages, Renaissance, and Reformation, vol. 2: Visions, Programs, and Outcomes*. Edited by Thomas A. Brady Jr., Heiko A. Oberman, and James D. Tracy, 641-681. Grand Rapids, MI: William B. Eerdmans, 1995.
Schnekenburger, Gudrun. *Über die Alpen: Menschen, Wege, Waren*. Stuttgart: Archäologisches Landesmuseum Baden-Württemberg, 2002.
Schobesberger, Nikolaus. "Mapping the *Fuggerzeitungen*: The Geographical Issues of an Information Network." In *News Networks*. Edited by Joad Raymond and Noah Moxham, 216-240. Leiden, Netherlands: Brill, 2016.
Schobesberger, Nikolaus, Paul Arblaster, Mario Infelise, et al. "European Postal Networks." In *News Networks*. Edited by Joad Raymond and Noah Moxham, 19-63. Leiden, Netherlands: Brill, 2016.
Scholz, Luca. *Borders and Freedom of Movement in the Holy Roman Empire*. Oxford: Oxford University Press, 2020.
Schwerhoff, Gerd. "Hexenverfolgung in einer frühneuzeitlichen Großstadt—das Beispiel der Reichsstadt Köln." In *Hexenverfolgung im Rheinland Ergebnisse neuerer Lokal- und Regionalstudien*. Edited by Thomas Becker and Stephan Lennartz, 13-56. Bergisch Gladbach, Germany: Thomas-Morus-Akademie Bensberg, 1996.
Scribner, Robert W. *For the Sake of Simple Folk: Popular Propaganda for the German Reformation*. Oxford: Oxford University Press, 1994.
Segal, Adam. "Bridging the Cyberspace Gap: Washington and Silicon Valley." *Prism* 7, no. 2 (2017): 66-77.
Sella, Domenico. *Salari e lavoro nell'edilizia lombarda durante il secolo XVII*. Pavia, Italy: Fusi, 1968.

Sellers Garcia, Sylvia. *Distance and Documents at the Spanish Empire's Periphery.* Stanford, CA: Stanford University Press, 2014.
Senatore, Francesco. *Uno mundo de carta: Forme e strutture della diplomazia Sforzesca.* Naples: Liguori, 1999.
Serra, Armando. "Corrieri e postieri sull'itinerario Venezia-Rome nel Cinquecento e dopo." *Archivio per la storia postale* 3, no. 7-9 (January-December 2001): 5-36.
Serra, Armando. "'Monopolio naturale': Di autori postali nella produzione di guide italiane d'Europa, fonti storico-postali tra cinque e ottocento." *Archivio per la storia postale* 5, no. 14-15 (2003): 14-15.
Sharpe, Kevin. "Thomas Witherings and the Reform of the Foreign Posts, 1632-40." *Historical Research* 57, no. 136 (November 1984): 149-164.
Shore, Chris, and Susan Wright. "Audit Culture Revisited." *Current Anthropology* 56, no. 3 (June 2015): 421-444.
Signorotto, Gianvittorio. "Stabilità politica e trame antispagnole nella Milano del Seicento." In *Complots et conjurations dans l'Europe moderne.* Edited by Yves-Marie Bercé and Elena Fasano Guarini, 721-745. Rome: École française de Rome, 1996.
Simmel, Georg. "The Sociology of Secrecy and of Secret Societies." *American Journal of Sociology* 11, no. 4 (1906): 441-498.
Snyder, Jon R. *Dissimulation and the Culture of Secrecy in Early Modern Europe.* Berkeley: University of California Press, 2012.
Soll, Jacob. "From Note-Taking to Data Banks: Personal and Institutional Information Management in Early Modern Europe." *Intellectual History Review* 20, no. 3 (2010): 355-375.
Stengel, Richard. *Information Wars: How We Lost the Global Battle against Disinformation and What We Can Do about It.* New York: Atlantic Monthly, 2019.
Stevens, Kevin. "New Light on Andrea Calvo and the Book Trade in Sixteenth-Century Milan." *La Bibliofilia* 103, no. 1 (2001): 48-49.
Stevens, Kevin. "Printers, Publishers, and Booksellers in Counter-Reformation Milan: A Documentary Study." PhD diss., University of Wisconsin, 1992.
Stix, Franz. "Zur Geschichte und Organisation der Wiener Geheimen Ziffernkanzlei." *Institut für österreichische Geschichtsforschung, Mitteilungen* 51 (1937): 131-160.
Taxis-Bordogna, Lamoral, and Erhard Riedel. *Zur Geschichte der Freiherren un Graffen Taxis-Bordogna-Valnigra und ihrer Obrist-Erbpostämter zu Bozen, Trient und an der Etsch.* Innsbruck, Austria: Wagner, 1955.
Terpstra, Nicholas. *Religious Refugees in the Early Modern World: An Alternative History of the Reformation.* Cambridge: Cambridge University Press, 2015.
Tessier, Alexander. *La poste, servante et actrice des relations internationaux (XVIe-XIXe siècle).* Brussels: Peter Lang, 2016.
Tiraboschi, Giampiero. "Lucca et Nicolo Comenduni: I corrier della magnifica Comunità di Bergamo nel Cinquecento." In *Ateneo Scienze, Lettere ed Arti di Bergamo.* 2020. https://ateneobergamo.it/lucca-et-nicolo-comenduni-2/.
Trivellato, Francesca. *The Familiarity of Strangers: The Sephardic Diaspora, Livorno, and Cross-Cultural Trade in the Early Modern Period.* New Haven, CT: Yale University Press, 2009.

Trivellato, Francesca. *The Promise and Peril of Credit: What a Forgotten Legend about Jews and Finance Tells Us about the Making of European Commercial Society.* Princeton, NJ: Princeton University Press, 2019.
Vaillé, Eugène. *Histoire generale des postes françaises.* 6 vols. Paris: Presses universitaires de France, 1949.
van der Linden, James. "The Thurn und Taxis Postal Administration in the Spanish Netherlands from 1492 to 1713: A Postal Historical Survey." In *I Tasso le poste d'Europa.* Edited by Tarcisio Bottani, 289–316. Bergamo, Italy: Corponove, 2012.
Verga, Ettore. *La Camera dei mercanti di Milano nei secoli passati.* Milan: Allegretti, 1914.
Verhoeven, Gerrit. "Wading through the Mire: Mobility on the Grand Tour." In *Connected Mobilities in the Early Modern World: The Practice and Experience of Movement.* Edited by Rosa Salzberg and Paul Nelles, 63–85. Amsterdam: Amsterdam University Press, 2023.
Vincent, David. *The Culture of Secrecy: Britain 1832–1998.* Oxford: Oxford University Press, 1998.
Virilio, Paul. *Speed and Politics: An Essay on Dromology.* Translated by Mark Polizzotti. Cambridge, MA: MIT Press, 2006.
Visceglia, Maria Antonietta. "'Farsi imperiale': Faide familiari e identità politiche a Roma nel primo Cinquecento." In *L'Italia di Carlo V: Guerra, religione e politica nel primo Cinquecento.* Edited by Francesca Cantù and Maria Antonietta Visceglia, 477–508. Rome: Viella, 2003.
Visceglia, Maria Antonietta. *Roma papale e Spagna: Diplomatici, nobili e religiosi tra due corti.* Rome: Bulzoni, 2010.
Vollmeier, Paolo. *Bolli prefilatelici di Milano dalle origini al 1850.* Padua, Italy: A. Ausilio, 1976.
Vollmeier, Paolo. *Repubblica di Venezia: Catalogo documentato (con storia postale).* Castagnola, Switzerland: Alfaprint, 2003.
Wallerstein, Immanuel Maurice. *The Essential Wallerstein.* New York: New Press, 2000.
"Wall Tapestry—The Legend of Our Lady of the Sablon." Brussels City Museum. http://www.brusselscitymuseum.brussels/documents/view/wall-tapestry-the-legend-of-our-lady-of-the-sablonpdf?id=157.
Walpole, S., ed. *A History of England.* London: Longmans, 1879–1886.
Weber, Max. *Economy and Society: A New Translation.* Translated by Keith Tribe. Cambridge, MA: Harvard University Press, 2019.
Weil, Rachel. *A Plague of Informers: Conspiracy and Political Trust in William III's England.* New Haven, CT: Yale University Press, 2014.
Williams, Megan. "The Perils of the Post Road: Diplomats, Diplomatic Couriers, and the Informational Fabric of Early Modern Europe." In *Information and Power in History: Towards a Global Approach.* Edited by Ida Nijenhuis, M. van Faasen, Ronal Sluijter, Joris Gijsenbergh, and Wim de Jong, 105–121. Abingdon: Routledge, 2020.
Wolpert, Hermann. *Schrifttum über das Deutsche Postwesen.* Munich: Ges. zur Erforschung der Postgeschichte in Bayern, 1937.
Yardley, Herbert O. *America's Black Chamber.* New York: Bobbs-Merrill, 1931.

Zegart, Amy. *Spies, Lies, and Algorithms: The History and Future of American Intelligence*. Princeton, NJ: Princeton University Press, 2022.

Zenobi, Luca. *Borders and the Politics of Space in Late Medieval Italy: Milan, Venice, and Their Territories*. Oxford: Oxford University Press, 2023.

Zwierlein, Cornel. *Discorso und Lex Dei: Die Entstehung neuer Denkrahmen im 16. Jahrhundert und die Wahrnehmung der französischen Religionskriege in Italien und Deutschland*. Göttingen, Germany: Vandenhoeck & Ruprecht, 2006.

Index

Page numbers in italics refer to figures.

Acquapendente, 157
Adrian VI (Pope), 51
Akkerman, Nadine, 194
Albani, Angelica, 142
ambassadors, 63, 66–67, 79, 209
Ancona, 69
Antelmi, Bonifacio, 107
Appiano, Ercole, 110–11
artistic endeavors, Tassis sponsorship of, *27*
audit cultures, 128, 152

Balbi, Giovanni Battista, 178–79
bandits/banditry, 77–79, 82–84, 126, 142, 145, 158, 206
bankruptcy, 14
Barnardiston, Nathanial, 274n16
Battista, 37
Behringer, Wolfgang, 9
Belgium, 26
Bellone, Francesco, 133
Bentham, Jeremy, 181, 213
Benzoni family, 22
Benzoni, Zuanne (Giovanni), 84
Bergamaschi, 31–32, 38, 91–92, 208
Bergamaschi couriers, 9, 20–22, 24, 37, 94–95
Bergamaschi diaspora, 16, 89, 94–95
Bergamasco, 9, 21–22
Bergamo (Lombardy), 7, 9, 19, 22, 24, 86, 190
Bernardello, 33
Bertoldo, Giuseppe, 83
Biblioteca Civica Angelo Mai (Bergamo), 190
Birghden, Johann von den, 147–48, 150–51, 182, 186, 194, 264n97, 264n99
Bishop, Henry, 185, 190
Bishop of Paris, 48
Bishop, William, 175

black chambers, 16–18, 183, 194–95, 197, 202, 204, 213
Bollino, 91, 107, 111
Bonamingo, Francesco (d. 1492), 232n114
Bonelli, Camerlengo Michele, 67–68, 70
Borro, Pietro Martire, 40
Borromeo, Charles, 90
Bors family, 276n39
Boyes-Watson, Carolyn, 131
Bozola, Giovanni Battista, 161
Brenner Pass, xviii, 140, *191*, 260n46
Breton, Nicholas, 198–200
bribes, 53, 71, 139
Brienne trove, 193
Britain. *See* England
Brussels (Belgium), Tassis couriers, 26
Buddenbrooks Syndrome, 115
Bundespost, 5
Burattino's Directions, 169, 189
Burckhardt, Jacob, 6
bureaucracy, 1, 5–6, 10, 13, 17, 152, 175
bureaucratization, 13, 211
Burgundy, 26, 35
Burman, Pieter, 173

Calepio, Giuseppe, 263n82
Camerata Cornello, 21–22
Campbell-Smith, Duncan, 183
Cantelli, Giacomo, 190–91
Capelleto, 42
Capilupi, Hippolito, 60, 238–39n49
Caracciolo, Marino, 41
Carafa, Carlo, 48
Carafa family, 49, 51, 54–55, 62–63, 212
Caravaggio, Giuseppe de, 138
Carne, Edward, 62
carozzeri, 94
Carrier's Cosmography (Taylor), 157
Cattaneo family, 252n56

INDEX

cavalcata, 107
cavallari, 11, 32–33, 42, 94, 96, 207, 248n93
chapel of San Giovanni Elemosinario, 22–23
Charles II (England), 186
Charles V (Habsburg), 8–9, 28–29, 31, 49, 68, 102, 104, 231n109
Charles VI (Habsburg), 192
Charles VIII (France), 28
Chifflet, Jules, 187, *188*, 190, 275n22
Christina (Queen), 275–76n30
Clement VII (Pope), 51
clowns, 19
coaches, 94, 154–55, 167–68, 171–72, 179, 266
    See also stagecoaches
Codogno, Ottavio, 1–2, 113, 116, 120–23, 134, 136, 139, 213
    duties of, 2–3, 113, 119–20, 124, 233n124
    and Lucina Cattanea Tassis, 103, 112–13, 137
    Pauluzzi on, 118–19
Codogno's post office, 1612 audit, 14
cokini, 7
Colonna family, 33, 48–49
commercial revolution, and the early modern post office, 10
commercialization, 13
communes, 8
communications, importance of, 4
communications infrastructure, 206
communications monopolies, 49–50, 63–64, 71, 93, 95, 98, 175–76, 207
communications technologies, role of, 4
Compendium of the Posts (Codogno), 2, 123, 159
Congress of Vienna (1814–1815), 184
conspiracies, 56, 92
contagion theory, 86
Contractor States, 100
contracts, top-down nature of, 99
contrascrittori, 40
corriero maggiore, 2, 21, 34, 42–43, 94, 125, 155, 209, 232n114
    Fioravante's campaign to become, 43
    responsibilities of, 40–41
    See also postmaster generals
corruption, 98, 207
    Spanish investigations of, 117, 122, 124, 134, 136–38, 254–55n82
    vs. patronage, 117

Coryate, Thomas, 158
Council of Trent (1545–1563), 45
Counter-Reformation era, 50, 90–91
Courier in the Distance (Mitelli), 11, *12*, 13
The Courier Waylaid (Il corriero svaligiato) (Pallavicino), 198–201
couriers, 2, 77, 79, 108, 168, 172–73, 207
    ancient, 5, 172–73
    arrests of, 66
    attacks on (*svaligiamento*), 77, 79, *80*, 82–85, 142, 144–45, 168, 242n19
    extraordinaries, 100, 134
    and extraterritoriality, 15, 49, 180–81
    as fifth column, 76, 91–92
    and Fioravante, 44
    Florentine, 8
    and fraud, 32
    German, *78*
    Haro's interviews with, 137
    influence of, 37
    jurisdictional disputes, 69
    land vs. sea routes, 88–89, 274n13
    local carriers, 178
    long-distance, 133
    and Milan, 24
    "ordinaries," 15, 68, 100
    papal interference with, 53–54
    and plagues, 86–89
    relays of, 40
    rider receipts, 143, *144*
    as smugglers, 90–91
    Spanish, 274n13
    trade organizations of, 11
    and treaties, 32
    in Venice, 22–23
    wages, 132–33, *135*, 138
    and weapons, 85
    See also specific subcategories or companies of
Cremona, *xviii*, 79, *80*, 81, 84, 93–94, 110, 247n83
cryptography, 49–50, 57, *58*, 183, 272n95
    tools for, 58–59
cursores, 7
cursus publicus, 3
Curzola, Giacomo Bandino da, 54–55
customer service, 170

d'Adda brothers, 110
dal Monte, Francesco, 138
Datini, Francesco, 8
Datini, Margherita, 8

INDEX

de Acevedo, Enríquez, 103, 117–18, 120–24, 255n83, 255n84, 255n85
de la Vega, Garcilaso, 48, 56, 58–59, 61, 64
de Leeuw, Karl, 195
de Leyva, Antonio, 231n109, 232n113
de Padilla, Sancho, 106
de Rabutin-Chantal, Marie, 195
de Rye von Taxis, Alexandrine, 89–90, 174, 185–88, 193–94, 275n24
de Sancti family, 232n114
de Soria, Lope, 36
decentralization, 29
decryption, 58–59, 60–61
Degli avanzi delle poste (1677), 199
del Vantaggio, Bartolomeo, 51
di Rossi, Giovanni Angelo, 133
Dialogue on the Two Chief World Systems (Galileo Galilei), 88
Different Posts of Italy, Germany, Spain, and France, 161
diligences, 169, 177, 210
diplomatic correspondence, 74, 158
  encryption of, 57, 58–59, 60–61
diplomatic envoys, Tassis as, 35, 115
diplomatic extraterritoriality, 15, 49, 63, 71
diplomatic history, 102
diplomatic immunity, 51, 63
dispatch notes, 128–29, 140–42, 143, 146–47, 153, 192–93, 261n52
distrust, 212
Dockwra, William, 176
d'Orville, Jacques-Philippe, 173
double-entry bookkeeping, 132
Duke of Alba, 47, 57, 58–59, 61–62

Early Modern Letters Online catalogue, 141, 173
economics, based on households, 115
economies of scale, 109, 145, 148, 151, 172
Eleanora of Toledo, 65
Elys, Edmund, 175
England, 162
  London Penny Post, 176
  postal interference in, 195, 202
  postal regulations, 196
  Restoration, 186
  and the Tassis family, 35
  Tassis pamphlets, 185–86
English postal service, 9, 271n80
espionage, 43, 120, 148, 151, 194, 213, 277n51

The European Mercury, 162
Evelyn, John, 157
extraordinary/ordinary binaries, 100, 207

Fabretto, Geronimo, 83
Facchinetti, Giovanni Antonio (d. 1591), 67–69
Falconi brothers, 242n19
fanti, 7
Ferdinand I (Holy Roman Emperor), 63, 104
Ferdinand II (Habsburg), 147–48
Fioravante, Ludovico, 43–44, 209, 232n114
Flacchio, Engelbert, 187, 189
Florio's, John, 77
"flying" (*volante*), 8
fourteenth century, 7–8
France, 277n51
  and the Carafa family, 54
  and England, 195
  Fioravante in, 43
  and Paul IV, 48
  and Simone Tassis, 36–37
  and Spain, 54
  and Venice, 60
Frankfurt post office, 147
Franzese, 56
Fray, David, 150
Frederick III (Holy Roman Emperor), 24
free commerce, 174–75, 177–79, 207
Fregulia, Jeanette, 112
French postal service, 9
Frey, Linda, 49
Frey, Marsha, 49
Frizzell, William, 274n15
Fugger family, 32, 79, 111, 127
Furlan, Bartolomeo, 83
Furlan, Ortensio, 83
Furlani, Baldo, 83

Gail, Jörg, 161–62, 267n27
Galileo Galilei, 88
Gallarato, Dioniseo, 138
Gamba, Giovanni, 32
Gamba, Pellegrino, 52
Gamba, Zuan (Giovanni), 79
Genoa, 139
Genovese power, Spanish concerns about, 111–12
Gerbier, Balthazar, 193–94
German postal service. *See* Bundespost

INDEX

German Road (*Via Claudia Augusta*), 140, 145–46, 150–51, 194
Germany, and postal coaches, 169
Gherardi, Mattia (Matteo) (d. 1582), 50, 64–67, 69–72, 209
Giupponi, Benedetto "Zippone," 70
Giuseppino, 138–39
Goldoni, Carlo, 19
Gonzaga family, 33
Grand Tour, 156, 191
Granvelle, Antoine Perrenot de, 105
Gregory XIII (Pope), 71
Griego, Zuan (Giovanni), 230n90
Gritti, Andrea, 38
Gustavus Adolphus, 15, 150, 180

Habsburg dynasty, 9, 15–16, 20, 26, 28, 31, 49, 102
hackneymen, 155–56, 166–67, 169
Haro, Felipe de, 116–18, 124, 131, 137, 254n81
Harvey, Eliab, 274n16
"haste haste haste" (*cito cito cito*), 8
Heinsius, Nicolaas, 173
Henot family, 151
Henot, Hartger, 149
Henot, Jakob, 148–49, 263n82, 271–72n90
Henot, Katherine, 149
Henry II (France), 49
Henry IV (France), 121, 157
Herodotus, 5
Heylyn, Peter, 171–72
Hill, John, 175–76
Hill, Thomas, 274n16
historical study, letter subfields, 11
Holy Roman Empire, 9
horses, 26, 157–58, 168, 170–71, 265n11

Il postiglione (1666), 199
imperial system, development of, 34
information sovereignty, 50–51, 67–73, 71, 95
information wars, 14, 16, 21, 33, 50, 206
Innocent IX (Pope). *See* Fachinetti, Giovan Antonio (d. 1591)
inns, 82, 157–58, 170–71, 234n17
in Milan, 178
"Institution Proposed by the Couriers in Service to the Venetian Dominion of an Ordinary for Milan by Way of Mantua and Cremona," 106

intelligence, 11–12, 34, 41, 57, 151, 278n58
intelligencing, 20–21, 183, 203, 207, 211
and black chambers, 183, 195
modern, 213
and postmasters, 52, 56, 119, 151
secret intelligences, 76
and women, 121
international diplomacy, 184
international trade, and courier reliability/speed, 13
Internet, 211
Introduction to the Italian Tongue (Torriano), 161, 167
Istrian fiefdoms, 26, 31, 38
Italian Renaissance state, 6
Italian Road, 17, 99–100, *101*, 102, 108–9, 111, 124–25, 127–28, 136, 210
Italian Wars, 9, 16, 30–31, 33, 36, 40, 49, 76, 100, 208–9
Italy, 6–8, 17, 28
Itinerarium Galliae, 163
Itinerary of the Posts throughout Different Parts of the World (Stella), 161, *164–65*

Jacobs, Margaret, 228n59
journalism, 147

Kahn, David, 59

Landriano, Gerolamo, 133
language, evolution of, 157
"The Latest News from Italy" (*Ultima Nova ex Italia*), 35
Légende de Notre-Dame du Sablon: La statue de Notre-Dame est conduite à l'église du Sablon, 27
Les marques d'honneur de la maison de Tassis (Chifflet), 187, *188*, 190
letters, 176, 211
costs to send, 10, 69, 104, 175, 248n100, 250n30, 259n26
disinfection of, 86–88, 245n57
domestic, 196
in the *Early Modern Letters Online* catalogue, 141, 173
on the German Road, 140–41
growth in, 5
merchants', 93
privacy of, 181, 192–93, 196
private, 107, 109, 126–27, 175

self-censorship of, 195
state letters, 104, 175
taxes on, 174
Linnarsson, Magnus, 275–76n30
Liscati, Giovanni Giacomo, 85
L'Italia con le sue poste (Cantelli), 190–91
literacy, growth in, 5
Lomboni, Vergilio, 69
London Penny Post, 176
Longho, Domenico, di, 96
Longo, Angelo, 52
Louis XIII (France), 121
Lupis, Antonio, 201

Maffei family, 22
magister cursorum, 24
mail systems, 74–75, 96–97
mail thefts, 79
mailbag novels, 198–204
mailbags, 126–27
maps, xviii, 276n36
  commissioned by postal officials, 15
  courier costs, *135*
  Italian Road, *101*
  L'Italia con le sue poste (Cantelli), 190–91
  of postal couriers attacked, *80*
  postal maps, 190, *191*, 192, 276n39
  transalpine routes, *130*
Marcandato, Viano, 133
Margaret of Austria (Archduchess, d. 1530), 30, 38
Maria Theresa (Empress), 192
Mariano family, 133
Marioni, Piero Antonio, 123
Maroton, Louis, 35
marriages, 29, 35, 89, 141
Martinengo family, 90–91
Martinengo, Giovanni Battista, 83
Martinengo, Giovanni da, 90
Marvels of Rome, 266n22
Marzi, Ottaviano, 86–87
Masius, Andreas, 53–54, 62, 236n31
master of the posts, 26
Maximilian I (Holy Roman Emperor), 24, *27*, 28, 30
Mayr, Georg, 162
Mazzini, Giuseppe, 202
Medici, Alessandro de', 41
Medici, Cosimo de', 52, 65
Medici family, 33, 53
Medici, Lorenzo de', 8

Medici, Ottavio, 272n95
Memmingen-Rome mail route, 26
merchant courier cooperatives, 7–8, 127–28
merchants, letter-carrying privileges, 91
messengership, late Middle Ages, 7
Middle Ages, mail in, 5
Milan, 76, 86–87, 91, *101*, 231n94
  chamber of merchants, 91
  Duchy of, 23–24
  extradition agreements, 83
  and the Habsburgs, 38
  inns, 178, 265n10
  and the Italian Road, 100, 210
  laborers in, 40
  and postal carriages, 168–69
  postal routes from, 73
  postal system, 23, 40, 109, 112, 134, 138
  Spanish post office in, 93–94
  state archives, 1
  under the Austrians, 178
  and Venice, 36, 107
Milan-Genoa postal route, 136, 139–40
Milan-Venice postal service route, 17, 106–7, 134, 173
Miselli, Giuseppe, 177, 189
Mitelli, Giuseppe Maria, 11, *12*, 172–73
mobility infrastructure, 155
Mont-Cenis Pass, xviii
Montaigne, 158–59, 166, 170–71
Monte, Giacomo, 137
Morland, Samuel, 196
Moryson, Fynes, 158–59, 172

nation-building, and the postal service, 177–78
Navagero, Bernardo, 49, 53–54, 62–63, 66
The Necessary Posts (Turlano and Bozola), 161
Netherlands, 264n98
New Itinerary of the Posts of the World (Codogno), 2, 4, 13, 15, 100, 113, 115, 131, 140, 151, 153, 159, *160*, 189
New Travel Booklet (Witzenberger), 162
"news from Parnassus" genre, 200
newspapers, 11, 147–48, 151–52, 175, 205, 209–10
Nicholas, Edward, 274n16
nobility, postmasters/mistresses as, 182
nolesini, 94
nomenclators, 58–59, 61
Nores, Pietro, 60–61

312 INDEX

Notre Dame du Sablon (Brussels), 26, *27*
Nouveau, Jerôme, 277n51
nuncius, 7

Occhi, Katia, 30
Odonuj de Taxo, 24
office leasing (*arrendamiento*), 110–11, 137, 184, 207
official secrecy, 181, 183–84, 192–97, 196–97, 202, 204
Orlando Furioso (Ariosto), 163

Paceco, Carlo, 56
Paceco, Francesco, 64
Padilla, Sancho de, 92–93, 119–20, 151
Padua, 247n83
Pallavicino, Cesare, 138–39
Pallavicino, Ferrante, 15, 61, 63–64, 198–99, 201–2, 212, 279n70
Pallavicino, Sforza, 60
pamphlet wars, 76
pamphlets, 185–86
Panizone Sacco, Oliver, 110
Papal Index of Prohibited Books, 50
Papal States, 50, 61–65, 68, 70–71, 106
  See also Rome
papermaking, 7–8
paperwork, 1, 5–6
Paris Peace Conference (1919–1920), 184
Parker, Geoffrey, 248n3
particolari, 129, 136, 212
Paul III (Pope), 65
Paul IV (Pope), 48–49, 53, 61
Pauluzzi, Antonio, 118–20, 255n88, 256n102
Peace Conferences of Westphalia (1645–1648), 151, 156, 174, 184, 273–74n11
Peace of the Pyrenees (1659), 185
pedoni, 23, 94, 127
Perrenot de Granvelle, Antoine, 52, 254–55n82
Philip I (Holy Roman Empire), 26, 35
Philip II of Spain, 38, 49, 59, 104, 112, 126, 148
pilgrimage guidebooks, 161
Pius IV (Pope), 67
Pius V (Pope), 67–68, 71
plague hospitals, 86–88, 245n57
plagues, 85–90, 113, 123, 210, 245n57, 246n63
political economy, 172, 186

polizza di cambiatura, 171
popes
  state-building, 50, 64
portalettere, 23, 94, 96–97, 127
Porto, Piero da, 96
post-books, 155, 157–59, *160*, 161–63, *164–65*, 166, 198
The Post-Boy Robbed of His Bag (Gildon), 199
post houses, 154–55, 183
The Post of the World (Verstegan), 162
"Post Office Scandal" (1884), 202–4
post offices, 2, 13–18
postal accounting, 131
postal conferences, 182, 185
postal disputes, records of, 96–97
postal history, 4–5, 179, 207–8, 214
postal infrastructure, 155, 158–59, 166, 183, 206, 210
postal interference, 180–81, 183, 193–94, 196, 202
  and Ferdinando Tassis, 192–93
  as fictional plot, 199
  between France and England, 195
  Gustavus Adolphus on, 180
  See also black chambers; official secrecy; privacy; secrecy of correspondence
postal itineraries, 13, 152, 159, 161–63, 166, 169, 172, 198, 200
postal lieutenants, 116, 131, 166, 178
postal lodges, 183, 197
postal markings, 8
postal officials, 145, 155, 196–97, 203, 209–10
  as bureaucrats, 211
  changing roles of, 129
  depictions of, 12
  and foreign policy, 100, 102
  and knowledge/intelligence, 12
  as professionals, 131–32
  recordkeeping, 132
  restructuring postal services, 176–77
  as spies, 15
  and travel, 159
postal roads, 79, 81–82, *101*
postal routes, 7, *101*, *130*, 139–40, 145–46, 168, 175, 185, *191*, 206, 211, 267n27, 267n28
postal systems, 3, 16, 172, 204, 208, 214
  commercialization of, 127–28, 154
  costs of, 8, 40, 96, 109, 128, *135*, 138, 248n100, 251n39
  English, 9

INDEX

foundations of, 99
French, 9
imperial regulations for, 40
and inns, 82
Italian, 8
land vs. sea routes, 88–89, 274n13
language of, 7, 177
many faces of, 198
mercantile vs. government, 11
modern, 205
and newspapers, 11, 147–48, 209–10
ordinary, 106, 109
and postal officials, 209
private use of, 126–27, 129, 131, 136, 145, 153, 174, 184, 257n1
as public services, 156
recordkeeping requirements, 128–29, 132, 152–53
standardization of, 173
state, 11, 13–14, 16–18, 26, 70, 90
and state power, 16
and transparency, 173, 177
and trust, 13–14, 75
See also travel; travelers
postal treaties, 185
postal wars, 50, 65, 67, 72–73, 86, 89, 99, 106, 209
postavvisi, 146–47
A Poste with a Mad Packet of Letters (Breton), 198–200
postilions, 14, 155–56, 166–67, 170, 198
posting, 7, 154, 158–59
postmaster generals, 2, 14, 16, 44–45, 178, 184, 190
See also corriero maggiore
postmaster lieutenants, 2
postmasters, 13–15, 113, 125, 156, 182, 234n15
arrests of, 47–48, 50–51, 55–56, 64, 72
authority of, 40, 42, 45–46
as bureaucrats, 211
correspondence between, 129
and intelligence, 34
and intelligencing, 52, 56, 119, 151, 207, 278n63
and the Medicis, 53
office leasing, 110–11, 137, 184, 207
papal postmaster, 55
and politics, 210
and postal standardization, 173
as professionals, 132

roles of, 21, 31, 34, 44–45, 50, 116–17, 140
social status of, 41
staffs, 40–41
state, 76
title as, 103
and travelers, 158, 168, 172
and weapons, 85
postmistresses, 89–90, 103, 112, 114, 116, 182, 184, 186–87, 253n66, 254n77
Practical Travel (Vidari), 169
privacy, 12–13, 193, 196, 212–14, 276–77n42
private letter carriers, 74, 95
Privilegium Maius, 28
procacci, 23, 94, 96, 127, 247n84
Provveditori di Comun, 22, 42–44, 69, 174
public/private identities, 14
public/private separations, 3–4
public transportation, 154, 157, 169, 179
Purdon, James, 202

quarantines, 85–86
Quattrocavi, Mario, 120

recordkeeping, 128–29, 132, 142–43, 146, 152, 178
See also postal accounting
Regensburg, postmaster, 37
relay policy (*polizza di cambiatura*), 171
religion, and state-building, 75–76
Renausea, Maddalena, 29
revolution, term, 205–6
Rhineland-Palatinate region, postal stations in, 26
Rimini, 69
Roelans, Jacob, 275n22
Roman Road (*Roemerstrasse*), 140
Rome, 47–48, 50–51, 50–53, 65–66
See also Papal States
Rose, Colin, 79
Roseo, Mambrin, 60
Rossetto, 33
Route Booklet (Mayr), 162
Rübsam, Joseph, 146–47
Rudolf IV (Duke of Austria), 28

Sacco, Oliver Panizone, 110
Safley, Thomas, 14
St. Gotthard Pass, xviii
Salierno, Vito, 197
San Martino, Giovanni, 133

INDEX

Sanudo, Marin, 32–33, 36–37
Savoyard archives, 88
scarselle, 23, 76
"schools" (Venetian corporate form), 22
secrecy, 14, 49–50, 60, 118, 181, 212
secrecy of correspondence, 181–82, 184, 202–3
secrets of state (*arcana imperii*), 183
selle della posta, 168, 268–69n45
senders, defining, 10
Servant of Two Masters (Goldoni), 19
Sforza Dukes, 8, 31, 35, 38
Sharp, Samuel, 170, 270n67
signorie, 8
Silvestre, Vincenzo Busio, 71
Simonetti, Gironimo, 69
Sixtus V (Pope), 71, 73
Smith, Thomas, 175, 195
Smollet, Tobias, 170
smuggling, 90–91
Snyder, Jon, 60
social discipline, and post offices, 13–18
Sola scriptura, 75–76
Spain
 and France, 54
 and the Tassis family, 31, 34, *39*, 55
Spanish-Papal accord (1557), 62
spies, 32–33, 60, 87, 120, 213
Spinelli, Tomaso, 35
Spinola, Ambrosio, 111
Splügen Pass, xviii
staffetta, 40, 107, 109
stagecoaches, 13, 81, 154, 157, 159, 167, 177, 210
 See also coaches
state-building, 75
states, 75–76, 271–72n90
 archives, 206
 and the early modern post office, 10
 histories concerning, 6
 postal systems of, 11, 13–14, 16–18, 26, 70, 90, 126, 183, 192, 210
stato, 8
Stella, Cherubino, 161
Stevens, Kevin, 90
Stix, Franz, 277n51
Suardo, Luigi, 138
Suárez de Figueroa y Córdoba, Gomez III, 36
surveillance
 and communications monopolies, 93, 98
 of mailbags, 183–84
 and official secrecy, 181, 183–84, 192–97, 196–97, 204
 and post offices, 13–18, 116–17, 174, 197
 and secrecy of correspondence, 181
 of travel, 179
svaligiamento, 77, 79, *80*, 81–85, 142, 242n19
Swedish postal service, 271n80

tabellari, 7, 11
Tamaius, Franciscus, 61
Tassignano, Francesco, 41–42, 209
Tassis, Agostino (d. 1510), *25*, 30–31
Tassis, Allegra, 29
Tassis, Antonio (d. 1619), 29
Tassis, Antonio (d. 1574), 52
Tassis bank, 24, 28, 227n40
Tassis, Cristoforo (d. 1486), *25*, 29–31
Tassis, Davide (d. 1538), *25*, 30, 34, 104–5
Tassis, Domenico (d. 1538), *25*, 27
Tassis family, 3, 7–9, 20, 22, *25*, 76, 104, 115, 125, 157, 184, 187, 208–9
 artistic sponsorship, *27*, 209
 and Birghden, 194
 courier heraldry, 77
 genealogy of, 16, *25*, 157, 182–84, 187, *188*, 189–90
 and the Habsburgs, 24, 30–31
 and information wars, 21
 intermarriage among, 29, 141
 internal correspondence, 194
 as nobility, 182–83, 187, *188*, 189–90
 pamphlets by, 185–86
 postal disputes between, 105, 110
 Sandri branch, 24, 30–31, 65, 209
 social status, 26, 28
 and the Venetian Company of Couriers, 30–31, 89
Tassis, Ferdinando (d. 1648), 87–88, 142, *143*, 144, 192–94, 275n22
Tassis, Filippo (d. 1603), 116, 246n66
Tassis, Francesco (d. 1517), 26, *27*, 35, 104
Tassis, Gabriele (d. 1536), *25*, 30–31
Tassis, Giovan Antonio (d. 1580), *25*, 47, 49–55, 73, 105
 as imperial postmaster (Rome), 63
 imprisoned, 62–63, 66, 72, 209
 Paceco on, 64
 torture of, 56–57, 209
Tassis, Giovanni Battista (d. 1541), *25*, 28–30, 34–35, 52, 104, 110
Tassis, Giovanni Battista (d. 1588), 189

INDEX   315

Tassis, Isabella (d. 1614), 29
Tassis, Janetto (d. 1517), 24, *25*, 31, 104, 226n32
Tassis, Lamoral I (d. 1624), 149–50
Tassis, Lamoral II (d. 1677), 187
Tassis, Leonardo I (d. 1612), 149
Tassis, Leonardo II (d. 1628), 148
Tassis, Lorenzo Bordogna (d. 1559), 53
Tassis, Lucina Cattanea (d. 1619), 2, 89, 103, 112–15, 121–22, 132, 136–38, 233n124
Tassis, Maffeo (d. 1536), *25*, 34, 104, 271n88
Tassis, Octavio (d. 1626), 141–42, 145–46, 148–51
Tassis, Ottavio (d. 1632), 116, 124
Tassis, Ottavio (d. 1691), 201–2
Tassis postal system, 182
Tassis, Raimondo (d. 1579), *25*, 28–29, 104–5
Tassis, Regina, 29
Tassis, Ruggero, 24, *25*
Tassis, Ruggero (d. 1514), *25*, 28
Tassis, Ruggero (d. 1583), 68, 102, 105
Tassis, Ruggero (d. 1588), 13, *25*, 92, 102–3, 105–6, 116–17, *144*
Tassis, Simone (d. 1563), 21, 28–29, 33–38, *39*, 56, 66, 104–5, 213, 231n109
  in Milan, 41–42, 52
  and Spain, 38–39, 45
Tassis, Vittorio (d. 1606), 116, 246n66
Tasso, Lauro, 96
Tasso, Maffeo (d. 1677), 169, 269n53
Tasso, Torquato, 20
Taube, Wilhelm, 275–76n30
Taxis, Adelheid von, 236n31
Taxis Bordogna, Lucia Ropele, 114
Taxis, Ginevra, 141–42, 149
Taxis, Josef (d. 1566), 53
Taxis, Juan (d. 1607), 115
Taxis, Leonhard I (d. 1612), 105
Taxis, Lorenzo di, 227n40
Taxis, Lucia Ropele Bordogna (d. 1688), 90
Taxis, Seraphin (d. 1582), 29, 249n12
Taxis y Acuña, Juan de (d. 1607), 109–10
Taxis y Peralta, Juan de (d. 1622), 115
Taylor, John, 157
Tealdo, Bartolo, 83
technocrats, 6, 20, 95, 102, 132, 210, 213
Tellier, François Michel Le, 196

Thirty Years' War, 17, 145, 147, 152–53, 177, 180, 207
Thurn und Taxis archives, 3, 118, 146–47, 185
Thurn und Taxis family, 10, 16, 20, 182, 187
Tiepolo, Paolo, 68
Timone, Bernardo, 32
Torriano, Giovanni, 161
tourism, 154, 156, 169
travel, 268–69n45
  pilgrimages, 161–62
  and postal systems, 155, 198
  posthaste, 158
  public transportation, 159
  Travel Booklet (Raißbuechlin) (Gail), 161–62
travelers, 154, 156, 208
  attacked, 79, 81–82
  customer service, 170
  and extortion, 166–67
  marginalia of, 163, *164–65*
  and postmasters, 158, 168, 172
treaties, and courier protections, 32
Treaty of Madrid (1526), 28
Treaty of Utrecht (1714), 192
Triulzi, Teodoro, 32
Troilus and Cressida (Shakespeare), 212–13
Truffaldino, 19
trust, 13–15, 75–77, 212
Tuke, Brian, 35
Turlano, Damiano, 161

United States, 5, 196, 203–4, 211
universities, and messengers, 7
utility theory, 18

Valle Brembana, 20–22, 208
Valois dynasty, 16, 20, 28, 49
Vantaggio, Antonio di Bartolomeo del, 11, 65
varletti, 7
Velasco y Tovar, Juan Fernández de, 117, 119–20, 122
Venetian Company of Couriers, 9–10, 20–22, 29, 68, 72–73, 76, 94, 98, 232n114
  communications monopoly of, 95
  on courier-related attacks, 84–85
  couriers of, 22–23, 70–71, 133, 225n16
  and Fioravante, 43–44

Venetian Company of Couriers (*continued*)
   and Gherardi, 70
   and the Italian Road, 100, 111, 114, 210
   Mariegola, 22–23
   privileges of, 23
   and Roman post offices, 51–52, 67
   and Ruggero Tassis, 106
   schedule, 69
   structure, 42–43
   and the Tassis family, 30–31, 89
Venetian State Inquisitors, 14, 119
Venice, 22–23, 68, 76, 86, *101*, 108–9
   communications monopoly of, 95–96
   courier locations, 23
   and decryption, 60
   extradition agreements, 83
   and the Imperial postal system, 36, 139–40, 145
   and Milan, 36, 107
   ordinary postal service, 107–8
   and the Papal states, 68, 70–71
   post office in Rome, 65–66
   and the Tassis family, 31, 36
   taxes, 174
Verona, 86, 95–97, 247n83
Verstegan, Richard, 162
Via Svizzera (Swiss Road), 145–46, 150, 194, 256n95
Vicenza, 247n83
Vidari, Giovanni Maria, 169, 177, 275n28
Vignale, Giovan Antonio (Il Sarto), 41–42, 53
Villano, Pietro Francesco, 137
Visconti family, 23–24
Visconti, Gian Galeazzo, 23

Voghera post, 42
von Stauding und Taxis, Susanna Jakob, 113–14, 116
Vrints, Gerard, 148, 152

Wachtendoch, Christine, 29
Wallerstein, Immanuel, 273–74n11
War of Spanish Succession (1702–1713), 195, 275n28
wars
   and couriers, 32
   See also information wars; Italian Wars
wax seals, 193, 196, 276–77n42
Weber, Max, 211
Wechel, Gese, 254n77
Westminster Review, 202–3
Wingfield, Robert, 35
Witherings, Thomas, 185, 189–90, 274n15
Witzenberger, Daniel, 162
Wolsey, Thomas, 32, 35, 63
women, 29, 112, 121, 141–42, 252n57
   See also postmistresses

xenophobia, 170, 228n59

Yardley, Herbert, 204

zanni, 19
Zapata, Christina, 29
Zapata, Diego Giacomo, 114
Zapata, Giovanni Battista, 29
Zapata Tassis, Victoria, 114
Zazzera, Francesco, 73, 187, 189–90
Zonio, Jacopo Filippo, 110

www.ingramcontent.com/pod-product-compliance
Lightning Source LLC
Chambersburg PA
CBHW030731230426
43667CB00007B/671